Greening People
Human Resources and Environmental Management

edited by
Walter Wehrmeyer

Above all, the resolution of human and societal problems remains in the hands of the citizens of all the society. We should be on our guards not to overestimate science and scientific methods when it is a question of human problems, and we should not assume that experts are the only ones who have rights to express themselves on questions affecting the organisation of society.

Albert Einstein

Greening People

HUMAN RESOURCES AND ENVIRONMENTAL MANAGEMENT

 *Greenleaf* **Publishing** *1996*

© 1996 Greenleaf Publishing unless otherwise stated.

Published by Greenleaf Publishing
Greenleaf Publishing is an Imprint of
Interleaf Productions Limited
Broom Hall
Sheffield S10 2DR
England

Typeset by Interleaf Productions Limited and printed on environmentally friendly, acid-free paper from managed forests by The Cromwell Press, Melksham, Wiltshire

British Library Cataloguing in Publication Data
  Greening people : human resources and environmental
    management
    1.Industrial management - Environmental aspects 2.Personnel
    management - Environmental aspects 3.Environmental
    engineering
    I.Wehrmeyer, Walter
    658.4'08

  ISBN 1 874719 1 52

Contents

Foreword

Dr Georg Winter

*I*F A COMPANY is to adopt an environmentally-aware approach to its activities, the employees are the key to its success or failure. If the employees are not persuaded of its benefits, the project will fail, no matter how well it has been otherwise prepared. If they are convinced of the value of environmental management, the project can virtually run itself. Staff will also become more enthusiastic if, in their daily routine work, they appear to be safeguarding the environment. No one can put their heart and soul into their work, unless they are sure that they are not destroying their surroundings.

Staff motivation and training must reflect the truth that, in the long term, a company can perform to high standards in its efforts to protect the environment only by maintaining consistently high standards of work in its traditional activities. Concern for environmental standards must, in practice, always progress in step with an increasing awareness of standards of workmanship in the conventional sense, that is, an inner commitment to work and ensuring that products are of a high quality.

In *Greening People*, Dr Wehrmeyer and his sterling set of contributors explore the role of human resource management at the core of the environmental practice in an organisation. Part 1 demonstrates the relationship between human resource management and environmental management. Part 2 provides insight into the psychological make-up of contemporary staff that may foster or hinder company-wide implementation of environmental measures and Part 3 addresses the shortcomings of current management training programmes and suggests new approaches for effective implementation of environmental human resource management. Finally, a selection of excellent case studies demonstrates how the concepts are being implemented in companies and local authorities.

The objectives of environmental human resource management might seem impossibly high given the limited time available to give to staff motivation and training in the daily struggle for survival in a competitive world, but failure to set ambitious targets often means that realistic objectives are not achieved either.

Greening People is an invaluable contribution to the greening of companies and other organisations: an objective that is absolutely crucial for all who are striving to achieve the goal of an environmentally-sustainable economy.

Foreword

Gilbert S. Hedstrom

*O*VER THE LAST two decades, the corporate record of environmental, health and safety (EHS) performance has been impressive. Though the level of success varies by company, extensive progress has been made across industry in developing the right management system, programmes and EHS staff to help protect the companies, their employees, local communities and the environment. In many ways, however, this build-up reflects a bygone era. The regulatory and public demands on companies were relatively new twenty-five years ago and companies responded by developing EHS initiatives to meet those demands—whatever the cost (up to 4% of sales in many industries today). Like other non-core parts of the organisation, the EHS function was often managed and measured separately from the business operations.

Not surprisingly, in today's changing business climate, the demands on the EHS part of the organisation are changing too. These are some of the harsh realities:

- Many companies have been through some kind of re-engineering or downsizing in the last few years, which can throw environmental (and other) programmes into tailspins.

- In many organisations, EHS budgets have joined other once-sacred functions—such as finance, legal and information systems—as candidates for rigorous cost-cutting and demands for greater productivity.

- Recent corporate experiences demonstrate that a so-called 'green wall' can pose a real threat to environmental progress, the 'green wall' being that point at which management refuses to move forward with its strategic EHS programme because of an uneasy fit or a rift between EHS and the business operations.

■ Though companies have made some progress in drawing line managers into the EHS management process and setting performance targets, the performance appraisal systems have not yet caught up with the new expectations.

Today, companies are actively seeking ways to improve the productivity of the resources they devote to managing their EHS activities. Their motivation is not just financial. Even in those industries not focused on downsizing, the best companies recognise that there is extensive 'upside potential' to be gained by managing EHS issues effectively and efficiently. Consequently, leading organisations are pushing line managers to make a 'paradigm shift' to view the environment as a potential business opportunity, not just a liability. Similarly, environmental managers are beginning to change the way they think about their roles, moving from technical advisors to business strategists. Part of that role is also to educate the organisation around the need to integrate the environmental strategy into the overall business strategy. Part of that role is also to take the lead in embedding EHS management and responsibility into operations, while adopting metrics to measure the real costs and business benefits of the EHS initiatives.

Tomorrow's EHS leaders will have transformed the culture of the company by developing a vision among line managers to convert environmental challenges into opportunities. Incentives and performance measurement schemes will be aligned to leverage the 'creative tension' that exists between current reality and the vision, thus helping pull the organisation toward that goal. A huge asset to be tapped in this process is the workforce who feel strongly about the environment (and the health and safety of their families and communities) and will be exhilarated by a new-found ability to express their personal values in the workplace. Companies will invest heavily in training and developing the skills of their staff so they can work more efficiently and effectively throughout the organisation.

In the long term, it is the creation of a learning culture, combined with bold vision and aligned incentive programmes, that will define the competitive winners. The issues will deal fundamentally with the core competencies of a business—and of the people who make it successful.

Greening People fills an important void in the corporate environmental, health and safety management debate. Organisational success can only be achieved in EHS management if the personal motivation of the staff is encouraged and channelled to improve performance and drive progress. Realistically, it is only through the energy, performance and personal commitment of each employee within an organisation that we will move toward sustainable industrial development.

Introduction

Walter Wehrmeyer

*E*NVIRONMENTAL management (EM) largely began as a result of public and legislative pressures on business, and early successes in improving environmental performance have been in economic areas such as waste and materials reduction, energy efficiency and emissions control. However, environmental problems have not gone away, nor have the efforts from industry thus far succeeded in answering public concern. In fact, the continued occurrence of environmental problems invites the question of just how successful or sincere EM is in its current approach.

Most technological development occurs within industrial corporations, which harbour the competence and financial capacities. However, if this innovation fails to take into account social, ethical or cultural concerns, the usefulness of these new technologies in the next generation of environmental problems is doubtful. Such concerns in the main are either outside the control of organisations or not immediately associated with economic benefits, and thus are relegated to the elusive and complex realm of 'sustainable development'.

It is a curious aspect of contemporary environmental business management that employees' personal values regarding the environment are not exploited to the full to maximise the success of corporate environmental initiatives, even though they have demonstrably positive effects for management. In fact, Sisson makes the point that the core role of personnel policy in corporate success has been made evident numerous times; it has been proven that 'the workforce is the most vital asset' and that 'the real, sustainable competitive advantage, or edge, has to come ultimately from the way capable and motivated teams put technology and capital to work.'[1]

The positive effects of increased staff involvement and recognition of personal values include: increased motivation, lower staff turnover, greater job satisfaction, closer identification with corporate goals and culture, and the improved status that derives from working for a company that cares about the environment. The personnel function, then, is and has been vastly and unjustifiably under-rated in the EM area, which in turn has contributed to the perception that the acceptance of environmental values in companies has been lacklustre and that the majority of environmental improvements have been purely economically motivated, rather than through ethical or soc The purpose of this book is to open the discussion on the range of benefits that arise from such actions and to investigate the methods. It should be noted that, ideally, the two areas of management interact, so that EM impacts on HRM activities, and in turn HRM activities, such as training, have been changed to accommodate EM matters.[2] This introduction covers four main areas of this interaction:

- **What is the role of personnel in environmental management?** In other words, what can personnel do to assist the EM function?

- **What is the role of environmental management in personnel?** Here we ask how EM has, as an emerging discipline, affected the functioning and the role of personnel, and of human resources management (HRM). In addition, this section supports the notion the environmental problems can only be solved successfully if the way in which we interact with, and perform within, the natural environment is considered. This includes a re-orientation of the role of technology.

- **Who is the environmental manager?** This section reports current trends towards staffing EM; in particular it focuses on areas of technical and managerial competence, payment, age structures and types of jobs.

- **How is the EM function organised** at the moment in leading companies? In particular, how is organisational structure and task allocation affected by this relatively new field?

In considering the issues identified above, environmental management is defined here broadly as the co-ordinated and organised approach to issues relating to the natural environment, from a business perspective with the aim of reducing those impacts deemed harmful to the natural environment. This includes the identification, documentation and elimination of these environmental effects. Similarly, personnel management is defined here using Torrington and Hall's definition as: 'a series of activities which: first enable working people and their employing organisations to agree about the objectives and nature of their working relationship and, secondly, ensure that the agreement is fulfilled.'[3] Storey and Sisson on the other hand, make a distinction between personnel management and human resources management (HRM) in terms of the respective emphasis on utilisation of resources and strategic significance; this book, much like Tyson, uses both terms as 'equivalent...whilst acknowledging HRM as a more modern title',[4] as the difference between the two is not critical for most of the discussions presented here.

■ *The Role of HRM in Environmental Management*

Broadly, the role of HRM in environmental management is to support the success of environmental activities. In the field of TQM, Schonberger[5] argues that changes in the HRM field itself are quintessential for TQM, and that these changes have to take place interdependently and in conjunction with the introduction of TQM. A similar case can be made for the interaction between EM and HRM. Figure 1 suggests three broad categories of HRM functions in which this can be analysed.

EHRM function	Activity
Supply competent staff	■ Job description ■ Requirement ■ Induction ■ Dismissal
Management of staff	■ Training provision ■ Health and Safety at work ■ Staff appraisal ■ Industrial relations ■ Motivate and reward ■ Grievance and discipline
Promote organisational dynamics	■ Monitor culture and attitudes ■ Promote environmental ethic ■ Support change management ■ Improve lateral thinking ■ Improve communication ■ Interpersonal and team skills

Figure 1: *Environmental HRM Functions*

The first function relates to the supply of competent staff to the organisation, and the main activities supporting this function cover the broad categories of job description, recruitment, induction and dismissal. Job description relates to the specification of job tasks with regard to social, personal and technical requirements of work. Here, a number of issues are to be considered: the inclusion of environmental protection duties, the allocation of environmental reporting roles and the allocation of health and safety tasks as part of the general job specification, which are all part of an HRM approach to EM.

Job description can also concern itself with the extent to which potential emissions are the responsibility of specific staff. If environment is part of everyone's job, then it must be part of everyone's job description. If EM (or parts of it) is peculiar to a particular department, then roles and relationships between this department and all other staff must be established. Environmental implications of job descriptions can also involve employees' actual exposure to harmful substances, which is usually covered by the health and safety regulations (e.g. COSHH). However, Field and Phillips note the absence of a consistent approach to designing an environmentally-beneficial environment for office workers—even though they cite studies that show 80% of workers suffer from at least one ailment that can be linked to poor office environments.[6] Recruitment involves matching job descriptions with personal attributes. Here, HRM can usefully ensure that not only has the job been designed with the environment in mind, but also that the ideal candidate has environmental competencies that are useful to the firm as well as fulfilling the specific job criteria. Many EM activities, such as environmental auditing, performance assessment or the understanding of ecological principles, are specialist competencies that are easier to buy in and can also be accumulated through new recruits rather than by investment in training. Barrett's survey of 210 environmental managers showed that all but 5% had been educated to degree level or above,[7] the majority of which had technical, engineering or natural science-based disciplines. Many of these competencies are difficult to come by in conventional occupational training packages.

Induction refers to the initial integration of new staff to the job and its organisational context. Here, the role of HRM in environmental management is to ensure that new recruits understand the EM approach, are familiar with the relevant health and safety arrangements, take the environmental components of their duties seriously and appreciate the corporate environmental culture. Many environmental impacts are aggregations of many very small decisions by employees, making the induction process and the initial training package critical in combating a lacklustre or half-hearted approach to the environment. 'Learning the ropes' organisationally begins on the very first day, especially with regard to work attitudes, personal motivation towards the job (and the organisation) and relationships with colleagues, all of which have a very strong bearing on successful EM.

If the employee's contract is terminated by the organisation (dismissal), the general debriefing should include an environmental dimension. Equally, if staff resign from the organisation, it is important for personnel managers to discover the reasons for this. Environmental factors may play a role, insofar as intrinsically-motivated staff, or highly-sought-after staff, often seek not only financial rewards, but also ethical or environmental involvement. The exit interview should investigate this.

Referring to Figure 1 again, the second function of HRM lies in the support of staff management in an organisation. This covers the general provision of training, the delivery and continuous update of health and safety regulations and practices at work, staff appraisals, union negotiations and industrial relations generally, the ensuing motivation and reward packages, and the handling of grievances and discipline.

Training is perhaps the one area where the role of HRM in EM has been acknowledged for the longest time. Accordingly, the availability of training materials has grown rapidly, and Alison Bird of the Institute of Environmental Management (Chapter 11) provides a good and practical overview of some of the issues involved. Her conclusion is that all training must be made relevant, applicable and appropriate, and her examples demonstrate often ingenious methods of training provision and mode of delivery.

With regard to industrial relations, Andrea Oates provides an introduction into this complex field and explores its interface with the environment (Chapter 5). She shows that the trade union, through its traditional health and safety interest, can offer strong support for environmental improvements, and as such can be a useful partner in EM, even though the majority of unions' environmental concern has in the past related to the workplace rather than ecology as a whole. In fact, many unions today regard themselves as members of the environmental movement and, most notably UNISON, have compiled model environmental agreements. It can be argued that the top-down approach of many EM systems corresponds with the approach adopted by many unions who feel themselves better able to negotiate for improvements at the top level. The Trade Union Congress has published a guide to environmental issues at work from the trade union perspective.[8]

Staff appraisal is generally defined as the process of reviewing past staff performance with the aim of future improvement. Given the inclusion of environmental activities and objectives into the job description and recruitment, it seems obvious that staff appraisal should cover environmental issues as well. Topics covered would include environmental incidents, the take-up of environmental responsibilities, and the success in communicating environmental concerns and company policy. Staff appraisal carried out badly or cynically is a waste of time for all involved, but the inclusion of environmental matters into the appraisal process is a good indicator of the seriousness of a company's EM approach.

The same can be said for staff motivation and incentives, where, as Milliman and Clair (Chapter 2) show, environmental factors in performance-related pay as well as the type of fringe benefits provided are good indicators of management's success in integrating environment into *all* aspects of a company. The importance of job rotation for training and motivation of staff has been recognised in EM as well: Peter James (Chapter 6) indicates that job rotation can be used as a means to train environmental executives or to familiarise potential Board members with the environmental side of operations and policy.

With regard to incentives, it seems obvious that environmental managers would not be too motivated by the promise of a company car if much of their time is spent on increasing energy efficiency, promoting car pooling of staff (a task for which the personnel department is uniquely equipped) or converting environmental impacts to their carbon equivalent. Nonetheless, more than a third of site environmental managers use a company car—a figure that rises with seniority.[9]

However, there are many ways in which company cars can be provided in an environmentally-friendlier manner. Such measures include the extension of mileage allowances to bicycle journeys, bicycle loans, the provision of financial substitutes for staff giving up their car allowances, car pooling or car sharing provisions, or limiting the use of company cars to journeys beyond the realm of public transport. Generally, a car is a strong and highly-visible symbol: why should shopfloor workers care about the environment personally if the boss (environmental manager) still gets *his* luxury car paid for by the firm?

The issue of staff grievance and discipline has so far received little environmental attention. However, staff should be given the opportunity to raise environmental concerns or areas of non-compliance in a non-conflictual way. So far, very few companies have followed the lead of National Westminster Bank, a company that encourages 'whistle-blowing' internally, but, environmentally, much more can be done. For high-risk operations, the ability to raise grievances of an environmental nature is vital for the safety record. The most obvious example to be cited here is the environmental disaster at Bhopal, where staff raised matters with superiors long before the incident. In addition, the enforcement of safety regulations and, by implication, EM rules and duties, should have disciplinary procedures attached to them in the event of non-compliance. The very existence of these procedures reinforces to the workforce the company's environmental commitment.

The third main function of HRM in environmental management lies in the promotion and support of organisational dynamics, in particular in the monitoring and shaping of the corporate culture, the support of change management, the improvement of communication and of lateral thinking, and, accordingly, of interpersonal and team skills.[10] This takes the position, as this Introduction hopes to prove, that it is not technology that makes for success, but people, and their attitudes and motives. As Friedman points out: 'many former activists from the 1960s, who accepted positions in regulated industries, brought an environmental ethic to industry, as well as an understanding of the difference between "scientific truth" and "regulatory truth".'[11] I have in earlier publications[12] and in Chapter 7 suggested that environmental care as an ethical value in companies originates with people, whereas TQM attitudes originate primarily with the company. Developments in the profile of environmental managers presented by Peter Dobers and Rolf Wolff (Chapter 13), as well as Peter James (Chapter 6), indicate that EM is not (if indeed it ever was) within the remit of managers with a clear view on the economic performance of the organisation.

However, the HRM function of promoting organisational dynamics underlies many of the specific examples outlined above, and forms part of the overall management approach rather than something uniquely environmental. The idea is, much like with TQM, to tap into and utilise the ingenuity, awareness and motivation of staff to improve corporate performance, be this in the delivery of customer satisfaction as in TQM, or in EM. The role of HRM in this field is that of facilitator and enabler, which makes use of its previous two functions, namely to supply and support competent staff, and to enable individuals to be a greater part of organisational success. To do this, recruitment and job description are perhaps the most critical yet most underrated HRM activities contributing to environmental success in companies.

In conclusion, the role of HRM in environmental management is a critical one. This has been argued on the grounds of: (a) the importance of people in environmental success generally; (b) the origin of environmental values inside companies; (c) the fact that technology itself is often less relevant to success than the way in which employees interact with it; (d) the often complex nature of environmental issues requiring special analytical and communication skills; and (e) that since much of EM is lateral to all existing business activities, it requires special negotiation and interpersonal skills to support others in their implementation.

■ The Role of Environmental Management in HRM

This section discusses the impact the environment and its management agenda has had on personnel, in particular the impact on recruitment, on compensation, on management of pension funds and on more strategic aspects of managing change, organisational learning and strategic HRM. In this discussion, the impact of HRM on EM and the impact of EM on HRM are seen as mirrored and interdependent processes. They are aspects of the same process—which makes a personnel case for environmental management and an environmental case for personnel that are both long overdue.

Recruitment is perhaps the most significant field in which environmental issues have impacted on HRM activities. Attitude surveys have shown that environmental concern has been a dominant trait of the public for some time;[13] equally, Charter[14] points out that, where other considerations are equal, high-achieving graduates do consider the environmental performance and reputation of a company. He found in a survey of UK university graduates that 74% were interested in working for a socially-responsible company and, if in the position to choose, 56% would rate the environmental track record as an important or very important criterion.

A similar finding came from Taillieu and Mooren's[15] longitudinal study of more than 1,500 students that showed the rise of environment as a decision-making criterion among high-flying business graduates—as defined as those from top European business schools and universities. This is not surprising, as high-quality staff are often intrinsically motivated by the non-monetary aspects of a job, such as company status, position, power, the nature of the work, or future career moves arising from a job.

If lower-quality graduates do not differ in principle but in the degree to which they are able to make choices between companies rather than being chosen, then staff recruitment is becoming increasingly difficult for firms with a below-average environmental reputation. This point has already been made for some time,[16] but increasing competition at the higher end of the job market has compounded the problem. This is part of a wider shift in graduates' expectations and a more fundamental change in the job market itself, namely that the career path is unlikely to be guaranteed with one company alone and is not exclusively based on education, but also on interpersonal and transferable skills; that more qualified women are finally entering the job markets; that work is increasingly seen as an area of personal self-expression as well as an economic basis of life; and that loyalty to a company has fallen, whereas loyalty towards societal concepts—such as religion, background and ethics—has, if anything, risen.

Hence, by improving the environmental performance of a firm and by introducing environmental management and protection into all aspects of business, EM assists HRM in its recruitment efforts, and can in turn enjoy the benefit of better-motivated or better-qualified staff. This may be part of a wider development in HRM where previously narrowly-defined jobs are becoming increasingly complex, diverse and multi-disciplinary. In line with this, Wolters *et al.*[17] see the environment as part of job enrichment.

Equally, EM has already had an effect on remuneration and pay. Some firms, as Milliman and Clair (Chapter 2) point out, have begun to include environmental issues into their performance-related pay (PRP) systems, either as an additional performance criterion or as a minimum standard to be achieved before qualifying for PRP. This is a welcome step, as it demonstrates the company's commitment over short-term gain. It also presents the view that good economic performance that works to the detriment of the environment should not be rewarded. In addition, pension fund managers can and do chose ethical investment funds as part of their risk-diversification strategies and for reasons of consistency with the environmental policy. Environmental pressure groups have already lobbied companies to avoid polluting industries in their fund portfolio, and there is a small number of firms excluding such investments from their portfolio altogether. Nonetheless, the financial investment community remains largely ignorant of the environmental management revolution,[18] even though there is not necessarily a financial premium on ethical investments.[19]

A critical area in which environmental factors have fundamentally augmented the number of alternatives in the design process of HRM managers is that of the working environment. What began as a matter of ergonomics and of motion studies to improve production efficiency in the assembly lines of the 1920s now covers issues as diverse as the use of natural lighting and planting in offices, climate and energy control in all buildings (where the storage area and the truck loading area are of particular concern), the use of energy-efficient lights, sound office architecture, and much more. There are economic reasons for this. For instance, Wilson[20] suggests a clear connection between environmental quality of the workplace and productivity, and Field and Phillips[21] cite four reasons to manage the office environment, namely: increased productivity, reduced staff turnover, reduced absenteeism, and the ethical responsibility for the wellbeing of employees.

Another area where the environment has impacted on HRM is the canteen—equally as visible to staff as the company car. Here, the provision of healthier food (be this organic, low fat or vitamin-rich), a more pleasant lunchtime environment, the display of health and fitness advice and the provision of vegetarian foods are all examples of an approach to personnel management that goes beyond the traditional notion of managing supply and demand of the human component of the socio-technical system.

These activities, where environmental issues have already affected HRM, relate to an approach to personnel management that perceives staff as human beings with particular needs that have to be satisfied so that a person can fully contribute to organisational success. Hence, humans are not only there to support the organisation to be paid in return for the inconvenience, but are recognised to be dynamic shapers of the organisational agenda at all levels and make valid contributions to the productivity and ethics (or lack thereof) of an organisation—as well as to serve the traditional functions of staff. This approach somewhat extends contemporary views on HRM, as it is quite distinct to the original HRM approach that saw staff as (human) resources to be utilised and whose utility is to be maximised for the organisational benefit.[22]

Inasmuch as the EM agenda has expanded the traditional view of the organisational environment to include natural ecosystems as they are affected by an organisation, so the view of the internal, social environment is expanded by the EM agenda to include personal beliefs, attitudes and ethical principles into the range of factors that affect, and are affected by, decision-making and ultimately organisational success. This is a new development that so far forms no part of mainstream HRM (or indeed EM), but is highlighted by ESB (see the case study on training needs analysis by Wehrmeyer and Vickerstaff, Chapter 17), which quite sensibly included staff and their spouses in personal development and growth training programmes.

From a theoretical perspective, this assumes that action and the environment within which it happens are not to be separated but are integral parts of an indivisible interaction between activity and its context—an argument that is well established in the complex systems view of organisation –environment interaction, where organisations are merely places of higher order than their surroundings, which depend on resources from the environment to maintain their status of higher order. In this, organisation and environment represent but one process of interaction, and the aim of this is not resource efficiency (measured in profit) but homeostasis—the maintenance of the equilibrium through the avoidance of undesirables. According to Morgan:

> The idea that organic forms evolve through a process of goal-oriented or instrumental adaptation to context is a myth fostered by the mechanistic mode of thought...Cybernetics shows us that organised forms do not actively seek or orient themselves toward achievement of a desired future state. Rather, they arrive at any given state through processes of adjustment which eliminate other possible system states.[23]

This radical perspective rejects anthropocentricity as well as the benefits of purposive, planned action, which can be compared with process theories of corporate strategy of Tyson.[24] It also argues a strong case against technology-oriented approaches to management as well as against corporate strategy as a plan of action, decided by some and implemented by all. According to Morgan again:

> Through the pursuit of profit, production, and other desired objects which are regarded as synonymous with success, the organisation may in fact be creating the conditions which underlie its demise...Goal-seeking organisations constitute positive feedback systems which influence and change their contexts in major and harmful ways, and thus find themselves forever solving the problems which their previous actions have created.[25]

This would also fit a more radical view on organisations as 'systems of destruction. They systematically destroy environmental value. This destruction cannot be dismissed...as an externality of production,'[26] which fits well with the proposed view of organisations as places of higher order whose positive feedback mechanisms have replaced the original purpose of homeostasis and now necessitate greater and greater resource transfer from their specific organisational environment.

This line of thought brings us to the argument that the environmental problems we have are essentially not due to technological or managerial efforts, but are related to the very way in which we perceive the natural environment—and act upon this perception. For example, Western society's collective perception of the natural environment is one that has largely been assembled from television images. This relationship finds its most extreme, and dysfunctional, expression in environment-orientated themeparks. Also relevant to this argument is Jung's famous quote that 'the world that we have made as a result of the level of thinking we have done so far creates problems we cannot solve at the same level at which we created them.'

Adopting this new perspective would offer several benefits to practitioners and academics alike. It would allow a better understanding of the dysfunctional side-effects of traditional, non-environmental management; it would offer greater opportunities for staff involvement and interaction; and it would allow a fresh and somewhat promising look at where environmental problems come from as well as what can constructively be done about them. This perspective also relates to the point that our use of technology prevents us from experiencing the natural environment in a functional manner; we prefer technological solutions that support or maintain, but do not question, our individual lifestyles. In this sense, we 'solve' the problem with the environment by redefining it. The same can be said for personnel: as long as we assume that work behaviour is fundamentally different to leisure behaviour, HRM will not be able to motivate staff fully towards continuous improvement, TQM or environmental action.

■ Who is the Environmental Manager?

The third field of interest in the discussion about EM and HRM is who the environmental manager is, what his or her background and demography is, which competencies are essential and which factors make for greater success in EM. This is the field where most research has been conducted, and this discussion relies on three landmark studies, namely the survey by Barrett for Environmental Data Services,[27] the European survey by Peter James (Chapter 6) and the most recent member survey of the Institute of Environmental Management (IEM) in 1995.

Barrett's 1993 survey of 210 environmental managers is indicative of the state of EM at the time. He showed that almost 30% of EM jobs had been created within the previous twelve months, and about 65% were in newly-created jobs. An even earlier report showed that significant skills deficiencies existed, mainly with respect to environmental legislation, environmental assessment and determining technical solutions.[28] Understanding environmental legislation appears to be a continuing problem.[29] Barrett also shows that about 23% of respondents, a higher percentage than in a similar survey of the Institute of Environmental Management in 1993, were working exclusively for the environment; in the list of other duties, health and safety dominate, with technical services and quality following.

Separating environmental managers into corporate, divisional and site environmental managers, it is found that the majority of the latter two work on activities related to environmental auditing and on training, where managers at the corporate level spend more time on statutory and non-statutory requirements. All three spend about equivalent time—roughly 18%—on the development and implementation of an EMS and its certification through BS 7750 or equivalent.[30] The time spent on environmental issues, is for all three managerial levels, equally split between air pollution, water emissions and waste management, followed by waste minimisation and, less importantly, product stewardship. Managers at the corporate and divisional level spend more time on the latter issue, along with contaminated land, whereas site environmental managers spend more time on noise and vibration.

As previously stated, this survey found a high level of education, with 95% of respondents qualified to degree level or above, most commonly in 'hard' sciences, and many managers had doctorates either in the 'hard' or 'soft' sciences. Not surprisingly, given the state of environmental education and training in the UK at the time of the survey, the majority of environmental managers develop their competence through publications and conferences rather than through specific training courses.

With regard to pay, the survey found salaries, depending on the type of industry, the level of seniority, the extent of non-environment duties of the job holder and the professional experience of the job holder, to range between £20,000 and £60,000 p.a., with median salaries between £28,000 and £35,000. Interestingly, more than two out of five environmental managers were given a company car. The age distribution of job holders is quite even, with a small peak in the 46–55 age bracket. More than 90% of respondents were male.

From this, it appears that the majority of environmental managers originate in engineering or technology-related or 'hard' science backgrounds, which may be indicative of a technology-oriented approach to environmental issues. This also correlates with the very low number of women in such jobs. Environmental managers are not 'tree-huggers', a finding that is supported by the low percentage of respondents being members of environmental pressure groups (under 10%), which is interestingly lower than the corresponding figure for environmental co-ordinators in the UK public sector.[31]

A similar survey was conducted by the IEM in 1995.[32] As a follow-up on a survey, also by the IEM, in 1993, and with 162 responses (18% response rate), the sample was comparable to Barrett's. Two years on, the survey found staff were increasingly qualified, in terms of both the level and type of educational background and the length of occupational experience. The number of environment-related degrees held by staff rose from 8% to 26% between 1993 and 1995. Their main motivation was improving the environment and raising environmental awareness as means to improve business success. Career prospects are perceived to be, on balance, improving.

The earlier picture of environmental managers who have duties in many diverse activities is gradually receding towards more full-time involvement. The main areas of involvement are policy formulation, internal and external communication, compliance, management, systems monitoring and auditing, and training. With regard to professional recognition, respondents cite membership of more than eighty different bodies, only two of which have a predominantly environmental remit, indicating the great diversity of backgrounds. The main barriers the respondents found in the 1995 IEM survey were conflicting priorities and lack of management and financial commitment.

Already in 1993, the picture of an environmental manager as a male of late middle age who 'had come up through the ranks but had reached a dead end in his career path, and so had been shifted sideways'[33] has fundamentally changed. It is now perceived as a job of greater complexity posing an intellectual and organisational challenge. This is reinforced by James, who in his chapter on environmental executives (Chapter 6) covers the EU rather than the UK, and focuses on the Board. He suggests that environment is no longer a career dead-end, but a positive career stepping stone, where younger executives learn and demonstrate their capacity to manage a complex and highly diverse agenda.

> [Since] improved environmental performance depends upon the actions of line managers and non-environmental staff, who usually cannot be ordered to take action but must be persuaded, ...most environmental executives see the secret of success more within their general management abilities...and top level support than in environmental knowledge *per se*.[34]

So, what makes successful environmental managers? James and Stewart argue that

> the successful environmental executive...is somebody whose educational background and industry experience commands respect amongst his or her fellow managers, has the interpersonal skills and contacts to gain their voluntary acceptance of the environmental message, but also the personal and organisational clout to win battles.[35]

A similar message comes from Dobers and Wolff, who in Chapter 13 identify four elements of 'ecological competence', defined as the ability to address ecological issues by:

1. Making use of an interdisciplinary scientific knowledge base.
2. Managing inter-organisational relationships.
3. Integrating ecological technology into multi-technological operations.
4. Creating and maintaining a value-driven discourse.

This is supported by Friedman[36] who identifies five basic characteristics that are quite similar:

1. To have a technical understanding of environment.

2. To be an advocate for ideas.

3. To appreciate the ethical understanding of environment.

4. To be credible.

5. To be knowledgeable about the law.

Interestingly, these characteristics and competencies profile the environmental manager as a widely-qualified and experienced change agent, a 'jack of all trades' who is intrinsically motivated by the environmental challenge, can effectively communicate and persuade others towards continued environmental improvement. The next section outlines some organisational aspects of the context in which this rather rare species operates.

■ *The Organisation of the Environmental Management Function*

The final aspect of the interaction between HRM and EM relates to the way in which environmental jobs and the environment as a managerial issue generally is organised. This, obviously, depends on a number of contextual factors specific to the organisation, such as the type of product, the market, the age and size of the company, the degree of environmental exposure, the company philosophy with respect to the environment and the extent of regulatory control on the firm. Thus, rather than prescribing a specific course of EM implementation, this section looks at two main areas of contention in the organisation of EM, namely:

a. Whether environment is a specialist or a generalist function and whether it should be organised in a centralised or decentralised manner.

b. The issue of 'turf'—since environment is a matter for all staff, who are accountable for the environmental improvements—and how much the traditional departmentalisation of roles and responsibilities are an obstacle in the pursuit of a lateral agenda, such as environment.

Many of these contextual factors can be reduced, by means of analogy, into a choice to see environment either as a motivator or as a hygiene factor. In studying what makes managers feel particularly good or bad about their jobs, Herzberg[37] found in the 1960s that there are factors in our jobs that satisfy us, and these affect us quite differently to those factors that dissatisfy us. He found that the absence of dissatifiers (he calls them 'hygiene factors') usually does not motivate us and that, equally, the presence of job satisfiers ('motivators') can motivate us to pursue a particular course of action. The analysis he provided was that not only were there two distinct types of work factors, they also motivate us differently. Given their organisational contexts, some companies may perceive EM as a 'hygiene factor'—a set of issues that must be addressed or negative implications may occur. However, these issues are not motivators; they are not issues that in themselves offer incentives over and above the absence of their negative effects. In this, health and safety and auditing are predominantly hygiene factors, and raising internal commitment to environment is likely to be a motivator.

The question of whether environment is a specialist or a generalist activity has misled the EM debate for some time. It somewhat mirrors the debate on the distinction between line and staff positions in traditional personnel management. The benefits of a specialist approach to EM lies in clear accountabilities—if all are responsible for the environment, then integrating these activities towards a combined unity of effort becomes important as the risk arises that perhaps few are actually doing anything environmentally noteworthy. With the full-time appointment of an environmental manager, the company ensures that at least one person in the firm is accountable in case of environmental bad news. This may be one of the reasons why in Germany all companies above a certain size must have an environmental manager (Umweltschutzbeauftrager) at Board level.

The drawback of the specialist approach is that staff who are not part of the specialist section may not feel that it is their responsibility to pursue environmental protection. Equally, the alienation of the specialist department is made easier and it may reduce the relevance of the environmental agenda to that of the health and safety officer. Early indications that 'there is little evidence to suggest that industry requires an "environmental specialist"'[38] have changed. The highly-complex and often quite technical nature of the environmental manager's job and its interpersonal challenge largely necessitates this.

The generalist approach argues the environment is the duty of all—with resulting widespread and decentralised activities but potential confusions over accountability, which in case of environmental crises may be a significant obstacle. Also, the training of staff in technical expertise necessary for the environment may not be cost-effective in a generalist approach.

It is argued here that both approaches are valid: there are activities on the EM agenda that are clearly specialist; others are of a generalist nature. For instance, the provision of technical knowledge related to the environment, such as risk assessment, audit methodologies, lifecycle impacts or Toxic Release Inventories in the US, is part of a specialist activity; the duties of environmental protection and awareness of environmental impacts are part of a generalist activity. Hence the organisation of EM should allocate specialist expertise to a dedicated section, accountable to the Board, but should also allocate generalist environmental duties to all staff. This split can now be observed in most organisations that approach environment systematically, and is consistent with BS 7750 and EMAS.

In this sense, a high degree of centralisation of the environment function would hamper the comprehensive implementation of environmental awareness and practice, whereas a decentralised approach would reduce the capacity of environmental leadership to be communicated from the top. Related to this is the top-level commitment and support for EM—a need that is now as famous as the confusion about the concept of sustainable development. This top-level support is more easily communicated (and more important) in a centralised organisation.

The issue of 'turf' is related to the specialist–generalist debate. If environmental managers need—as Miller (Chapter 15) and James (Chapter 6) argue—to convince others of the need for environmental action, then a significant proportion of the success of EM lies outside the control of the environmental managers held accountable for it. In other words, how can environmental managers demonstrate success and value for money attributable to their departments if most of their initiatives rely on making other departments more successful? (see Rees, Chapter 18). This is part of the wider question of how the performance of an enabling and facilitating department can be measured. There is no clear answer to this, except if environmental performance is reviewed not on a departmental but on an organisational level[39] which allows a tracking of progress but still leaves the challenge of accountability.

However, the traditional departmentalisation of roles and responsibilities in an organisation is 'perhaps the biggest and least-discussed obstacle'[40] for EM, as it has generated distrust in divisional managers towards corporate initiatives, caused staff jealousies and confusion in cases of overlapping duties and a general suspicion that environment is merely a Trojan Horse for greater centralised control and interference. As EM is inevitably a lateral activity affecting all areas of business, such defensive reactions are dysfunctional and require the very profile of environmental managers outlined above. This is of particular importance where environmental activities result in a re-organisation or reduction of powers, such as in the introduction of a centralised purchasing section with appropriate environmental policies or the introduction of a regular auditing or environmental reporting schedule.

The solution to such problems cannot be found in EM itself but in a shift in the general approach to the division of labour. The TQM revolution has already made significant inroads towards the breakdown of traditional organisational barriers in the decentralisation of decision-making power and the harnessing of individual initiative and enthusiasm towards organisational success. EM can and has built upon these developments, and a further integration of EM with HRM is only to be recommended. Here, the breakdown of internal departmental barriers coincide with an external fragmentation of career paths and a decline of uni-disciplinary university education.

Given the great number of areas in which EM and HRM interact and interdepend, it is sad that HRM and EM have so far not been integrated to a greater degree. This lack of integration demonstrates the somewhat naïve belief that current managerial approaches and uses of technology to solve environmental problems are doing enough to address the issue of environmental protection. This approach reinforces, and is product of, a technological optimism that may assist organisations in their economic performance, but does not create a path towards sustainable development as it does not address ethical and attitudinal change. This lack of integration is, curiously, also detrimental to the economic success of organisations, as it negates the opportunities that can be gained from a more ethical and participative approach to environmental and staff management. The greatest benefits— namely, higher staff motivation, lower turnover, a greater degree of job satisfaction, more innovations and improved customer services—are due not to improved technology but to people. In this, the danger of an excessively technological approach lies in 'suboptimisation': the constant improvement of a system that should perhaps not be improved at all but scrapped.

This book aims to redress this imbalance and to publicise an emerging but so far undervalued field of EM. It should help environmental managers towards 'greening people' in their interpersonal roles and initiatives, but should also help HRM managers in understanding and applying the environmental issues that already affect their jobs. The book follows on from the success of a Special Issue of *Greener Management International* on HRM and the Environment (No. 10), which was published in April 1995, and contains many additional articles published elsewhere or written specifically for this edition. The case studies at the end of the book highlight some approaches towards environmental HRM.

The book is structured in four parts, covering: the relation between EM and HRM; managing people; training and skills towards environmental improvement; and case studies. In the main, the book aims to proceed from theory to practice.

In the first part, Milliman and Clair (Chapter 2) review the US experience in HRM with regard to EM, arguing that many EM programmes are implemented less successfully than could be hoped for because HRM support is not forthcoming or is provided in an unchanged, traditional and therefore less suitable way. James (Chapter 1) provides a useful outline of the interaction between quality management and EM, in particular the HRM implications of TQM, emphasising the need to change staff roles and performance expectations, as well as a review of the HRM department itself, covering its role and objectives and the way in which it is organised. This somewhat mirrors Barrett and Murphy's article (Chapter 3) on the interplay between environmental policy and HRM in the UK, arguing that, since environmental policy implementation comprises a significant shift in attitudes, culture and practice, HRM must be an integral part. In this, they argue for greater support of HRM towards EM through a process of redefining HRM practices and purposes, an issue upon which all three chapters agree.

Milliman and Clair and Barrett and Murphy share the view that HRM should support policy, a view that is contrasted by Wehrmeyer and Rees (Chapter 4) who report the experience of Local Government Environmental Co-ordinators in implementing Local Agenda 21. Here, *environmental human resources management* is very much a missing link between corporate intention and organisational practice—a finding that makes the theoretical implications of the previous three articles even more relevant. Many of the traditional activities of HRM concerned union negotiations, so it is only appropriate that Oates (Chapter 5) outlines the industrial relations dimension of environmental management in UK businesses, arguing cogently that there is a long tradition of environmental concerns among trade unions, which somehow have not been publicly recognised as such since they were part of the health and safety agenda or the overall improvement of working conditions.

The second part of the book, on managing people, begins with Peter James' second contribution to the book (Chapter 6), in which he outlines the characteristics of environmental executives in Europe. His argument—that environmental executives are successful because of interpersonal competencies and their ability to persuade others of the benefits of new working practices—points to the greater need for such training and education opportunities, as outlined in the third part of this book. Wehrmeyer and Parker (Chapter 7) outline a method of tracking environmental attitudes in a company and outline the relevance of such personal attitudes for the corporate culture and for the success of environmental policy in companies. This is followed by Hart (Chapter 8), who, as a HRM practitioner, outlines the HRM perspective on EM and how the job of HRM practitioners has been enriched and diversified by the EM agenda—a potential EM has for most job holders. Mawle (Chapter 9) then presents the case for women managers to have a much greater role in EM. Her argument fits well with the tenor of this Introduction: that women managers have a skill mix that is often quite distinct to that of male managers and that it is these particular skills that can help in an EM approach more based on changing values and attitudes than on technological or engineering-oriented solutions.

This section of the book is concluded by Klinkers and Nelissen (Chapter 10), who have researched the effectiveness of different environmental campaigns in organisations. Their conclusions on how best to conduct such environmental campaigns also provide a very useful bridge to the third part of the book, which covers training and skills towards environmental improvement. In this part, Bird (Chapter 11) from the UK Institute of Environmental Management produces a concise outline on training provision, which she illustrates with a large number of company examples. North (Chapter 12) then follows this with a more theoretical comparison of the training provision in UK and German firms, which are usefully supported by comparative case studies. Dobers and Wolff (Chapter 13) follow this with a valuable theoretical and practical introduction of 'ecological competence', the skills and knowledge necessary in the EM field—a necessary step in an environmental training needs analysis or an environmental job design.

Ulhøi and Madsen (Chapter 14) then report from their study on the way in which EM is taught at European management schools and universities, suggesting that many business schools, rather than demonstrating leadership in the provision of management education, are lagging behind the EM education needs. The pressing needs for appropriate skills are also evidence in Miller's contribution (Chapter 15), where she, supported by presentations from a one-day conference in Lausanne, argues that environmental education is as much about transferable and interpersonal skills as it is about education in 'hard' sciences or the technical and specialist knowledge required for EM. In this, she supports both contributions of James, as well as this Introduction.

The fourth section of this book contains four specific case studies. Even though many of the chapters preceding this part are based on, or refer to, case study material, it was felt that the practical relevance of this book's message could be enhanced through dedicated case studies. Here, Pollack (Chapter 16) reports from Rover's integration of EM and HRM in a Quality Management philosophy—a case of a UK organisation leading in this integration of the three dimensions. A similarly advanced firm is analysed by Wehrmeyer and Vickerstaff (Chapter 17) presenting details of training needs analysis, the HRM tool perhaps most widely used by EM practitioners. A public sector account is given by Rees (Chapter 18), showing how the largest employer in Kent is coming to terms with EM. His contribution not only shows the particular approach taken by a specialist department, it also demonstrates the similarities between public- and private-sector EM. The case by Beatson and Macklin (Chapter 19) is of Cable and Wireless, one of the few firms to allocate EM into its HRM section.

I am grateful to a great number of people who have either been involved with this book or have been patient throughout its production. First of all, I would like to thank all contributors for their efforts and punctuality. I am also very grateful to Pauline Climpson and John Stuart from Greenleaf Publishing who endured my propensity to miss deadlines and who provided critical encouragement when it was needed most. I would also like to thank Sue for her never-ending patience and support.

■ Notes

1. J. Storey and K. Sisson, *Managing Human Resources and Industrial Relations* (Buckingham, UK: Open University Press, 1993), p. 1.

2. See U. Steger, 'Organisation and Human Resources Management for Environmental Management', in P. Groenewegen, K. Fischer, E.G. Jenkins and J. Schot (eds.), *The Greening of Industry Resource Guide and Bibliography* (Washington, DC: Island Press, 1996); R.J. Schonberger, 'Human Resources Management Lessons from a Decade of Total Quality Management and Re-engineering', in *California Management Review*, Vol. 36 No. 4 (1994), pp. 117-23.

3. D. Torrington and L. Hall, *Personnel Management: A New Approach* (Englewood Cliffs, NJ: Prentice Hall, 1987), p. 11.

4. S. Tyson, *Human Resource Strategy* (London, UK: Pitman, 1995), p. 2.

5. *Op. cit.*

6. R. Field and N. Phillips, 'The Environmental Crisis in the Office: Why aren't Managers Managing the Office Environment?', in *Journal of General Management*, Vol. 18 No. 1 (Autumn 1992), p. 36.

7. J. Barrett, *Environmental Managers in Business* (London, UK: Environmental Data Services Ltd, 1993), p. 9.

8. Trade Union Congress, *Greening the Workplace* (London, UK: TUC, 1991).

9. See Barrett, *op. cit.*

10. See E. Datschefski and the Environment Council, *Environmental Sense is Commercial Sense* (London, UK: The Environment Council, 1993).

11. F.B. Friedman, 'The Changing Role of the Environmental Manager', in *Business Horizons*, Vol. 35 No. 2 (April–May 1992), p. 25.

12. W. Wehrmeyer, 'Environmental Management Styles, Corporate Cultures and Change', in *Greener Management International*, No. 12 (October 1995).

13. See R. Worcester, 'European Attitudes to the Environment', in *European Environment*, Vol. 4 No. 6 (1994), pp. 3-9.

14. M. Charter (ed.), *Greener Marketing: A Responsible Approach to Business* (Sheffield, UK: Greenleaf Publishing, 1992).

15. T. Taillieu and H.C.M. Mooren, *International Career Orientations of Young European*

Graduates: A Survey of Opinions and Aspirations (Tilburg, The Netherlands: University of Tilburg, Department of Psychology, 1990).

16. See J. Elkington, P. Knight and J. Hailes, *The Green Business Guide* (London, UK: Victor Gollancz, 1991); Charter, *op. cit.*; G. Winter, *Blueprint for Green Management* (Hamburg, Germany: McGraw-Hill, 1995).

17. T. Wolters, M. Bouman and M. Peeters, 'Environmental Management and Employment: Pollution Prevention Requires Significant Employee Participation', in *Greener Management International*, No. 11 (July 1995), pp. 63-72.

18. See Business in the Environment and Extel Financial Ltd, *City Analysts and the Environment: A Survey of Environmental Attitudes* (London, UK: Business in the Environment, 1994); C. Ryall and S. Riley, 'Green Investment: An Incentive for Business', in *Greener Management International*, No. 5 (January 1994), pp. 16-21.

19. See F. Dunham, 'Ethical Funds No Bar to Profit', in *Accountancy*, June 1990, p. 111.

20. S. Wilson, 'Making Offices Work', in *Management Today*, October 1987.

21. *Op. cit.*

22. See Tyson, *op. cit.*

23. G. Morgan, 'Rethinking Corporate Strategy: A Cybernetic Perspective', in *Human Relations*, Vol. 36 No. 4 (1983), p. 347.

24. *Op. cit.*

25. G. Morgan, 'Cybernetics and Organization Theory: Epistemology or Technique', in *Human Relations*, Vol. 35 (1982), p. 534.

26. P. Shrivastava, 'Castrated Environment: Greening Organisational Studies', in *Organisational Studies*, May 1994, p. 721.

27. *Op. cit.*

28. ECOTEC Consulting Ltd, *The Impact of Environmental Management on Skills and Jobs* (Report for the Training Agency; Birmingham, UK: ECOTEC, 1990).

29. See Environmental Data Services, 'Many Directors Acknowledge Ignorance of Environmental Laws', in *ENDS Report*, No. 240 (January 1995).

30. See Barrett, *op. cit.*

31. W. Wehrmeyer and S. Rees, 'Who's Afraid of Local Agenda 21? A Survey of UK Local Government Environmental Co-ordinators' Background, Values, Gender and Motivation', in *Greener Management International*, No. 10 (April 1995).

32. Institute of Environmental Management, 'Members' Annual Survey', in *Journal of the IEM*, Vol. 2 No. 4 (1995).

33. Barrett, *op. cit.*, p. 60.

34. P. James and S. Stewart, 'The European Environmental Executive: Technical Specialist or Corporate Change Agent?', in *Corporate Environmental Strategy*, Vol. 2 No. 3 (1995), p. 69.

35. *Ibid.*, pp. 69-70.

36. *Op. cit.*

37. F. Herzberg, *Work and the Nature of Man* (London, UK: Staples Press, 1968).

38. ECOTEC, *op. cit.*, p. iv.

39. See W. Wehrmeyer, *Measuring Environmental Business Performance: A Comprehensive Guide* (Cheltenham, UK: Stanley Thornes, 1995).

40. Friedman, *op. cit.*, p. 26.

Part 1

Environmental Management and Human Resources Management (HRM)

1

Total Quality Environmental Management and Human Resource Management

Peter James

*T*HERE IS a growing interaction between corporate environmental management and quality management. This is most advanced in the US, where leading companies have established the Global Environmental Management Initiative (GEMI) as a networking centre for the application of quality principles to business. These and other activities have created new acronyms—total quality environmental management (TQEM) and quality environmental management (QEM)—several new journals, such as *Total Quality Environmental Management* and *Pollution Prevention Review* and a number of books and reports.[1]

This chapter examines the human resources implications of this interaction. The first section discusses the principles of total quality management and their relevance to environmental management. The second section analyses the effects of TQM on people management, while the third concluding section identifies some limitations of traditional TQM and argues for a transition to sustainable quality management—a transition in which human resources have a major part to play.

■ Total Quality Management and the Environment

The house of quality has many mansions and it is important to distinguish between them. The oldest is what can be called the highly-skilled **engineering quality** tradition which is most closely associated with Germany and permeates that country's approach to environmental problems.

Total quality management (TQM) came into being as a response to the difficulties of reconciling engineering quality with the rapidly expanding, unskilled or semi-skilled workforces of wartime US and post-war Japan.

TQM is aimed at enhancing organisational performance through increased customer satisfaction. This requires a better understanding of what customers want and actions to remedy the defects they do not want in products or services. These are partly achieved through rigorous systems and procedures—as when management systems require the clear allocation of responsibility for responding to defects, or when statistical process control techniques are used to gain a better understanding of process variations.

However, TQM is also a management philosophy that sees organisational problems—such as workers with little autonomy to introduce improvements, internal barriers between departments and external barriers between the organisation and its customers—as a key reason for poor quality.[2] One of the founders of TQM, Joseph Juran, was told when working as a quality inspector that remedying defects was not his job. His boss informed him that 'we're the inspection department and our job is to look at these things after they are made and find the bad ones. Making them right in the first place is the job of the production department.' Juran and others have since argued that high quality is achieved when staff are motivated to seek improvement and have freedom to introduce changes to achieve it—a state often referred to as 'empowerment'. This must be supported by mechanisms such as cross-functional teams to break down the barriers within the organisation and encourage sharing of information and co-operation to solve quality problems.

One important component of TQM is the introduction of systematised procedures to detect quality failures and ensure that they do not recur. In recent years a number of standards for such procedures have been developed in both the quality and the environmental areas. Environmental standards have been developed by the British Standards Institute (BS 7750) and are being developed by the International Standards Organisation (ISO 14000). Some writers on the subject have tended to equate such **environmental management systems** as being synonymous with a quality approach, but this ignores some of the broader implications of TQM, for which management systems are but a part.

One reason that TQM has seemed relevant to environmental problems is a belief that it produces radical improvements in the performance of any activity to which it is applied. However, there are also more specific connections between the objectives and practice of TQM and environmental management. These are:

■ TQM's emphasis on the importance of **customers** and its broadening of the term beyond mere purchasers of a product provides a useful framework for considering and responding to the demands of environmental stakeholders.

■ TQM's emphasis on commitment to **continuous improvement** is very helpful to organisations wishing to move beyond mere compliance with environmental regulation.

■ TQM's focus on eliminating the **root causes** of problems rather than their symptoms fits with the growing awareness that pollution prevention is often a better approach to environmental problems than 'bolting on' pollution control equipment.

■ TQM's belief that quality is **everyone's responsibility** within a company fits well with the growing awareness that all employees have to make a contribution to environmental performance.

■ TQM's concern with calculating the **cost of (non-)quality** provides a useful framework for considering the total costs and benefits of environmental action or inaction.

Customers

One of the central features of TQM has been its extension of customer from external purchasers to any recipient of an product or service within or outside the company. An environmental quality approach extends this definition further by also considering external stakeholders such as communities, regulators and environmental groups as customers for the environmental service. One consequence of this approach is to place greater emphasis on communicating with, and receiving feedback from, such customers through environmental reporting, corporate/advisory panels and other means.

Continuous Improvement

TQM aspires to meet or exceed actual or latent customer expectations of a product or service, which are always changing. This is a demanding goal, which requires a constant search for opportunities to improve. The same requirement is present in the environmental area. New issues are always emerging and new demands are always being made by environmental groups, regulators and others. Many companies have found that merely complying with regulations makes them ill-equipped to deal with this situation. Indeed, strict liability legislation such as Superfund in the US means that, if past environmental actions (or inaction) causes subsequent problems, the legality of those actions is not a defence. The polluter must still pay. Hence, the least risky option is to move beyond compliance to internal standard-setting. A number of companies have therefore introduced internal targets that are more demanding than much national legislation or, less frequently, are in areas that are not currently regulated. In some cases, companies will set targets equivalent to the most stringent environmental legislation in the world (usually California, Germany or Japan), while others will derive it from their own calculations.

TQM sees performance measurement—and subsequent target-setting—as a powerful driver of continuous improvement.[3] A number of companies have also set targets for energy and water consumption, solid waste generation and use of recycled materials. One of the most advanced examples of performance measurement is probably that of Baxter, which tracks its year-by-year progress towards predefined 'state-of-the-art' standards.

One important tool for continuous improvement is frequent and systematic **benchmarking** of one's own performance with others. Until now, environmental benchmarking has been impeded by the perceived sensitivity of environmental performance and lack of comparative data. However, the public availability of TRI and other data has reduced the need for secrecy and created a standardised basis for benchmarking, and several companies are now undertaking it.[4]

■ Tackling Root Causes

A fundamental tenet of TQM is that it is cheaper in the medium to long term (and sometimes even in the short term) to eliminate the causes of problems rather than deal with the symptoms. There is a growing realisation that this is especially true of pollution, and that tightening legislation and other factors make it desirable to prevent it rather than by 'bolting on' pollution control equipment. This can be done by substituting materials, redesigning processes and products, improved monitoring and control of processes, and in other ways.

■ Quality is Everyone's Responsibility

In the old days, quality was the preserve of the quality control department. TQM seeks to downgrade or abolish this function by 'getting it right first time', i.e. eradicating defects at source. This requires that all employees see quality as their responsibility. Pollution prevention, ecodesign and many other environmental actions also require the involvement of many people, in many different departments, within companies, and therefore require a similar spreading of responsibility. This has significant implications for environmental managers, who become much less technical specialists and more change agents working across functional boundaries. However, one recent study suggests that this change is less pronounced in Germany—

which continues to achieve good environmental performance through 'engineering quality', that is, widespread and deep specialist knowledge of environmental issues—than in UK-, Dutch- and US-based companies, which have been more influenced by TQM ideas.[5] If this cross-functional approach is indeed important to continued environmental progress, it may be that German companies will experience some problems in maintaining their record in coming years.

■ Cost of (Non-)Environment

It was no easier to persuade people of the value of, and opportunities for, higher product or service quality in the 1970s and 1980s than it is to convince them of the need for environmental action today. One central aspect of a TQM approach is the winning over of sceptics by demonstrating the costs of the status quo and the benefits of change. This includes calculating costs of inspection, reworking, etc. which can be avoided by eliminating defects at source. Often these costs are not allocated to products but lost in general overheads. The same can be done for environmental issues, both through identifying current costs of poor environmental performance (such as high energy and materials and waste costs) and potential future costs, such as liability for contaminated land. A number of methods are now available; for example, the US Environmental Protection Agency has developed a valuable Total Cost Assessment methodology for calculating the costs of (non-)environment.[6] When applied to several potential investments in wastewater treatment in the paper industry—which had failed the company's conventional investment appraisal process—the methodology identified a number of hidden costs and benefits that made the real return extremely attractive.

■ European Quality Award

The tenets of TQM have been operationalised by the European Foundation for Quality Management (EFQM), which is modelled on the Baldridge Quality awards of the US and earlier Japanese precursors. The Foundation has developed a standardised template that can be used to assess the overall performance of an organisation. It offers an annual European Quality Award (EQA) to the organisation that achieves the highest marks when judged against the template.

The template allocates points (with a possible total of 1,000) for different aspects of performance. With only 150 points (15%) allocated to the conventional measure of performance, i.e. business results (for example, levels of turnover and profit), the template is intended to focus attention on non-financial aspects of performance, such as the fundamental *enablers* of leadership, people management, policy and strategy, resources and processes (allocated 500 of the total points) and the non-financial *results* of people satisfaction, customer satisfaction and impact on society (allocated 350 of the total 500 points for results). The inclusion of impact on society—which covers environmental as well as social issues and is absent in the US and Japanese versions—is therefore an overt recognition of the links between environment and quality. Although some have seen the 60 points allocated to this category as being inadequate—it is only 6% of the total—others argue that it at least forces organisations to pay attention to the issue and that there is no reason why environment cannot be dealt with under other categories as well as impact on society. James[7] discusses the relationship in detail with regard to an award winner, ICL's D2D subsidiary.

■ TQM and Environment: The Best Approach?

One problem with a TQM approach is that only a minority of schemes are delivering their anticipated benefits. Research suggests that this is because organisations are misunderstanding that successful TQM is not a set of tools and techniques but a radical management philosophy. In the words of Binney, 'to achieve continuous improvement, companies need a holistic approach to change: focusing on customers *and* practising fact-based management *and* creating an environment in which people bring to work the same energy, ability and commitment that they display in their life outside work.'[8] This also counters the critics who equate a quality approach with BS 7750 and criticise it for being overly mechanistic and bureaucratic. They are right that introducing systems without an underlying commitment to change organisational values is unlikely to succeed, but wrong in supposing that the management systems approach is the whole of quality. TQM supporters, while recognising the usefulness of systems as a component of quality problems, are equally aware of the dangers of creating a 'bureaucracy of quality'.[9]

Of course, it still may be—as Welford[10] among others has argued—that TQM is too incremental an approach to deliver the scale of change that is needed to achieve sustainability. This is certainly true of a limited **environmental management systems** approach that sees the introduction of a system such as BS 7750 as being synonymous with the whole of quality. However, results from companies who take a wider view suggest that a TQM approach can at least create impressive environmental achievements. In particular, the creation of a philosophy of continuous improvement, and of tracking progress towards it, creates momentum to move beyond compliance and do more to meet the demands of external stakeholders.

■ Human Resource Implications of TQM

The essence of TQM is a belief that people are capable of higher performance than in traditional organisations and can realise this potential in appropriate organisational settings. It is therefore a philosophy of human resource management as much as anything else.[11] Schonberger[12] has summarised the human resource alterations demanded by TQM as:

- Changes in people's **roles**
- Changes in **performance expectations and management**
- New objectives and practices in **human resources departments**
- New principles of **decision-making and strategic development**

The following sections discuss each of these points in detail and provide environmental examples—wherever possible from published sources—from companies that have been influenced by TQM.

■ Changing Roles

This encompasses three main changes:

- Empowerment of employees
- Greater use of team-working
- Creation of quality champions

Empowerment. One central tenet of TQM is that the people closest to processes—typically the front-line workers—have the greatest knowledge of possible improvement opportunities.[13] Realising these opportunities depends upon their being motivated and able to take action and having the data needed to identify appropriate solutions.

McGee and Bhushan[14] have given one example of this in practice. A large chemical company asked operational staff to consider ways of achieving good environmental performance in a new plant. They concluded that three important factors were: handling of raw materials; regular visual inspection of key equipment; and some autonomy for operators to change the process parameters. It also became clear that it would create more understanding and ownership if operatives conducted much of the environmental monitoring and data analysis. As a result, operators' jobs were redesigned to incorporate the new tasks and training programmes put in place to help achieve them.

Team-working. TQM makes heavy use of teams for two reasons. First, many improvements require the bringing together of a number of insights or pieces of information that can be difficult for a single individual to achieve. The second is that one of the main barriers to improvement is the internal boundaries between departments, which can create territoriality and impede the flow of information. By bringing previously separated people together within a constructive, problem-solving context, TQM can help reduce these barriers.

Teams can be either one-off, dealing with specific issues, or permanent. Examples of the former include the environmental quality teams that are regularly formed at the US furniture manufacturer Herman Miller.[15] According to Azzarello, the company has a tradition of participative management that has allowed it to develop a system of ad hoc environmental improvement teams. These bring together professional, managerial and shopfloor staff to address specific environmental issues. After the issue has been addressed, the team either disbands or tackles another one. The company estimates that, as a result of the teams and other environmental initiatives, it has saved $3 million per annum and taken a pioneering role in areas such as eliminating tropical hardwoods from furniture and leaving conservation areas around its plants.

The computer company ICL has created a permanent team of its product developers and designers, environmental champions and staff from its in-house recycling centre to develop a 'cradle-to-grave' approach to its products and the materials used within them. According to one of the members interviewed by the author:

> [The workshops] act as a kind of think tank. We talk about our latest experience, informally benchmark ourselves and ask where we should be going. It's important to have this cross-fertilisation...the workshops are bringing internal suppliers and customers together. The recyclers are the final customer for our product developers.

Another example is provided by the 'Problem Stoppers' team from Sylvania Lightings' plant in York, Pennsylvania, which won the 1992 US National Team Excellence award.[16] The eleven-member team was permanent and multi-level and multi-functional. Members met for one hour weekly and were also allowed one hour per day for data collection and analysis. To enable this, all members had training in relevant statistical techniques and problem-solving approaches. To maintain interest, and allow everyone to take on the role of project leader, several projects were run at the same time. One of these projects was to reduce the amount of waste glass from the furnace. After extensive investigation, the team found that installation of new equipment could recycle 800,000 pounds per annum of cullet and save the company $80,000 per annum.

Many people can initially find it difficult to switch to such team-based approaches, particularly in individualised countries such as the UK and US. Success often depends upon training in topics such as team dynamics and listening and other interpersonal skills. In organisations with personalised reward and recognition systems, success also depends upon team contributions—which can often be difficult to observe and assess—being given equal weight to individual achievement. HR professionals have a vital role in both these areas.

Quality champions. Although TQM sees quality as a collective responsibility, it also recognises that change needs to be seeded by committed and enthusiastic individuals. A key aspect of TQM is therefore the creation of a network of quality champions in all sections of the organisation, including the very top. Sometimes these are full-time posts, but more often they are committed individuals who provide quality leadership in addition to their existing activities. In all cases, their brief is to link the activities of their particular area with overall quality objectives and to provide inspiration and, where necessary, information and assistance to their colleagues.

The aircraft division of the US company Northrop provides one interesting example of how this can be done.[17] In the early 1990s, Northrop had an urgent need to improve its hazardous waste practices and ensure that less was generated. This required a major educational effort among its 5,000 employees. However, both the corporate environmental and training departments were over-stretched. The solution adopted was to select 25 individuals from line positions in key waste-generating areas. The environmental 'Focal Points', as they were described, were chosen for their knowledge of waste, business credibility and communications and other training-related skills. They were put through a 'train the trainer' programme of approximately one week's duration, designed by environmental and training experts, and then conducted training sessions for all staff within their particular areas. Within a short period, the Focal Points grew from being environmental trainers to environmental champions within their departments and established their own network, with quarterly meetings and representation on the company's Environmental Management Committee.

▮ Performance Expectations and Management

TQM is focused on improving performance. An important part of this is to create an expectation that quality is important for its own sake and that it is therefore natural to seek improvement wherever possible. However, ambitious quality initiatives are unlikely to succeed if their objectives are not translated into individual or collective performance management and reward systems. The starting point for this is the incorporation of quality into job descriptions and performance objectives. Next is the linkage of good performance—either individual or collective—to material or non-material rewards. According to Sandra Woods, Vice-President of EHS at Coors Brewing:

> If any single element can be isolated and held up as an example of a successful pollution prevention effort, it is...rewards and recognition. We have worked hard to make sure every employee who has contributed to a successful waste minimisation effort has been publicly rewarded. We give many awards, and we give them often. The company's senior officers have presented these awards to employees during task force meetings. Recipients have been given publicity in the company newspaper, and, whenever possible, we try to share an employee's success with his or her peers.[18]

Woods also notes that waste minimisation efforts have made a significant contribution to the company's recent cost savings and therefore employee returns from a profit-sharing plan.

One key point is that team-based efforts require team-based rewards to maintain motivation and foster a sense that collective endeavour is more fruitful than individual self-seeking. However, many companies have also started to relate individual rewards to personal objectives. One example is Richard Monty, director of environment, health and safety at Huntsman Chemical. Half his incentive pay—which he describes as 'significant part of my overall compensation'—is tied to overall corporate profitability and half to specific environmental goals.[19] These are: compliance, emissions reduction and implementation of the Chemical Manufacturers' Responsible Care programme.

Whether rewards are team- or individual-based, one important point is to take as holistic a view of performance as possible. Environmental champions, for example, are trying to change the attitudes and behaviours of bosses and colleagues and their efforts may be rated less highly by them than by environmental observers. Effective TQM therefore implies some kind of 360-degree feedback process so that views can be sought from team colleagues, internal customers and others who are absent from normal appraisal processes.

Rewards should not only be entirely for performance. There is a growing trend for at least part of the reward package to be related to the acquisition of designated skills or competencies, on the grounds that these are important factors in long-term performance. This is certainly the case with environment where, for example, knowledge of environmental legislation or environmental chemistry among front-line staff can prevent illegal emissions or serious accidents. Building environmental factors into skill-based reward schemes is therefore a particularly important task for HR professionals.

New Roles for Human Resources Staff

TQM introduces two major changes for traditional functions such as human resources or marketing. The first is the transfer of as much operational responsibility as possible to line staff, with the functions becoming advisers and co-ordinators. The previously discussed Northrop case provides an example, with the training division foregoing the operational task of organising environmental training and instead enabling line staff to do this through a 'train the trainer' programme. The second change is a move from separate, specialism-based decision-making to a style based more on cross-functional discussion. The chemical company discussed above provides an example, with changes to job descriptions and objectives being determined not only by human resources staff and line managers, but becoming a more collective output of a quality improvement team.

While these changes diminish the traditional role of human resources in some ways, they also provide an opportunity to break out of traditional patterns and expectations to become more proactive and strategically-oriented 'people champions' of the business. This is particularly true in the environmental area, where several studies have found little interaction between environmental managers and human resource departments.[20] As previous discussions have suggested, there is considerable scope for human resources staff to:

- Suggest modifications to recruitment and selection procedures and criteria to ensure that environmental awareness, team-working skills and other quality-related attributes are prioritised

- Facilitate training in environmental issues, problem-solving and statistical techniques and other enablers of quality environmental management

- Suggest modifications to job descriptions and reward and recognition systems to take quality and environmental considerations into account

To be consistent, they also need to internalise the ideas they are supporting within human resources processes themselves. For quality generally, this primarily means identifying internal customers and ensuring their needs are met. For environmental quality, it means examining the environmental implications of current human resource activities and the opportunities for improvement—not least through the implementation of some of the ideas discussed in other sections of this book.

A more specific role for human resource professionals is with regard to recruitment, succession planning and performance management of environmental staff. The process-based, cross-functional approach of TQM has the same implications for the roles, recruitment and training of environmental managers as it does for their human resource equivalents. James and Stewart,[21] for example, have suggested that a specialist background becomes less important and general management credibility and industry knowhow more important and that employers should recruit accordingly. Conversely, the competencies required of successful environmental leaders are sufficiently similar to those required of top managers for the posts to be a useful source of experience for high fliers. They can therefore be built into mainstream succession planning and career management activities to a greater degree than in the past.

Decision-making and strategy. TQM is only completely successful when its principles have been internalised and, to a degree, routinised and thereby guide everyday behaviour. This occurs when the values of the organisation are aligned with those of its customers and its employees, when staff, and senior managers in particular, actually practise the views they espouse, and when the performance management systems are closely aligned with overall quality objectives. The same points apply to successful quality-based approaches to environmental issues, and human resources staff have an important part in achieving them.

■ Values and the Environment

TQM sees shared values as partially replacing traditional methods of achieving performance and co-ordination within enterprises. However, Western TQM often appears to lack some of the value content that seems to have been present in the Japanese version. For many people, the term 'total' is less than accurate if it does not touch upon fundamental questions such as a company's purpose and contribution to society—questions that are increasingly being asked in Europe and North America by educated employees and external stakeholders.[22] Many Japanese have seen TQM as having a quasi-spiritual dimension—such as helping society through helping customers and helping maintain the existence of both organisations and the Japanese nation—which greatly assisted its implementation in their companies. Westerners are more cynical about such matters and often tend to see TQM-type innovations as merely a means of increasing profitability and management power. This is undoubtedly one of the main reasons for the failure of so many TQM schemes and it may be that TQM has to develop a deeper intellectual rationale and value content if its potential is to be truly unleashed in environmental and other areas in the West.

Ecology may hold the key to this transformation. A widespread recognition of the nature and fragility of ecosystems may not only be a necessary addition to the application of TQM in the environmental area but also a source of metaphors to understand the general changes in management practice which 'deep' TQM requires. Businesses increasingly need to understand that they are components of a social as well as a natural ecosystem and that their wellbeing depends upon recognising the inter-dependence of all its components (for example, companies and their suppliers and customers) and the linkage between the survival of components and that of the system as a whole. Ecosystems are also dynamic and the responses of species—for example, adaptability to a wide range of habitats or occupying specific niches—have many parallels with those of corporate responses to market conditions. Above all, the holistic, systems perspective that naturally arises from the study of ecosystems is also one that is needed to make sense of 1990s business conditions.[23]

The paradoxical conclusion, therefore, is that, in future, TQM may be influenced by environment as much as environmental management uses TQM. Sustainable quality management—a holistic, value-centred approach that recognises the need to maintain human and natural systems as well as the individual customers within it—may be the key not only to achieving sustainable development but also to unleashing the full potential of the intellectual and organisational revolution that TQM and other innovations are creating. Human resources staff have a major role in both championing its development and guiding its detailed implementation through the people practices of organisations.

■ Notes

1. For example, the President's Commission on Environmental Quality, *Total Quality Management: A Framework for Pollution Prevention* (Washington, DC: US Government, 1993); J. Willig, *Environmental TQM* (New York, NY: McGraw-Hill, 1993).

2. See R. Grant, R. Shani and R. Krishnan, 'TQM's Challenge to Management Theory and Practice', in *Sloan Management Review*, Winter 1994, pp. 25-35.

3. See P. James and M. Bennett, *Environment-Related Performance Measurement in Business* (Berkhamsted, UK: Ashridge Management Research Group, 1994); W. Wehrmeyer, *Measuring Environmental Performance: A Comprehensive Guide* (London, UK: Stanley Thornes, 1995).

4. See James and Bennett, *op. cit.*

5. See P. James and S. Stewart, *The European Environmental Executive* (Berkhamsted, UK: Ashridge Management Research Group, 1995).

6. See C. Tuppen (ed.), *Environmental Accounting in Industry* (London, UK: BT, 1996).

7. P. James, 'Quality and the Environment: The Experience of ICL', in K. North (ed.), *European Case Studies in Environmental Management* (London, UK: Prentice-Hall, 1996).

8. See G. Binney, *Making Quality Work: Lessons from Europe's Leading Companies* (London, UK: Economist Intelligence Unit, 1992).

9. Binney, *op. cit.*

10. R. Welford, 'Breaking the Link between Quality and the Environment: Auditing for Sustainability and Life-Cycle Assessment', in *Business Strategy and the Environment*, Autumn 1993, pp. 31-38.

11. See Grant *et. al.*, *op. cit.*

12. R. Schonberger, 'Human Resource Management: Lessons from a Decade of Total Quality Management and Reengineering', in *California Management Review*, Winter 1994, pp. 109-23.

13. See J. Cramer and B. Roes, 'Total Employee Involvement: Measures for Success', in *Total Quality Environmental Management*, Autumn 1993, pp. 39-52.

14. E.C. McGee and A. Bhushan, 'Applying the Baldrige Quality Criteria to Environmental Performance', in *Total Quality Environmental Management*, Autumn, 1993, pp. 1-18.

15. See J. Azzarello, 'Long-Time Environmental Leadership Pays Off in Many Ways at Herman Miller', in *Total Quality Environmental Management*, Winter 1992/93, pp. 187-91.

16. See D. Caplan, 'Sylvania's GTE Products Problem Stoppers', in *Total Quality Environmental Management*, Winter 1992/93, pp. 159-64.

17. See B. Weise, 'Integrating Total Quality Principles into an Environmental Training Program', in *Total Quality Environmental Management*, Spring 1992, pp. 245-51.

18. S. Woods, 'Making Pollution Prevention Part of the Coors Culture', in *Total Quality Environmental Management*, Autumn 1993, pp. 31-38.

19. See J. Snyder, 'More Execs Find Pay Linked to EHS Goals', in *Environment Today*, October 1992, pp. 1, 22-23.

20. T. Lent and R. Wells, 'Corporate Environmental Management Shows Shift from Compliance to Strategy', in *Total Quality Environmental Management*, Summer 1992, pp. 379-94; James and Stewart, *op. cit.*

21. *Op. cit.*

22. See Royal Society of Arts, *Tomorrow's Company* (London, UK: RSA, 1994).

23. See P. Senge, *The Fifth Discipline* (New York, NY: Doubleday, 1990); M. Wheatley, *Leadership and the New Science* (San Francisco, CA: Berrett-Koehler, 1992).

2

Best Environmental HRM Practices in the US

John Milliman and Judith Clair

ORGANISATIONS are experiencing increasing pressures for environmentally-sensitive products and operations. Unfortunately, many organisational efforts in this direction fail because human resource management (HRM) practices are left unchanged during the implementation of environmental programmes. To suggest a pathway to overcome this flaw, this chapter describes the methods used by the most progressive corporations in the US to develop environmental HRM practices. First, the strategic context for environmental management is described. Secondly, best environmental practices in training, performance appraisal, and reward systems are discussed. Thirdly, suggestions for future practice in each of these areas are offered.

■ Introduction

Many researchers agree that the planet faces a significant ecological crisis. As a major source of this environmental damage, corporations are increasingly pressured to develop 'green' practices by government regulators, environmental activists, business competitors,[1] and consumers.[2] In developing green programmes, research suggests that a systems approach is crucial to programme success. Put simply, all organisational systems must be aligned to fulfil environmental goals. Thus, environmental programmes often require significant internal and external organisational changes. These changes include the alteration of core internal organisational systems, the creation of 'green' operations and products,[3] and the development of new relationships with various environmental stakeholders.[4]

In line with this systems approach, a business organisation must also adjust its human resource management (HRM) practices.[5] Consultant E. Craig

McGee of the Gauntlett Group and Xerox Environmental manager, Abhay Bhushan state: 'This dimension covers the systems for empowering people at all levels to monitor their own work and suggest improvements, creating reward systems that take environmental performance into account, and training managers for environmental accountability'.[6] In fact, training, incentives, and evaluation are among the most important aspects of an effective environmental management programme,[7] especially as a tool for communication of expectations about integrity, ethical behaviour and competence.[8] Nevertheless, many organisations still implement environmental management programmes without an integrated HRM component.[9] Furthermore, until recently, little was known about links between HRM practices and organisational environmental effectiveness.

Thus, the purpose of this chapter is to explore the role of HRM in environmental management programmes. We do this by discussing best practice environmental examples in US organisations. Best practice studies involve the analysis of processes and practices in organisations that are proven and successful. Organisations are selected for benchmarking that are known in their industry as having superior performance in a particular environmental practice.[10]

Our review includes organisations with innovative environmental practices that have been selected for publication or presentation in leading industry journals and conferences in the US. This literature review suggests that the implementation of environmental HRM involves four steps, as shown in Figure 1. The first precondition for environmental HRM is the development of the organisation's environmental vision and its associated goals. In turn, effective environmental HRM programmes are designed to facilitate employee attainment of the environmental vision through: (1) training that provides employees with the requisite environmental skills and knowledge; (2) performance appraisals that make employees accountable to environmental performance standards; and (3) rewards that provide incentive to accomplish environmental objectives. Data from performance appraisal and reward systems are also used as feedback on the organisation's environmental goals and to help refine and set new goals. The first precondition concerning the organisation's strategic environmental context is explained next. Following this section, the literature on best practices in these three areas of environmental HRM in North American organisations is reviewed and suggestions for future practice are offered.

■ Environmental Strategic Context

Our survey of the literature of corporate best practices suggests that a critical precondition for successful environmental programmes is executive

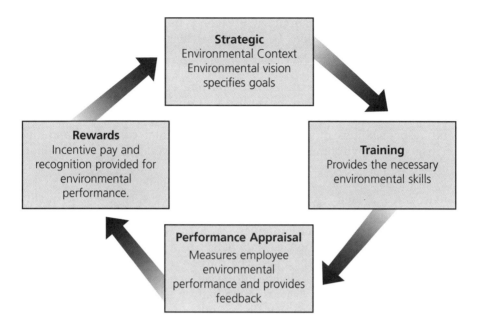

Figure 1: *Overview Model of Environmental HRM Practices*

management development of, and commitment to, an environmental vision statement for the organisation.[11] 'The continuous interest and support of top management is the major key to the long-term success of the [environmental] programme,' observed William Parker, director of environmental programmes at EG&G, a company that manufactures laboratory and electronic equipment. Such interest on the part of corporate executives is expressed through an environmental vision statement. The environmental vision sets the organisational objective to either meet or exceed compliance requirements[12] and relates environmental initiatives to the firm's business strategy. As Jane Hutterly, Vice President for Environmental and Safety Actions of S.C. Johnson & Son declared, 'First, we needed to determine what S.C. Johnson wanted to be environmentally as we approached the 21st century. Senior management dialogs provided the impetus to translate our philosophies into specific environmental policy and principles'.[13] The S.C. Johnson & Son environmental vision states that it is committed to increased recycling, to support for environmental education programmes, and to the reduction of specific chemicals, packaging materials, raw materials, and a variety of solid wastes.

As stated above, an environmental vision is important to S.C. Johnson & Son and other organisations because it provides the direction and call to action that can energise employees to implement successfully a comprehensive environmental programme. However, to be effective, it also needs to be translated by executives into concrete environmental goals[14] and specific practices that can be utilised throughout the company.[15] For example, Kodak's environmental vision specifically defines various roles and responsibilities of its corporate environmental committee and line managers on environmental management practices.[16] To further facilitate the accomplishment of environmental objectives, an increasing number of US organisations are applying quality management principles to the environmental area, spawning new programmes such as total quality environmental management (TQEM) and environmental re-engineering.[17]

To make environmental initiatives—such as TQEM and re-engineering, effective, organisations must institutionalise them as a part of the company's core systems, culture and values. The purpose of institutionalisation is to ensure that organisational change efforts become part of the new corporate status quo. Regarding environmental initiatives, experts agree that effective institutionalisation requires that the organisation's training, appraisal and reward systems be modified to ensure that the organisation's environmental vision and values are actually implemented.[18]

While many organisations have made significant efforts to improve their environmental practices, the institutionalisation efforts are far from complete. A recent empirical study of over 800 firms in four industries in the US revealed that there was a significant difference between the rhetoric that managers espouse about the *need* for environmental management practices and the development of *actual* environmental management practices, such as HRM. In fact, the greatest difference between corporate rhetoric and action on a number of different dimensions of environmental management was in performance appraisal and reward systems. Without the development of such HRM systems, environmental management initiatives are in some danger of being seen as another US management 'fad'.[19] In the next sections of this chapter we discuss best practices toward institutionalisation of environmental initiatives in three core HRM systems: training, performance appraisal and rewards.

■ Environmental Training

■ Translating the Environmental Vision into Training Objectives

Once an environmental vision is developed, employees need to be instructed on its implementation. Environmental education programmes provide employees with the capabilities and information required for the implementation of green programmes. Such an emphasis on training is consistent with the fourth principle of the International Chamber of Commerce (ICC) Business Charter for Sustainable Development which states that organisations should 'educate, train, and motivate employees to conduct their activities in an environmentally responsible manner'.[20] Consultants Judy Cook of Mac Technical Services Co. and Brenda Seith of ERM Northwest take this principle further by expressing that 'A training programme can be the single most important element of a company's compliance strategy. By carefully identifying regulatory requirements, company goals, and employees' needs, the training assures that these can all be satisfied.'[21] Thus, training appears to be an absolutely critical component in the success of environmental endeavours.[22] Perhaps this is the reason why US firms have instituted more environmental training programmes than any other aspect of HRM.[23]

Once an organisation commits to environmental training, an environmental training programme objective that is consistent with the organisation's environmental goals and strategy must be established.[24] Polaroid provides a good example of a clear environmental training objective that is related to organisation's vision for regulatory compliance. The company's environmental training goal is 'the creation of an environment where every member is provided with the proper knowledge and training to increase awareness of environmental issues and to assure full compliance with the regulatory requirement'.[25]

■ Environmental Training Needs Analysis

Following the articulation of the environmental training objective, an environmental training needs analysis should be conducted to determine the nature, composition and delivery of the training programme. A number of steps are required to conduct an environmental training needs analysis effectively and these are summarised in Figure 2.

This figure indicates that, first, it is important to determine what environmental knowledge and skills employees need to meet the company's overall environmental objective and related programme goals.[26] There are a number of ways to determine these knowledge and skill requirements. One method is to appoint a team of specialists to analyse the training needs of employees and the company; for example, a corporate environmental training committee, composed of executives, training experts and environmental professionals investigates training needs at Duke Power.[27] A second method is to survey employees on their level of environmental knowledge and other relevant management skills.[28]

1. **Environmental knowledge and skills are determined.**
   a. Corporate Environmental Committee assesses employee training needs.
   b. Survey employee environmental and managerial skills.

2. **Employees needing training are identified.**
   a. Identify who will receive training and the content of the training.
   b. Implement plans to ensure training is carried out.

3. **Training programme delivery is planned.**
   a. Decide who will conduct the training.
   b. Determine location and length of training sessions.
   c. Select an appropriate presentation format.

Figure 2: *Key Steps in Environmental Training Needs Analysis*
Source: Based on Judy Cook and Brenda Seith, 'Designing an Effective Environmental Training Programme',
in *Journal of Environmental Regulation*, Autumn 1992, pp. 53-62.

As shown in Figure 2, the second step in an environmental training needs analysis is to determine which employees are to be trained. A key question here is: should all employees participate, or should only certain types of employees in selected departments or management levels receive instruction?[29] In some organisations, plant and middle-level managers are given the responsibility to determine which employees are to be trained.[30] Line managers are also frequently given the responsibility for ensuring that their employees take the appropriate training.[31]

A third key step is to determine how the training programme will be delivered. Key questions here include: Who will conduct the training? Where will the training be conducted? How many training sessions will be held and how long will they be? What media and types of presentations (e.g. lecture, case studies, discussion, tours, exercises, etc.) are most effective in promoting environmental learning for the different groups of employees in the organisation? Some organisations have sought to avoid a packaged training approach by developing modular training's in which employees receive education only in the areas needed. With a modular approach, specific training components can also be more easily changed to include new information on frequently changing environmental regulations.[32]

■ *Major Types of Environmental Training Programmes*
The next step in the process is to implement the environmental training programme. Our literature review indicates that the three most prevalent

environmental training programmes used in US organisations are on regulatory requirements, employee awareness and TQEM.

Environmental Regulatory Training. Environmental regulatory training typically involves technical training on state, federal and local regulations regarding air, water and solid-waste emissions[33] as well as instruction on emergency response procedures.[34] In the US many of these regulations are mandated at the federal level by the Environmental Protection Agency (EPA), Occupational Safety and Health Administration (OSHA) and the Department of Transportation (DOT) as a result of environmental laws such as the Clean Air Act, Safe Drinking Water Act, the Clean Water Act, the Toxic Substances Control Act (TSCA) and the Resource Conservation and Recovery Act (RCRA). In addition to the federal level, there are numerous state and local regulations and environmental agencies in the US that must be communicated to employees.[35] Environmental training is considered the best vehicle for dissemination of this information.

Nevertheless, regulatory-based training is particularly challenging for four reasons: (1) it is required by the governmental agencies rather than initiated voluntarily; (2) the laws constantly change; (3) the laws often conflict between the different governmental agencies;[36] and (4) the regulations can be vague or ambiguous.[37] For example, William Parker, Director of Environmental Programmes at EG&G, commented: 'Several EPA programs list a total of over 800 hazardous compounds, and these lists are frequently revised.'[38] For these reasons, an important challenge for the environmental training staff is to research and keep abreast of regulatory changes,[39] and, in addition, extensive training records must be kept to ensure compliance.[40]

Environmental Awareness Training. Perhaps second in importance to regulatory training are those education efforts intended to increase employee awareness of environmental issues and policies. For many organisations, environmental management practices are still relatively new, and some employees may question whether their company is simply paying 'lip service' or is truly committed to proactive environmental management practices.[41] For these reasons, companies such as Duke Power[42] have developed environmental awareness training programmes to increase employees' awareness of the company's commitment to environmental protection, to ensure that environmental issues are kept uppermost in employees' minds while they cope with daily business challenges,[43] and to enhance employee motivation to implement proactive environmental practices.[44] Research suggests that environmentally-aware employees are more likely to take pride in performing their jobs in an environmentally-responsible manner, to share their positive attitudes with other employees,[45] and to provide more ideas and suggestions.[46]

Effective communication tools and media are a key component of environmental awareness programmes to ensure that employees understand the importance of environmental issues. Such communication can take many different forms; for example, Xerox educates its employees through CEO communications, the company environmental, health and safety (EHS) newsletter, employee environmental publications, company electronic mail networks, employee forums, and videos.[47] Duke Power also communicates the importance of environmental issues via the organisation's electronic bulletin board, interdepartmental task force communications, the placement of environmental questions on employee opinion surveys, and company celebrations and other social events.[48] Other organisations communicate the importance of environmental issues in their annual reports and through the delivery of training in naturalistic settings.[49]

Training on Environmental Quality Management. A third popular topic for environmental training involves environmental TQM or TQEM. Cathy Stevenson, Manager of Health, Safety and Environmental Audit at Allied-Signal, Inc., observes that '[environmental] TQM is a journey from innocence to excellence. To use TQM, companies must first understand the tools of the process and then the application of each tool. The journey begins with education for everyone.'[50] Because TQEM often involves major changes in employee roles and organisational systems, the level and type of training needed depends on the capabilities and knowledge of the employees assigned to implement it. Employees who understand quality management techniques require little additional training. In contrast, employees lacking in quality management experience require much greater up-front training for TQEM. For example, one organisation trained its employees on basic reading, writing and maths skills to prepare them to apply TQEM principles effectively.[51] In addition, since TQEM requires greater employee involvement, organisations with a top-down decision-making style may need to address how to improve employee empowerment, participation and input in their training.[52]

Another hurdle in TQEM training is employee cynicism. Quality management programmes have frequently been perceived as a management 'fad' in the US. Thus, employees sometimes withhold their full support or commitment to such programmes because they see them as short-lived and as an obstacle in their daily work, rather than as an opportunity for performance improvement. However, resistance to TQEM can often be addressed by showing the importance of environmental issues and by identifying the relationship between environmental goals and the company's overall business strategy.[53]

In most TQEM training, employees first receive instruction on quality management techniques such as customer focus, process evaluation, problem-solving, measurement, and taking corrective action.[54] For instance, Xerox implemented intensive training of its employees on quality tools, including interactive skills, teamwork, quality goal-setting, measurement and monitoring, systematic defect and error-prevention processes, and statistical and analytical tools.[55] Similarly, TQEM training at EG&G, Inc. included continuous improvement, how to address the most solvable problems first, and how to involve stakeholders into decisions.[56] Training plays a particularly important role in ensuring that employees have the knowledge and skills to implement more complex TQEM tools such as benchmarking. At Allied-Signal, employees receive extensive training to ensure they conduct effective and efficient benchmarking studies that achieve optimum results.[57]

TQEM training often must also involve the promotion of employee interpersonal and communication skills: 'Training in the use of technical tools and the development of behavioural, people-oriented skills are critical and necessary for the TQM process to succeed.'[58] Examples of interpersonal skills emphasised in TQEM training include: leadership, how to work in teams, goal-setting, listening, presenting and meeting management.[59]

The most effective TQEM training programmes include skill development and application, rather than just information about the various quality management techniques. Tina Worley, a training manager at Duke Power, observed, 'our approach is moving from knowledge-based to performance-based training. Instructors now teach skills in the context of how employees will use them on the job.'[60] Skill-oriented training techniques at Duke Power include small group exercises, role-playing, games and case studies. In comparison, Allied-Signal, Inc. seeks to ensure the effective application of training skills to the workplace through the development of support groups and the selection of organisational problems and projects that are manageable.[61]

■ Summary of Current Best Practices

Our study indicates a number of common characteristics of effective environmental training programmes which are summarised below and in Figure 3. Though no one organisation demonstrates all of these characteristics, together they comprise the total approach to environmental HRM currently employed in the organisations surveyed. First, the company's environmental vision must be carefully translated into concrete environmental training objectives. Second, a systematic training needs analysis is performed which clearly states the environmental knowledge that needs to be learned, the specific employees to be included in the training, and how the training programme is to be delivered. Third, an organisation develops a three-part training strategy which includes information on: (1) environmental regulatory requirements to help ensure that the company meets its legal requirements; (2) employees' awareness to ensure that environmental issues are perceived as an integral part of the company's culture and philosophy; and (3) TQEM or some other programme that enables a corporation to make continual improvements in its environmental practices and results.

I. Training

1. Translate company environmental vision into concrete environmental training objective.
2. Conduct a systematic training needs analysis that specifies the skills to be gained, who will be included in the training, and how the training will be delivered.
3. Conduct training on three key areas: regulatory requirements, employee awareness, and a programme for improving environmental processes and systems, such as TQEM.

II. Performance Appraisal

1. Include quantitative environmental measures in appraisals so that employees have clear and specific targets to attain.
2. Prevent excessive focus on a few numerical goals by having a broad number of goals, include qualitative goals, and take into account external factors and cultural differences.
3. Carefully link performance appraisals to organisational environmental audits and management information system (EMIS) to obtain the most accurate and comprehensive environmental measurement information.

III. Rewards

1. Develop a reward system for environmental performance that includes financial, recognition and non-traditional incentives to maximise the motivation of a diverse workforce.
2. Ensure that a significant portion of an employee's incentive package is based on environmental performance.
3. Ensure that environmental rewards are highly visible and are offered on an individual, team and company-wide basis.

Figure 3: *Summary of Findings on Effective US Environmental HRM Practices*

■ Future Environmental Training Practices

Besides improving skill development and application in training sessions, it is important to consider other ways companies can improve their environmental training programmes. Our review of the literature indicates that relatively little was said about specific evaluation practices. Therefore, a first implication for future practice involves how to develop systematic ways to evaluate the effectiveness of environmental training programmes. Such an evaluation process should ideally involve a multi-pronged approach including analysis of how the training programme was conducted, the extent of skill or knowledge acquisition by the participants, and the degree of actual improvement in environmental performance by employees and the organisation.

A second issue is to determine if there are other important environmental training needs that have not been addressed extensively thus far in organisations beyond those on regulations, employee awareness and TQEM. Since companies have to deal increasingly with external environmental stakeholders, one important future training need may involve the development of corporate officials' abilities to communicate effectively to and obtain feedback from representatives of regulatory agencies, the media, and citizen activist groups. Multinational corporations may also need to include more international components and considerations into their environmental training programmes.

A third issue companies will need to address is whether their environmental training needs should be conducted up-front at the beginning of an environmental initiative or in a 'pull' or 'just-in-time' manner in which training is provided on an as-needed basis for employees during the implementation of the environmental programme. This dilemma can be resolved by addressing the following question: In which way do employees learn the best—obtaining the bulk of the information first or by getting the information in parts as they begin each new environmental task? The answer to this question will vary according to type of organisation and industry.

A final and related concern is how best to deliver environmental training in terms of both learning and cost. As organisations face increasing competition and pressure, they must attempt to accomplish more with fewer resources. What type of training (e.g. lecture, role-playing, case studies, problem-solving, etc.) most promotes the transfer of learning on environmental tasks from the classroom to the workplace? Does the most effective method of training vary depending on the purpose (e.g. regulatory, awareness, TQEM, etc.) of the training session? If so, how? In terms of cost-savings, one promising direction might be look how companies use new technologies (e.g. interactive TV, computers, videos, electronic mail, etc.) to deliver more effective training while utilising fewer resources.

■ Environmental Performance Appraisals

One of the greatest challenges with an environmental management programme is its longevity. To ensure that a programme can last, a third step in environmental HRM is for organisations to hold employees accountable for their environmental duties in performance appraisals.[62] 'Without accountability managers are either oblivious to or less concerned about compliance issues that are critical to a facility's operation and livelihood.'[63]

■ Managerial Environmental Performance Appraisals

Thus far, most environmental appraisal systems appear to be primarily limited to plant managers, division managers and executives. For example, at EG&G, Inc. the division manager is held accountable for all environmental goals set at the division level.[64] Similarly, Kodak has developed a self-appraisal programme that allows plant managers to judge their environmental performance against company standards and to identify any performance gaps.[65] Environmental results of plant managers' performance appraisals should also be communicated to staff employees to demonstrate a relationship between their unit's outcomes and their own environmental efforts.[66]

To measure environmental performance effectively, quantitative environmental goals are often included as key criteria in appraisals. However, including difficult quantitative measures in appraisals can create extensive pressure on managers, to the extent that they may distort the system to show that they reached all of their goals. Primarily quantitative appraisals can also cause managers to focus almost exclusively on the numerical objectives and ignore the qualitative aspects of environmental initiatives.[67]

To prevent an excessive focus on quantitative performance outcomes, Browning-Ferris Industries (BFI) has developed a sophisticated environmental performance appraisal system for its regional and facility managers. First, BFI managers are evaluated on the following aspects of environmental management: management systems, compliance programmes, government and community affairs, permit management, risk management/loss control, environmental training, contingency and preparedness, and environmental monitoring. Having a diverse number of goals and accountabilities prevents managers from focusing on a few aspects of environmental management to the exclusion of other important areas. Secondly, managers receive points in each of the above areas of environmental management on a low, medium or high basis, depending on the level of accomplishment. In this way, managers can receive some credit in their performance appraisal even when they have only partially accomplished a goal. Thirdly, the performance appraisals take into account external factors (e.g. delays in permit approvals) which are beyond the immediate control of managers, since interaction with government agencies and regulators is frequently required.[68] These latter two steps take much of the pressure off managers and thereby decrease their need to distort appraisal systems.

In addition to accounting for external factors that influence a manager's environmental performance, another challenge of performance appraisals involves how accurately and consistently to measure performance standards across different units of the organisation. This is a particularly important issue for multinational corporations (MNCs), because environmental expectations and regulations vary extensively by country. For instance, Amoco found itself in a dilemma in when it sought to ban personnel from wearing beards in areas of the company that contain toxic gas. Holding managers accountable for the implementation of this policy became a problem in the company's operating units in Muslim countries in the Middle East where wearing beards is a cultural custom. Roy Hutson, Senior Environmental Consultant at Amoco, recalled: 'you suddenly find that you have run headlong into a culture that holds beards to be part of its religion. Now what do you do?'[69]

Amoco dealt with this issue by instituting new corporate-wide environmental performance standards for on-site use policies, waste management plans, environmental audits and waste reduction. Although Amoco's standards are customised to some degree to each country's culture and regulations, they are still considered to be proactive because a number of the countries have little or no environmental requirements.[70]

■ Integrating Appraisals with Audits and Information Systems

Another important issue in performance appraisals is how to obtain accurate and objective data on managers' environmental performance: 'All organisations face the same challenge: how to identify measures that track and quantify change in an effective and useful way.'[71] In response to this need, many organisations have developed environmental management information systems (EMIS)[72] and environmental audits,[73] both of which are discussed below.

The purpose of an EMIS is to track effectively the vast number of pollution, energy and regulatory requirements that the company faces.[74] Once an EMIS is developed, it is important not just to use it for the company's reporting purposes, but also to link it to managers' performance appraisals. Thus, one of the first steps of EMIS is to organise and prioritise the company's various environmental data so that it can be utilised in an effective and time-efficient manner. This step is complicated by the fact that environmental data must frequently be obtained from many existing sources, including energy utilisation, water consumption, accident rates, environmental expenditures and pollution releases.

A second important EMIS challenge is to develop quantitative measures for each specific customer need. For example, regulatory agencies generally prefer indexed metrics, while the general public prefers the total amount of waste released into the air, water and land.[75] Organisations need to decide carefully which type of measures are most appropriate for accurately assessing the environmental performance of their various employees.

A third need for EMIS and appraisal systems is to keep abreast of the many changes in environmental data and performance indicators: 'What you measure today may not be what you measure two years from now. Times change, environmental science evolves, priorities of a company may change, finances may change, and you need to evaluate your indicators on a regular basis.'[76]

Environmental audits and environmental management system reviews are other mechanisms by which organisations collect data to assess environmental performance. For example, the Union Carbide environmental audit programme involves an environmental procedures and protocols examination, environmental hazards ranking, analysis of causes and findings of environmental pollution, review of action plans, and field audits.[77] Audits are typically conducted every one to four years. However, corporate plants that receive low audit ratings are audited more frequently. Many corporations use a combination of corporate and local business unit employees and outside consultants to conduct audits to obtain both diverse perspectives and ensure independent assessment.[78] As with EMIS, audits provide another opportunity for firms to collect data on the company, as well as on the performance of their managers.

In sum, environmental audits and EMIS programmes can provide valuable information for the organisation and its employees. First, at the organisational level, the audit and EMIS programmes allow a company to evaluate the effectiveness of its existing environmental management programmes and to ensure consistent adherence to company policies across different operating units.[79] For example, the results from the performance measurement process at Church & Dwight are used to set higher environmental goals, to refine methods for achieving the goals, and to share knowledge acquistion across the company.[80] Secondly, EMIS and audit results can lead to specific recommendations for how to improve environment systems and processes. Thirdly, data from the EMIS can also enable a company to better report results to various external stakeholders, such as regulators and consumers.[81] Finally, information from audits can provide employees with the opportunity to raise recurring problems in environmental systems, to receive feedback on past performance, and to obtain coaching and direction for future performance.[82]

◼ Summary of Current Best Practices

Companies with effective environmental performance appraisals have the following characteristics, as shown in Figure 3. First, effective organisations include quantitative environmental criteria to ensure that employees have specific and clear measures. Secondly, to prevent any negative side effects of quantitative goals, organisations should carefully take several steps.

1. Set a diverse number of environmental goals to be measured in appraisals.

2. Emphasise difficult-to-measure, but important, qualitative objectives, such as teamwork and information-sharing.

3. Take into account external factors.

4. Consider cross-cultural issues in the appraisal systems of multinational corporations.

Finally, link information from environmental audits and EMIS systems to individual employees' performance appraisals.

◼ Future Environmental Performance Appraisal Practices

Though corporations are making some important strides in environmental performance appraisals, there are still many key issues that should be addressed. First, feedback from external stakeholders such as regulatory agencies, citizen activist groups and public officials should be included in the environmental performance evaluation of a corporate official, such as a plant manager or Director of Environmental Affairs. This is important because these various external groups can wield a significant influence on corporate decisions. Obtaining feedback from these groups in appraisals can help ensure that a company is responsive to their concerns. Ontario Hydro in Canada does this to some degree by obtaining feedback on the utility company's environmental performance from an environmental advisory board and through survey research on a number of its customer groups.[83] Nonetheless, a key issue concerns the conditions and situations under which such feedback should take place and how it is linked to specific managers' performance appraisals.

Performance appraisals and 360-degree goal-setting may be one avenue by which organisations can systematically receive more feedback from their various environmental constituents. The requirement of 360-degree goal-setting is that a manager sets specific goals with each internal and external customer (or stakeholder) with whom the manager interacts at the beginning of the year. In some companies, the goal-setting is formalised into a contract or written agreement between the manager and his/her customers.[84] At the end of the year, a sampling of these customers provides feedback on how well the manager has performed on the goals. By directly involving customers into goal-setting and performance appraisals, the 360-degree approach can make a manager more accountable to his/her customers.[85] Such a system could be developed by including key community, regulatory and interest group officials into the goal-setting and performance appraisal systems of managers with strong environmental responsibilities, such as the Director of Environmental Affairs.

A second issue for appraisals concerns how baseline measures of environmental performance can be developed so that an organisation can more accurately compare the environmental performance of managers in different plants or units within the organisation. Questions regarding this issue include:

- What criteria is most essential in the environmental performance of a Director of Environmental Affairs versus those that are most crucial to a plant manager?

- What measures can an organisation develop that are comparable between managers who are responsible for different types of pollution (e.g. air, water and solid waste)?[86]

- What changes need to occur in the company's EMIS, audit programme, and performance appraisal to facilitate these comparisons?

A third major challenge for a company is how to develop effective goals and performance measurement systems for all employees throughout the organisation, not just middle and upper-level managers. The issue is to determine how to set meaningful environmental goals for supervisors and rank-and-file employees such as assembly line and manufacturing personnel. One possible method to accomplish this is to use the 'management by objectives' (MBO) approach, whereby objectives at each level of the organisation are translated into more specific and concrete objectives for the next lower level of the organisation. When conducted properly, the MBO approach, has been found to be highly successful in converting organisational objectives into more specific goals for departments and individual employees.[87] The MBO process could also be implemented for environmental objectives. Employees throughout the organisation could then be held accountable for these environmental goals in their performance appraisals.

Environmental Rewards

As shown in Figure 1, a final step in environmental HRM is the development of reward programmes to provide further incentive for employees to be ecologically proactive.[88] To ensure that employees are rewarded on a performance contingent basis, reward systems should be tightly linked to the attainment of goals in performance appraisals. Bruce Gantner, Director of Environmental Compliance at BFI, states: 'Performance goals are the critical foundation for any incentive plan.'[89] To date, organisations have primarily developed monetary-based and recognition-based rewards for environmental performance.[90] Research indicates that these rewards have primarily been implemented for managers, rather than employees.[91] Below we discuss both types of rewards, along with some non-traditional rewards that are being developed by a small number of innovative firms.

Financial Rewards for Environmental Performance

Providing financial rewards for environmental performance can be one of the most important ways to generate employee involvement and commitment to environmental programmes,[92] but only a few organisations have done so thus far: 'Linking pay to environmental performance is a sure way to reinforce the company's environmental message—but most aren't doing it.'[93] Part of the reason why companies are slow to develop performance-based environmental incentives may be that most companies still have relatively new environmental appraisal systems, as indicated previously. James Snyder of *Environment Today* observed: 'The greater the comfort level with performance measurement systems, the more specific the EHS manager's incentive pay is honed.'[94]

BFI, with a well-developed environmental appraisal system, is a prominent exception to this trend. At BFI, a significant portion of a facility manager's bonus is contingent on environmental performance outcomes. Furthermore, a manager does not receive any bonus when personal environmental goals remain unmet.[95] Similarly, it is possible for employees at Coors to receive increases in the company profit-sharing plan when their environmental efforts decrease overall costs.[96]

Recognition Rewards for Environmental Performance

In contrast to the paucity of financial rewards, recognition rewards for environmental performance have been developed in many organisations, including Monsanto, Dow Chemical, and ICI Americas, Inc.[97] Important to the success of these rewards is a provision for company-wide public recognition. Such attention increases employee awareness of environmental accomplishments[98] and sends a powerful message about the importance of the environmental efforts throughout the entire organisation.[99]

There are a number of ways in which an organisation can communicate environmental excellence throughout the organisation. For instance, senior managers at Coors present awards in highly-visible meetings to employees who participate in successful environmental task forces.[100] Similarly, Tina Worley of Duke Power states that, in her company, 'Recognition is noted in various ways, such as communicating achievements in company news articles; giving mugs, T-shirts, or monetary awards; and providing recognition lunches with management.'[101]

Another key to the success of recognition rewards is offering them at different levels within the company. For instance, CEO environmental awareness rewards are given annually to the individual, team and division with the most outstanding contributions to waste reduction at EG&G, Inc. In addition, division-level managers are encouraged to include environmental achievements in their divisional award programmes.[102] Similarly, Xerox has awarded a number of environmental teams company-wide team excellence awards for efforts such as the development of environmentally-sound packaging, re-use of materials and packaging, and the marketing of recycled paper for Xerox copiers. Finally, Xerox has also developed an 'Earth Award' to recognise achievements in innovations of waste reduction, re-use and recycling.[103]

■ New and Innovative Environmental Rewards

Some organisations have implemented non-traditional ways to reward employees for environmental performance. For instance, The Body Shop pays its employees to perform community service throughout its worldwide operations. Employees are also kept informed on environmental and social issues via company newsletters and are given the opportunity to attend environmental events and rallies.[104] These types of rewards appeal to employees who place a higher value on social activism above more traditional incentives such as money.

■ Summary of Current Best Practices

Our research indicates that effective environmental performers embrace the following reward system characteristics, which are also summarised at the bottom of Figure 3. First, financial recognition and non-traditional rewards are developed to appeal to the interests of a diverse workforce. Secondly, a significant portion of a manager's bonus is based on his or her environmental performance, and a manager is not eligible for a bonus if environmental objectives are not attained. Thirdly, recognition awards are given in a highly-visible manner and communicated company-wide to show the central importance of environmental efforts to the organisation.

Future Environmental Rewards

Though at least some organisations have made advances, we have identified several other ideas for the future practice of rewarding environmental performance. First, like recognition, monetary rewards for environmental performance should be provided simultaneously on an individual, team and plant-wide basis. It has been suggested that individual monetary rewards are best for motivating employees to exert greater effort, but can cause competition between employees. In contrast, team- and plant-wide rewards are generally viewed as being better at motivating employees to share information and to work together.[105] A key issue is to determine what combination of these rewards (individual, team and plant-wide) is most effective in getting employees to exert maximum individual effort *and* be a team player on environmental initiatives.

Secondly, those responsible for designing reward systems should determine which major type of reward—monetary or recognition—creates greater motivation in their employees to accomplish environmental goals. Some quality management advocates argue that individual monetary rewards inherently create employee competition and other negative side-effects.[106] Research needs to be conducted on whether one type of these rewards is more effective than another in relation to environmental management programmes.

A related question is: What rewards—other than financial—should be used to motivate employees? Our research indicates that some companies, such as The Body Shop, have developed non-traditional incentives such as paid time off to volunteer in social and environmental causes. Similarly, an increasing number of US organisations are offering sabbaticals to employees. For instance, Federal Express allows employees to take paid leave up to three months every five years to work on projects that mutually benefit themselves and the company.[107] Such a policy could be used to allow employees with environmental interests to pursue a green project for the benefit of themselves and their organisation. The challenge is for organisations to find other new and novel ways to reward the increasing number of employees who have strong environmental values. Much has been said about the younger generation in the US having different values and interests to older employees, including a deeper interest in environmental issues. What new rewards should organisations develop to motivate this younger cohort of people toward key organisational performance objectives, including environmental initiatives?

Finally, organisations need to determine how rewards, such as promotion, can be linked to employee environmental performance. What career ladders are available to employees with strong environmental interests? How can organisations promote the career development of managers with extensive environmental responsibilities and interests?

■ Summary

Organisations must systematically change a number of HRM practices to implement effective environmental management initiatives successfully. Although the majority of firms in the US still lag behind, a small but increasing number of companies have implemented proactive environmental HRM practices. US companies, probably due to in large part to legal pressures, have to date developed the most extensive and sophisticated HRM practices in regulatory training. Other major training efforts include employee awareness of environmental issues and preparing employees to implement TQEM.

In contrast to training, environmental practices in performance appraisals and monetary rewards still appear to be relatively underdeveloped. Nonetheless, some cutting-edge firms are including environmental criteria as a key part of managers' performance appraisals and are linking these criteria to financial incentives. Further, a promising trend is that many organisations have developed sophisticated recognition rewards for environmental performance at individual, team and plant levels.

A critical first step in the success of these various HRM practices seems to be for top management and key environmental professionals to translate the organisational strategic environmental vision into more specific and concrete objectives for environmental training. Secondly, these organisational objectives must also be translated into meaningful environmental targets and standards for the various employees throughout the company and included into these employees' performance appraisals. Thirdly, companies must recognise and financially reward employees based upon their environmental performance.

Developing effective environmental training, performance appraisal and reward systems is not an easy task; it takes considerable time, resources, and the combined efforts of staff and managers systematically to develop each of these areas. In addition, each HRM system must be carefully linked to each other and aligned with the overall corporate vision as well as other organisational systems, such as EMIS and environmental audits. An ideal environmental management system clearly informs employees what their environmental objectives are, provides training to give them the skills necessary to perform those objectives, measures their performance on those objectives in appraisals, and then rewards them on those objectives. By interlinking these various HRM practices, a company can provide a powerful system to motivate employees at all levels to accomplish the environmental goals of the organisation. Such a systematic and integrated HRM approach can play a major role in enabling organisations to improve their environmental and financial performance.

◼ *Notes*

1. See K. Dechant and B. Altman, 'Environmental Leadership: From Compliance to Competitive Advantage', in *Academy of Management Executive*, Vol. 8 No. 3 (August 1994), pp. 7-27.

2. See J. Fiksel, 'Quality Metrics in Design for Environment', in *Total Quality Environmental Management*, Vol. 3 No. 2 (Winter 1993/94), pp. 181-82.

3. See Dechant and Altman, *op. cit.*; C.B. Hunt and E.R. Auster, 'Proactive Environmental Management: Avoiding the Toxic Trap', in *Sloan Management Review*, Winter 1990, pp. 7-18.

4. See J.F. Milliman and J.A. Clair, 'Total Quality Environmental Management (TQEM): Implications for Research and Practice', in *Proceedings of the International Association of Business and Society Conference*, Hilton Head, SC, March 1994, pp. 442-47.

5. See J. Cahan and M. Schweiger, 'Product Life Cycle: The Key to Integrating EHS into Corporate Decision Making and Operations', in *Total Quality Environmental Management*, Vol. 3 No. 2 (Winter, 1993/94), pp. 141-50.

6. E.C. McGee and A.K. Bhushan, 'Applying the Baldridge Quantity Criteria to Environmental Performance: Lessons from Leading Organisations', in *Total Quality Environmental Management*, Autumn 1993, p. 6.

7. See W.H. Parker, 'Continuous Improvement at EG&G: The Waste Reduction Pays (WARD) Initiative', in *Total Quality Environmental Management*, Vol. 3 No. 4 (Summer 1994), pp. 421-31.

8. See R.S. Greenberg and C.A. Unger, 'Environmental Management, Internal Control, and TQEM', in *Total Quality Environmental Management*, Vol. 5 No. 2 (Winter 1993/94), pp. 223-28.

9. See Milliman and Clair, *op. cit.*

10. See C.A. Stevenson, 'Training for Benchmarking: The Allied Signal Experience', in *Total Quality Environmental Management*, Summer 1993, pp. 397-403.

11. See Hunt and Auster, *op. cit.*; R.P. Wells, P.A. O'Connell and S. Hochman, 'What's the Difference between Reengineering and TQEM?', in *Total Quality Environmental Management*, Spring 1993, pp. 273-82.

12. See Hunt and Auster, *op. cit.*

13. J.M. Hutterly, 'Creating an Environmental Vision', in *Proceedings of the Global Environmental Management Initiative Conference*, Arlington, VA, March 1993, p. 1.

14. See B.A. Gantner, 'Evaluation of Facility Managers Using TQEM', in *Proceedings of the Global Environmental Management Initiative Conference*, Arlington, VA, March

1992, pp. 149-56; W.R. Woodall, 'Environmental Management System Assessment', in *Proceedings of the Global Environmental Management Initiative Conference*, Arlington, VA, March 1994, pp. 127-39.

15. See Hutterly, *op. cit.*

16. See T.J. Dagon and J.W. Kleppe, 'Product Stewardship in Photoprocessing', in *Proceedings of the Global Environmental Management Initiative Conference*, Arlington, VA, March 1994, pp. 17-22.

17. See Wells, O'Connell and Hochman, *op. cit.*

18. See W.E. Stead, J.G. Stead, A.S. Wilcox and T.W. Zimmerer, 'An Empirical Investigation of Industrial Organizational Efforts to Institutionalize Environmental Performance' (Paper presented at the *International Association of Business and Society Conference*, Hilton Head, SC, 1994).

19. See Stead *et al.*, *op. cit.*

20. International Chamber of Commerce, *The Business Charter for Sustainable Development* (Paris, France: ICC, 1991).

21. J. Cook and B.J. Seith, 'Designing an Effective Environmental Training Program', in *Journal of Environmental Regulation*, Autumn 1992, p. 53.

22. See Cook and Seith, *op. cit.*; B.M. Thomlinson, 'Church & Dwight Does the Environmentally Correct Thing', in *Food Processing*, September 1993, pp. 33-37.

23. See Stead *et al.*, *op. cit.*

24. See Cook and Seith, *op. cit.*

25. B. Schwalm, 'Apply Total Quality and Strategic Planning Techniques for Improved Compliance and Performance at Polaroid', in *Total Quality Environmental Management*, Vol. 3 No. 2 (Winter 1993/94), p. 163.

26. See Cook and Seith, *op. cit.*

27. See T. Worley, 'Promoting Employee Environmental Awareness and Involvement', in *Proceedings of the Global Environmental Management Initiative Conference*, Arlington, VA, March 1994, pp. 141-45.

28. See 'How Hyde Tools' Quality-Oriented Culture Produces Pollution Prevention Results', in *Business and the Environment*, Vol. 4 No. 8 (August 1993), pp. 5-6.

29. See Cook and Seith, *op. cit.*

30. *Ibid.*

31. See Worley, *op. cit.*

32. See Cook and Seith, *op. cit.*

33. See B. Filipczak, 'Toxic Training', in *Training*, July 1992, pp. 53-56.

34. See A.C. Pierce, 'Guidelines for Corporate Environmental Performance', in *Journal of Environmental Regulation*, Summer 1992, pp. 421-24.

35. See Filipczak, *op. cit.*

36. *Ibid.*

37. See M.E. Marshall and D.W. Mayer, 'Environmental Training: It's Good Business', in *Business Horizons*, March/April 1992, pp. 54-57.

38. Parker, *op. cit.*, p. 422.

39. See Filipczak, *op. cit.*

40. See Marshall and Mayer, *op. cit.*

41. See Milliman and Clair, *op. cit.*

42. See Worley, *op. cit.*
43. See Marshall and Mayer, *op. cit.*
44. See Worley, *op. cit.*
45. See Cook and Seith, *op. cit.*
46. See Gantner, *op. cit.*
47. See A.K. Bhushan, 'Employee Awareness and Training: Motivating and Training Employees for Environmental Leadership', in *Proceedings of the Global Environmental Initiative Conference*, Arlington, VA, March 1994, pp. 81-88.
48. See Worley, *op. cit.*
49. See 'How Hyde Tools' Quality-Oriented Culture...' in *op. cit.*
50. See C.A. Stevenson, 'TQEM Education and Communications: The TQM Journey Begins with Education', in *Proceedings of the Global Environmental Management Initiative Conference*, Arlington, VA, March 1992, pp. 19, 24.
51. See 'Building a Corporate Culture that Promotes Environmental Excellence', in *Business and the Environment*, Vol. 4 No. 8 (August 1993), pp. 2-3.
52. See Stevenson, *op. cit.*
53. See J. Cahan, J. Friss, M. Schweiger and P. Neiroth, 'Environmental Health and Safety Training and Education: TQEM Style', in *Proceedings of the Global Environmental Management Initiative Conference*, Arlington, VA, March 1992, pp. 25-30.
54. See Stevenson (1992), *op. cit.*
55. See Bhushan, *op. cit.*
56. See Parker, *op. cit.*
57. See Stevenson (1993), *op. cit.*
58. Stevenson (1992), *op. cit.*
59. *Ibid.*
60. Worley, *op. cit.*, p. 144.
61. See Stevenson (1992), *op. cit.*
62. See Hunt and Auster, *op. cit.*
63. Gantner, *op. cit.*, p. 149.
64. See Parker, *op. cit.*
65. See Dagon and Kleppe, *op. cit.*
66. See A. Wolfe and H.A. Howes, 'Measuring Environmental Performance: Theory and Practice at Ontario Hydro', in *Total Quality Environmental Management*, Summer 1993, pp. 355-66.
67. *Ibid.*
68. See Gantner, *op. cit.*
69. R. Hutson, 'Establishing International Performance Standards', in *Proceedings of the Global Environmental Management Initiative Conference*, Arlington, VA, March 1993, p. 119.
70. *Ibid.*
71. Wolfe and Howes, *op. cit.*, p. 355.
72. See Wells *et. al.*, *op. cit.*
73. See G.D. Carpenter, 'Global Deployment and International Consistency of EHS Management for Multinational Corporations', in *Proceedings of the Global Environmental Management Initiative Conference*, Arlington, VA, March 1994, pp. 7-10.

74. See Schwalm, *op. cit.*
75. See Fiksel, *op. cit.*
76. Wolfe and Howes, *op. cit.*, p. 365.
77. See P.D. Coulter, 'The Use of Union Carbide's Audit Program as a Management Tool', in *Proceedings of the Global Environmental Management Initiative Conference*, Arlington, VA, March 1994, pp. 95-98.
78. See Carpenter, *op. cit.*; Coulter, *op. cit.*
79. See L.B. Cahill, 'Evaluating Management Systems as Part of Environmental Audits', in *Total Quality Environmental Management*, Vol. 2 No. 2 (Winter 1992/93), pp. 171-76; B.J. McGuinness, 'Moving toward Management Systems Auditing: DuPont's Environmental Audit Programs', in *Proceedings of the Global Environmental Management Initiative Conference*, Arlington, VA, March 1994, pp. 113-19.
80. See Thomlison, *op. cit.*
81. See Wells *et al.*, *op. cit.*
82. See McGuinness, *op. cit.*
83. See Wolfe and Howes, *op. cit.*
84. See J.F. Milliman, R.A. Zawacki, B. Schulz, S. Wiggins and C. Norman, 'Customer Services Drives 360-Degree Goal Setting', in *Personnel Journal*, June 1995.
85. See J.F. Milliman, R.Z. Zawacki, C. Norman, L.C. Powell and J. Kirksey, 'Companies Evaluate Employees from All Perspectives', in *Personnel Journal*, November 1994.
86. See Wells *et al.*, *op. cit.*
87. See S.P. Robbins, *Organizational Behaviour: Concepts, Controversies and Applications* (6th edn; Englewood Cliffs, NJ: Prentice Hall, 1993).
88. See Wells *et al.*, *op. cit.*
89. Gantner, *op. cit.*, p. 150.
90. See Milliman and Clair, *op. cit.*
91. See Stead *et al.*, *op. cit.*
92. See J.M. Cramer and T. Roes, 'Total Employee Involvement: Measures for Success', in *Total Quality Environmental Management*, Vol. 3 No. 1 (Autumn 1993), pp. 39-52.
93. 'Pay for Environmental Performance', in *Environmental Manager*, August 1994, p. 4.
94. J.D. Snyder, 'More Execs Find Pay Linked to EHS Goals', in *Environment Today*, October 1992, p. 22.
95. See Gantner, *op. cit.*
96. See S. Woods, 'Making Pollution Prevention Second Nature to your Nature', in *Proceedings of the Global Environmental Management Initiative Conference*, Arlington, VA, March 1993, pp. 51-56.
97. See 'How Hyde Tools' Quality-Oriented Culture...', in *op. cit.*; H. Whitenight, 'Integrating Total Quality and Environmental Management: A Story of Applied Learning', in *Proceedings of the Global Environmental Management Initiative Conference*, Arlington, VA, March 1992, pp. 101-104.
98. See Bhushan, *op. cit.*
99. See 'Building a Corporate Culture', in *op. cit.*
100. See Woods, *op. cit.*

101. Worley, *op. cit.*, p. 145.

102. See Parker, *op. cit.*

103. See Bhushan, *op. cit.*

104. See B. Burlington, 'This Woman Has Changed Business Forever', in *Inc. Magazine*, June 1990, pp. 34-48.

105. See E.E. Lawler, 'The New Pay', in *The University of Southern California Center for Effective Organizations* (Paper G84-7; Los Angeles, CA, 1984).

106. See Milliman and Clair, *op. cit.*

107. See 'Corporate Sabbaticals: Some Companies Reward Employees with Time Off', in *Wall Street Journal*, 8 August 1995, p. A1.

③

Managing Corporate Environmental Policy:
A Process of Complex Change

Susan M. Barrett and David F. Murphy

*T*HIS CHAPTER presents some initial findings of a research project on the implementation of corporate social responsibility policies in a sample of companies. The School for Policy Studies and New Consumer Charitable Trust are jointly undertaking this study, which is funded by the Economic and Social Research Council (ESRC).[1]

The chapter presents four main arguments. First, we demonstrate the importance of economic considerations in the adoption of corporate environmental policies. Second, we show how personal and organisational values influence the policy process. Third, we illustrate the link between the management of complex change, risk and uncertainty, and policy effectiveness. Finally, we suggest that strengthening the organisational capacity to develop appropriate knowledge and skills, and to cope with uncertainty and change, will be key factors influencing effective policy implementation. Although there is a growing recognition of the importance of organisational and human resource dimensions in effecting change, these aspects are not yet generally seen as an integral part of policy development. Human resource managers must recognise that environmental policy is not a matter that can be left to technical experts. Indeed, all senior managers need to be more closely involved in the process of engaging and motivating those individuals upon whom action depends.

We have selected three environmental policy case studies from phase one of the project which illustrate well the themes that are emerging from the wider research. The cases were chosen to offer contrasting examples of environmental policy development in terms of sector, company size and scope of activity, and the focus of the policy itself.

Case 1: Iceland Foods. The importance of the leader in the development of an environmentally-responsible organisational culture (see Fig. 1 on page 78).[2]

Case 2: JT Design Build Ltd. The collective leadership of the Board and the personal drive of a policy champion in 'going green'. (see Fig. 2 on page 80).[3]

Case 3: DIY–WWF Alliance. The catalytic roles of an environmental organisation and a market leader in developing a sector-wide policy initiative (see Fig. 3 on page 82).[4]

Each is described in greater detail in Figures 1–3.

■ Current Trends in HRM

The concept of human resources management (HRM) received considerable attention in the 1980s with the publication of a number of influential management books beginning with *In Search of Excellence.*[5] An excellence movement was launched which brought issues such as organisational culture, leadership style and teamwork to the fore. Despite initial reservations, HRM academics and practitioners embraced this movement as a means of enhancing the status and influence of strategic human resource issues in enterprises, academic institutions and other organisational settings.[6] HRM has recently been defined as an approach that 'is concerned with the totality of organisational co-ordination and integration of strategic human resources'.[7] Key characteristics of the HRM model include: 'business need' as prime guide to action; emphasis upon customer orientation; facilitation as a 'prized skill'; increased communication flows; teamworking; reducing conflict through culture change; and learning companies.[8]

Underlying this are three very important themes in the HRM literature:

■ The promotion of links between individual and organisational values and needs in order to realise greater enthusiasm, productivity and commitment on the part of employees[9]

■ The integration of employee management with an analysis and understanding of organisational culture, so that the former reinforces the latter[10]

■ The emphasis on organisational learning as the key process in fostering unity of organisational purpose and structure, as well as corporate survival and growth[11]

Another important message in HRM literature is the complex combination of factors that influence organisational learning: for example, the interpretation of the external context, the analysis of past organisational actions and the power of key decision-makers to promote change.[12]

In the following sections we present some of our preliminary findings which reinforce a number of the HRM themes mentioned above. These include: the importance of external and internal factors in mobilising individual and company action; the central role of values and organisational culture in the policy process; and the effective management of change and uncertainty.

■ Policy Origins and Motivation for Action

Where does the motivation for environmental policy come from? This is an important initial question for people concerned with the analysis and management of corporate environmental policy. In all three of our cases, the motivation for environmental policies could be argued to be simply a matter of economic self-interest or good strategic planning, albeit in response to a changing social and environmental context.

While the specific factors that influenced the adoption of the policy initiative may have been different in each case, all three demonstrate a commitment to long-term company health. The proactive stance of the companies can be argued to represent good strategic planning, which has meant anticipating their future operating environment and planning for it. Companies that practice good strategic management are concerned not only with short-term profits, but also with the longer-term implications of customer demands, impending legislation, maintaining public image, market share or other business needs. Strategic business leaders need to be able to see how economic growth, bottom-line profits and sustainable development can be brought together so that taking environmental issues on board makes sense for business.

In 'Iceland', the origins and motivation for the CFC policy initiative within the company can be linked to a number of related factors: impending legislation, public image, competition and corporate values. As a frozen food and fridge-freezer retailer, Iceland finds itself in a highly-competitive retail sector. It is also very dependent on refrigeration techniques and materials. The writing was on the wall regarding the phasing-out of CFCs, so it was really a matter of when, rather than whether, the company acted. In the retail trade, it is very difficult for public companies such as Iceland to stand still. They must always look for growth and opportunities to expand their market share. Where social or environmental concern can lead to good public relations and contribute to sales, Iceland has no hesitation in exploiting this, and no excuses are made for taking that advantage.

JT Design Build Ltd, similarly, saw the development of environmental policy as a way of 'doing well by doing good'. In a climate of increased public awareness of environmental issues, the company judged that sooner

Case 1
Iceland Foods
The Importance of the Leader and the Organisational Culture Created

ICELAND defines itself as a specialist food retailer. From its origins with a single shop selling loose frozen foods, the company has expanded into a nationwide chain employing around 17,000 people. Expansion through take-over has enabled it to include sales of freezers and refrigerators, 'value-added' frozen and chilled foods, convenience groceries and fresh produce in its predominantly high street stores. Iceland is now a public limited company with UK sales of over £1,180m in 1994. In many ways, however, it retains the culture and management style of its small business origins through the values and direct, personal and entrepreneurial approach to decision-making of its founders, one of whom still leads the company as Chairman and Chief Executive. Company culture is deliberately fostered as a valuable asset. Core values are explicitly set out in the company philosophy as 'A commitment to protect the environment and preserve the quality of life', and 'Linking efficiency with a social conscience and profitability with good business ethics'.

A mission statement emphasising profitable growth, long-term customer satisfaction, honest value for money and friendly efficient service is issued to all employees on a plastic card. Environmental policy initiatives include: CFC recovery and alternatives; energy management; recycling; litter control; and waste management. The company has also supported a Greenpeace anti-whaling boycott of Norwegian goods by cancelling a £1 million contract for Norwegian prawns. In this chapter, the focus is on the CFC policy.

Iceland's policy on CFCs resulted in the introduction of a recycling scheme for gas from redundant refrigerators and freezers in the late 1980s. This was followed by the development of a portable CFC recovery unit, which by 1993 had led to the establishment of its own cleaning system to recycle gas for re-use within the business. By reducing its CFC requirements, Iceland was laying the ground for the pending phase-out of CFC usage by the end of 1994. The publicity generated by these actions and Iceland's own lobbying of chemical companies accelerated research and development of CFC alternatives. All new cold store and shop-floor freezers operate on the least hazardous gases currently available, often entailing substantial extra costs. Iceland has also given a commitment to Greenpeace and other NGOs that it will also phase out the use of CFC alternatives that contain fluorocarbons, ensuring that all future refrigerants are non-fluorocarbons—ammonia, hydrocarbons and air.

Much of the drive for innovation and change was linked to the personal values of the founder, combining a strong commitment to environmental issues (e.g. Greenpeace membership) with entrepreneurial drive, tempered by pragmatic recognition of the limits of what is possible in a highly-competitive sector. Perceived limits to Iceland's future commitment to environmental concerns include: economic recession; the impact of recent expansion through acquisitions; and the influence of 'City interests', given its public company status. Together these factors could mean that a caring company with certain moral values may have to avoid any causes that might jeopardise its profitability. However, underlying the process are moral imperatives, exemplified by policies that were undertaken because the Founder-Chairman and other members of the Board believed that they were things that had to be done.

Figure 1: *Iceland Foods*

or later the industry would have to address issues such as energy efficiency, pollution and waste in relation to design and construction. At the same time, JTDB saw the development of environmental policy as a means of raising company profile and gaining a competitive edge as the construction industry started to feel the effects of economic recession and competition more intensely.

In the third case, the origins of the policy on wood product sourcing were similar in all of the Do-It-Yourself (DIY) home improvement retailers. All identified environmental pressure group tactics and customer questions and letters as being significant. Both activists and members of the general public wanted to know which wood products were being sold, their origins, and what the corresponding company policies were. The DIY retailers relied on timber products for a significant percentage of turnover—increasing consumer and environmental group pressure could affect sales and profitability. The catalytic role of the World Wide Fund for Nature (WWF) in providing a means for competitors to work together on a specific environmental issue was also significant. By signing agreements with WWF, most of the DIY retailers were no longer targeted by protesters, and signing up to the 1995 target represented a public commitment to change existing practices. WWF also achieved one of its policy objectives by forming a politically-significant group of companies to move its forests campaign forward.

The three cases, thus, illustrate an interesting motivational mix of opportunity and threat.

- On the one hand, the potential threat of external pressures from either impending legislation, implementation deadlines, or pressure from consumers and environmental groups
- On the other, the opportunity to use good image/moral high ground as a selling point for getting one jump ahead of the competition, or as a means of keeping up with a market leader
- This kind of interpretation is lent support by the commercial realism and limits to policy development shown by the case study companies. Each is interpreting and assessing risk to company profitability—balancing investment in change necessitated by policy shift against calculated benefits.

Market position is clearly another important factor, limiting or constraining the scope for action. A small or medium-sized company, such as JT Design Build Ltd, in the highly-competitive but conservative construction sector[13] cannot afford the risk of innovation on its own, hence the policy emphasis placed on raising client and industry awareness of environmental

Case 2
JT Design Build Ltd
The Collective Leadership of the Board and Personal Drive of an Individual Employee

THIS MEDIUM-SIZED construction company, established in the early 1960s, was one of the pioneers of the re-emergence of the design and build approach to construction. This means a single company taking responsibility for the entire construction process from design conception, through detailed specification and materials ordering, to construction and delivery of the finished building. The two founders conceived JT Design Build Ltd (JTDB) as a multidisciplinary organisation with in-house design and project management skills, which would grow and succeed (as it did) on the basis of its reputation for high-quality design, combined with cost-efficiency, responsiveness and accountability to clients. At the time their environmental policy was developed, JTDB had an annual turnover of over £50 million, and a total staff of around 170 people.

After being commissioned by a development company to work on the design and construction specification for an 'environmentally-responsible' office building, the JTDB Board decided to take a closer look at environmental issues. Other factors were the anticipation of future environmental legislation and regulation and the need for a competitive edge in a period of recession. Their policy stance was also highly cost-conscious. This pragmatic approach was necessary, given that not all Board members were enthusiastic about environmental issues. The Board identified and prioritised those issues which were essential for the credibility of the company's environmental position.

At an early stage in the process, the Board made an explicit commitment to reduce the environmental impact of JTDB's activities. This was published as an environmental statement aimed primarily at clients. Awareness-raising was given priority, not just among clients, but in the industry generally and within JTDB itself. The original project architect for the 'green' building was given responsibility for policy development—and its translation into practice. His motivation and enthusiasm proved to be an important factor in the initiatives developed. As well as the initial statement, there were a series of staff seminars to raise awareness of the issues, which included:

■ A public and industry awareness campaign which promoted green construction issues and which raised the profile of the company as a market innovator

■ An environmental review and audit of company activities to provide the basis for developing procedures in line with BS 7750—the British Standard for Environmental Management Systems

■ The production of a 'green' construction guide setting out the environmental impacts of a range of construction materials and processes, and the alternatives available, to enhance company capacity in green design and construction

The Board allocated £100,000 for policy development, which included salary costs of the environmental architect, the awareness campaign, and consultancy costs of the environmental audit and construction guide. The awareness campaign took place over an eighteen-month period, and was highly successful in raising the company's profile.

The audit formed the basis for participating in the piloting of BS 7750, and for establishing internal priorities for action. Short-term, inexpensive measures to reduce environmental impact were implemented. However, relatively little was achieved in terms of either environmental design contracts or in respect of changing JTDB's own design and build practices. The severity of the economic recession affected the level of priority accorded to environmental aspects of construction. Difficult market conditions precipitated a management buy-in, and subsequent company restructuring has placed the more ambitious aspects of the policy on hold. The environmental architect was head-hunted and became an environmental manager with a company in a different sector.

Figure 2: JT Design Build Ltd

issues while taking a very cautious and incremental approach to changes requiring any significant risk investment.

Equally, however, degree and focus of action can be seen to relate to the source of pressure for change (e.g. moral or consumer pressure; impending regulation), and judgement about the potential impacts of responding or not responding. The joint agreement between WWF and the DIY retailers was both a carrot and a stick. When the market leader B&Q signed up, the others felt they had to follow. It seems that the public relations penalties of not joining were perceived as greater than any future costs—which were difficult to estimate at the outset.

The participation of all leading DIY retailers in the WWF 1995 Group demonstrates the extent to which business is increasingly being challenged by groups and individuals who feel they have a stake in the activities of the corporate sector. Making such forms of 'stakeholder partnerships' both operationally and strategically significant is not a traditional public relations exercise. Companies such as those in the WWF 1995 Group are beginning 'to consider the effects of their actions on future generations and on people in other parts of the world'.[14]

Although economic factors were important in all three cases, this still does not adequately explain why companies chose to act in the way they did; it does not explain the factors that have shaped the scope and focus of policy and relative success of its implementation. The economic argument, while plausible, does not explain why other companies in the same sector have not acted at all. Here we suggest that there is an important and complex contingent relation between personal values, organisational culture and the cultural as well as the economic context. This is tempered by the power relations between them which are a function of existing structures of control and accountability between individual, group and society. In the following section, these issues are explored in greater detail.

■ Values, Power and Influence Systems

Our research is beginning to suggest that values at the personal and organisational level may be an essential factor in explaining, at least, perceptions of the need for innovative action. This fits with existing business and management literature on what makes for 'excellence' and the ability to learn and adapt to changing conditions.[15] A key figure in the move towards excellence is the 'product champion'.

The 'product champion' is a 'believer', committed to the need for, and direction of, change and who will take responsibility to ensure that action is taken.[16] The concept of 'product champion' can be translated into 'policy champion' as a necessary condition for the development of environmental policy initiatives. The existence, somewhere in the story, of a committed and

Case 3
Wood Products Alliance
The Catalytic Role of an Environmental Organisation
in Bringing Competitors Together

IN 1991, the World Wide Fund for Nature (WWF) established the end of 1995 as a target for all wood and wood products traded in the UK to come from well-managed forests. Later that same year, WWF established the 1995 Group, a working group of companies whose Boards had agreed to a number of requirements. These include: the phase-out of the sale and use of all products that do not meet the target; a written action plan; the timely submission of six-monthly progress reports to WWF; and the immediate phase-out of all labels and certificates claiming sustainability or environmental friendliness, until such a time as a credible independent labelling system is established. As part of the monitoring process, WWF also responds individually to each company commenting on progress and indicating areas where further effort is required.

The first company to sign up to the target was B&Q, the leading UK retailer of do-it-yourself (DIY) products. Its Board formally adopted the policy in September 1991, and gave its environmental co-ordinator free rein to look at the whole product range and recommend action. In order to meet the deadline, he initiated an intensive audit of its supply chain. Six other major DIY retailers have subsequently joined the group: Texas Homecare in mid-1992, Do It All and Homebase in late 1992, and Great Mills in late 1993. One of these companies was excluded from the 1995 Group for six months in 1993/94 for failing to meet reporting requirements. In late 1994, Wickes, a related DIY building supplies company, joined, shortly followed by Magnet. In early 1995, B&Q's original Environmental Co-ordinator was promoted to Quality and Environmental Controller.

Within the DIY sub-group, company representatives have agreed for the most part to standardise supplier surveys and to share some strategies for meeting the target. In early 1994, four of the DIY retailers and WWF signed a joint accord on the sourcing of wood products 'to send a clear and consistent message' to over 500 wood product suppliers in the UK and overseas. In early 1995, an updated Retailers Accord on Wood Product Procurement was signed by six of the DIYs, three other major retailers and WWF.

Progress is being monitored in two ways: database development and product certification. Databases enable companies to gather data to identify which sources should be dropped or certified. This introduces a new role for buyers, for whom the source of timber was not previously important. A number already have some certified wood products in their systems. However, the long-term cost implications of certified timber are not yet fully known. (B&Q insists that the extra cost of certified timber could be as little as 10p on a door retailing for £50.) There are also differences of opinion about who should pay for certification. Most companies argue that certification is a quality-assurance cost that should be paid for by suppliers or producers. In some cases, considerable resources have been allocated to certification, either by underwriting the process or allocating additional staff time to product research and to communication with suppliers.

DIY retailers are learning the practicalities of buying and selling independently-certified timber, which is proving to be a difficult process. WWF has learned that progress on complex international policy issues is possible through collaboration with industry. In early 1996, 1995 Group members participated in the launch of the independent certification logo of the Forest Stewardship Council, the new international standard for sustainable forest management. There is uncertainty, however, about the extent to which most timber buyers have integrated the policy into their buying function. In five of the seven companies (including Wickes and Magnet), the policy champion is either an environmental or quality-assurance manager, not a timber buyer. Company achievements remain dependent upon the relative power position of responsible individuals and a supportive organisational culture. Those with more power have achieved more; those with less power have achieved less. The highly-competitive DIY retail sector still has some way to go before all companies can be certain that all their wood products are being sourced from 'well-managed forests'.

Figure 3: *DIY–WWF Alliance*

enthusiastic individual taking a leadership role in policy innovation features in all three of the cases described here. In Iceland, the motivation for action on CFCs came from the company's Chairman and Chief Executive. JTDB's policy champion was a professional team leader at middle management level. Within the DIY group of companies, it is clearly one individual in one company that has led the initiative. B&Q's Quality and Environmental Controller has championed the policy both within his own company as well as in the wider DIY–WWF Alliance. In addition, WWF's Forest Conservation Officer has been instrumental in getting all of the DIY retailers involved and in monitoring their progress.

While the commitment and motivation of individuals is crucial for policy development, their scope for action will be facilitated or constrained by their power position and the culture of the organisation in which they are operating. The value and power context facing policy champions at the wider structural or societal level also influences their ability to achieve cultural change. Below we review the links between values, culture and power in each of the case studies, as well as showing how external factors influence environmental policy in different corporate settings.

Iceland's Chief Executive has a strong personal value commitment to environmental responsibility. As one of the founders, he has shaped company culture and used his positional power to initiate action. Policy design and implementation in JT Design Build Ltd were largely the product of a committed and enthusiastic individual within the company—but, crucially, supported and facilitated by a Board committed in value terms and willing to commit resources and trust the ideas developed from below.

In the DIY–WWF Alliance, B&Q has clearly led environmental policy development within the DIY sector. Some of the other DIY companies have taken a more cautious stance. Whereas B&Q's Quality and Environmental Controller has been given increasing responsibility by the Board for both quality and environmental matters, most of his counterparts in the other DIY companies have not been granted such a free rein. Such discrepancies mean that individual policy champions within the various DIY retailers have different levels of power and influence to effect change in their organisations.

For the policy champion to become an effective change agent, legitimacy and support is therefore needed from the top of the organisation. This point is dramatically illustrated by another of our case studies, which we have been unable to proceed with. The company concerned had made major advances in using lifecycle analysis techniques to re-appraise its relationships with suppliers. It was about to embark on further work in the area of wood product sourcing. A change in the US parent company boardroom, and a subsequent shift in values and priorities, resulted in all environmental policies being scrapped, the policy champion transferred to a company outpost and his environmental team disbanded. A policy shift toward short-term shareholder profits has meant that long-term environmental considerations have fallen off the company's policy agenda.

The theme of the need for support from the top is familiar in the HRM and organisational change literature.[17] However, even this may not be enough if the innovation is too challenging to the prevailing organisational culture.

While individuals may bring new values and ideas into organisations, the individual is also shaped and influenced by the existing organisational culture. By culture, we mean 'the deeper level of basic assumptions and beliefs that are shared by members of an organisation, that operate unconsciously, and that define in a basic "taken-for-granted" fashion an organisation's view of itself and its environment'.[18]

In more everyday language, culture can be seen as 'the way we do things here', comprising the often internalised and unspoken beliefs and norms that shape the way an organisation functions. External societal attitudes and norms also permeate and influence internal attitudes and practices. In all three cases, the influence of various external factors has contributed to the decision to take environmental policy issues on board. The growing influence of environmental groups and the corresponding increase in general societal concern for the environment are two external forces that are beginning to permeate the cultures of some of the case study companies.

Nevertheless, there will also be distinctive features of organisational culture contingent on the particular functional sector (e.g. manufacturing versus service) or subdivisions within it (e.g. retailing versus construction). Subsystems within the organisation introduce additional contingencies, reflecting different internal groupings, professional orientations and interests, including the influence of individual management styles.[19] When new values are introduced into established organisational cultures, however, the extent to which they are taken on board depends upon the power and influence of the policy champion in relation to others in the organisation.

For example in JT Design Build Ltd, the idea of environmental responsibility was in tune with, and seen by the Board as an extension of, the company culture of profitability through quality and responsibility to clients. It was relatively uncontroversial to make a commitment in principle to reducing the environmental impact of construction activity, yet even here there was by no means universal support within the company. Designers tended to be most enthusiastic, seeing opportunities for new and creative approaches to design. Materials buyers and marketing staff were less so, worrying about their lack of knowledge and potential costs to clients of changed practices.

In the DIY–WWF Alliance, all companies have agreed to the same policy goal through their membership in the 1995 Group. By signing the WWF-Retailers' Accord on Wood Product Procurement, they have all declared publicly that they share identical objectives to reach the 1995 target. There are, nevertheless, quite different approaches within each company to the implementation of the policy. These differences reveal considerable diversity in organisational cultures and in the respective power positions of the policy champions within each company.

As alluded to earlier, B&Q has invested the most resources into the policy initiative, giving its Quality and Environmental Controller the power and influence to get things done. B&Q had an established organisational commitment to environmental issues before it joined the 1995 Group. A number of the other companies have had some success in developing systems to trace wood product sources, but most have not yet been able to use this policy initiative as a catalyst for developing an overall environmental strategy for their companies. The wood sourcing issue appears to be a relatively low business priority. One of the companies went so far as to reject the policy champion's request for funding to support environmental awareness training for the product managers and timber buyers—key individuals who needed to be brought on board.

A policy champion thus needs a compatible organisational culture. The ability of the individual agent to act is not just a function of formal power position, or a matter of top-level endorsement, but also depends on the cultural context. Within broader economic and cultural constraints, what is achieved at organisational level may depend to a large extent on the way that innovation and change is perceived, approached and managed—with obvious implications for human resources management. The rest of the chapter focuses on these aspects.

■ Environmental Policy, Complexity and Managing Cultural Change

Adopting environmentally-responsible practices is likely to involve significant change in organisational values, practices and procedures, breaking entrenched habits of thought and practice to take on board new ways of thinking about what is done, why and how.[20] In this section we look at the characteristics of the kind of change we are talking about and we introduce some of the implications for human resource management.

Environmental responsibility, if taken seriously, involves reviewing all aspects of a company's activities, internal and external, from sourcing, through value-added processes, to distribution of outputs and disposal of waste. Just this basic process of identifying what and how activities impinge on the environment requires human resource inputs of time, knowledge and expertise, and may be very complex. This point is well illustrated by the following quote from one interviewee in the DIY–WWF case:

> Essentially what we were all trying to do was to do an inventory of all our products that contained timber and where it came from. In our case we had about 3,000 products, so really we were trying to trace all of them back to forests of origin, and that's really the starting point...It is very difficult for the suppliers to get the information...There was one supplier who supplied us stuff through the UK. I think they were paint brushes. He bought his paint brushes from a company in Germany who bought the timber from a company in Italy who bought it from a company in America who bought it from a range of sawmills in America who bought it from an even wider range of forests. So essentially it was a bit of a nightmare.

The complexity is thus not merely about identifying all the different components of a particular product or process, but also in tracing all the connections involved from the production and sourcing of each component back to the origins of raw materials and methods by which they have been obtained.

There is also the question of whether, and how much, control can be exercised to bring about change. The review process must also include identifying the network of relationships involved in each product or process—and the nature of each relationship in terms of power and dependency. For example, in JT Design Build Ltd, the internal audit suggested that major energy savings could be made by changing the system of heating and air conditioning. However, in the short run this was not possible, since the company, as a tenant of its office space, could not act without the support of the landlord.

In this case, following the consultant's presentation of the initial audit, the company 'ranked' all the areas identified for action according to both cost–benefit and relative difficulty–feasibility of taking action, to arrive at short-, medium- and long-term priorities for action. Even with good technical information, it is still a matter of 'deciding between apples and pears' rather than priorities being self-evident, and very often technical advice itself is ambivalent.

The sheer scale of the audit process as well as the kinds of complexity described have immediate human resource management implications, not just in terms of staff time and cost involved, but the whole issue of knowledge and expertise, and how best to obtain or develop it. A company starting out on the road to environmental responsibility may have motivated individuals, committed managers and a supportive culture, but is unlikely to have in-house the necessary environmental expertise or to be able to commit adequate time and resources to the task.

JTDB's environmental architect had the advantage of some previous research and development work on a commission for the design of an environmentally-friendly building; but even here the basic audit of company activities, and the production of the 'green' construction guide was commissioned from consultants. In the DIY–WWF Alliance, WWF's policy champion is a professional forester. In order to enhance his capacity to assist the DIY retailers in reaching the 1995 target, WWF hired a full-time consultant (also with forestry training) in late 1994. This person has assumed the role of 1995 Group Manager and meets regularly with the designated person in each company to help overcome some of their day-to-day difficulties with the timber sourcing process. B&Q has also been instrumental in providing technical support to its competitors, particularly on supplier audits and database development. While WWF's and B&Q's advice has not always been acted upon by the other DIY companies, there has been no shortage of technical expertise and practical advice available to them.

Although probably inevitable, the use of consultants brings its own problems of how to transfer external expertise into an internal capacity for action, and the risk of both enthusiasm and expertise being confined to a 'special élite' rather than commitment and ownership of environmental initiatives permeating the whole organisation. We return to this issue below.

■ Risk and Uncertainty

The discussion so far suggests that, as well as complexity, there is substantial risk and uncertainty involved in developing environmental responsibility in practice. First is the uncertainty of making judgements about relative impacts of different products and processes, and in assessing relative costs and benefits of different alternatives. Some of this uncertainty arises from lack of knowledge and expertise about what is possible or feasible. However, it is also a function of the 'state of the art' in a developing and dynamic arena: as understanding and knowledge increases, so perceptions, attitudes and standards change. Apparently solving one problem may over time be seen to have created others, as is rapidly being recognised in the area of paper and newsprint recycling, and use of unleaded petrol.

The unpredictability associated with the dynamics of changing understanding and technologies makes investment in environmental responsibility potentially high-risk and open-ended. It may be possible to know where you want to get to—but difficult to say with any certainty what you are getting into; what will be involved in terms of changes to current practice; or the costs and benefits of different courses of action. For example, what started in Iceland as a fairly limited good-practice exercise to dispose of CFCs safely took the company into its own R&D and into the whole area of CFC alternatives for its own refrigeration plant at substantial extra cost. A quality assurance manager with one of the DIY retailers further demonstrates the unpredictable nature of the environmental policy process:

> Where you are breaking new ground, you don't know what you
> are going to come across in the future...Operationally it was
> actually quite difficult to see where it was going to lead us to.

It will also be difficult to plan ahead in relation to the timescale and pressures for change. Changing perceptions of environmental impacts affect attitudes to the issues (often precipitated by crises), in turn exerting pressure for developing new alternatives for action, and thus changing the position of issues on political and legislative agendas.[21] In all three cases, judgements were made about the likely importance and timescale of pressures for change: in Iceland with relative certainty, since the phasing-out of CFCs was already fixed. In the others a more speculative calculation was required, given the absence of specific impending legislation for their sectors. In this context, it is not surprising that the basic policy stance in JT Design Build Ltd—a relatively small company in a highly-competitive industry—was a cautious one: deferring to the longer-term action that would involve significant investment for little tangible short-term return. In the DIY–WWF Alliance, the more gradual approach of some of the DIY retailers is also better understood. The influence of environmental and consumer pressures may have offered hints of future UK or EU legislation; however, the wood-sourcing policy remains a voluntary scheme that each DIY company is implementing in its own way.

In this sense, companies have to walk a tightrope in respect of the credibility of their environmental stance in the eyes of their own personnel, customers, suppliers and, not least, environmental pressure groups in the wider society. At the same time, companies have to reassure shareholders (or holding company) about continuing profitability when it is by no means certain what will be involved. The WWF Forest Conservation Officer illustrates this point well. He recalls how he brought the DIY company representatives on board:

> It was a leap of faith for these companies...A key [in the early
> stages] was coming up with something that was clear enough

so that the DIY retailers had a rough idea of what they were doing, but not so specific that they felt they couldn't do it.

This strategy enabled the WWF representative to tie his business counter-parts to a process. This was important, given that uncertainty leads to higher levels of anxiety among those upon whom action depends: not just employees, but also suppliers, distributors, etc.

Change is always destabilising since it changes the status quo of power and influence networks. When change involves both the values and practices of a company, it will create particular anxieties related to:

- Implied criticism of past practice inherent in environmental reviews and audits

- Lack of knowledge of alternative methodologies or techniques

- Ability to learn or cope with new ways of doing things

- Underlying concern that developing new processes and techniques may be used for rationalising or at least making change in existing status quo of power and influence relations via changes in organisational structures and procedures

In an atmosphere of uncertainty and anxiety, the basic physiological reaction is the classic fight–flight response. This can be manifested as aggressive hostility to, or the belittling of, change initiatives, ignoring change and hoping it will go away; or 'digging in' and holding on to the familiar, however unsatisfactory. Apparent hostility to change may therefore reflect feelings of insecurity as much as genuine conflicts of interest.[22]

From all this we can conclude that the process of implementing environmental policy is concerned crucially with managing uncertainty and cultural change, both of which are central to the current concepts of human resources management described earlier.

■ The HRM Implications of Managing Change

Eco-efficiency is not achieved by technological change alone. It is achieved only by profound changes in the goals and assumptions that drive corporate activities, and change in the daily practices and tools used to reach them.[23]

Our research so far lends support to Stephan Schmidheiny's argument. The three cases suggest that the effectiveness of policy implementation will in a large part be determined by the extent to which individuals and organisa-tions are willing to take on board innovation and change, with obvious human resource management implications. Effective managers of human resources must therefore be centrally involved in the policy development and implementation process. They need to know what kinds of people make things happen and what kinds of skills are required. They also need to answer a very difficult question: How do you change unsustainable practices that have been learned over decades as being the norm?

A key part of the process is translating the particular into the general, building environmental criteria into the list of things that business people automatically consider when introducing a new product. This is easier said than done. The preceding sections have identified some factors that appear to have been important in shaping the policy process in the three cases, all of which are essentially dimensions of effective human resources management.

All cases have shown that there is a need for commitment from the company's leadership. Without the support of the CEO and Board, many of the policy initiatives would never have got off the ground. This commitment must then be translated into resource allocation—both time and money. In some companies, quality assurance managers have had environmental policy added to their job descriptions without reducing any of their ongoing responsibilities. In others, new environmental managers, project co-ordinators or internal consultants have been hired. Both ongoing and newly-created posts require new operational funds for policy implementation. As one of the DIY retailers illustrates, a highly-motivated new environmental manager with no budget for staff environmental awareness will not be able to implement policy effectively and will become frustrated in the process. In this situation, the following questions need to be asked: How far is organisational commitment to the policy real and long term? To what extent is the initiative tokenistic or symbolic and only short term?[24]

Even where senior managers are committed to change, there is still the major problem of developing the knowledge and expertise necessary to handle both the complexity and uncertainty inherent in moving to environmentally-sustainable practice. In all cases, we can see problems in managing the diffusion of knowledge, and thus ownership of policy initiatives, from a select and committed few into the 'mainstream' of company practice. The identification of policy innovation with a particular individual may prove counter-productive over time. If understanding, knowledge and expertise are confined to a single individual, then the whole impetus for policy development is at risk if that person leaves—as happened in JT Design Build Ltd—before the idea has taken root in the organisation. This emphasises the need for staff development to be recognised and managed as an integral part of policy formulation and implementation rather than something added on after decisions have been made and initiatives embarked upon.

Our three cases have illustrated the way in which existing cultural values and practices have helped or hindered policy development and implementation. We have suggested that the process of adopting environmentally-responsible and sustainable practices needs to be regarded as a process of cultural change. We have also referred to the high levels of uncertainty and unpredictability associated with environmental innovation and how this can potentially increase resistance to such change if people are left in a state of anxiety about their own future within the new culture.

We would argue that none of these issues can be dealt with in isolation. Cultural change cannot easily be imposed, but will emerge over time out of positive exposure to new ideas and experience in practice. In all our cases, this has been recognised to a certain extent in the attention paid to raising awareness (JTDB and DIY–WWF) and to fostering company culture through training and staff development (especially Iceland). The certainty of unambiguous commitment from the top will also facilitate acceptance of change; however, if change is going to be accepted and adopted as a part of normal practice, then knowledge and expertise must be 'home grown'— planted and fostered as an integral part of a strategy for organisational development.

Developing environmental responsibility is a long-term process of essentially incremental change—moving in the direction of sustainable practice but through the gradual development of awareness, knowledge and confidence across the whole organisation to create what is referred to in HRM literature as a 'culture of organisational learning'. This has important implications for the way in which the whole process of policy development and implementation is conceived and managed.

First are implications for the concept of policy. Policy implementation will never be complete; experience will change aspirations, and knowledge the possibilities for action. Policy needs to be seen as a 'framework for directing an ongoing process of change, which combines clarity of goals with flexibility for innovation, adaptation to changing circumstances and learning'.[25]

Such a framework is more like the 'loose–tight' approach advocated by Peters and Waterman,[26] providing a clear 'bottom line' to inform the limits of risk and choice at the same time as allowing for innovation and creativity from the bottom up. This kind of approach is embodied in the recent BS 7750 as a standard for environmental management systems; it does not refer to absolutes, but the notion of continuous improvement towards what are inevitably changing and developing goals.

Second, this view of policy also has profound implications for the way that policy is introduced and implemented within organisations. Traditionally, implementation tends to be seen as a 'top-down' command-and-control process, whereby decisions at Board level are communicated and executed through the hierarchical line management structure of the company. The need to generate commitment to change and capacity for innovation through learning suggests that 'top-down' management needs to be combined with more participatory and negotiative approaches to change. This shift in practice may also have ramifications for styles of human resources management.

Finally, there are major implications for the meaning of education, training and learning. The policy process is evolutionary; organisational learning is also an ongoing process. As we have pointed out earlier, in all three cases, neither the policy champions nor anyone else in their companies could be specific about policy implementation at the outset. While there were some general targets set, the companies appeared to operate in a more incremental way within the context of an agreed strategic direction. Much has been learned by doing; there is also recognition that this must continue.

The success of the policy initiative is further dependent upon developing an organisational capacity to learn. In JT Design Build Ltd, the policy champion left and the company itself was restructured before environmental values and policies could become part of the organisational fabric. While external factors are also important determinants of success, the organisation needs to develop a culture that empowers staff to respond to an ever-changing external environment. Bob Garratt[27] notes that 'learning' is 'being seen increasingly as the key commodity necessary to guarantee organisational survival in the medium to long term'[28] and that 'the keys to organisational survival and growth must lie within the hands, hearts and minds of all those who are members of the organisation'.[29] The implications for HRM and environmental policy are that companies must begin to place greater emphasis upon investment in organisational 'learners' as opposed to plant infrastructure, for example. Developing this organisational capacity to learn remains a weak area in all three cases. Most of these companies have yet to reach a point where the required changes in organisational culture have become institutionalised.

Traditional ways of thinking about education and training, therefore, need to be challenged. As well as formal training related to procedures, people need to be equipped to participate in the overall change process. An organisational learning approach means that education and training activities must draw upon the enthusiasm of those upon whom action depends. These people are not necessarily the policy champions. The environmental and quality assurance managers (and, in one company, a senior timber buyer) in the DIY companies are still trying to bring the product managers, timber buyers and suppliers on board. Training and awareness programmes must recognise the concerns of all who play a part in the implementation process. This means acknowledging individual anxieties and involving those responsible for implementation in the design of monitoring and evaluation tools. Commitment to the policy initiative is further enhanced, as is individual capacity to implement the required changes. Extensive participation in the change process also provides a means of reducing conflict, apathy and inaction.[30]

What challenges and opportunities lie ahead for companies committed to the environment and learning organisations? The DIY–WWF example may offer a new learning model for the implementation of corporate environmental policy with environmental NGOs acting as both watchdogs and partners of industry.[31] The other two cases also hint that business–NGO relations may be becoming more collaborative—from the Greenpeace membership of Iceland's Chairman and the company's support for boycotts, to JT Design Build's environmental awareness campaign. The latter included participation by NGOs such as the Council for the Preservation of Rural England (CPRE) and Transport 2000, and prominent 'greens' such as Jonathan Porritt and Herbert Giradet.

In the DIY–WWF Alliance, the facilitating roles of WWF's Forest Officer and 1995 Group Manager have been a key part of policy implementation, both in providing much of the initial technical and practical advice on timber sourcing and in offering a safe ongoing forum for competitors to share and develop strategies. While a number of the retailers now have internal timber technology expertise, WWF continues to play an important monitoring and advisory role. Individual companies continue to struggle with the problems of trying to identify the sources of all their wood products and to determine whether the original trees were sourced from well-managed forests. WWF offers the DIY retailers ongoing access to its extensive global forest networks, which is essential given the inherent complexity in attempting to trace the original local source of even a paint brush handle.

■ Conclusion

In this chapter, we have demonstrated that there is no blueprint for the corporate environmental policy process. What works in one business will not necessarily be acceptable nor appropriate in other settings. Understanding how policy development and implementation is approached and handled in a particular organisation is therefore crucial.

At the beginning of this chapter, we introduced four main lines of argument about corporate environmental policy implementation and HRM:

- The importance of the economic context for policy motivation
- The role of personal and organisational values
- The link between managing change, risk and uncertainty, and policy effectiveness
- The need to strengthen organisational capacity to develop knowledge and skills

In this section, we present our conclusions based upon the three case studies and our wider research on the implementation of corporate social responsibility policies.

Our analysis of the three case studies demonstrates that the organisational and human resource dimensions of effecting change have not yet become an integral part of environmental policy implementation. All three case studies reveal complex relationships between values, power, culture and learning in attempting to translate policy into action. Our central message is that the technical aspects of environmental policy are not the major obstacles to implementation. The real barriers lie in the human resources, values, attitudes, relationships and related practices that need to be changed. HRM literature and the lessons from our research provide an indication as to how this can be achieved.

We have grouped our conclusions around the four general themes highlighted in the introduction and point to some of the strategic and practical implications of the environmental policy process for human resources management.

1. Economic context. Effective environmental and corporate social responsibility policies depend upon a supportive economic and commercial context. Such policies will not be sustained when the bottom line is threatened. While there is evidence of new financial and human resource investments for policy development in all three cases, the development and integration of environmental considerations into company practice remains vulnerable to external commercial forces. Among these external forces are consumer demands. If the customer is willing to pay more for environmentally-responsible products and services, then companies will provide them as long as there is a demand. However, there may also be scope to redefine the market as illustrated by the DIY–WWF case. All the major retailers have agreed to an environmental policy based upon a new 'bottom line' for the DIY trade in wood-based products. How the 'bottom line' is perceived will vary depending upon corporate attitudes to two inter-related issues: a short-versus long-term view of investment and benefits; and a shareholder versus stakeholder view of social responsibility. A stakeholder analysis has the potential to broaden corporate time horizons to encompass the needs of future generations. Such an approach also challenges the notion that the economic context is the over-riding factor influencing the adoption of environmental policies.

2. Values. Environmental policy does not implement itself. In each of the three cases, genuine support for policy development appears to be linked to the presence of a supportive organisational culture where environmental and social responsibility values thrive. In some cases, such values emanate from the top of the organisation. In others, key individuals—policy champions and others upon whom action depends—have been instrumental in creating a climate where these new corporate values can grow. Without support from the top, or where policy champions lack sufficient power or influence, dominant organisational cultures may stifle effective policy implementation. The Iceland case aptly illustrates how consistent corporate values that integrate environmental and economic considerations can lead to effective policy implementation. Values on their own, however, will not ensure policy success. In all three cases, scope for action has depended upon the power position, organisational culture and industrial context in which policy champions operate.

3. Managing change. Environmental policy is about complex and innovative organisational change. The implementation of environmental policy usually involves new internal processes and procedures, and altered roles and relationships both internal and external to the company. Such change creates anxiety on the part of individuals involved in the process. The need for a strategic overview of policy development and implementation is therefore essential. Both management and employees need to know where the organisation is heading. Human resource managers need to create a secure context in which to enable both managers and their employees to step into the unknown and to know that they will have support from the top of the organisation. Without an organisational commitment to manage the process carefully and intelligently, then little in the way of substantive organisational change will occur.

4. Organisational capacity. Linked to all of the above is the need to enhance the organisation's long-term capacity to respond to ongoing environmental marketing and value shifts. In order to become learning organisations, responsive companies must invest wisely in their human resources. Learning organisations are based on people who have the confidence and skills to adapt to their changed roles and who are enabled to make effective use of new environmental technologies or processes. Organisational learning capacity is further enhanced by bringing a wider range of stakeholders into the corporate environmental policy process—environmental NGOs, clients, consultants, customers, suppliers and even competitors. In all three cases, external and internal consultants have been hired to develop new organisational knowledge and skills. Building this expertise into organisational capacity remains a challenge. By including a wider range of stakeholders in the organisational policy process, capacity to implement may be strengthened. At the end of the day, however, companies require internal leadership to integrate all external resources effectively into the organisational culture and ongoing operations.

Managing the environmental policy process is essentially a function of HRM. Effective environmental policy development and implementation in corporate settings depends upon a supportive strategy for human resources management. If a company is really serious about adopting good environmental policy and practice, then those responsible for policy development need to engage human resource managers to plan for organisational learning and cultural change. Senior management should not assume that its own commitment to values and power to implement will be enough to bring about the change. For their part, human resource managers need to recognise that environmental policy is not a matter that can be left to technical environmental experts. The formulation and implementation of a strategy that will work within a particular company setting must be the product of engaging and motivating all the human resources upon which action depends.

■ Notes

1. This research is developing a body of case study information on UK companies which will contribute to an understanding of social responsibility in corporate practice. This qualitative study explores why and how companies have adopted environmental and/or social policies and the extent to which companies and their stakeholders judge these to have been successfully implemented. The research also explores how innovation and change have been approached in the context of current theories of organisational process and the strategic management of change. It builds upon previous work in which a series of case studies was prepared for management teaching purposes (see SAUS and *New Consumer, Good Business? Case Studies in Corporate Social Responsibility* [Bristol, UK: SAUS Publications, 1993]).

2. See also D. Parry, *Iceland—Plaudits or Profits? What Makes a Responsible Company?* (Corporate Social Responsibility Research Working Paper; Bristol and Newcastle, UK: School for Policy Studies and *New Consumer*, 1995).

3. See also S.M. Barrett, *Constructing a Green Profile: The Case of JT Design Build Ltd* (Corporate Social Responsibility Research Working Paper; Bristol and Newcastle, UK: School for Policy Studies and *New Consumer*, 1995).

4. See also D.F. Murphy, *Doing It Together for the World's Forests: A WWF–DIY Alliance*

on the Sourcing of Wood Products (Corporate Social Responsibility Research Working Paper; Bristol and Newcastle, UK: School for Policy Studies and *New Consumer*, 1996).

5. T. Peters and R. Waterman, *In Search of Excellence* (New York, NY: Harper & Row, 1982).

6. See P. Blunt, 'Recent Developments in Human Resource Management: The Good, the Bad and the Ugly', in *International Journal of Human Resource Management*, Vol. 2 No. 2 (1991), pp. 45-59.

7. T.H. Roback, 'Personnel Research Perspectives on Human Resource Management and Development', in *Public Personnel Management*, Vol. 18 No. 2 (Summer 1989), p. 138.

8. J. Storey, 'HRM in Action: The Truth is Out at Last', in *Personnel Management*, April 1992, pp. 28-30.

9. See Roback, *op. cit.*

10. *Ibid.*

11. See B. Garratt, 'Learning in the Core of Organisational Survival: Action Learning is the Key Integrating Process', in *Journal of Management Development*, Vol. 6 No. 2 (1987), pp. 38-44.

12. See M.A. Lyles and C.R. Schwenk, 'Top Management Strategy and Organisational Knowledge Structures', in *Journal of Management Studies*, Vol. 29 No. 2 (March 1992), pp. 155-74.

13. Our description of the construction industry as 'conservative' is confirmed by a recent study by Biffa Waste Services (*Snakes and Ladders? A Benchmarking Report on Waste and Business Strategy* [High Wycombe, UK: Biffa Waste Services, 1994]) and the University of Strathclyde, which found that the construction sector was lagging behind the rest of UK industry in its commitment to waste management practices and awareness. Of companies surveyed, 45% expressed no interest in waste minimisation programmes and 42% do not recycle any materials.

14. S. Schmidheiny, *Changing Course: A Global Business Perspective on Development and the Environment* (London, UK: MIT Press, 1992), p. 86.

15. See T. Peters, *Thriving on Chaos: Handbook for a Management Revolution* (London, UK: Pan Books, 1989); R.M. Kantor, *The Change Masters: Corporate Entrepreneurs at Work* (London, UK: Unwin Paperbacks, 1985); *idem, When Giants Learn to Dance: Mastering the Challenges of Strategy, Management, and Careers in the 1990s* (London, UK: Unwin Paperbacks, 1990); Garratt, *op. cit.*; D. Garvin, 'Building a Learning Organisation', in *Harvard Business Review*, Vol. 71 No. 4 (July/August 1993), pp. 78-91.

16. See D. Frey, 'Learning the Ropes: My Life as a Product Champion', in *Harvard Business Review*, Vol. 69 No. 5 (September/October 1991), p. 46.

17. See Peters and Waterman, *op. cit.*; Kantor, *The Change Masters*; C. Handy, *The Age of Unreason* (London, UK: Business Books, 1989).

18. E. Schein, *Organisational Culture and Leadership* (San Francisco, CA: Jossey Bass, 1985), p. 6. See also P.H. Frissen, 'The Cultural Impact of Information in Public Administration', in *International Review of Administrative Sciences*, Vol. 55 (1989), pp. 569-86.

19. See P.J. Frost, L.F. Moore, M.R. Louis, C.C. Lundberg and J. Martin (eds.), *Reframing Organisational Culture* (London, UK: Sage, 1991).

20. See Schmidheiny, *op. cit.*

21. See W. Solesbury, 'The Environmental Agenda', in *Public Administration*, Vol. 54 (Winter 1976), pp. 379-97.

22. See S.M. Barrett and L. MacMahon, 'Public Management in Uncertainty: A Micro-Political Perspective of the Health Service in the UK', in *Policy and Politics*, Vol. 18 No. 4 (1990), pp. 257-68.

23. Schmidheiny, *op. cit.*, p. 10.

24. See M. Edelman, *Politics as Symbolic Action* (Chicago, IL: Markham Publishing Company, 1971).

25. S.M. Barrett, 'Information Technology and Organisational Culture: Implementing Change', in *International Review of Administrative Sciences*, Vol. 58 (1992), p. 370.

26. *Op. cit.*

27. *Op. cit.*

28. *Ibid.*, p. 39.

29. *Ibid.*, p. 42.

30. See Storey, *op. cit.*

31. See T.A. Hemphill, 'Strange Bedfellows Cozy up for a Clean Environment', in *Business and Society Review*, No. 90 (Summer 1994), pp. 38-44. The issues raised by the DIY–WWF case study are explored in greater detail in D.F. Murphy, 'In the Company of Partners: Businesses, NGOs and Sustainable Development: Towards a Global Perspective', in R. Aspinwall and J. Smith (eds.), *Environmentalist and Business Partnerships: A Sustainable Model?* (Cambridge, UK: White Horse, 1996), pp. 45-72; and Murphy, *op. cit.*

Who's Afraid of Local Agenda 21?[1]

A Survey of UK Local Government Environmental Co-ordinators' Background, Values, Gender and Motivation

Walter Wehrmeyer and Stephen Rees

*T*HE INITIAL experience of Local Government Environmental Co-ordinators in implementing sustainable development and Local Agenda 21 (LA21) into the UK is reviewed in this chapter, based on a postal survey. Following an introduction into the current state of UK local authorities, we report that the vast majority of staff are highly and intrinsically motivated individuals who are relatively new to their posts and originate primarily from the Environmental Health function. A Principal Component Analysis revealed that the two most important factors determining motivation are gender (with women more motivated towards LA21), and professional values. The respondents' view of the role of local authorities generally is documented as the 'five Cs', namely to care, collaborate, create, communicate, and control. Various human resource implications for each of these roles are identified in the belief that such HRM support is essential if LA21 as a catalyst for organisational, regional and social change is to be introduced.

■ Introduction

> Sustainable development means carrying on with anything you like but justifying it with clever arguments.
>
> *A Local Environmental Co-ordinator*

Sustainable development, it increasingly appears, is a concept whose relative ease of international acceptance by politicians does not reflect the complexities and contradictions encountered by those implementing it at a local level. This is not to deny the urgent need for such implementation.

Although non-governmental organisations and industry are quite active, the implementation of sustainable development in the UK is firmly on the governmental side, and, according to the Local Agenda 21 process, within the remit of local government with the official support of central government.[2] The structure of UK local government—being split into borough/district, metropolitan and county-wide or regional administrative areas with increasing geographical scope and variations in statutory duties—is an important facet in this strategy.

This chapter presents a number of preliminary findings of an ongoing research project into the management context of Local Government Environmental Co-ordinators (LGECs) and the Local Agenda 21 (LA21) process. This chapter has these aims:

- To identify organisational traits of those in charge of implementing LA21

- To analyse what motivates and stimulates LA21 implementers, both personally and organisationally

- To identify organisational roles of local authorities and identify their human resource implications for sustainable development

Assuming the popular Brundtland Report definition, sustainable development combines the values of environmental protection, intergenerational and inter-regional equity and quality of life. Agenda 21 is the document that emerged at the 1992 UNCED conference in Rio outlining how sustainable development can be introduced into the national contexts of developing and developed countries. In this, Agenda 21 recognises local government as pivotal in delivering the majority of actions recommended and this is endorsed by the UK Government. In fact, Chapter 28 of the text specifically requires local governments to initiate a Local Agenda 21 process by 1996.

However, the success of local governments in implementing the LA21 process depends crucially on the motivation, understanding, authority and resources of those individuals in charge of it. At the moment, from an organisational point of view, support for local government from the UK central Government appears to be less forthcoming. Apart from the organisational constraints on local government, the development of LA21 represents a classical management problem—how to motivate staff towards a new set of issues and criteria without change becoming threatening or an imposition.

■ *Background to UK Local Authorities*
■ *Local Government Review (LGR)*

To set the context for this preliminary report, it is necessary to outline briefly the structures and changes that are taking place in local government in the UK. The last major overhaul of local government took place in 1974. The 1990s have seen another overhaul with the Local Government Review (LGR). Through a phased programme of review, certain (non-metropolitan) regions have been under scrutiny by a Royal Commission with a view to dissolving two-tier structures (districts and counties) and replacing them with 'unitary authorities'. At no time in this process has local 'sustainability' been taken into account, although the Royal Commission has encouraged action in authorities which might have implications for the Local Agenda 21 process—for example, the better devolution of responsibility and supply of information to parish councils.

This process has created a considerable amount of disruption in local government, diverting strategic, financial, administrative and political resources to deal with the threat and process of change in both districts and counties. The inherent rivalry between counties and districts has also been problematic in developing partnerships. This agenda has had a considerable impact on UK local authorities and an opportunity to integrate 'sustainability' criteria into the review process seems to have been missed. Nevertheless, where new 'unitary' authorities are designated, it would seem an ideal opportunity for environmental management and 'sustainability' objectives to be taken on board at the outset.

■ *Compulsory Competitive Tendering*

Compulsory Competitive Tendering (CCT) was a feature first born out of the Local Government and Housing Act of 1989. The attempt to bring 'competition' into local authority services started with blue-collar activities. This new approach encourages a formal contractual division between the **'purchaser'** (the local authority) and the **'provider'** (a local authority Direct Labour Organisation or external contractor) as directed through a contractual process. The process of 'competition' has now been extended to the white-collar professions with local authorities required to commit 35% of their white-collar services to open competition with the private sector. Where LAs have been affected by the Local Government Review, CCT for white-collar services must be completed within 24 months of the final decision. In promoting this process of CCT or 'competition', central Government has chosen to omit environmental or 'sustainability' criteria. CCT has also had a dramatic impact on the strategic, administrative and political resources available to address the sustainable development agenda.

■ Research Method

In designing the research, efforts were made not to prejudge the opinions of LGECs responding. Accordingly, the inductive research method was that of a questionnaire comprised of a large number of personal and organisational attitude statements, as well as open-ended questions. It was sent by mail to all 453 LGECs[3] in the UK. 180 LGECs responded, of which 153 were valid replies (29% of which were female). The data was computerised and subsequently used for a content and statistical analysis. The sample of this survey thus consists of those LGECs in the UK responding to the survey request. Given the size of the sample and its spread across the geographical, functional, gender-based and age-related dimensions of the sample, the survey can be seen as broadly representative.[4] The main methods of analysis are content analysis, statistical inferences on the cross-tabulations and Principal Component Analysis (PCA).[5] In a forthcoming second stage, and to qualify the written and numerical responses, semi-structured interviews will be conducted with a subset who have indicated their willingness to partake in such a process.

■ Results

As it can be seen from Figure 1, the majority of the 153 respondents are from district/borough councils. Given the much larger number of such councils, this is expected. Equally, as Figure 2 shows, the majority of respondents are environmental health officers, commonly charged with implementation rather than strategic or policy issues. It also reinforces earlier research by

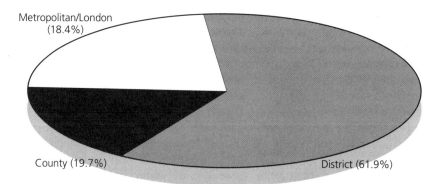

Figure 1: *Responding Organisations*

Crabb,[6] who found that human resources managers saw environmental issues predominantly as factors of health and safety, non-smoking areas and unleaded petrol in (company) cars. The distribution of respondents, both across the type of organisation and across job categories, could be expected, as it largely reflects the statutory role attributed to the various parties.

With regard to age and length of service, the majority of respondents were under 35 years old (Fig. 3, see overleaf) and were in their current job for less than four years (see Fig. 4, see overleaf). Given the nature of their work, planners and policy-makers had on average a slightly longer experience with their workplace, and environmental co-ordinators and health officers were relatively newer to their posts (typically by 2–4 years). As Figure 4 shows, the majority of respondents have held their current posts for less than four years (57.8%), yet almost a fifth (19%) have held their posts for six or more years. The empirical findings of this survey are categorised into two main sections:

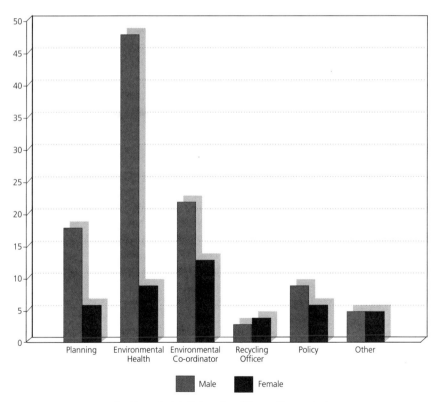

Figure 2: *Job Categories of Survey Respondents*

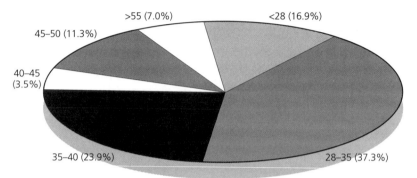

Figure 3: *Age of Survey Respondents*

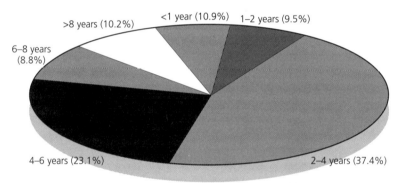

Figure 4: *Length of Stay in Current Position*

- Overall findings and organisational aspects of LA21 implementation in the UK

- Motives (values) and motivation of Local Government Environmental Co-ordinators (LGECs)

Organisational Aspects of LA21 Implementation in the UK

The survey responses had a broadly representative spread from the three types of organisations—in order of decreasing geographical cover and level of abstraction in policy-making: county, metropolitan authorities and London boroughs as well as district/borough councils. Respondents came predominantly from the latter (62%), but the metropolitan and county authorities were equally well represented with 18.4% and 19.7% respectively (see Fig. 1).

With regard to the gender distribution (Fig. 2), the majority of female respondents work as environmental co-ordinators but are comparatively under-represented in planning and in the environmental health sections. Even though male respondents appear slightly older, no such difference could be identified in the length of stay. Equally, men and women were represented in roughly equal percentages from the metropolitan areas, but women were represented at a slightly greater level from the district at the expense of slightly less representation at county level.[7]

However, gender appears to be less of an issue as age progresses. Female respondents appear to value their education and their mobility significantly more highly than their male co-workers. In addition, younger staff are more concerned with party politics[8] and are apparently more aware of their ideological background, but show significantly less concern for the local community from which they originate.

It also appears that staff with low duration in their current job tend to criticise short-termism significantly more often as an organisational obstacle to sustainable development.[9] The same group also showed greater sympathy towards 'fair trade' as an option towards LA21 implementation. No meaningful and statistically significant correlation between income and age, length of stay, gender, place of work or job type could be identified.

■ Individual Motivation and Relevance of Personal and Work Factors
To better understand the motives of LA21 implementers, it was decided to offer respondents a range of cultural, work-related and motivational factors (such as ethnic group, family, political party, intrinsic work motivation, job satisfaction, personal education, corporate values or income) and to ask how strongly these influence daily life either as a background (motivational) factor (column 2 of Fig. 5) or work-related factor (column 3 of Fig. 5). This variety of factors was then transformed into principal components, the results of which are displayed in Figure 5.

■ Background and Motivation of LGECs
The results suggest that LGECs are, not unexpectedly, not motivated by the financial but rather by the intrinsic rewards of their professions. In asking where their motivation came from:

- 95.2% suggested job satisfaction.
- 92.5% suggested the challenge of environmental issues.
- Interestingly, 82.1% suggested the opportunity to alter corporate culture.

	Background and Motivation	Work Factors and Goals
Component 1 (Name)	Female (sex, gender background, gender values)	The Self (personal ambition, education and status, career and status goals)
Proportion	15.9%	21.9%
Component 2 (Name)	Esprit de Corps (professional values and corporate culture)	Environmental challenge, reject pay as work factor (Intrinsic Motivation?)
Proportion	13%	11.2%
Component 3 (Name)	Work Values (professional values, work, reject family values)	Self Experience (personal health, freedom, time and access to environment)
Proportion	7.9%	8.9%
Component 4 (Name)	Spirituality ('one earth', religion, culture, reject the Self or place of work)	Sustain family (Food), power but not vocation or academic challenge
Proportion	7.9%	5.8%
Component 5 (Name)	Traditional values (family, wider family, political parties)	Faith and Food (religion and sustain family financially)
Proportion	5.8%	5.5%
Component 6 (Name)	Personal background (family, own history, education)	Cultural Identity and Sustain Family
Proportion	5%	4.6%
Component 7 (Name)	Religion, local community; job code, but not wealth	Job Satisfaction, reject cultural identity or access to technology as goal
Proportion	4.7%	4.2%
Cumulative Proportion	62.6%	62.1%

Figure 5: *Motives of LA21 Implementers*

Equally, 75% were not motivated by the example of their work colleagues and 75% were not motivated by the financial rewards of working in the public sector.

Cultural values are, as Cernea has shown,[10] critically important for social motivation towards sustainable development. However, 83% of respondents did not identify with their ethnic group; 77% did not perceive themselves to be influenced by religion; and only 20% identified strongly with their local community.[11] The finding that LGECs appear culturally inactive may prove an intangible and inhibiting factor for Local Agenda 21, particularly since the family provides much stronger social influence than wider cultural values: 92% identified (very strongly) with their family; 83% were unwilling (unable?) to sacrifice their family support system; and 73% felt the influence of increasingly popular family values. In fact, only 60% thought of themselves as having a cultural identity.

The Principal Component Analysis identifies and ranks those factors that explain the data variability more than others. The first such factor for the individual background and motivation is whether or not the respondent is female. That women have quite different and often stronger environmental awareness and attitudes has been shown in several other studies[12] and in fact, this component analysis result is further reinforced by the respective cross-tabulations where 87% of males rejected their gender values, yet 65% of female respondents strongly associated with such values.

The second group of motivational factors is associated with work and consists of factors 2 and 3, comprising about 21% of the data variability. The values of work and of the corporate culture are thus recognised and appreciated by the respondents as deciding factors. This includes the emergence of an environmental profession[13] or the increasing profession-alism of Local Agenda workers. This may reflect a task-oriented rather than a people-oriented approach,[14] yet, more importantly, is ample evidence for the intrinsic motivation of LGECs to pursue their task. This vocational aspect is also evidenced in the above percentages, where even though only about 60% supported a 'vocational call', 23.8% showed strong support.

The third group of motivating factors are mainly ethical and concern family and religious values in changing permutations with political party influence and 'deep green' environmental ethics.[15] These factors 4–7 together account for about 23.4% of data variability and are arguably focused on socio-psychological factors of 'the Self'. This mixture has a relatively strong emphasis on family values which, as combined sets of values, are either mixed in with political ideologies or with personal education. Equally, the spiritual aspects of such motivation appear strong; yet, again, substantially more research is required to explore fully the relationship between personal spirituality and the motivation towards sustainable development.[16] Cernea's[17] cultural factors necessary for sustainable development thus reappear here as motivators towards Local Agenda 21 implementation.

■ *Relevance of Work Factors and Goals*

Interestingly, and in line with the relevance of personal and social background, in the range of work factors perceived as important, the Self plays the single most important role explaining about one-fifth of the data variance. Personal ambition, the pursuit of a career and the perceived status and relevance of the environmental agenda are seen as important factors at work. In a sense, this may point less to the career-oriented environmental co-ordinator and more to the relatively high status and organisational relevance environmental issues may enjoy.

However, it was also noted from the written responses that a number of LGECs felt as if they were working in relative isolation: the 'Environment Department' was perceived as having a comparatively lower status and a poor political position. This may suggest that their comparably lower career ambition could be related to a lower career expectation. The question remains: does this make 'environmental co-ordination' an organisational role of high skills but low prospects?

An alternative interpretation of the role of career development is that staffing choices made by the relevant human resources departments simply reflect the broad skills, age structure and experience an LGEC may enjoy. The importance of this factor may also indicate that, in this context, staff may feel that their individual values and skills matter and that they can be acted upon—at least to some extent.[18]

The second set of factors relevant for work generally and goal-setting in particular concern the environment. 'Saving the world' as an intrinsic part of the job plays an encouragingly prominent role. That the environmental challenge is related to a general rejection of pay and work conditions as a stimulating factor reinforces the intrinsic motivation that can be derived from the work. It also indicates the strength of the *intrinsic* character of the motivation—working on Local Agenda 21 'despite the odds' (or pay), and refers to the personal motivating factors as identified in the previous section's Principal Component Analysis and hence supports the promising notion of highly-motivated staff in this area.

The third factor is equally interesting as it refers to work values outside work but, like the first factor, related to the Self. Even though the first factor was more concerned with the background of an individual, this factor is more concerned with what staff are doing on a daily basis. Here, personal health, time and having access to the environment are *work* factors considered of importance. Subsequent factors are more instrumental and less values-based. They tend to focus around pay (sustaining the family economically), the ability to influence an organisation positively, religion, and cultural identity.

In this set of factors, the strength with which cultural and spiritual factors appear is both surprising and consistent with the personal motivators indicated above. In this, it appears that, arguably, working as an environmental co-ordinator is part of the cultural identity of staff—a conclusion that in turn may indicate success for the LA21 process. If, as it has been argued earlier, sustainable development is a matter of values rather than techniques, then the development process leading to LA21 is inevitably and essentially a cultural process, which is probably more related to personal sustainability than the proponents of a more technology-oriented approach would care to admit. Conversely, the introduction of performance-oriented 'competition' has fostered this very technology-based approach, as has a focus on legislative compliance.

In addition, the emphasis on intrinsic job satisfaction (in factors 2, 3 and 7) is encouraging for the LA21 process as, by implication, the human resources function has staffed the process with appropriate (and motivated) manpower. However, the enthusiasm of staff may be seen as isolated from the social and organisational context, where the Self as a work factor appears more relevant than the work itself (or the professional context of colleagues): self-interest ranks in importance over and above the environmental challenge. This may reflect a personal emphasis of LGECs, namely to implement their own personal understanding of sustainable development into the local context.

■ *How do LGECs see the Role of Local Authorities in Sustainable Development?*

An important part of this research is the identification of language and the use of concepts in promoting LA21. One part of this was to study what respondents saw as their personal definition of sustainable development—the subject of a later paper. Here, the role of local authorities in the LA21 process is analysed as it is perceived by LGECs. This is important for human resources as the latter should be co-ordinated and integrated with these various management roles.[19] From the qualitative responses, five main roles for local authorities could be identified (see Fig. 6).

Probably the most prominent, but not necessarily best-implemented, of such roles is that of **care**, where the needs of the economically and socially disadvantaged are addressed through a wide range of measures to ameliorate physical and mental suffering and to support environmental, social or economic casualties in the provision of basic and tailored needs.

Care
■ As defender, provider, carer, steward and protector

Collaborate
■ As enabler, facilitator, participator and partner for projects, ideas and activities

Create
■ As initiator, example-setter and educator for pilot and ongoing activities and action

Communicate
■ Externally as lobbyist, awareness raiser, arbitrator, conflict resolver and informer. Equally to communicate through other roles.

Control
■ As appraiser, auditor, planner, designer, manager, monitor and regulator

Figure 6: *Local Authority Roles as Perceived by LGECs*

The second role of local authority as seen by its environmental co-ordinators is that of **collaboration**. Here, new projects and ideas are introduced by means of partnership projects, and new activities are initiated with local authorities as enablers and facilitators of community-initiated or -directed activities. Here, local authorities are partners.

The ability to **create** new projects and action is a further role of local government. Here, the functions of initiation, setting examples and educating are somewhat distinct as they presume a leadership function in authorities.

Another substantial role of local authorities is that of **communication**, be it internally to report to higher authorities or externally to inform about events, action or ideas, to raise awareness, to support its networking function, to arbitrate but also, in an intermediate way, to resolve conflicts among parties.

Finally, local authorities have a considerable influence in their **control** role, where activities, be these planned, anticipated or ongoing, are appraised, audited, designed, managed and regulated. This includes the statutory duties of UK authorities in the planning, environmental health and waste management process.

It should be noted that many aspects of these roles overlap, yet in many cases it is difficult to perform several such roles at the same time, as they can contradict each other.

It is now possible to identify how human resources management may support the performing of these roles towards sustainable development.[20] This has been summarised in Figure 7, where the various roles are supported by HRM activities and examples are given for this in current practice.

■ Discussion and Preliminary Conclusions

The Local Agenda 21 process is set out to introduce sustainable development principles and practices in a large number of countries. The role of local government in pursuing this environmental challenge has been recognised by the Agenda as well as by the UK Government, which placed the onus of implementation firmly into the hands of local authorities. However, from a HRM viewpoint, the staffing of this task with highly-motivated employees has arguably *de facto* succeeded in that, even if not all employees work on the process full-time, the level of enthusiasm and intrinsic motivation is encouraging.

LA21 also sets out to introduce value changes and a different view of the (organisational, social and environmental) world. This requires the establishment of personal and organisational sustainability indicators and an

Local Government Function	Human Resource Management Contribution	Examples of Action
Care	■ Establishing criteria for 'personal' sustainability ■ Allow and support 'ownership' of issues ■ Establishing responsibility for environment ■ Staff attitude and awareness ■ Meeting fear of threats from LA21 ■ Change measures of success ■ Train to deal with cultural and gender barriers	■ Community care plan ■ Service provision (fire, police, health, social services) ■ HRM support structure within organisation ■ Design of sustainable communities
Collaborate	■ Better representation of disadvantaged groups in LA21 ■ Political networking ■ Participation and empowerment ■ Develop partnership and collaboration skills ■ Consensus-building—common sense	■ Partnership projects ■ Pump-priming funds ■ Local Agenda 21 ■ Forums for change (internal and external) ■ Support information exchange
Create	■ Pilot alternative projects ■ Develop managerial, creative and lateral skills ■ Support management systems and targets through staffing and staff performance appraisal	■ Environmental education—curriculum-related activities ■ Business–education partnerships ■ R&D—in-house pilot projects and services
Communicate	■ Assess perception levels in electorate ■ Avoid 'eco-babble' (make language user-friendly) ■ Develop presentation and communication skills ■ Educate about environment	■ Environmental Information Regulations 1992: review of information needs and delivery of practical information ■ Consumer monitoring ■ Information/reporting on environmental performance
Control	■ Include environment in staff appraisal ■ Integrate environment into management system ■ Foster preventative and proactive approach ■ Review training to include environment into all forums for staff development ■ Seek political acceptance of sustainable development	■ State of the environment—monitoring and reporting ■ Environmental Protection Act 1990: implementation of 'Duty of Care' on waste ■ Environmental appraisal of development plans (PPG 12) ■ Inputs into CCT process

Figure 7: The HRM Function for Sustainable Development

implementation of sustainable development into all aspects of local authorities. The preliminary conclusions of this research find the process so far to be largely disappointing with (non-LGEC) staff interpreting LA21 as an additional duty rather than as a fundamental change. In this, it remains an add-on rather than an opportunity for a substantial re-think of all operations and activities. This is not necessarily a surprise, as the considerable and far-reaching changes of Compulsory Competitive Tendering and, particularly in Wales, of Local Government Review have already introduced the very climate of uncertainty and of an organisational threat that is more important than the introduction of a what some see as a nebulous process[21]—which will depend on HRM in the development of a 'learning culture'.

One of the most surprising findings of this research is the role of gender in the motivation and socio-psychological composition of staff, where women often work in lower roles with less scope to initiate change, yet are more environmentally concerned and may provide particular skills conducive to sustainable development. Even though this issue has been recognised as important in the literature, no coherent empirical research has been conducted so far. Given this, further speculation on what may be the causes and effects of this 'male dominance' of the LA21 process is, despite its importance, premature.

It was also found that, even though intrinsic motivation is there and higher than in many other jobs, the Self appears much more important in daily organisational life. This finding contrasts somewhat with the above notion of intrinsic motivation of employees. Even in the environmental area—as relevant and important for individuals' futures as any—short-term ambitions and careers are predominant over intrinsic (environmental) factors. The concept of 'personal sustainability' and the power of the Self remains an over-riding factor. This is ameliorated somewhat by the finding that pursuing an environmental career is not considered to be a dead end or, by implication, a professionally marginal issue. For the future of environmental management, this may suggest ensured capacity to attract motivated and qualified staff.

With regard to motivation, it was found that LGECs participating in the survey are highly personally-motivated individuals who are inspired by the task, following more concrete social values emanating from their families and personal knowledge. Interestingly, career prospects, personal wealth, professional recognition or economics appear not to be influencing factors. However, for the introduction of such a complex and, as yet, vague concept as sustainable development, it may prove an obstacle that those charged with its concretisation are themselves less influenced by abstract social and more by technology-oriented values. How can a values-based approach of sustainable development be introduced by technology-oriented staff? The predominance of environmental health officers, planners and technical officers in the response begs the question as to how far the social sciences and education practitioners have been brought on board to foster community or organisational development issues. Only about a quarter of respondents are involved in policy and long-term decision-making, which by implication may mean that LA21 is seen as an operational rather than a strategic issue. Local authorities currently translate sustainable development into a topic of little local scope and local organisational diversity—an implementation approach that is in striking contradiction to the content of such implementation—enabling and empowering local decision-making. Hence, 'Think Globally, Act Locally' translates into 'Implement Nationally, Act Accordingly'. Given the relative youth of environmental management and the Local Agenda 21 issue, and given the national organisational and financial hierarchy of local government, this is not necessarily a surprise but, from a human resources viewpoint, it will be interesting to further clarify the interpretation by organisations as to what LA21 is all about.

From the above tables on the various roles of local authorities in sustainable development, it was evident that staff felt strongly the need for including and integrating HRM in the development of organisational capacity towards the LA21 process. In that, LA21 is promoted here as an integrated concept that does not fit easily with unchanged organisational priorities and practices. A number of implications of this can be formulated.

First, and only after careful further research, LA21 could be supported by a greater inclusion of gender issues in those implementing it.

Secondly, the motivational levels appear high, so that the role of HRM lies more towards the provision of organisational incentives to foster LA21 implementation, such as undertaking a review of performance-related pay, staff appraisal processes or contractual agreements with regard to their respective environmental impacts.

Thirdly, it appears that the instrumentalisation of the LA21 process indicates that staffing has strangely taken the 'wrong attitude' to LA21, namely that it can be implemented into the local context without considerable attitude and structural change. Such change may include the role and influence of local authorities on local economic systems and on the access to local resources—as recognised by LA21 itself. However, this is not within the statutory remit of local authorities, so that, given the role of local government as implementer, there is little they can do but to see LA21 as a set of issues to be implemented into the existing context, rather than to change the very fabric of local government. In this, sustainable development is misinterpreted not only by central Government but also locally by (HRM) staff: *operationalisation* of a set of requirements is favoured over a wider change of priorities and preferences.

Fourthly, and given the motivation and competence of LGEC staff, HRM is here more concerned with facilitation and reward than with job specification and control, whereas the opposite is the case for other local authority staff.

However, generally, the concept of sustainable development itself is in need of further definition and refinement. As it stands now, and concluding from the data set, the concept is in danger of misinterpretation due to hasty implementation. At present, the uncertainties and insecurities incidentally introduced by CCT and LGR pose substantial barriers for sustainable development implementation. Efforts towards continuous environmental improvement are difficult in a political and organisational context that favours short-term fixes and presentable results. This highlights the further problem for LGECs that much of their work is concerned with facilitating and supporting other groups' work—a task that helps these groups in their performance but makes the environmental co-ordinator's performance assessment intrinsically difficult. Hence, how can one foster a function designed to help others in a climate of attributing individual and 'hard' results to individual staff? This may reflect an emphasis of changing outcomes rather than processes and may lead to cynical staff responses to the LA21 process.

In this, ways to show the performance of facilitating (staff) functions is necessary as this topic is an established field of management theory. This may (and should?) lead to areas of performance-related pay for environmental management, and ways to attribute environmental success (in whatever definition) to individual staff. A further area of research is the career expectations of LGECs—a matter that is apparently not of overarching importance to the respondents, but is critical if 'environment' is to be seen as a central and not a marginal area of local government. HRM has a vital role to play in the implementation of LA21 in the UK. This process and the process of finding coherent responses to the challenge of sustainable development constitutes perpetual learning processes, the study of which is presented here with, as yet, only preliminary results.

■ *Notes*

1. The research described in this chapter received the support and endorsement of the UNED-UK Committee, The International Council for Local Environmental Initiatives (Toronto), The UK Local Government Management Board (LGMB) and the Environment Council (UK). The authors are grateful for these contributions and

the responses received from the Local Government Environment Co-ordinators.

2. See Department of the Environment, *Sustainable Development: The UK Strategy* (Cm 2426; London, UK: HMSO, 1994).

3. LGECs are defined here—rather narrowly—as anybody participating in the LGMB network.

4. However, a potential bias of non-respondents on postal surveys cannot be excluded, although no statistical support for such a bias was found. Theoretically, such bias could exist, particularly with regard to knowledge, awareness, and implementation efforts towards sustainable development. Those not responding may be less active generally and less involved in sustainable development implementation or the Local Agenda 21 process.

5. The main aim of this method is to convert the existing data set into a new set of transformed variables so that, ideally, 'the variation in the data set can be adequately described by the few [principle components] with variances that are not negligible' (B.J.F. Manly, *Multivariate Statistical Models: A Primer* [London, UK: Chapman & Hall, 1986], p. 58). In a sense, PCA is a mathematical procedure to identify 'important' factors or factor combinations in explaining data variability, where 'importance' is defined as the capacity of such factors (components) to explain data variability.

6. S. Crabb, 'Has Industry Seen the Green Light?', in *Personnel Management*, April 1990.

7. It appears that there is an age factor in the gender distribution where young age is positively correlated with female gender ($r^2 = 0.3300$; significant at 99.9% level) and, conversely, males are positively correlated with length of stay in their current place ($r^2 = 0.2587$; significant at 99.9% level).

8. $r^2 = -0.3552$; significant at 99.9% level.

9. Curiously, this could be a function of short-term contracts for such staff which may make respondents more aware of potential shortcomings of short-term strategies.

10. M.M. Cernea, 'Culture and Organisation: The Social Sustainability of Induced Development', in *Sustainable Development*, Vol. 1 No. 2 (1993), pp. 18-29.

11. These high figures do not necessarily contradict the PCA results, as they are based on cumulative percentages rather than frequency distributions. In other words, the percentages show little difference between responses indicating strong or very strong agreement to an attitude statement. PCA, however, would show different results in these cases because PCA is based on the 'distribution of agreement' rather than the sum of all those who agree, no matter how strong.

12. See K. Peattie, *Green Marketing* (London, UK: Pitman, 1992); M. Charter (ed.), *Greener Marketing: A Responsible Approach to Business* (Sheffield, UK: Greenleaf Publishing, 1992).

13. In another section of the questionnaire, the notion of 'ecobabble' as a language of the environmental professions was mentioned and the majority of respondents recognised such a phenomenon and rated it as distracting from the original purpose of facilitating LA21 ownership and participation to as many as possible.

14. See C.B. Handy, *Understanding Organisations* (3rd edn; Harmondsworth, UK: Penguin, 1985).

15. See T. O'Riordan, *Environmentalism* (2nd rev. edn; London, UK: Pion, 1981).
16. Equally, more research is necessary to understand the role of family values as a motivating factor for environmental issues.
17. *Op. cit.*
18. This is an interesting result of this research, where earlier research has indicated that cultural factors of staff attitudes were significantly different to those of the individual—the 'employee' had different values to the 'parent', the 'shopper', or the 'voter' (see W. Wehrmeyer, 'Personal Environmental Attitudes and Corporate Environmental Cultures: Where Do they Come from and How Do they Mix?' [Paper present to the *Third Annual Conference on Business Strategy and the Environment*, Nottingham, UK: 15–16 September 1994]).
19. See D. Torrington and L. Hall, *Personnel Management: A New Approach* (London, UK: Prentice Hall, 1987).
20. The view of HRM taken here is that of an organisational function that provides strategic, tactical and operational support for the core roles of the organisation (see K. Sisson, *Personnel Management in Britain* [Oxford, UK: Blackwell, 1989]).
21. Even though external threats can be triggers for organisational change, it is argued here that this non-environmental threat preoccupies attention and somewhat counterbalances the motivation of staff to initiate large-scale environment-oriented change of structures and processes.

5

Industrial Relations and the Environment in the UK[1]

Andrea Oates

CONCERN over environmental issues began to turn to action in the United Kingdom in the early 1970s. Public awareness about the effects of pollution on the environment increased, and environmental pressure groups, including Greenpeace and Friends of the Earth, were formed. Since this time, a series of major disasters, both in the UK and abroad, including the explosion at a chemical plant in Flixborough, UK, the poisonous gas leak at the Union Carbide plant in Bhopal, India, and the nuclear accident at Chernobyl, have brought into focus industry's potential for ecological devastation. Closer to home there was a series of food scandals that brought widespread criticism of agricultural practices, including the use of pesticides and fertilisers that resulted in contamination of food and water supplies by pesticide residues and nitrates.

However, despite the various pressures, the proportion of UK companies with a corporate environmental policy, or a policy of carrying out environmental auditing, remains low. And employers are generally reluctant to involve unions in what has traditionally been considered a management area—as a survey carried out by the Labour Research Department in 1991[2] shows: only 7% of employers had involved unions in environmental auditing.

Perhaps partly because of the dominant political philosophy during the recent period, and the associated hostility to trade union organisation, the concern expressed by individuals has not been translated into collective action as far as industrial relations is concerned. While trade unions have been involved in action to protect the environment since the 1970s, early examples were confined to a number of significant but isolated single-issue campaigns which were related to health and safety concerns of the membership of those unions. These included campaigns against the use of hazardous and environmentally-damaging substances, including pesticides and asbestos, and the refusal by seamen and transport workers to handle nuclear waste destined for disposal in the North Sea.

More recently, the TUC Environmental Action Group, which was only formed in 1989 and reported for the first time in 1990, has called for environmental rights for workers, and national unions have mounted high-profile campaigns demanding that employers recognise that workers and their representatives have a right to be involved in environmental issues at their workplace.

The second wave of union representation is all-embracing, with a shift in emphasis toward the collective green agreement, which addresses environmental issues at work in a comprehensive and structured way. This approach is in the early stages and there are very few negotiated agreements giving trade unions rights of involvement in environmental issues so far. The UK trade union movement is conscious that, in order to play a more active role in environmental protection, they must challenge the individual and consumerist response and develop it into one of collective action.

■ The Legal Framework

There is very limited provision within the formalised legal framework of industrial relations in terms of employee–employer consultation in the UK. There are no legal bodies representing a company's workforce, and protective legislation on working conditions is very selective and undergoing revision. Regulatory legislation is concerned with areas that include collective action, health and safety at work, and contracts of employment.

Legislation on employee involvement is very underdeveloped in the UK compared to countries such as Germany. There are no rights of the workforce to be consulted and informed about training issues or personnel issues, for example. Limited rights of consultation regarding changes in operations at a plant that have health and safety implications are provided within the Health and Safety at Work Act 1974. Further limited rights to information and consultation are provided in the Transfer of Undertakings Regulations and the Employment Protection Act 1975, which both enable unions to receive information on changes planned at the workplace, particularly where job losses are envisaged. More recently, the Companies Act of 1985 and the Employment Act of 1982 require companies with more than 250 employees to include in their annual reports a statement describing particular arrangements made to encourage employee involvement. It is fair to say, however, that, in the field of environmental protection, no comparable rights to consultation or participation have been extended to representatives of the workforce.

Legislation on the Working Environment

The Health and Safety at Work (HSW) Act came into force in 1975. It provides a comprehensive, integrated system of law, dealing with the health, safety and welfare of people at work, and of people affected by work activities. Under the Act, employers have a general duty to ensure the safety, health and welfare of their employees, and to consult them concerning arrangements for joint action on health and safety matters. These consultation and information rights are through the unions, not through any separately-elected body.

In 1978, the Safety Representatives and Safety Committees Regulations came into effect and gave recognised unions the legal right to appoint workplace safety representatives who have the right to represent their members' interests in relation to any matter affecting their health and safety, to make representations to their employer on health, safety and welfare matters, and to obtain necessary information from their employer to enable them to carry out their functions. Safety representatives are entitled to carry out periodic inspections, investigate accidents and dangerous occurrences, and receive time off with pay to carry out their job as safety representatives and to undergo TUC- or union-approved training. In comparison, there are no clearly definable and enforceable environmental rights available to workers and their representatives. For example, there are no legal rights to paid time off for environmental training. While union education courses covering environmental issues are being developed, often as part of health and safety courses, an employer can refuse a safety representative training leave if the course does not exclusively address health and safety matters as prescribed under the 1977 Safety Representatives and Safety Committee Regulations.

Legislation covering hazardous substances has been introduced within the legal framework on health and safety. The Control of Substances Hazardous to Health (COSHH) regulations cover: substances classified as very toxic, toxic, harmful, corrosive or irritant; substances that have been assigned a maximum exposure level or an occupational exposure standard; micro-organisms arising from work activities that are harmful; substantial concentrations of dust; and other substances that create a comparable hazard.

The regulations require employers to carry out an assessment of the health risks presented by exposure to hazardous substances at work. This involves identifying what hazardous substances are used in the workplace, the risk presented by the use of such substances, how workers may be exposed to them, and what control measures are necessary in order to reduce the risks. The regulations require employers to provide information, instruction and training to employees who may be exposed to hazardous substances on the 'risks to health created by such exposure and the precautions which should be taken'. Workers are also entitled to know the results of monitoring of the work environment and the collective results of any health surveillance. In contrast, there are no rights for workers to be informed of the results of monitoring of emissions and discharges into the environment. The regulations have resulted in increased access to information on hazardous substances. The general approved code of practice to the regulations states: 'Employees or their representatives at the place of work should be informed of the results of the assessment.'[3] Again, there is no such requirement with regard to informing employees or their representatives of any environmental impact assessments under the EPA.

■ *International and European Guidelines*

At international level, there have been developments in industrial relations and the environment. The United Nations Economic Commission for Europe (UNECE) conference took place in Bergen in May 1990. Representatives of governments in Western and Eastern Europe and the US and Canada, and representatives from industry, labour, environmental, scientific and youth organisations took part. The result was a 'Joint Agenda for Action', to which the British Government is a signatory. This aims to promote sustainable development and covers a variety of issues relevant to industrial relations, which include:

- The promotion of environmental awareness, which includes promoting public participation in decision-making and the 'active involvement of people in the processes and decisions affecting their lives and environments'
- The achievement of clean production, including 'mechanisms for consultation and co-operation between management and labour' to prevent industrial accidents and hazards
- Drawing up environmental audits on which employers should consult workers and their trade union representatives
- The provision of full training for workers, their trade union representatives and managers on the environmental aspects of their work

The 1990 International Labour Conference passed a resolution on 'environment, development, employment and the role of the International Labour Organisation' [ILO],[4] which spoke of the need for tripartite co-operation at national and international level to create links between environmental protection and employment creation. It stressed that the working environment formed an important and integral part of the general environment as a whole and called for integrated policies based on 'full collaboration' between—among others—employers and trade unions. The resolution also stated that the restructuring of enterprises to take account of the need for better environmental performance should be promoted, while maintaining or increasing, as far as possible, the number of jobs.

Recently, the EC has started to link the issues of industrial relations and the environment. The Commission's 1990 annual report on Employment in Europe contained for the first time a chapter on environment and employment. This is seen as confirmation that there is a 'social dimension' to environmental control.

The EC's Structural Funds were identified as being suitable instruments for bringing about change. The distribution of these funds is undertaken on the basis of formal consultation with a number of bodies, including trade unions and employers.

■ Voluntary Agreements between the Industrial Actors

The United Kingdom has no written constitution, and therefore no entrenchment of fundamental rights and freedoms, which applies in the industrial relations field as well as elsewhere. There is no automatic right of recognition of trade unions in the UK: a trade union is 'recognised' for statutory purposes if it is recognised to any extent by the employer for the purposes of collective bargaining. The Trade Union and Labour Relations Act 1974 sets out the matters that the law considers may be the subject of collective bargaining, which is carried out on a voluntarist basis. Collective agreements are at present not legally binding on either side, although there is a presumption that those items that are capable of being incorporated into an individual contract are legally enforceable. Procedure-type agreements are not legally binding and are therefore legally unenforceable.

■ Agreements on Participation in Environmental Issues

The involvement of the trade unions with environmental issues has developed over the last twenty years or so. Early action tended to be very reactive and concentrated into significant, but isolated areas of industrial action and campaigning. Environmental bargaining has tended to be ad hoc and subject-specific, reflected in a series of successful union campaigns promoting the use of non-toxic chemicals, recycling, and the use of lead-free fuel.

The collective green agreement has only recently been sought by unions with the second wave of union representation which began with the first report of the TUC environmental action group presented to Congress in September 1990. In this approach, the emphasis has shifted towards all-embracing bargaining and green agreements that address environmental issues at work in a comprehensive and structured way. The 'model green agreement' outlined by the TUC is typical of green agreements that unions—including the general union (GMB) and Manufacturing, Science, Finance (MSF)—are attempting to negotiate with employers.

Bargaining initiatives have been launched by three of the large UK unions. The GMB, which represents around 900,000 members across a wide range of industries, and whose general secretary chaired the TUC environmental action group, launched its 'Green Works' initiative in 1991. Twenty-five companies have been identified, including local authorities and chemical companies, which the union wants to sign its model environmental agreement. The agreement contains provisions for joint union/employer environmental auditing, training for union representatives on environmental issues, and the provision of information for employees, the local community and the media. The full text of the *Environmental Action Model Agreement* can be seen in the Appendix at the end of this chapter.

As part of the initiative, negotiators in all the union's industrial sectors will be issued with checklists providing a step-by-step guide to 'greening' the workplace. Union representatives are encouraged to raise environmental issues with the membership. The initiative recognises that, although people are generally more aware of environmental issues, and many are involved in campaigns to protect the environment, trade unionists do not necessarily see the union as a vehicle for their concerns.

MSF, which has 650,000 members in manufacturing and the public sector, and which represents workers in the chemicals industry, has approached chemical companies asking for initial talks on involvement of the unions in environmental affairs, while producing an information pack for negotiators. The union's annual pay claim to ICI in 1991, which was negotiated at national level with the company, included a request for the setting-up of an environmental committee. Again, a model environmental agreement has been produced, which includes the establishment of this environmental committee to act as a forum for discussion between the company and MSF on environmental matters. It contains provisions for the environmental committee to be informed on environmental protection investment, development of clean technologies, pollution and emissions, health and safety issues, environmental auditing activity, compliance with environmental legislation, storage and transport of hazardous materials, waste management and environmental education.

The communication union, NCU (now the Communications Workers Union [CWU] following the merger with the Union of Communication Workers [UCW]), which represents some 150,000 communication workers, has launched a green code for its union officials. This green code includes the discussion of environmental issues at meetings, rudimentary environmental audits as part of safety inspections, measures for ensuring enforcement of environmentally-sound measures, programmes for boosting awareness among members, and suggestions on how environmental work can be made more effective by linking up with local pressure groups. This is intended to provide a framework for more detailed negotiations at local level. The union has also reached an agreement with British Telecom (BT) for the joint monitoring and discussion of environmental initiatives launched by the company. This includes a joint forum for the union and the company to give impetus to the initiatives being put forward by both organisations.

However, there are major difficulties facing unions attempting to play an active role in environmental protection, and it is clear that national policies and initiatives have not yet been translated into collective action at local level. There is currently no requirement for companies to carry out environmental auditing, which has been identified by the TUC as the main area in which unions can be involved in environmental protection in the workplace. Many organisations in the UK have yet to assess their environmental performance, or have not yet developed an environmental policy. Even where companies do carry out auditing, the tendency so far has been to do this without the involvement of the unions. A survey by the Labour Research Department in 1991,[5] which looked at the involvement of unions in environmental issues at workplace level, found that only 17% of employers in the survey had carried out an audit, and only 7% had carried out joint management/union audits.

Although the Labour Research Department survey found that almost half the employers negotiate with unions on environmental issues, the survey was fairly heavily weighted towards the public-sector practice: 74% of responses came from union representatives in the public sector and 26% from the private sector. Also, the survey only covered unionised workplaces, and, as such, is likely to reflect best practice rather than give an overall picture of industrial relations and environmental issues. The survey found that over half the negotiations took place on the safety committee, which suggests that the negotiations were mainly on health and safety issues, where there are legal rights for union involvement. Only a very small number of employers (less than 2%) had set up an environmental committee where negotiations with the unions on environmental issues took place.

Lack of access to information is also a serious difficulty. Employers are currently under no obligation to give workers or union representatives access to information on any aspect of the environmental impact of the workplace, apart from information on hazardous substances under the COSHH regulations.

The Labour Research Department survey showed that, as well as a very low number of employers carrying out joint environmental auditing, only 3% had provided training on environmental issues. This suggests that employers are reluctant to give information to trade unionists on the environmental impact of the company, or provide training and education to encourage workers to become involved in environmental issues at the workplace.

However, in spite of the difficulties outlined, there are examples of joint action and co-operation between employers and unions on environmental issues. The Labour Research Department survey found six examples of environmental committees set up in workplaces where management and unions discussed environmental issues. These were all in public-sector workplaces. The survey also found 23 workplaces in the private and public sectors where joint management/union environmental auditing is carried out, and twelve employers providing training and education on environmental issues. A number of examples of joint action and co-operation are outlined below.

West Wiltshire District Council (a local authority) discusses environmental issues at the local joint consultative committee, along with equal opportunities, leave and health issues. An environmental strategy was drawn up in February 1991, after consultation with the unions, and, as a result, recycling schemes have been set up in the area. At Dunlop Ltd, which manufactures rubber products, environmental issues not related to safety are discussed along with safety-related issues at the safety committee. Recycling of waste has been discussed with GMB representatives and a scheme has been implemented.

Energy-efficiency initiatives, including insulation and improved heating systems, were initially raised at the safety committee by Institute of Professionals, Managers, and Specialists (IPMS) safety representatives at the Natural Environmental Research Council. These issues were then discussed at the local Whitley committee (joint consultative committee) before being taken up by management. A waste recycling working group was set up as a sub-committee of the joint consultative committee at Sheffield Polytechnic to examine the implementation of a higher-grade paper collection and recycling scheme.

There are also examples of workplaces where green groups and community groups have been involved in the implementation of environmental improvements. At SCM Chemicals in Humberside, a chemicals plant producing titanium dioxide pigments for paint, the joint shop stewards committee, comprising of representatives including the Transport and General Workers Union (TGWU) and general union GMB, successfully negotiated an improvement in the company's waste disposal methods.

During the negotiations, the unions contacted Greenpeace and arranged a meeting with senior managers, the green group and the unions to discuss solutions to the problem of discharge of chemical waste into the Humber Estuary. And at another company, Amerlite Diagnostics, local site liaison committees are held with local community groups.

■ Policy Statements, Demands and Campaigns

■ Employers' Organisations

The Confederation of British Industry (CBI) is the central organisation of employers in the UK and seeks to represent the interests of its members at national and international level. The CBI is not a negotiating body, but seeks to formulate and influence policy on industrial and economic matters. In 1989, the CBI took a decision to take a greater leadership role and actively promote better understanding of the environment and more consistent high performances throughout British business. An Action Plan for the 1990s was drawn up—*Environment Means Business*[6]—and an environmental management unit was established in March 1990. Its main role is to promote good environmental practice through the provision of guidance and promotional material on key environmental issues and to establish links with other expert groups.

The Environmental Policy Unit of the CBI advises that companies need a sound environmental management system, accompanied by a thorough review or audit of the company's activities that effect the environment, and a written statement showing the company's policy on the environment. However, it says that corporate environmental performance strategies will only be successful with the commitment and support of senior management from board level and the involvement of all employees. And in common with issues such as quality, it says that enhanced staff morale and higher productivity can be the direct results of environmental improvement measures within the workplace where employees are encouraged to become directly involved, both during the execution and follow-up, and advocates suitable education and training schemes at work.

Action that the CBI says companies could be taking is summarised as follows:

- Ensuring adequate communication with employees in all aspects of the environmental performance of the company, particularly those areas regarded as sensitive

- Making the environment one of the key issues for discussion at existing consultative meetings and, if necessary, setting up a specific committee to address environmental issues, with representatives drawn from all functions of business

■ Initiating a suggestion scheme on environmental issues and, where appropriate, 'rewarding' personnel whose ideas are adopted

■ Ensuring that employees of all departments of the company are involved in the continuous process of environmental reviewing from the start. The commitment will contribute towards the successful outcome of improvement plans that the process is designed to generate.

It recommends a far-reaching and voluntary review of operations and products from an internal point of view, backed up or 'validated' where appropriate by an independent body and then published as an authoritative document for internal and external consumption. This, it says, should be a continuous internal process that measures performance against a set of objectives identified by the company.

However, the CBI is wholly opposed to mandatory environmental auditing and to the involvement of the unions in auditing on the grounds that auditing, should be a management tool for assessment and control tailored to the circumstances of the company in question. This approach means that some companies may well believe that there should be a formal role for the trade union representatives in auditing, while others would regard it as a management task. The CBI does not believe that legislation is appropriate to deal with the process of environmental reviewing. The CBI recognises that there is a great deal of public pressure for more information on the environmental performance of companies, as well as for greater openness of information. However, it sees the real question for companies is to what extent new information should lead to a distinctive new role for the trade unions in decision-making.

■ Management and Employer Response to Environmental Protection

Businesses are coming under increasing pressure to pursue environmentally-sound practices. To ensure that this is publicised, having a 'green label' is seen as increasingly important. An increasing number of UK companies have produced corporate environmental policies and are conducting environmental reviews of their performance. The consequences of environmental pollution can be disastrous for companies, both from a financial and public relations viewpoint.

However, the proportion of companies with environmental policies remains low, and the policies are not always put into practice. This is confirmed in a number of surveys that have examined the response of managers and directors of UK companies to increasing pressures on environmental issues. A survey carried out in 1990 by KPH Marketing of 107 managers from the UK's top companies[7] showed that, while interest in corporate environmental matters has increased sharply, some 36% of the companies surveyed had not introduced environmental policies. The main inducement for companies to adopt green policies is said to come from consumers, with employees second and trade unions least influential. The survey also showed that employers are finding that their attitude to the environment is fast becoming an important factor in the recruitment and retention of staff.

The Labour Research Department survey[8] showed that there was a high proportion of employers taking some forms of measures to improve environmental performance, reflecting a high degree of awareness. However, an analysis of the types of measures taken by employers tended to be in areas related to health and safety—for example, the substitution of hazardous substances—or in areas not requiring major changes: for example, purchasing environmentally-friendly materials, providing recycling facilities and improving energy conservation. The survey found much less activity in areas involving major changes to the processes.

A CBI survey of 250 firms[9] showed that environmental awareness is increasing, though less so among smaller firms. Of those surveyed, 35% regarded environmental issues as 'very important', but half did not have specific management structures for dealing with environmental issues. Just under half said they had undertaken or were planning to undertake major capital investment on green matters. Some 65% said that local authorities would have the greatest impact in driving their attempts to reduce air and water pollution and the disposal of hazardous wastes. The survey also suggests that management did not perceive the workforce as a major influence on organisational change.

Cranfield School of Management carried out a survey[10] that indicated that small companies do not really regard environmental issues as their problem. Only 2% of small companies surveyed felt they produced a 'lot of pollution' and nearly half said they took almost no measures to protect the environment. Less than a third of non-manufacturing companies saw the environment as 'very important', and only 14% of manufacturing companies had carried out environmental audits.

There appears to be a reluctance on the part of management to involve workers and their representatives in environmental issues. The CBI produced a paper on corporate environmental policies and environmental statements of nineteen companies in May 1991.[11] Of these, only two of the companies outline their environmental policies in relation to employees.

James Cropper plc, a paper manufacturing company based in Cumbria in the North of England, set up an environmental audit group in 1990 to survey its industrial site, and established an environmental policy in which it states that the company will inform suppliers, customers, the workforce and the public about the measures taken to protect the environment and seek their co-operation in meeting the company's objectives. Procter & Gamble's environmental policy includes assurances that the company will ensure that products, packaging and operations are safe for employers, consumers and the environment, and that consumers, customers, employees, communities and public interest groups and others will be provided with relevant and appropriate factual information about the environmental quality of Procter & Gamble products, packaging and operations.

Information availability on a company's environmental record is further limited because Her Majesty's Inspectorate of Pollution (HMIP) has a policy of constructive engagement with companies rather than fining them for pollution offences. Also, inspection activity by the HMIP is low, with fewer than 500 visits by HMIP inspectors to registered works in 1988/89, which represents a small proportion of the total number of workplaces.

Although companies are claiming commitment to environmental protection in their corporate environmental policies, environmental pressure groups, and the company's prosecution record, have shown that this is not always the case. Cleanaway is signatory to the Chemical Industries Association's 'Responsible Care Programme' and has an environmental policy that is again outlined in the CBI paper. However, it is one of the companies whose polluting activities in the Mersey basin area have been highlighted by Greenpeace, as they have been consistently dumping excess effluent into the sea.

Greenpeace launched *Greenpeace Business*, a bimonthly newsletter, in June 1991, which outlines that the organisation has a track record of exposing environmental abuse, and intends to expand such activities into the realm of company practice, making use of the legal system, shareholder and investor pressure. The newsletter says it will highlight sound industrial practice and expose activities of companies that harm the environment.

■ Workers' Organisations and Representatives

The Trade Union Congress (TUC) is the central co-ordinating body for the trade union movement and is composed of individually affiliated trade unions. Around 90% of all union members, representing around 40% of the working population in the UK, belong to TUC-affiliated unions. Among the TUC's affiliates are unions representing workers in the nuclear power industry, and in the coal and oil sectors. While the National Union of Mineworkers (NUM) points to the poor safety record of the nuclear power industry, unions representing nuclear power workers point to the burning of fossil fuels as the cause of global warming. TUC policy is in favour of a phasing-out of nuclear energy over fifteen years by a future Labour Government. An attempt to overturn this commitment at the 1991 Congress was defeated by 4.59 million votes to 3.213 million.

In recent years, particularly since the establishment of the Environmental Action Group (EAG) in 1989, the TUC has concentrated on the involvement of unions at workplace-level negotiations. In 1990, the first report by the group[12] contained an overview of environmental issues faced by working people, the proposed role of trade unions, and made proposals for 'Greening the Workplace'. This included demands for trade unions to be consulted on environmental audits and for extended rights for trade union representatives. The EAG report outlined that the working and living environment are linked and that most external environmental concerns originate in the workplace, therefore trade unions should have the right to participate in decision-making. It proposes that the role of safety representatives should extend to cover environmental issues, and outlines new environmental rights under which workers would have the right to:

- Know the environmental impact of products and processes they are using and producing

- Be informed and consulted on the environmental strategies of their company

- Initiate and participate in environmental policies, audits and inspections, and have a legal entitlement to call in independent inspectors

- Negotiate changes in production and work organisation

- Refuse, without recrimination, to undertake work with potentially harmful environmental effects

- Expect paid time off to receive necessary education, training and retraining

The TUC have identified environmental auditing as the main area in which unions can become involved in environmental issues at the workplace. It says that audits should cover the use of raw materials and energy consumption, harmful emissions during the production process, waste generation and disposal, the substances and materials used throughout the workplace, and the environmental impact of the product itself. The TUC believes that environmental auditing should be carried out in consultation with union representatives, and that information for this purpose should be made available.

The EAG submitted its views to the now defunct National Economic Development Council in 1991, acknowledging that both sides of industry must work together to achieve higher standards of environmental performance. The EAG believes that Government must play a more supportive role and work in partnership with industry, local government and unions. The group says that there should be an integration of environmental policy with industrial and employment policies in an open spirit of partnership and co-operation. They have called for a national environment education and training programme, but also considered that there was an urgent need for trade unions to be better informed of workplace environmental issues and given practical advice on what was required to raise standards.

The group therefore produced a 'greening the workplace' guide which provides a 'working kit' for unions wanting to build on their environmental activities.[13] This outlines that it believes a consensual approach is necessary to deal with environmental issues and that the union response 'extends to an awareness of the possible impact that environmental adjustments will have on wage negotiations, on training needs and workloads'. The guide aims to assist unions in bringing environmental issues onto the bargaining agenda. The TUC believes that this can result in potential opportunities to discuss and establish union legitimacy in related issues, facilitate closer links with the local community and other outside groups, and make a contribution to the union's image and recruitment. The TUC has called on all its affiliated members to:

- Ensure that trade union policies and activities fully reflect environmental considerations and priorities

- Seek to achieve higher environmental and health and safety standards in the workplace by way of co-operation and partnership with the employer and outside organisations

- Develop joint environmental strategies (by way of a 'green agreement' or otherwise) that spell out both the challenges and responsibilities of the employer and trade union

- Agree a framework for implementing an environmental strategy that provides for access to information and regular, structured communications and discussions between management and union representatives

- Assess and evaluate the environmental performance and impact of workplace activities by undertaking jointly-agreed environmental audits or reviews

- Raise awareness of environmental issues and the implications both inside and outside the workplace

- Promote the active participation of all employees in joint action to improve environmental performance

- Publicise their activities on environmental issues to the workforce, media and local community

■ Ensure that the environmental education and training needs of the workforce are adequately met

■ Seek paid time off for union representatives to attend education and training courses on environmental issues

It is worth noting that the TUC began running Environmental Education Courses as part of its National Education Programme in October 1992.

According to the Government's 1991 Labour Force Survey,[14] the proportion of British workers (employees) in trade unions and staff associations had declined to 37%, from 38% in 1990 and 39% in 1989. One of the reasons why unions are seeking to extend their role into the area of environmental protection is to re-establish their legitimacy and increase recruitment, and to further extend their role into related issues such as investment and training. Trade unions are increasingly taking the view that environmental issues are likely to remain on the political agenda and changes in the way industry operates are inevitable. The unions want to ensure that their members are involved in progressing the changes.

Recent years have seen trade union campaigns on the environment gain momentum. Most of the largest twelve unions—in particular GMB, MSF, NCU (now CWU), TGWU and NALGO (now UNISON)—have been particularly active in this area. They have launched initiatives to translate national policy into action at workplace level and put environmental issues firmly on the bargaining agenda. The campaigns have tended to be run along two lines. High-profile approaches have been made to employers demanding that the union's role in environmental issues is recognised, and that employers negotiate with unions, carry out joint environmental auditing, and provide access to information on the company's environmental impact. At the same time, training and information has been provided in order to educate the membership in order for them to be able to negotiate at workplace level.

There has been a change in emphasis from campaigning on particular environmental issues towards demanding all-embracing green agreements, reflecting TUC policy. Within the last few years, following an increased level of awareness among the membership of unions, which has resulted in the adoption of resolutions on environmental issues, unions are beginning to adopt comprehensive environmental policies.

Because of the reactive nature of early examples of industrial action taken by their members on environmental issues, national unions have found themselves in the dilemma of attempting to support workers on opposing sides of conflicts between environmental protection and job preservation. An example of this occurred in 1989 when dock workers, members of the

Transport and General Workers' Union (TGWU), refused to handle imported toxic waste destined for incineration at a waste incineration plant in Wales. The union also represented workers at the incineration plant, situated in an area of high unemployment, and were therefore caught in the classic conflict of representing workers taking action to protect the environment, and workers opposed to the action on the grounds of job preservation.

The TGWU has since made clear its position on toxic waste importation: 'The TGWU says that positive immediate action is needed to eliminate this trade in which profits are being put above the safety of workers, communities and the environment. The TGWU says no to Britain being used as the world's toxic waste dump.' The TGWU has also formed an environmental policy group, ENACTS, to look at policy across its trade groups.

Manufacturing, Science and Finance (MSF), which represents around 650,000 workers, including workers employed in the chemicals industry, produced a policy statement which recognises that, in the short term, the introduction of more stringent environmental protection policies could have an adverse effect on its members' job security. However, it believes that companies will need to alter their operations to comply with stricter environmental legislation and consumer demand, and invest in new product development, identify new markets, clean up processes and re-train employees in order to survive. MSF is also promoting the development of 'clean technologies' as a solution to environmental problems in industry. The union held a conference on clean technologies in the Summer of 1990, which concluded that MSF has a crucial role to play in the process, as it represents thousands of scientists, designers and technologists with particular expertise. The union campaigns for the establishment of a UK Environmental Protection Executive to oversee all aspects of the environment, directed at prevention of pollution, with an effective system of penalties for breaches of legislation.

NALGO (now UNISON), the union representing workers in local government, public services and recently-privatised utilities, has had a lengthy and varied involvement in raising environmental awareness and developing constructive initiatives. Doubtless this reflects the particular interests and competence of NALGO (UNISON) activists, many of whom work in environmental protection, either in local government or in utilities with critical environment links such as the water, gas and electricity industries. Hence, the union has been campaigning for some time for the establishment of an Environmental Protection Agency. (It provided the funds for the Labour MP Ann Taylor, who at the time was the opposition

'Shadow' Minister for the Environment, to produce her book *Choosing our Future*,[15] which sets out her plan for an Environmental Protection Agency.) The union set up an Environment Action Group in 1990 to co-ordinate its environmental campaigns and to develop policy proposals. Its education department was among the first to develop and implement environment training courses. Finally, it is worth noting that NALGO (UNISON) has undertaken an environmental audit of its own head office in London.[16] It is believed to be the first British union to have taken such an initiative.

Unions, including NALGO (UNISON), the Inland Revenue Staff Federation (IRSF; now part of the Public Services, Tax and Commerce Union [PTC] as a result of a merger with the NUCPS) and the Civil and Public Services Association (CPSA), have all been affiliated for some time to environmental pressure groups at national level. UK unions are drawing on comparisons in Europe, and using examples of gains made by unions, particularly in Denmark and Germany, to press companies for the same agreements in the UK. The NCU (now CWU) points to the agreement between its sister union in Germany, the DPG, and the Ministry of Posts and Telecoms. And MSF are attempting to negotiate an agreement with ICI that has been negotiated with the German chemical union, IG Chemie.

■ Attitudes of Trade Unionists to Environmental Issues

It is clear that national union and TUC policy on the environment has not been translated into collective action at workplace level; and debate at union conferences shows that there is still some reluctance on the part of trade union members to 'take on' environmental issues.

The issue of job security is obviously a major concern. The debate on affiliation to Greenpeace at the Civil and Public Services Association conference in 1991 reflected opposing views of delegates. While the resolution to affiliate was carried, several delegates opposed it on the grounds that Greenpeace campaigns for the scrapping of nuclear energy and therefore 'for jobs to be taken away from CPSA members'. While there are fears that, in the long term, environmentally-damaging industries may be forced out of business, there is also fear that, in the short term, improving environmental performance is costly and could lead to closures in particular sectors. At a recent conference, one National Union of Mineworkers (NUM) delegate said that, at the colliery where he worked, there was considerable community opposition to sea pollution from colliery waste. However, as union members, the workforce saw that other, more costly methods of waste management would increase costs and could lead to closure, and hence felt unable to take any action on improving the situation.

The lack of access to information and lack of education and training on environmental issues are mitigating against union involvement. There has been a lack of guidance available on how to tackle issues, although practical advice and information is starting to be produced by unions. While the results of exposure to harmful substances are often evident because of the effects on workers, the results of environmental pollution are not so immediately obvious. This may mean that workers do not view the pollution outside of the workplace as an issue appropriate to industrial relations, particularly where access to information is severely restricted.

Examples of industrial action by union members has highlighted the concern felt on environmental issues, particularly related to safety concerns. For example, seamen and transport workers have refused to handle nuclear waste destined for disposal in the North Sea; and trade unionists have refused to allow the importation of toxic waste destined for incineration in the UK. However, it is unclear how trade unionists see trade unions as the vehicle to convey environmental concerns, and how far they see environmental issues as an issue for the bargaining agenda. While the LRD survey[17] suggests that, at least in the public sector, trade unionists are raising environmental issues at bargaining forums, particularly safety committees, the extent to which this is happening in general remains unclear.

A survey by Touche Ross[18] suggests that employees feel less empowered to influence their firms' environmental policy, though Touche Ross argue that this is changing and that, under a future Labour Government, environmental matters could become a much more important aspect of industrial relations.

■ *Interaction with Environmental Activists and Community Organisations*
In the LRD survey, only 4% of respondents indicated that green groups had been involved in implementing environmental improvements at the workplace: Greenpeace and Friends of the Earth were the groups involved. However, guidance from green groups was being used in the drawing-up of environmental policies, particularly by local authority employees. The relationship between green groups and industry tends to be adversarial, with companies' poor environmental record being publicised, particularly by Greenpeace. However, the launch of *Greenpeace Business* claims that good practice as well as bad will be highlighted. Traditionally, the relationship between unions and green groups has also tended to be adversarial, particularly because of the 'jobs versus environment' conflict. However, unions and green groups are attempting to work together, and alliances have been formed.

At national level, a number of unions have affiliated, and therefore give financial support to Friends of the Earth: fringe conferences have been organised at the TUC where union leaders and environmental pressure group members have shared a platform. It is perhaps worth mentioning that health and safety officers from the largest two unions, GMB and TGWU, have taken up posts in environmental pressure groups, Friends of the Earth, and World Wide Fund for Nature.

A 1989 report on trade unions and green groups by Greenpeace[19] said that, where political agreement does occur, it usually involves conflict rather than co-operation, although there are exceptions. The report highlighted areas where trade unions and green groups have been able to co-operate. Green groups and unions have also worked in co-operation in campaigns opposing the privatisation of water and electricity services. The campaigns on toxic waste, pesticides and asbestos also lead to trade union and green group co-operation. However, the report also outlines problem areas experienced where co-operation was not found to be possible. These included particular unions' policies on nuclear power because of job preservation; TUC opposition to the Titanium Dioxide Directive (1983) because of perceived job and competitiveness threat to UK plants polluting the North Sea; and the close relationship between the unions and employers in opposition to radical action on power station pollution control to prevent acid rain.

The report outlines difficulties mitigating against co-operation between the two groups, including the job preservation issue and mutual mistrust, but concludes that co-operation is mutually beneficial, and is possible in areas including co-funding of research, jointly campaigning on issues and sharing information.

■ Summary and Recommendations

The shift in public opinion in the UK in favour of environmental issues has resulted in increased pressures on industry to improve environmental performance. This has augmented the increasingly stringent legislation on pollution control being initiated at European level, notably the Environmental Protection Act 1990. However, this general increase in environmental awareness has yet to be translated into collective action, and environmental issues do not appear to have yet pervaded the system of industrial relations to any considerable degree.

It is only relatively recently, within the last few years, that the unions have campaigned for the involvement of unions on all aspects of workplace environmental issues. Previously, campaigns tended to focus on specific issues, such as the banning of pesticides, or the disposal of nuclear waste at sea. The second wave of union representation has been to campaign for collective green agreements that give unions rights of involvement in this area. However, workers and their trade union representatives have no legal rights of involvement in environmental issues at the workplace, and it appears that few, if any, employers have signed collective green agreements and voluntarily allowed union involvement in all areas of the company's environmental impact. Clearly, this situation is likely to remain while there are no legal requirements on employers to involve unions in environmental issues. There is political hostility to the involvement of trade unions in environmental issues on the part of employers, as outlined by the CBI, who see that this would lead to a broadening of the collective bargaining agenda and lead to union involvement in areas such as investment and other areas of company decision-making.

Trade unions do not have any rights of representation on bodies responsible for developing policy and formulating new legislation on environmental protection, as is the case on health and safety, where the TUC nominate two representatives to the Health and Safety Commission. Information availability on a company's environmental record is limited, as only a small amount of information has to be kept in public register, there is low prosecution activity, and the information is not computerised at present, which further restricts access. This means that, while a company may claim to have a good environmental record, it is extremely difficult to find out, whether as an employee or a member of the public, if this is in fact true. It has generally been green groups who have exposed companies' polluting activities. Currently, there is no legal protection for employees who 'blow the whistle' on poor environmental practice, which means that they could be dismissed for breach of confidentiality. These areas need to be addressed if greater freedom of access to information on environmental issues is to be achieved.

There is a serious lack of training and education on environmental issues provided to employees, which needs to be addressed by both employers— the CBI says that a corporate environmental policy will only be successful with full employee commitment and involvement—and by unions, who are urging their members to negotiate collective green agreements giving rights of involvement in all aspects of a company's environmental impact. The issue of re-training for employees who may lose jobs in polluting industries due to the closure of 'dirty' workplaces has not been seriously addressed, despite a large potential market for environmental industries: for example, the manufacture of pollution control equipment.

It is perhaps surprising that, in view of the lack of access to information and lack of training and education, more co-operation between trade unions and green groups is not in evidence. However, it appears that the main obstacle to building alliances in this area is the 'job preservation versus environmental protection' issue. It is difficult to assess the attitude of trade unionists to environmental issues as it appears there have not been extensive surveys carried out in this area. However, it seems likely that the lack of legal rights on involvement in environmental issues at the workplace, and lack of training, education and information, are reasons why national union policy has not been translated into collective action at local level.

In conclusion, the integration of environmental issues into the system of industrial relations is in the very early stages in the UK. It is unclear at present how far employers will enter into voluntary agreements with unions, and indeed how far unions at workplace level are attempting to negotiate on these issues.

■ *Notes*

1. This chapter was first published in 1993 in a European Foundation publication dealing with national experiences of industrial relations and the environment in Europe. Some of the references to particular pieces of legislation may now be out of date, and the chapter refers to the state of play in 1991. However, although further initiatives have been taken in this area since the chapter was written, the general conclusions concerning the extent to which environmental issues have pervaded industrial relations systems still hold for the situation today.

2. Labour Research Department, *Trade Unions and the Environment Survey: Bargaining Report 108* (London, UK: Labour Research Department, July 1991).

3. From the general approved code of practice on the Control of Substances Hazardous to Health (COSHH) (London, UK: Health Service Commission, revised 1995).

4. A resolution adopted by the 77th Session of the International Labour Conference, 1990.

5. Labour Research Department, *op. cit.*

6. CBI, *Environment Means Business: A CBI Action Plan for the 1990s* (London, UK: CBI, 1990).

7. KPH Marketing Ltd, *The Greener Employee* (Alton, UK: KPH, 1990).

8. *Op. cit.*

9. CBI/PA Consulting, *Waking Up to a Better Environment: A Report on the Survey of British Industrial Attitudes Concerning the Environment* (London, UK: CBI, 1992)

10. C. Barrow and A. Burnett, *How Green are Small Companies? A Survey by Cranfield School of Management* (Working Paper No. SWP 1/91; Cranfield, UK: Cranfield School of Management, 1991).

11. CBI, *Corporate Environmental Policies/Environmental Statements* (London, UK: CBI, 1991).

12. 122nd Annual Trade Union Congress General Council Report, *Environment Action Group* (London, UK: TUC, 1990).

Appendix: Full Text of the 'Environmental Action Model Agreement'

The union and the employer recognise the increasing impact of environmental issues on the employer's operations.

They agree that the need to meet higher environmental standards also presents an opportunity to achieve better levels of environmental quality and business efficiency.

The responsibility to achieve higher environmental standards rests with the employer. This requires the employer to make significant improvements in the quality of its environmental management and to develop new skills in the workforce. This is best achieved by the active co-operation of the union.

Such an approach can only succeed if there is a clear, joint strategy that spells out both the challenges for the employer and the ways in which workers and managers will respond to these challenges.

The union's input into this strategy will be via the joint Health and Safety Committees (or any other joint body if agreed by both parties).

This agreement lays down the framework within which the strategy will be developed.

Joint Environmental Policy

Any environmental strategy will need to be flexible enough to cover different challenges within all parts of the organisation. However, the signatories believe that the following issues will need to be addressed:

a) The environmental impact of the employer's current and proposed activities, ranging from the workplace and its immediate surroundings to the international level. Consideration will need to be given to:

- Waste or by-products (liquid, sold or gaseous) from the employer's operations
- Products and raw materials used by the employer in the course of its activities
- Disposal, re-use and recycling of products when they have ended their initial 'working life'

b) Challenges and threats to the employer's activities from legal, social, commercial, economic and other similar developments

c) Opportunities for the employer to develop new products, processes and services, as well as competitors' efforts to exploit similar opportunities

d) Action by the employer or the union to influence and anticipate public debate on environmental issues

Joint Examination of the Issues

The signatories agree that regular, structured communications and discussions between management and union representatives are essential to the success of a joint environmental strategy.

These discussions will reassure and inspire employees and provide management and union representatives with insights that are essential to the success of a joint environmental strategy.

They should take place through the official joint Health and Safety Committee, or any other joint body as agreed by both signatories. Both signatories can place any relevant issue on the agenda and have that issue fully discussed, without in any way committing either side to support a particular idea.

In order to gain the most from these discussions, it will be necessary to make use of a range of expert advice, for example, employer or trade union federations, environmental consultants, academics and public agencies, both local and national.

Some aspects of the employer's activities may be commercially or otherwise sensitive and therefore the discussion of issues or the supply of data will sometimes need to be governed by principles of confidentiality.

However, both parties believe that the test applied to any question of disclosure should not be 'the need to know' but 'the need not to know'. Disclosure of information is a good thing and information should not be withheld simply because of possible 'embarrassment'.

Environmental Audits and Impact Assessments
The parties agree that decisions about environmental action must be made on the basis of hard facts, not emotion.

They agree that both internal and external audits of existing operations and impact assessments of proposed operations are an essential tool in strategic planning.

Both sides accept that such studies, although sometimes involving the commitment of considerable short-term resources, tend to more than pay for themselves in the medium or long term. They also accept that independent verification and expertise may sometimes benefit these exercises.

The parties believe that audits and assessments will encourage managers and union representatives to take a longer-term view of all aspects of the employer's activities, leading to significantly improved all-round performance.

They also agree that audits and impact assessments will benefit from the maximum possible input from, and openness to, local authorities, community and environmental groups and regulators.

Training and Education
It is vital that union and employer representatives have a good working knowledge of environmental issues.

The employer therefore agrees to co-operate with attempts by union representatives to gain knowledge and receive training about the complex issues under discussion, and to ensure that its managers also receive appropriate training.

Such co-operation may include:

- Paid time off for union representatives to attend educational courses
- Funding of training for both sides' representatives
- Working with experts to advise both signatories' representatives and to inform the workforce
- Producing material for employees that outlines 'green' challenges and opportunities for the employer
- Developing an information campaign aimed at persuading the local community, the media and regulatory authorities that the employer is taking seriously its environmental responsibilities

This agreement will run until amended by the agreement of both signatories or revoked in writing by one signatory with six months' written notice.

13. TUC, *Greening the Workplace: A TUC Guide to Environmental Policies and Issues at Work* (London, UK: TUC Publications, August 1991).

14. 'Union Density across the Employed Workforce', in *Employment Gazette*, January 1993, pp. 673-89.

15. Ann Taylor, *Choosing our Future: A Practical Politics of the Environment* (London, UK: Routledge, 1992).

16. NALGO, *An Environmental Review of the National and Local Government Officers' Association* (London, UK: NALGO, April 1992).

17. *Op. cit.*

18. Touche Ross, *Heads in the Clouds or Heads in the Sands? UK Managers' Attitudes to Environmental Issues: A Survey* (London, UK: Touche Ross, 1990).

19. Greenpeace UK, *Trade Unions and Green Groups: From Conflict to Co-operation* (London, UK: Greenpeace, September 1989).

Part 2

Managing People

⑥

The European
Environmental Executive:
Technical Specialist or Corporate Change Agent?

Peter James and Stephanie Stewart

*T*HE EXPERIENCE, training, motivation and other attributes of environmental staff are a critical factor in successful environmental management.
Several recent studies have explored these topics for general environmental staff in the UK and USA.[1] However, there has been little research
about the key player in corporate environmental management, the senior
environmental executive; yet their ability to provide environmental
leadership can make the difference between poor, average and 'best-in-class'
performance. We therefore conducted in-depth—and anonymous—interviews with the senior environmental executives of 32 leading European
companies in electronic manufacturing, chemicals, oil and gas and consumer
products. The sample was further subdivided into UK, Dutch and German
companies and the European subsidiaries of US-based companies.

■ Portrait of the European Environmental Executive
We discovered broad similarities between countries and industries in the
background of our sample. The typical European environmental executive
is male (only one of our sample was female), has scientific or technical—but
not environmental—qualifications, has transferred into environmental
management from other areas (particularly research and production) and
has been with his company for an average of eighteen years. He also has
considerable job satisfaction.

Every interviewee commented on the wide variety of activities they were
involved in, the new challenges with which they were always being faced
and the diversity of contacts they had both within and outside the
organisation. While this creates considerable pressure, most saw it as a
central attraction of the post. Others enjoyed contributing to the strategic
direction of the company. One energy executive observed that:

It's enjoyable to make decisions about whether we do things.
They're not about high levels of expenditure and individually
they may not be important but they're ultimately about what
kind of company you want to be.

Around half the interviewees mentioned contributing to environmental
improvement as a major source of job satisfaction. While all would no doubt
have had done so if prompted, it probably reflects a real difference between
those executives who have a personal enthusiasm for the subject and those
for whom it is ultimately another position within the company.

We also asked about negative aspects of the job. Two issues stood out:
financial and other resource constraints and the slow pace of change within
the organisation. Both have been made worse by recession, although several
respondents pointed out that cutbacks have affected environment less than
other departments in the company. The concern about resource constraints
was not that they jeopardised meeting basic objectives, such as avoiding
accidents or complying with legislation, but rather with excessive demands
on staff and the risk that strategic initiatives could be driven out by
operating pressures. The slow pace of change was a concern, not only
because of the recession-induced emphasis on the bottom line, but also
because of the non-executive, advisory role that corporate environmental
executives now play in many highly-decentralised companies and the wide
range of responsibilities they have been given. As one executive remarked:
'The environmental issue develops so rapidly it's almost impossible to cope
with all the problems that are parachuted here. How do you set priorities?'

Our interviews suggested that environmental executives can be categorised
by the extent of their business background and awareness and the degree of
their environmental competence. This produces four basic types (see Fig. 1)

- Generalists
- Environmental generalists
- Environmental specialists
- Non-environmental specialists

Generalists are executives with a considerable range of business experience
who spend part of their careers in the environmental area. Over half of our
sample were in this category, and seven could be classified as 'experienced
managers' in their late forties and fifties who had been appointed either to drive
a step change in performance or, less positively, for non-environmental
reasons such as corporate re-organisations and final postings prior to
retirement. The 'step change' brief was well put by an executive in a

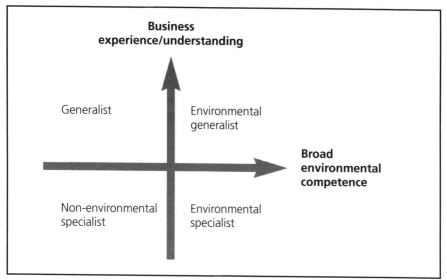

Figure 1: *A Typology of Environmental Executives*

divisionalised chemical company: 'They wanted someone who could tell CEOs how to run their businesses. My predecessor was a technically first-class guy who understood pollution control but wasn't being listened to.'

Six generalists were interesting examples of 'young Turks': that is, executives in their thirties and forties who had moved into environment after amassing considerable experience in other areas and who will probably move into other posts after a few years. A chemical executive exemplified this when he explained that 'I come from production and engineering, but to get a broader experience and knowhow, I have this job. Then I go back in the line organisation. Probably in site management or production.'

The young Turks saw their trajectories both as an appropriate means of integrating environment with the rest of the organisation and as providing an interesting personal career development opportunity. The former view was crystallised by an older generalist environmental executive with senior management experience when he commented that:

> Personally, I'm against having EHS specialists in this kind of position. In the past we've done that, but we didn't get the best people and they were easily forgotten. People with a line background have more credibility with their peers. Bring them in for three or four years and then let them infect the rest of the company with their EHS germs!

The career opportunities were highlighted by a British young Turk, who observed how taking the post 'enhanced my visibility inside and outside the group. I have a page in every issue of [the company magazine]—it was the same space as the annual results in the last issue!'

Non-environmental specialists are executives with considerable specialist knowledge in non-environmental areas or narrow environment-related disciplines (for example, toxicology), but limited general business experience and—prior to taking up the post—limited exposure to broad environmental issues. A quarter of our sample was entirely in this category with four of them being in German companies. Most executives in this category had moved into environmental management in the 1970s and 1980s, and their high representation probably reflects the fact that few environmental specialists were around at that time.

Two of our sample could be termed **environmental generalists**, that is, people with general business experience and/or well-developed business awareness who also have considerable environmental competence, for example, specialist qualifications or a long-standing personal interest in environmental issues.

Finally, only one of our sample—with a background in biology and wetland ecology—could be classed as an **environmental specialist**: that is, someone with considerable environmental competence but limited business experience. Perhaps not coincidentally, he was also one of the few interviewees who was uncertain as to whether the environmental executive position was the right one for him or not.

■ The Role of the Environmental Executive

We asked interviewees to describe their environmental responsibilities. Although their answers were varied, almost all identified two basic roles:

- ■ **The policy maker**, who is concerned with monitoring external developments and developing and implementing an environmental policy

- ■ **The co-ordinator**, who must operate both within the environmental function—for example, by aligning site activities with corporate goals— and between the environmental and other functions. The latter involves managing cross-functional teams and other activities in order to gain corporate 'buy-in'.

Around two-thirds of interviewees also mentioned three other roles:

- ■ **The communicator**, concerned with selling the environmental message within the organisation and influencing the views of external stakeholders

■ **The controller**, with a primary concern that all organisational actions are in compliance with legislation and corporate policies. While some will be surprised that any executive would not see this as a central role, it can be explained by the growing maturity of auditing and environmental management systems and the less punitive legal regime in Europe, and the consequent decentralisation of controlling responsibilities in a number of European companies.

■ **The consultant**, providing specialist advice on legislation, best practice and other topics to business units and sites

Three roles also explicitly identified by a number of executives were:

■ **The line manager**, of sometimes considerable environmental departments

■ **The change agent**, with an explicit brief of achieving a step change in environmental performance, perhaps as a result of adverse publicity or new legislation

■ **The strategist**, concerned with linking environment into the organisation's strategic objectives so that it can become a source of competitive advantage

■ *The Successful Environmental Executive*

There have been several attempts to define the critical skills that environmental managers need to possess, for example:

■ Kraaijveld[2] of Shell Petroleum distinguishes between three broad categories—skills, knowledge and awareness—and identifies sixteen specific competencies within these.

■ The UK Institute of Environmental Management[3] has identified key competencies as the basis for its professional accreditation procedures. They have identified six broad categories—strategic vision, business awareness, management skills, motivation/training/leadership, external communications and contingency planning.

However, the senior environmental executive position is distinctive and, as with every other top management position, success is always the product of a number of factors, including:

■ Personal attributes

■ Background

■ Company circumstances

■ Broader industry and societal circumstances

In order to better understand the more specific competencies required by senior environmental executives, and their relative importance compared to other factors, we asked interviewees to rate the importance of 21 different aspects of successful environmental management. They included general organisational factors, the nature of corporate environmental management and personal attributes of environmental executives. The results from such a small sample are indicative rather than representative, but nonetheless provide useful insights. The ten highest-ranked aspects were all concerned with general management abilities and top-level support (see Fig. 2). By contrast, factors such as the organisation of environmental management, workers' attitudes, a broad business background, environmental qualifications and previous experience in environmental management were considered to be less important. Indeed, undergraduate or postgraduate environmental education was seen as the least critical factor in British, German and US companies and was near the bottom of the Dutch ranking.

The findings were encapsulated in extreme form by a US executive (with a degree in toxicology) who commented that:

> as with so many management positions, you need good communication skills, an understanding of psychology, a broad understanding of technical issues and science and a capacity to absorb a certain amount of vernacular...if I had to do it over again I'd major in psychology and communication. Anybody can pick up science.

■ Leadership and motivation skills (of environmental executives)

■ Interpersonal skills (of environmental executives)

■ General management attitudes towards the environment

■ Broad environmental understanding (of environmental executives)

■ CEO–Director relationships (of environmental executives)

■ Comprehensive environmental policy

■ Teamworking skills (of environmental executives)

■ A long-term environmental vision (of environmental executives)

■ Industry knowhow (of environmental executives)

■ Quantified environmental results

Figure 2: *Critical Requirements for Successful Environmental Management*

A more measured summary was provided by a German who argued that an ideal environmental executive should have:

> a great knowledge of production or chemistry. He should have been production manager before and to be able to make contacts within the company and outside the company, to government and the public. He should also be able to make compromises.

In general, the findings show a modest difference between, on the one hand, Dutch- and German-based companies and, on the other, UK- and US-based ones. The former recognise the management aspects of the job as important but appear to place more emphasis on its specialist dimension and less emphasis on formal management systems and structures (even though these are usually present in their companies). This probably reflects the stringent regulation of Germany, the stronger environmental awareness in Germany and the Netherlands—which creates inner motivations to action—and the limited influence in both countries of TQM, which stresses the importance of cross-functional activities and formalised measurements and systems.

The question also revealed some interesting industry differences.

■ The **chemical** industry placed the least emphasis on the importance of environmental education and broad environmental understanding of any sector. This may reflect the feeling that a chemistry/chemical engineering background (which all our chemical industry interviewees had) provides a good foundation for environmental knowledge and has worked well so far, but could also explain why the industry sometimes fails to connect with its environmental critics.

■ **Consumer products** companies placed much more emphasis than others on the importance of external relationships, environmental vision and broad business background, no doubt reflecting their marketing and public relations orientation. Conversely, they placed less emphasis on a comprehensive environmental policy or quantified environmental results—perhaps suggesting that they may need to do more in this area in future.

Nonetheless, the overall message is clear: most environmental executives see the secret of success more in their general management abilities, company and industry understanding (which is often related to scientific and technical background) and top-level support than in environmental knowledge *per se*. This is because improved environmental performance depends upon the actions of line managers and non-environmental staff, who usually cannot be ordered to take action but must be persuaded. The successful environmental executive, therefore, is someone whose educational background and industry experience commands respect among his or her fellow managers, has the interpersonal skills and contacts to gain their voluntary acceptance of the environmental message, but also the personal and organisational clout to win battles when this is absolutely necessary. While this combination is by no means impossible for environmental professionals, the narrow scientific and technical orientation of many educational and training programmes in environmental management, and the ease with which they can be stereotyped as specialists, makes it difficult to achieve.

The following sections discuss the ten highest-ranked contributors to successful environmental management in detail.

■ Leadership and Motivation Skills

Environmental executives have to set and achieve corporate-wide goals without any direct authority over the main parties who influence those goals. Environmental leadership thereby requires credibility within the organisation, so that sometimes reluctant managers are persuaded to take action. For a consumer products executive, this came from understanding of, or experience in, line management:

> What is important is the trust people have, when you approach from the environmental position they have a different trust. If you have had a line position, it helps to establish the authority. This has all to do with culture change. It's much more than to reduce emissions. You can't bring culture change if you don't know the culture.

His point was echoed by a British executive whose office, unusually, was located at a factory:

> 75% of the requirement for my job was knowing the company's sites and issues. I'm greatly helped by being at a site rather than corporate headquarters. We're down in the trenches with everyone else—and sympathise with what they have to endure.

In many industries, credibility requires a similar background to the majority of managers, such as chemistry or chemical engineering qualifications in the chemical industry or a manufacturing background in engineering.

Another key aspect of leadership is the ability to reconcile attention to detail and day-to-day activities with a 'helicopter' perspective and awareness of medium- to long-term objectives. The point was made with feeling by an electronics executive:

> In my own group, there are people who are so detailistic, to the point of the comma...as a manager, it is my job to have a feeling for details but to also overview the total. This can't be learned. It's character, experience.

An oil executive commented that:

> you do need an ability to have quite a helicopter view ... to see issues in a broad way. Too narrow a technical focus, you won't be able to do the job. You have to relate it to the general societal aspects.

However, Friedman,[4] who is Vice-President for EHS at Occidental Petroleum and has written extensively on environmental management, believes that it can be difficult for line managers to make this transition:

> An operating manager who can speak the language of other operating managers can also be helpful in implementing and selling a program. However, the former operations manager needs to step back and think conceptually in order to engage in more than a fire-fighting operation.

Finally, the environmental executive also has an informal leadership and motivational role with regard to his or her 'dotted line' reports: the environmental professionals and champions at sites or in divisions. As one oil executive observed:

> You also have to be able to communicate well with EHS folks at the facilities, some of whom are full time and some part time. You have to coach them and support them, keep their spirits high, give them the feeling they're part of a team, try to get them empowered in their own organisations, raise their profile so that they can talk to the right people and get involved in the real business.

■ Interpersonal Skills

The lack of direct authority means that environmental executives must be adept at communication and persuasion. As a chemical executive noted:

With the range of activities I'm involved in, influencing skills are critical. I don't have any line authority so I'm totally dependent on my ability to influence others, whether they're board members, line managers or politicians.

An oil and gas executive also stressed: 'The ability to get a fairly widespread group of people to undertake the implementation of policies which, on the face of it, they may not see the need for.'

One attribute noted by a number of interviewees was the ability to get on with a wide range of people. As a Dutch executive observed, 'You should be not too reactive, with some patience. This is the same for every job. You have to deal easily with all kinds of persons and important persons.' Another Dutch executive observed that 'You should be a diplomat. Talk with people on the floor, with people in government, people in management...You use a different lingo for each group.' The point was equally well made by a wily German executive who noted that:

> From Germany to England, if we have a new idea and we bring it to managers, they close the front door. We are doing a job like a sales representative. He has to try the rear door. It's very similar to a salesman job. You have to convince people...[you also need] a feeling of how, to whom and together with whom you can go. This is important and also, how to go. With managers, if you pick the wrong day or hour, he may say no. You have to know his secretary to get his time.

■ General Management Attitudes

The environmental executive's task is made easier when fellow managers understand the need for, and are willing to support, environmental initiatives. General management attitudes are particularly important within a TQM approach, whose aim is to make environment everyone's responsibility. Hence a Dutch executive's ambition was to:

> establish a regular culture and attitude towards environmental issues. It should become part of the quality circle. If this succeeds, the rest will automatically follow. What matters is their receivers for the issues. When there are no receivers it's like a preacher in an empty church.

However, the recession of the early 1990s has created conflict between environmental and business goals in a number of organisations. The time and business performance pressures on line managers can mean that, irrespective of their personal feelings, environment is squeezed out of their day-to-day activities. It remains to be seen whether these problems will end with recovery or whether—in the leaner, more focused organisations that have emerged—the tension will persist.

■ Broad Environmental Understanding

Our respondents scored this very highly, but placed very little importance on having specialist environmental knowledge. One chemical executive, for example, was categorical in his statement that 'I would never give the environmental manager job to someone with an environmental background. I would bring him from operations.' This was based on a feeling that business experience and an industry-relevant scientific/technical background were both more important attributes and made it possible to assimilate quickly the specifics of environmental management. For one electronics executive, a critical factor is:

> The ability to understand environmental issues, whether technical or legal, and appraise, translate, apply them to one's business environment in a logical, cohesive but pragmatic way...I'm managing the system. I'm not a technical expert in every area.

However, this view could reflect a bias by managers without environmental training and there are dissenters from it. Friedman[5] has written that:

> A person need not be a professional environmental manager to function in an environmental position, although the best manager usually combines broad understanding of the corporation with professional environmental skills.

While this belief may be coloured by the author's background as a lawyer in a country with highly-developed environmental legislation, it was echoed by a few of our interviewees. Several of these dissenters were in consumer products companies (where the importance of a scientific/technical background is perhaps less than in other sectors). One household goods executive, for example, thought that a good environmental background meant that one avoided the risks of taking actions that are fashionable, although he went on to say that he personally had more environmental expertise than was really needed.

■ Senior Management Relationships

Our interviewees felt that their relationship with the chairman, chief executive and directors was a crucial requirement for success. A consumer products executive spoke for many when he stated that 'My main objective is to make the environmental plan the property of the chairman. He is responsible for it happening.' When senior management provide strong backing for environmental policies, the signals reach all sections of the organisation and provide environmental champions with a weapon for overcoming inertia. Conversely, when their backing is half-hearted, environment can easily be driven out by day-to-day operating and cost pressures. Most of our respondents felt that they did have senior management backing.

◼ Comprehensive Environmental Policy

While the broad trend in environmental management is to push responsibility down the line, all the environmental executives saw the need for corporate guidelines to achieve minimum standards and guard against major disasters. A well-written environmental policy can help achieve this. It also provides environmental executives with a 'founding charter' which can be of considerable political advantage. This is especially true when the policy has been developed with the participation of business units and facilities. A comprehensive policy can also be useful in directing organisational attention to issues that might otherwise be neglected: for example, those concerned with raw materials or the use and disposal of products.

However, policies have to be tempered by organisational realities. The units of decentralised companies value their autonomy and will often wish to have their own. Environment will also be of varying levels of importance. One electronics executive observed that 'we can't have 100% in all areas. It depends on priorities. We must keep a minimum standard but there is not a problem to have different levels.'

◼ Teamworking Skills

The wide-ranging nature of environmental issues, and the frequent need for co-ordinated action by a variety of departments and individuals within an organisation, mean that the environmental executive is often a member— and sometimes a leader—of cross-functional teams. As a German executive noted:

> there is a lot of teamwork because solving environmental problems means you are engaged in a sector that requires interdisciplinary work: production people, sales people, legal people. A full range of people, even research people. With new projects you chair a team and you have to convince and make sure the time schedule works out.

The development of TQM approaches, and the growing emphasis on collaboration between different organisations within the product chain, will make this competency even more important in future.

■ *Long-Term Environmental Vision*

A clear environmental vision forms the basis for broad corporate policies and detailed plans and programmes. Environmental issues are complex and long term and can be pigeonholed even by sympathetic employees facing relentless short-term demands. Even within the environmental area, a desire for immediate solutions can easily lead to the adoption of 'end-of-pipe' technologies rather than exploring the longer-term solutions of pollution prevention. As one of our sample remarked:

> You need someone with some vision, because environmental management does mean that you have to look at a timescale that is longer than the day-to-day business. For most companies, this is a change in attitude. Most companies don't think that long. Short-term environmental issues are three to five years: for companies this is a long time. Production managers think three months.

An electronics executive also felt that 'You have to have a broad picture of where you want to go. You are seldom directed from above. You have to be self-driven. I could sit and do nothing all day.'

A German executive—one of the few from that country to stress this topic—linked vision to personal commitment: 'First of all, in his personal characteristics he should be really convinced. He should be emotionally involved. You have to be convinced of what you are doing, so people know you feel it.' However, important as a vision is, it has to strike a fine balance between environmental optimality and business feasibility. The need to balance these tensions was well made by an oil executive:

> You have to have the bridge between EHS performance and business realities. It doesn't help to be a green prophet, who has a mission to green the organisation. Equally you can't just accept compliance and the minimum possible.

The actions of companies are driven by the characteristics of the industries they are in and the markets they serve. An understanding of these factors—and their influence on the attitudes and behaviours of managers within the company—is therefore an essential competency for the environmental executive. Indeed, one Dutch executive saw environmental management becoming more rather than less industry-specific in future:

In the past we've had a heavy weight on the management to install and use management tools and to have a big overview. Now the environmental manager has to be quite, to an extent, an expert. He must know his company and industry. His professional background will be dictated by industry type.

Industry knowhow is also helpful in creating and developing contacts with other companies and trade associations. These can be important when co-ordinated action is required—such as lobbying European or national decision-makers—and as sources of information and ideas.

■ Quantified Environmental Results

It is no longer sufficient for companies merely to state their environmental good intentions: they must increasingly prove their commitment by measuring their performance. Environmental executives are also finding that measurements and quantified targets among the best ways to drive continuous improvement in environmental performance.

■ The Environmental Executive as Scientist/Technologist

During our interviews, a majority of environmental executives commented on the importance of a scientific or technical background. The perception is clearly relevant to the high scores given to industry knowhow. This is perhaps unsurprising, given that almost all our respondents had such a background.

A chemical executive felt that:

> a technical background is almost needed. Its very important. It is not necessary that he must be a chemist, but it is better. There are necessary chemical processes behind environmental issues. It would be difficult if you were a law student or an economist.

For an electronics executive, the key competency is a background in:

> the technical aspects of production and manufacturing. He also has to know the process of product development. He must feel it. If he hasn't worked in such a process, he can't understand the motivation of the technical people, engineers and manufacturing people.

However, a minority of executives did dissent from this view. One oil executive with a legal background believed that 'You can't just be a technical specialist who they [line managers] delegate EHS to. I don't think you need technical expertise. You need access to it but you don't have to have it yourself.'

The conclusion is perhaps that environmental executives believe there is a triangle of relevant attributes—general business and management awareness, environmental knowledge and relevant scientific/technical background (see Fig. 3). Most of our interviewees agreed that all of these were important, but that general business and management awareness were most important, and detailed environmental knowledge the least. The precise centre of gravity within the triangle will be influenced by the importance of scientific and technical factors within an individual company. Figure 3 provides speculative examples for the chemicals and consumer product sectors.

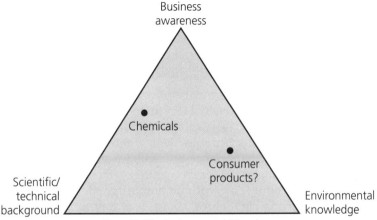

Figure 3: *The Environmental Triangle*

However, the views of current environmental executives on environmental qualifications and training are certainly debatable, and may reflect a bias by individuals who do not have such a background and therefore tend to underplay it. Certainly, many environmental professionals would argue that, whatever the position until now, future environmental demands on business will increase the value of a specialist background.

■ The Future

As in the US, European corporate environmental management is in **transition**, from a specialist, self-contained function to an activity that is more strategically integrated and cross-functional in nature. Many of our interviewees expect that:

- There will be a continuing need to reduce **emissions and wastes** even further. This will lead to increased emphasis on pollution prevention.

- **Environmental awareness** will need to be developed still further within organisations, both across functions and in international subsidiaries, particularly in the Third World.

- The focus of environmental management will shift from the organisation and its operational processes to the **product chain** and the need to work with suppliers and customers to minimise lifecycle impacts.

- The **weight of legislation** will continue to increase, requiring greater use of sophisticated decision tools such as lifecycle analysis and environmental cost–benefit analysis.

Previous sections have demonstrated that the work of environmental executives is influenced by their organisational, sectoral and national context. This situation is likely to persist in future. German executives in particular are likely to remain more specialised and task-oriented than their UK, US and Dutch equivalents and more regulatory-driven than UK and Dutch executives.

On the other hand, our survey also reveals considerable similarities in many key aspects of environmental executives' views and behaviour. Both are greatly conditioned by the fact that executives must influence many parts of the organisation's activities with limited or nonexistent formal authority. The resulting importance of credibility and influencing skills in achieving environmental goals was recognised even by German executives. The importance of **influencing without authority** will be increased further by some of the trends highlighted above. It is central both to enhancing organisational awareness and integrating with suppliers and customers and is also an important part of the move towards pollution prevention approaches in dealing with emissions and wastes.

These changes will all increase the relative importance of the change, communication, co-ordination and strategic roles of environmental managers. Even more than at present they will need to be:

- **Outward-looking**, in order to manage effectively product chains and deal with the changing needs of external stakeholders. This places a premium on communications and networking skills and experience in both process and product areas.

- **Politically adept**, in order to develop and maintain support across the organisation, but particularly among senior management

- Capable of **managing tension**, such as that between the autonomy of business units, facilities and national subsidiaries and the need for common corporate standards

■ **Business oriented**, so that the costs of environmental management can be minimised and the potential benefits maximised

■ **Visionary**, in directing organisational attention towards the long-term challenge of sustainability

The challenge will be to develop these roles while still maintaining broad control of corporate environmental actions and adequately providing the specialist consultancy advice that will remain important as environmental challenges become more complex.

At first sight, this conclusion may seem unexceptional. Senior functional executives of any kind have always had to balance the specialist and generalist aspects of their jobs. However, there are two points that will be surprising to some.

■ An emphasis on the business and managerial aspects of the position challenges the view of many environmental professionals that environmental management is a highly-specialised activity.

■ The environmental executive's position of having to influence without authority is one that is spreading to other business functions. Today's environmental executives may therefore be pathfinders for the job descriptions of many of tomorrow's functional managers.

■ The Environmental Executive: Specialist or Generalist?

The view of most of our interviewees that the environmental executive position is as much a general manager as an technical specialist—and the likelihood that the generalist aspects of the job will become more important in the future—creates a challenge for business and environmental professionals. Our sample may be rather atypical, for the authors' personal experience suggests that a number of companies define the post as a specialist one and recruit accordingly. Many incumbents and potential recruits then internalise these conceptions. This may be inappropriate even for today's environmental pressures and could be more so for tomorrow's.

Of course, there is no reason why individuals with specialised environmental backgrounds and knowledge—**environmental specialists** in our terminology—cannot develop general management skills, and a good number do in practice. Many such specialists would also argue that the growing complexity of environmental issues—and the need to align business activities with sustainable development—will place even more of a premium on environmental qualifications and knowledge in future. In practice, however, there is a risk that, in more advanced companies, and in the absence of the management experience and training that could turn them into **environmental generalists**, they may lose out for senior environmental executive positions to rising or mature **generalists** who have a more attractive mix of business credibility, scientific and technological background and broad environmental understanding. The challenge for human resource professionals and the environmental management community itself is to ensure that the training and development opportunities are available to broaden environmental specialists into managers who can hold their own with all parts and levels of the organisation.

■ *The Environmental Fast Track?*

The necessary competencies for today's, and, still more, tomorrow's environmental executives are remarkably similar to those that recent studies suggest will be necessary for all of tomorrow's business leaders.

■ According to Peter Drucker,[6] the fundamental change required from future managers is 'to learn to manage in situations where you don't have command authority, where you are neither controlled nor controlling'. Environmental executives already have little control over others and in most cases also have considerable autonomy within their work.

■ The ability to understand and manage external stakeholders is also second nature to many contemporary environmental executives. It will become ever more valuable to all managers in a world of partnerships, closely-integrated supply chains and an enhanced sense of corporate responsibilities to society.

■ As companies become more international, a global perspective—and the ability to deal with differences between individuals—becomes ever more critical. Environmental issues are not constrained by national boundaries and therefore lead naturally to an international perspective. In addition, environmental executives in multinational companies are well used to dealing with different national operations.

■ A key task for tomorrow's senior managers will be the ability to develop and communicate a long-term vision to staff and stakeholders while successfully managing day-to-day commercial and operational realities. This mix is also central to the work of many environmental executives.

Add to these points the corporate-wide perspective and experience that environmental management creates and it becomes feasible to imagine the environmental executive post becoming a valuable training ground for tomorrow's business leaders.

Our impression is that several of the current environmental executives whom we class as 'young Turks' are aware of this and see their current positions as springboards for high-level futures. Indeed, for some individuals at least, the environmental executive post could be a fast-track post for progression to the very top of an organisation. There is surely no better way to ensure that environmental issues are given the weight they deserve in the boardrooms of the 21st century.

▪ Notes

1. J. Barrett, Environmental Managers in Business (London, UK: Environmental Data Services, 1993); M. Gilboy and A. Bourner, 'Environmental Management in the '90s', in Hazmat World, October 1991, pp. 56-61; Institute of Environmental Management, 'Members Annual Survey', in Journal of the Institute of Environmental Management, Vol. 2 No. 4 (1995).

2. H.J. Kraaijveld, 'Shell International Petroleum', Paper presented to the *United Nations Environmental Programme Conference on Environmental Resource Management: Educating the Business Leaders of Tomorrow*, Paris, France: European Institute of Business Administration, INSEAD, 11–12 October, 1990.

3. Institute of Environmental Management, *Standards of Competence* (Edinburgh, UK: Institute of Environmental Management, 1993); see also P. James, 'The Competencies of Specialist Managers: A Study of European Environmental Executives', in *Competency*, Summer 1995, pp. 19-23.

4. F. Friedman, *Practical Guide to Environmental Management*, (Washington, DC: Environmental Law Institute, 1992).

5. *Ibid.*, p. 60.

6. P. Drucker, *Post-Capitalist Society* (London, UK: HarperCollins, 1993).

This chapter is based upon a longer report of the same title, published by Ashridge Management Research Group, Berkhamsted, Herts HP4 1NS.

7

Identification and Relevance of Environmental Corporate Cultures as Part of a Coherent Environmental Policy[1]

Walter Wehrmeyer and Kim T. Parker

*T*HE ROLE of Human Resources Management in the process of environmental management is essentially one of implementing, facilitating and managing change into the work processes and motivations of staff. In this, the attitudes of staff towards environmental management[2] and to work generally[3] have critically important functions in this process of managing environmental change. However, to ensure motivation of staff towards the organisation generally, and towards environmental management in particular, it is relevant that personal work attitudes and the perceived organisational culture have substantial overlaps and are at least in most aspects congruent to each other.[4]

It is the purpose of this chapter to present one way in which such cultures can be identified and located across an organisation and to discover what characterises corporate cultures with a significant environmental content—here labelled 'environmental corporate cultures'. This has obvious relevance for HRM, as Sadgrove[5] succinctly put it:

> In environmental management, *the personnel department has an important role to play, in ensuring that key appointments are made, and in developing environmental employment policies. Moreover, personnel will need to guide line management in ensuring that environmental policies are implemented with full staff co-operation* [emphasis added].

It is precisely this 'full co-operation' that necessitates staff enthusiasm, role identification, motivation towards performing a job, and goal and value congruence between personal and organisational goals and values.[6]

This chapter outlines one quantitative approach towards analysing corporate cultures and reports the main findings of a comparative study of five UK paper producers by describing the core cultural beliefs and their dispersal within these organisations. After a description of those organisational features that were found to be positively associated with improved environmental performance, the chapter outlines characteristics of environmental corporate cultures. The chapter concludes with a critique of the implications of this research for environmental ethics.

■ What are Corporate Cultures?

There are probably as many different definitions of the concept of corporate cultures as there are cultures. One of the more popular ones is Edgar Schein's, who has defined corporate cultures as 'the basic assumptions and beliefs that are shared by members of an organisation [which] are learned responses to a group's problems of survival in its external environment and its internal integration'.[7] Notwithstanding the semantic differences, similar definitions can be found in Deal and Kennedy,[8] Ouchi,[9] Pascale and Athos,[10] Dyer[11] or Hofstede.[12] The importance of such cultural influences on decision-making has long been established.[13]

In a general review article, Sinclair[14] argues that ethical behaviour in organisations can better be facilitated assuming 'shifting coalitions of subcultures' rather than fostering a unitary cohesive culture. Liedtka[15] analyses the origin of organisational cultures in the interplay between organisational and personal values. She suggests that different value systems as well as value congruence are significant and substantial factors in how individuals and organisations perform. This has been suggested earlier by Beyer[16] and Deal and Kennedy.[17]

Using Liedtka's value congruence model, Posner and Schmidt[18] argue that 'managers who felt clear (consonant) about their personal values and organisational values reported positive attitudes about their work and the ethical practices of their colleagues and firms', thus reinforcing Liedtka's initial idea, even though environmental issues were absent from the original definition of ethical behaviour. The interplay between personal and organisational values takes an additional turn according to Gabriel,[19] who provides an interesting psychoanalytical (and hence individual) interpretation of organisational (and hence collective) culture.[20]

Even though changes in cultures can be initiated and directed, corporate cultures themselves are not conscious and deliberate creations of certain members of the firm, but are produced by everybody. Corporate cultures evolve as spontaneous social systems where espousal of some to a cultural pattern shared by all members results in an (often tacitly) agreed predominance of that cultural pattern over others. They are those complex systems of which von Hayek[21] has said that 'we do not owe all beneficial institutions to design'.

From a systemic viewpoint, corporate cultures originate by agreement with an initial preference in decision-making which is then adopted, repeated and, by doing so, reinforced.[22] The characteristics of the initial pattern are relevant for the type of culture to emerge, but are largely irrelevant for the process to occur.[23] Once the pattern has emerged, a dialectic process of continuous testing and adaptation is observable, where individual behaviour is guided by that cultural pattern and, if successful, the cultural values and the particular behaviour are reinforced.[24] This allows individual behaviour to change according to 'standard practice'. It also allows the continuous testing and adapting of culture.

This continuous process of 'enacting values'[25] allows a culture to evolve and change. However, the *change of culture by behaviour* is usually more difficult than the *change of behaviour by culture*, because, by definition, the corporate culture is used by all employees as a reference point, which makes individual behaviour change easy if not desired (socialisation), whereas changing culture itself is more difficult—how does one change a reference point continuously in use by many? Organisationally, 'old habits die hard'.

Even though it is difficult to identify origins in a recursive and interdependent process, it can be argued that, if environmental values are predominantly introduced as a conscious effort by parts of the organisation to change values, such alterations are likely to be more difficult than if environmental attitudes are resident in all employees but are activated as part of a value change programme. It follows that new situations, new people or new perspectives make corporate culture change easier.

■ Method

In the design of this research, it was decided that the method of identifying corporate cultures should be only marginally, if at all, influenced by assumptions about how an environmental culture should appear. It was not intended to test hypotheses based on the researchers' beliefs about what form environmental cultures should take, but rather to let such cultures emerge from the data collected. A number of cultural modes in environmental ethics do exist, most notably those depicted in O'Riordan,[26] who separates anthropocentric and eco-centric modes into four subcategories (see Fig. 1). Even though these modes have somewhat informed the research, there were no preconceptions that the actual organisational cultures would fall into any of these categories; indeed, they could well be a mixture of several such modes.

Eco-centrism		Technocentrism	
Deep Ecology		**Shallow Environmentalism**	
Gaianism	**Communalism**	**Accommodation**	**Optimism**
Intrinsic importance of nature for humanity of humans	Emphasis on small scale and self-reliance	Belief that economic growth and resource consumption can be reconciled with environmental protection and care	Belief that humans can always find a way out of any difficulties
Ecological (and other) laws dictate human morality	A belief that integration of work and leisure within communities are part of corporate policy	Economic growth is beneficial to environmental protection if economic system is improved using better taxes, better legal rights for environmental protection and satisfactory compensatory arrangements. Existing policy evaluation criteria need improvement but are inherently worth modifying.	Economic goals define rationality of policy formulation.
Biorights (rights of non-human species or ecosystems to stay 'un-humanised'			
Scepticism towards modern large-scale technology and its demands on élitist expertise, central state authority and inherently anti-democratic institutions.			Faith that scientific and technological base provides guidance for economic, social and political development
Belief that materialism for its own sake is wrong; economic growth can be geared to providing for the basic needs of poor.			Belief that all impediments can be overcome given a will, ingenuity and sufficient resources arising out of growth; suspicion of attempts to widen participation in policy review to non-specialists

Figure 1: *Modes in Environmental Ethics*

Sources: D. Pepper, *The Routes of Modern Environmentalism* (London, UK: Routledge,1984); T. O'Riordan, *Environmentalism* (2nd rev. edn; London, UK: Pion, 1981).

The sector chosen for this research was the paper manufacturing industry in the UK, in which five companies were asked to participate. In total, 141 completed questionnaires were returned and analysed. Figure 2 gives an overview of the distribution of responses within the firms. Note that the categorisation of responses into classes largely followed the organisational functions in these firms, whose identities have been deliberately withheld at their request and are hence named 'Eagle', 'Kingfisher', 'Hawk', 'Falcon' and 'Merlin'. However, with regard to ownership pattern, organisational size (as measured in turnover, production volume or staff numbers), geographical location and type of product, the participating firms can be broadly seen as within the industry average of this sector.

Companies						
Number of responses	Kingfisher	Hawk	Falcon	Merlin	Eagle	Total
Directors	4	5	4	4	4	21
HRM and Finance	7	2	6	3	3	21
Environment and Analysis	3	1	7	6	2	19
Production	5	2	10	8	5	30
Marketing	6	2	6	5	3	22
Engineering	3	3	7	2	3	18
Other	1	3	4	1	1	10
Total	29	18	44	29	21	141

* Values = number of responses

Figure 2: *Summary of Responses*

One of the prime aims is to identify particular corporate cultures by means of this questionnaire-based enquiry. In such a context, it is thus necessary to find particular patterns of responses to certain questions. Respondents who hold views that are consonant with a culture will tend to answer some questions in one way and some in another, but the general pattern should be broadly the same for all who are part of that culture. For example, those associated with an eco-centric culture (assuming such a culture exists), would attach high importance to environmental conservation and thus return high scores for all questions related to valuing the environment. Conversely, they would probably give low scores on those questions asking about the importance of industrial production.

Although such an aim is relatively easy to understand, there is a considerable problem of analysis and interpretation, especially with a complex questionnaire of 129 questions. The multivariate technique of principal components analysis was chosen precisely because it can satisfy these requirements. The predominant view in the literature is that principal components analysis is a purely mathematical way of describing the original data which can 'simplify with minimal loss of information'.[27] The technique explicitly searches for a small number of new variables, which are formed as combinations of the original data (in our case, responses to particular questions), but which retain as much as possible of the original information.

Once principal components analysis has been performed, there is a problem of just how many components to use, striking a balance between completeness and simplicity. There are no unambiguous tests and, ultimately, researchers have to use their judgement.[28] When the most important components have been chosen, they then have to be interpreted. In this study, they were looked at closely to see which particular questions on the original questionnaire made the greatest contribution. It was thus possible to build up a picture of how high-scoring respondents viewed their firm. As described in the next section, these pictures, in fact, formed a coherent description of clearly identifiable cultures. This approach has also been used earlier by Pugh *et al.*[29] to identify the relevance of certain organisational characteristics (such as specialisation and differentiation) on the organisational ability to change.

Once the principal component scores had been calculated for each respondent, indicating the degree to which they adhered to certain cultures, it was also possible to attribute the corporate cultures to the respective firms in terms of their positions on the principal component axes, simply by averaging the component scores of all the respondents working for that firm. Similarly, it was possible to identify corporate cultures between functions and across firms. In the following, the four most important cultures are described, and these cultures attributed to the participating firms.

■ *Results of the Survey*

When the analysis was performed, it was found that the first four of the components (3% of the 129) accounted for some 35% of the total variation in the sample. Some of the important factors in these cultures are presented in Figure 6, where importance is technically defined as the relative contribution of certain questions to a particular principal component. It should be noted that the descriptions relate to high component scores. Principal components retain as much information as possible by emphasising contrasts, and thus there will be respondents at both ends of the scale: for example, just as there will be some who perceive their firm as co-operative environmentalists, there will be those whose firms are viewed as non-participative, not caring about the environment and formal.

Generic Corporate Culture	Description
Co-operative Environmentalism	Employees perceive firm as participative, co-operative, 'caring' for environment and employees alike; uses informal processes to supplant formal planning; has hierarchical boundaries with little significance; and has environmental protection as a defining characteristic.
Technological Growth-Orientation	Strong focus on growth and short-term profit; 'following the customer' is main source of corporate policy; environmental compliance is primarily achieved by technological upgrading; no anticipatory and proactive policy towards the environment; profit maximisation is prime organisational purpose; quality is prime competitive advantage.
Centralised Damage Limitation	Economic survival is of immediate and everyday importance; considerable inertia towards innovation and change; strong tendencies towards centralisation; crises occur relatively often; cost-cutting as prime competitive advantage.
Socially Concerned Administration	Prime drive is attempt to satisfy all (internal and external) pressure groups; little leadership; very little organisational structure (and, hence, little coherence); some environmental activities but little integration into overall policy, which is only crudely formulated; growth of little importance; innovation favoured but not necessarily facilitated.

Figure 6: *Generic Corporate Cultures*

These four generic cultures are the most important cultures as identified from the 141 responses to the questionnaire. As stated, there are many more, but it was decided to limit the analysis to these four as additional components ('cultural archetypes') shed little light on the variety of environmental cultures, but added to the number of considered factors. It is possible that different companies might produce different cultures; therefore it should be stressed that the four generic cultures are not the only ones possible for any firm.

However, by calculating the extent to which each respondent follows these cultures and averaging these for each of the five firms, it was possible to attribute the extent to which each firm follows any of these cultures. This method has already been used in similar studies by Sackmann[30] and Pugh *et al.*[31] A similarly quantitative approach to studying corporate cultures was pursued by Nystrom[32] and Posner and Schmidt.[33] This procedure allows us to 'map' the five firms into the four-dimensional space defined by these four principal components. Two projections of this mapping are shown in Figures 3 and 4. The companies showed significant differences in the extent to which they followed the principal components as can be seen by Figure 5.

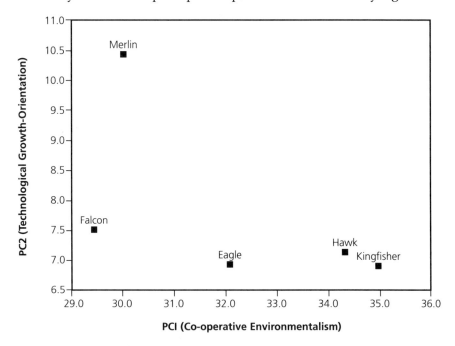

Figure 3: *Component Score of Co-operative Environmentalism and Technological Growth-Orientation*

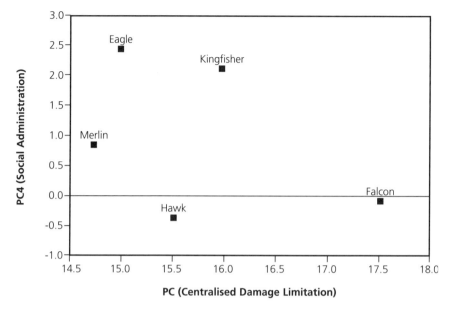

Figure 4: *Component Score of Centralised Damage Limitation and Socially Concerned Administration*

Principal component	F-value (4 and 136 degrees of freedom)	p-value
Co-operative Environmentalism	9.50	0.000
Technological Growth-Orientation	8.13	0.000
Centralised Damage Limitation	3.02	0.020
Socially Concerned Administration	5.85	0.000

Figure 5: *Analysis of Variance, Differences in Firms' Principal Component Scores*

As can be seen from Figure 3, the component score of Co-operative Environmentalism is relatively evenly spread between the companies, with Kingfisher and Hawk following this culture, and Falcon and Merlin being at the lower end of this scale. Such a spread could be expected, given the mechanisms for deriving this culture. However, the same figure depicts that Technological Growth-Orientation is not followed by any firm except Merlin, which embodies this culture while, at the same time, scoring at the low end of the Co-operative Environmentalism axis. Formal analyses of variance were performed in order to ascertain whether there significant differences between the firms in terms of their principal component scores. Indeed, the differences were found to be statistically significant for all four components (see Fig. 5). From this, one can infer that Merlin appears to follow predominantly Technological Growth-Orientation (in contrast to the other four which do not), but not Co-operative Environmentalism. In terms of Co-operative Environmentalism, Falcon and Merlin, and Hawk and King-fisher formed two opposed pairs, the latter two appearing to follow this culture.

Figure 4 shows that Falcon follows Centralised Damage Limitation but not Socially Concerned Administration. Equally, Kingfisher and Eagle seem to follow Socially Concerned Administration, whereas Hawk follows neither Socially Concerned Administration nor Centralised Damage Limitation. Using statistical means to support these inferences, it was concluded that Kingfisher's culture appears as a mixture of Co-operative Environmentalism and Socially Concerned Administration, that Falcon's culture follows Centralised Damage Limitation, Eagle follows Socially Concerned Administration, Hawk follows Co-operative Environmentalism and Merlin follows Technological Growth-Orientation. These findings, together with a discussion of the relative strengths and weaknesses of each empirical culture, were presented to each company at Board level.

Because of relative similarities between Co-operative Environmentalism and Socially Concerned Administration, it was decided that these cultures would be summarised under 'Order-Seeking', a name derived from their principal characteristic of trying to find order among activities and trying to make sense of these. Early research into the structuring of organisations has found a number of approaches corresponding to Order-Seeking. These have been labelled organic management styles. In addition, Order-Seeking was found to be comparable to more recent approaches to integrating complex systems theory into management thinking.[34] A summary of how Order-Seeking relates to earlier approaches of management theory, and in particular to well-established models of decision-making, can be found in Figure 7. It can be shown that, at least in theory, there are similarities in the decision-making approaches of organic management systems[35] and ecocentric modes of environmentalism.[36] 'Order-Seeking' has been described by Morgan[37] using the concept of systemic wisdom:

> [Systemic wisdom] is based on an understanding of contexts, an orientation of action away from noxiants, finding value in systems relations rather than instrumental ends, and fostering joint rather than individual action.

According to	Organising	Order-Seeking
March and Simon	Routinised decision-making	Problem-solving
Simon	Programmed decision-making	Non-programmed decision-making
Thompson	Computational strategy for decision-making	Judgmental strategy for decision-making
Burns and Stalker	Mechanistic management system	Organic management system
O'Riordan	Technocentric mode of environmentalism	Ecocentric mode of environmentalism
Pearce and Turner; Turner	Anthropocentric environmental ethic	Ecocentric environmental ethics
Capra	The Newtonian world machine	Complex systems' view of life

Figure 7: *'Organising' and 'Order-Seeking' in Context*

Sources: J.G. March and H.A. Simon, *Organisations* (New York, NY/London, UK/Sydney, Australia: John Wiley, 1958); H. A. Simon, *The New Science of Management Decision* (Hemel Hempstead, UK: Prentice Hall International, 1977); J.D. Thompson, *Organisations in Action* (London, UK/New York, NY: McGraw-Hill, 1967); T. Burns and G.M. Stalker, *The Management of Innovation* (2nd edn; London, UK: Tavistock, 1966); T. O'Riordan, *Environmentalism* (2nd rev. edn; London, UK: Pion, 1981); D. Pearce and R.K. Turner, *Economics of Natural Resources and the Environment* (London, UK: Harvester Wheatsheaf, 1990); R.K. Turner, 'Environment, Economics and Ethics', in D. Pearce (ed.), *Blueprint 2: Greening the World Economy* (London, UK: Earthscan, 1991), pp. 209-24; F. Capra, *The Turning Point: Science, Society and the Rising Culture* (Glasgow, UK: Collins, 1983).

Likewise, Technological Growth-Orientation and Centralised Damage Limitation were summarised under the term of 'organising', because of both cultures' reliance on technocratic and mechanistic tools and, generally, their attempts to superimpose their interpretation of activities onto their environment. This could be equally be compared with earlier management approaches, such as the mechanistic management styles of Burns and Stalker[38] or routinised decision-making[39] (see Fig. 7). The difference, then, between organising and Order-Seeking is the direction of influence in the interaction between an organisation and its specific environment. In essence, Simon[40] sums it up:

> If we want organism or mechanism to behave effectively in a complex and changing environment, we can design into it adaptive mechanisms that allow it to respond flexibly to the demands the environment places on it. Alternatively, we can try to simplify and stabilise the environment. We can adapt organism to environment or environment to organism.

Each model, then, must have different environmental effects—is it environmentally friendlier to superimpose organisational values and approaches onto its specific environment, or is it environmentally friendlier to try organisationally to adapt to fluctuations in the environment as they happen? This choice appears initially as a trade-off between economies of scale in environmental improvement, which are more prevalent in organising, and greater adaptability and higher local specificity which is more common in Order-Seeking.

To assess this problem, the obvious question is: what is the environmental performance of the companies, and to what extent are their corporate cultures influencing the relative environmental performance of each of the participating firms? To answer this, the relative environmental performance of the companies was assessed using Wehrmeyer's[41] methodology. This method integrates physical data (resource use, emissions, etc.) in a mathematical model to derive a single score where low values represent 'better' environmental performance and vice versa. Here, less is better, and organisational size certainly influences the environmental performance—as one can expect.

A full description of the mechanism and methodology is beyond the scope of the discussion here, yet it was found that Merlin had the lowest score and thus best environmental performance. However, it is also a company that is substantially smaller than the other four companies which, incidentally, had very similar production volumes. From the analysis of emissions, production volumes and resource consumption, it was concluded that the size-adjusted environmental performance ranking showed Kingfisher with the best and Hawk, Eagle, Merlin and Falcon, in that order, to follow. In a subsequent step, the environmental performance scores were compared with the predominant corporate cultures as identified above. This is shown in Figures 8 and 9. However, Merlin is a special case, producing very specialised, high-value low-output products, and was therefore excluded from the following analysis.

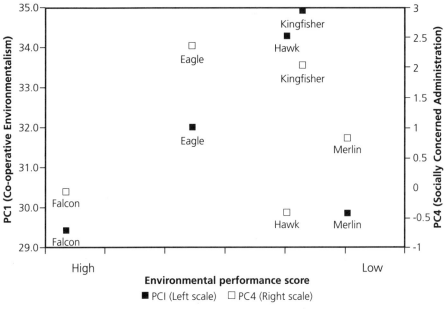

Figure 8: *Order-Seeking and Environmental Performance*

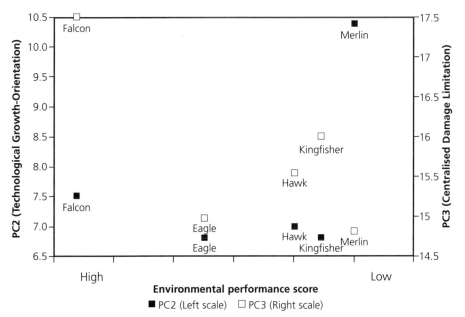

Figure 9: *Organising and Environmental Performance*

Figure 8 shows a relationship between Co-operative Environmentalism (and, to a lesser extent, Socially Concerned Administration) and lower environmental performance. Kingfisher and Hawk have both the highest scores on Co-operative Environmentalism and the best environmental performance. In addition, Kingfisher, together with Eagle, shows very high scores on Socially Concerned Administration. Falcon, with the worst environmental performance, follows Order-Seeking to the least extent, as represented by the two generic management styles. However, the converse relationship to the suggested link between low environmental performance and Order-Seeking as an active corporate culture, was less conclusive. Figure 9 shows that the environmental performance seems indifferent to Technological Growth-Orientation culture, yet there is support for the notion that strong indications of Centralised Damage Limitation seems to be associated with relatively larger environmental impacts (lower environmental performance scores). Thus, with the exception of the 'environmentally indifferent' Technological Growth-Orientation and excluding Merlin for the above reasons, organising cultures had somewhat higher environmental impacts and, moreover, Order-Seeking relatively lower ones. An overview of the relationship between environmental ethics, generic and theoretical management styles can be found in Figure 10. Dismissing what is here called organising, Morgan[42] has theoretically argued this relation a decade earlier:

Modes of environmental ethics		Theoretical management style	Generic management style
Eco-centrism	Gaianism (Co-evolution)	*Order-Seeking*	*Socially Concerned Administration*
	Communalism		*Co-operative Environmentalism*
Techno-centrism	Accommodation	*Organising*	*Centralised Damage Limitation*
	(Technological) optimism		*Technological Growth-Orientation*

Figure 10: *The Relation between Generic Management Styles, Theoretical Management Styles and Modes in Environmental Ethics*

Source: T. O'Riordan, *Environmentalism* (2nd rev. edn; London, UK: Pion, 1981)

The idea that organic forms evolve through a process of goal-oriented or instrumental adaptation to context is a myth fostered by the mechanistic mode of thought...Cybernetics show us that organised forms do not actively seek or orient themselves toward achievement of a desired future state. Rather, they arrive at any given state through processes of adjustment which eliminate other possible system states...The traditional goal-oriented concept of organisation and strategy projects and expresses a deep-seated desire: that human beings can and should exercise control over their destiny...Cybernetic epistemology shows us the systemic difficulties and paradoxes which result from attempts to exert such control over context, and offers an alternative approach...Whereas traditional conceptions...emphasise the importance of gaining unilateral control *over* systems relations, the cybernetic conception suggests the importance of finding control *in* relations.

■ Conclusions from the Research

Identifying corporate cultures in a more or less objective manner and without undue interference from the researchers' beliefs remains a task as important as it is difficult. However, before the mechanisms of such analysis and its subsequent intervening effects can be discussed, the question remains why organisations should be bothered about a congruence between personal and organisational values. The reasons are simple.

The first reason is that integrating environmental protection into existing cultures helps making existing environmental improvement programmes 'stick' and thus more likely to be successful. This instrumental reason sees the role of personnel management as one that supports the environmental management functions. This in effect calls for a 'learning culture' to be developed or utilised within organisations.

The second reason for maintaining goal congruence between personal and organisational environmental values is that such coherence helps to improve the environmental (and economic) performance of the organisation by improving cohesion, co-ordination and motivation of staff towards corporate policy attainment. The rationale behind this operational reasoning lies in greater staff commitment and motivation, not only towards environmental management goals but towards organisational success generally.

The third reason relates to the interplay between personal and societal values (*zeitgeist*): if environmental values have become a permanent feature of society at large, then organisations should be concerned with developing cultures that reflect the changing nature of societal cultures. Otherwise, organisations are likely to 'lose touch' with new developments or become inflexible towards changing social and societal attitudes. This developmental reason relates to organisational development and an organisation's adaptability to changes in its social and ethical environment. It is probable that successful organisations do that anyway as an inevitable process of cultural assimilation.[43] Other authors have also argued that this cultural interplay is not a one-sided affair. In fact, Galbraith has argued as early as 1967[44] that organisations actively try to export corporate values into society.

The literature on corporate social responsibility states that if business is to be (and remain) an integral part of the societies it serves and from which it resources itself, then the 'greening of business cultures' is a necessity.[45] This necessity, then, is not argued on grounds of traditional business values but because of the responsibilities of business to these very communities. This strategic reason only applies if organisations see this responsibility and their role beyond earning money.

The proposed method of identifying and assessing culture thus presents one possibility, albeit rather mathematical in its approach. However, this research uncovered several important correlations between the corporate culture of a company and its relative environmental performance.

There are many reasons why this research is more indicative than it is conclusive, yet the most significant relationship between *worse* environmental performance and traits in corporate cultures was that of Centralised Damage-Limitation. This is arguably due to its inherent 'fire-fighting' approach to organisational life; yet, notwithstanding the effect of this feature, there are other elements of this cultural trait, which indicates that there is more than one factor contributing to this environmental performance, such as its inertia-dominated approach to innovation.

On a more positive note, the relationship between Order-Seeking in general and Co-operative Environmentalism in particular and *better* environmental performance is equally critical. While there are potentially many other predominant cultures that could possibly emerge from the research, particularly if other sector industries are analysed, the following features may be distilled for 'environmentally-friendlier corporate cultures'.

The conclusions drawn here are tentative, but nonetheless drawn on the empirical findings presented, and are based on the perspective that corporate cultures are complex, self-organised systems with their own dynamic as autopoietic systems.[46] In this, one can infer the following characteristics:[47]

1. Management sees itself not as all-important but part of a greater whole. This conclusion is a direct inference of the introductory quote of

Morgan,[48] where greater environmental impact is caused by subsystems trying to superimpose unilateral control over the whole system. This systemic argument has not only implications for management but for the interaction of humans with their environment generally.

2. Since organisation does not necessarily derive from design but evolves from interaction, **the opportunity to make mistakes and the ability to learn from these** is critical—for the continuous improvement mentality as well as for the integrity of management systems. Environmental corporate cultures, in this respect, are cultures that are adaptive and perhaps not 'green' in themselves, but merely faster in responding to societal attitude change towards environmental protection, and are probably necessary if any 'greening' is to take place. Such cultures also inevitably **recognise ignorance**—at least initially—and are commonly oriented towards **continuous improvement**.

3. **Environmental corporate cultures show strong leadership and are clearly communicated.** Paradoxically, the impetus to decentralise, delegate and allow continuous improvement at all levels requires initially a clear and more decisive top management approach, because most management approaches are designed around **defensive routines**[49] and geared towards maintaining the status quo under changing circumstances rather than adaptive behaviour. The majority of corporate cultures are, for historical reasons, not geared towards environmental management. Hence, environmental corporate cultures are at least initially concerned with the management of change and thus require the precise leadership contradicting the 'green' and 'grass-roots' approaches it ultimately may envisage.

4. **Environmental corporate cultures enable, facilitate and support rather than monitor, control and dictate.** The above argument leads to the conclusion that management must depart from its traditional 'command and control' approach in order to achieve less environmental impact. Indeed, management styles and their cultural contexts must be more geared towards allowing staff to enact their values at the workplace rather than to waste efforts on keeping the ethics of the 'the employee' separate from those of 'the citizen', or other behavioural archetypes. This has, as argued, important effects on the motivation, identification and intrinsic rewards for staff.

5. The emphasis of such cultures lies in the **process of organisation** rather than its outcome. This implies a departure from the 'bottom-line obsession'. Equally, it was shown in comparisons between US and Japanese firms that an overtly strong focus on the 'bottom line' often results in worse economic performance than those firms who perceive the bottom line only as

verification of action rather than as a means in itself. A similar argument can be made for environmental management and its performance indicator.

These traits can be summarised in the staff attitudes towards profit and quality. Those companies that saw profit as the prime and core cultural value had, perhaps expectedly, worse environmental performance and vice versa. Surprisingly, these firms also had below-average economic performance. In turn, those firms that put emphasis on quality and did things because they were 'right' rather than 'profitable' had better environmental (and economic) performance. This is somewhat mirrored in the existing literature on Total Quality Management.[50] This does not, however, necessarily mean that environmental performance equates with economic success.

The repeated referral to 'right' and 'wrong' as tacit yet powerful criteria within decision-making indicates the strong influence of such cultural and ethical considerations within environmentally 'better' companies. It also suggests that environmental ethics may play a far larger role in the emerging Environmental Management discipline than its current role may suggest. Unfortunately, none of the (empirical) organisational cultures matched sufficiently with the (theoretical) modes of environmental ethics.[51] This either suggests that the modes are more complex than previously assumed or simply different. Alternatively, the sample size of this study may have been too small for an assessment of the working of environmental ethics modes at the workplace. This is certainly true, but that does not necessarily disprove the existence of different ethical modes.

The spurious absence of *environmental* factors in the empirical literature on personal and organisational ethics has already been commented upon. Liedka,[52] Posner and Schmidt,[53] Sackmann[54] and Nystrom[55] are examples of such omissions which, different from earlier authors, should not necessarily be explained through the novelty of environmental considerations in management.

With the presented method, it is not possible to identify causes and effects of different corporate cultures. Further, it is not possible to identify whether cultural changes are causing different corporate environmental performances or whether environmental management has an effect on the respective culture. Liedtka,[56] however, shows the importance of congruence in this interplay. Likewise, it is at the moment not conclusive whether these cultural changes are causing different environmental performances as a result of environmental management or other factors, such as comparably better management of change of organisational adaptability. However, the proposed method can be seen as one step into a direction that is likely to increase in relevance in the future.

From the above discussion, it emerges that establishing environmental cultures in a firm is an important part of implementing environmental protection in a firm. In this, the discussion about environmental management becomes a matter of intervention and the management of change. Hence, it is also far less easy than early approaches from the literature may have suggested. This chapter argues that the reason for this difficulty lies in the predominance of 'non-environmental' cultures in business contexts. Hence, the management of intervention is reduced to the simple question of how to change culture.

There are no easy and universal answers to this question, and Nelissen and Klinkers[57] show but one way of introducing attitude change. Trompenaars[58] discusses this in greater detail as well. The reason why this chapter argued from a systemic perspective towards understanding culture lies in the dual nature of the decentralised feedback processes by which attitudes and values are enacted and behaviour is adjusted. On one side, this mechanism is probably the greatest asset in stabilising cultures. Yet, it also makes it much more difficult to change existing cultures rather than to introduce new cultural elements, so that new situations, new people or new contexts allow a 'fresh' start and behaviour can be influenced through new cultural elements.

This emphasis on culture change through action or events (be they new events or new interpretations of existing phenomena) is a critical issue for environmental management for several reasons. First, many environmental programmes are about avoiding effects, such as programmes to minimise waste, avoid accidents or reduce emissions. It is in most cases more difficult to raise awareness about the problems than to 'declare success' of such programmes in a way that is as clear and visible as the original problem.[59] In other words, it is easier to see the smoke bellowing out of a chimney than to appreciate clean air or, to take an example from the political sphere, how many nuclear power stations have not been built because of public opposition, energy conservation programmes and increased energy efficiency?

The second reason derives from the way in which environmental information is treated in existing data and information management systems and which, often inadvertently, act as a filter: it is highly unlikely that we will see people dying directly because of global environmental issues such as desertification, global warming or the famous hole in the ozone layer. As a crass example: people do not perish simply because there is a hole in the ozone layer, but indirectly from skin cancer ; similarly, desertification itself does not kill, but rather the famine and hunger it may give rise to. How can organisations show their progress if the time series by which we measure success is not immediate but has many additional factors contributing to each variable?

The third reason is related to the previous one: many environmental impacts of organisations are not salient events, in that they are dispersed in space and time, which makes it difficult for us to perceive these and act upon them. For example, it has been estimated that on Britain's roads, there are about 450 fatalities every month. This is equivalent to a jumbo jet crashing every month. This does not attract as much attention than if, in fact, every month a jumbo jet were to crash with no survivors. In a sense, we have come to accept such environmental effects as part of our 'risk society'[60] and hence reduced the likelihood of learning from these events in their current interpretation. It is hoped that many of the more recently emerged environmental topics are not suffering the same fate. Recent events surrounding the Brent Spar oil platform and French nuclear testing give rise to more hope than this chapter may have indicated.

■ Notes

1. This chapter is based on a previous article by the authors, published in *Business Strategy and the Environment*, Vol. 4 No. 3 (July–September 1995), pp. 144-53. Parts are reprinted with the permission of Wiley.

The authors wish to express their gratitude to the participating companies as well as to the Esmée Fairbairn Foundation for their generous support of this research.

2. See: W. Hopfenbeck, *The Green Management Revolution: Lessons in Environmental Excellence* (London, UK: Prentice Hall, 1992); K. North, *Environmental Business Management: An Introduction* (Management Development Series, No. 30; Geneva, Switzerland: ILO, 1992); S. Schmidheiny and the Business Council for Sustainable Development, *Changing Course: A Global Business Perspective on Development and the Environment* (New York, NY: MIT Press, 1992).

3. See C.B. Handy, *Understanding Organisations* (Harmondsworth, UK: Penguin, 1985); D.A. Buchanan and A.A. Huczynski, *Organisational Behaviour: An Introductory Text* (London, UK: Prentice Hall, 1985).

4. See: A.J. Hoffman, 'The Importance of Fit between Individual Values and Organisational Culture in the Greening of Industry', in *Business Strategy and the Environment*, Vol. 2 No. 4 (Winter 1993), pp. 10-18; F. Trompenaars, *Riding the Waves of Culture: Understanding Cultural Diversity in Business* (London, UK: Nicholas Brealy, 1993); Handy *op. cit.*

5. K. Sadgrove, *The Green Guide to Profitable Management* (Aldershot, UK: Gower, 1992), p. 175.

6. See B.Z. Posner and W.H. Schmidt, 'Values Congruence and Differences between the Interplay of Personal and Organisational Value Systems', in *Journal of Business Ethics*, Vol. 12 (1993), pp. 341-47.

7. E.H. Schein, *Organisational Culture and Leadership* (San Francisco, CA: Jossey-Bass, 1985), p. 6.

8. T.E. Deal and A.A. Kennedy, *Corporate Cultures* (Reading, MA: Addison-Wesley, 1982).

9. W.G. Ouchi, *Theory Z* (Reading, MA: Addison-Wesley, 1981).

10. R.T. Pascale and A.G. Athos, *The Art of Japanese Management* (New York, NY: Simon & Schuster, 1981).

11. W.G. Dyer, 'The Cycle of Cultural Evolution Organisations', in R. Kilmann *et al.* (eds.), *Gaining Control of the Corporate Culture* (San Francisco, CA: Jossey-Bass, 1985).

12. G. Hofstede, *Culture's Consequences: International Differences in Work-Related Values* (London, UK: Sage, 1980).

13. See Handy, *op. cit.*; D.S. Pugh *et al.*, 'Dimensions of Organization Structure', in *Administrative Science Quarterly*, Vol. 13 (1968), pp. 65-105.

14. A. Sinclair, 'Approaches to Organisational Culture and Ethics', in *Journal of Business Ethics*, Vol. 12 No. 1 (January 1993), pp. 63-73.

15. J.M. Liedtka, 'Value Congruence: The Interplay of Individual and Organisational Value Systems', in *Journal of Business Ethics*, Vol. 8 No. 4 (1989), pp. 805-15.

16. J. Beyer, 'Ideologies, Values and Decision-Making in Organisation', in J. Starbruck and P. Nystrom, *Handbook of Organisational Design* (New York, NY: Oxford University Press, Vol. 2; 1981), pp. 166-202.

17. *Op. cit.*

18. *Op. cit.*

19. Y. Gabriel, 'Organisations and their Discontents: A Psychoanalytical Contribution to the Study of Organisational Culture', in *Journal of Applied Behavioural Science*, Vol. 27 No. 3 (1991), pp. 318-36.

20. See also G. Morgan, *Images of Organisation* (London, UK: Sage, 1988).

21. F.A. von Hayek, *Law, Legislation and Liberty* (Complete edn; London, UK: Routledge & Kegan Paul, 1982).

22. See H. Haken, 'Can Synergetics be of Use to Management Theory?', in H. Ulrich and G.J.B. Probst (eds.), *Self-Organisation and Management of Social Systems: Insights, Promises, Doubts and Questions* (Berlin, Germany/New York, NY/Tokyo, Japan: Springer Verlag, 1984); G. Morgan, 'Cybernetics and Organization Theory: Epistemology or Technique?', in *Human Relations*, Vol. 35 No. 7 (1982), pp. 521-37.

23. The description of corporate cultures originates in complex systems theory and is similar to some approaches within chaos theory.

24. See R.G. Klimecki and G.J.B. Probst, 'Entstehung und Entwicklung der Unternehmenskultur', in C. Lattmann (ed.), *Die Unternehmenskultur* (Heidelberg, Germany: Physica Verlag, 1990), pp. 41-65.

25. C. Argyris and D. Schön, *Organisational Learning: A Theory of Action Perspective* (Reading, MA: Addison-Wesley, 1978).

26. T. O'Riordan, *Environmentalism* (2nd rev. edn; London, UK: Pion, 1981).

27. B. Everett, *Cluster Analysis* (Oxford, UK: Heinemann Educational Books, 1974), p. 4; C. Chatfield and A.J. Collins, *Introduction to Multivariate Analysis* (London, UK: Chapman & Hall, 1980), ch. 4.

28. See B.G. Tabachnik and L.S. Fidell, *Using Multivariate Statistics* (2nd edn; New York, NY: Harper Collins, 1989), pp. 634-36.

29. *Op. cit.*

30. S.A. Sackmann, 'Uncovering Culture in Organisations', in *Journal of Applied Behavioural Science*, Vol. 27 No. 3 (1991), pp. 295-317.

31. *Op. cit.*

32. P. Nystrom, 'Differences in Moral Values between Corporations', in *Journal of Business Ethics*, Vol. 9 (1990), pp. 971-79.

33. *Op. cit.*

34. See G.J.B. Probst, *Selbst-Organisation: Ordnungsprozesse in Sozialen Systemen aus Ganzheitlicher Sicht* (Zürich, Switzerland: Paul Parey, 1987).

35. See T. Burns and G.M. Stalker, *The Management of Innovation* (2nd edn; London, UK: Tavistock, 1966).

36. See R.K. Turner, 'Environment, Economics and Ethics', in D. Pearce (ed.), *Blueprint 2: Greening the World Economy* (London, UK: Earthscan, 1990); O'Riordan, *op. cit.*

37. 'Cybernetics and Organization Theory', p. 345.

38. *Op. cit.*

39. See March and Simon (1953).

40. H.A. Simon, *The New Science of Management Decision* (Prentice Hall International; Hemel Hempstead, UK: 1977), p. 25.

41. W. Wehrmeyer, 'Ranking Corporate Environmental Programme in the Paper Industry' (Paper presented at the *First Annual Conference on Business Strategy and the Environment*, Leicester, UK: 1–2 September 1992); W. Wehrmeyer, *A Comparative Study of Management Styles and Environmental Performance in Paper Manufacturing Industries* (PhD Thesis; Canterbury, UK: University of Kent, August 1993).

42. 'Cybernetics and Organization Theory', pp. 347, 357-58.

43. See. H. Mintzberg, 'The Case for Corporate Social Responsibility', in *Journal of Business Strategy*, Vol. 4 No. 2 (1983), pp. 3-15.

44. J.K. Galbraith, *The New Industrial State* (London, UK: Hamish Hamilton, 1967).

45. Cf. D. Smith (ed.), *Business and the Environment* (London, UK: Paul Chapman, 1993).

46. Cf. Probst, *op. cit.*; M. Zeleny (ed.) *Autopoiesis: A Theory of Living Organisation* (New York, NY: North Holland, 1981).

47. Cf. W. Wehrmeyer, 'Strategic Issues', in M. Charter (ed.), *Greener Marketing: A Responsible Approach to Business* (Sheffield, UK: Greenleaf Publishing, 1992).

48. 'Cybernetics and Organization Theory'.

49. See C. Argyris, *Strategy, Change and Defensive Routines* (Boston, MA: Pitman, 1985).

50. See, for example, R.M. McNealy, *Making Quality Happen* (London/Glasgow, UK: Chapman & Hall, 1993); P. James, 'Quality and the Environment: From Total Quality Management to Sustainable Quality Management', in *Greener Management International*, No. 6 (April 1994), pp. 62-71.

51. See O'Riordan, *op. cit.*

52. 53. 54. 55. 56. *Op. cit.*

57. L. Klinkers and N. Nelissen, from *Environmental Campaigning: How to Promote Employee Participation in Environmental Policies*, in *Greener Management International*, No. 10 (April 1995), pp 96-109.

58. *Op. cit.*

59. See. W. Wehrmeyer, *Measuring Environmental Business Performance: A Comprehensive Guide* (Cheltenham, UK: Stanley Thornes, 1995).

60. See U. Beck, *Risk Society* (Frankfurt/Main, Germany: Suhrkamp, 1980).

The Role for the Personnel Practitioner in Facilitating Environmental Responsibility in Work Organisations

Tim Hart

*T*HE PROBLEM of our destruction of the natural environment and the difficulty of moving towards a more sustainable relationship within the ecosystem is a fundamental issue requiring urgent attention. The causes of such destructive behaviour are complex and widespread and involve all of our major institutions. This chapter examines the need to change one of these key institutions: the workplace. It specifically focuses upon how the personnel practitioner can contribute to environmental action at work.

■ Paper Recycling, Low-Energy Lightbulbs and All That

While it is true that such limited initiatives will not save the planet— and their significance is probably more symbolic than practical—they do encompass two crucial issues. First they indicate a perception of the need to do something about the damage we are doing to the environment; secondly they involve a change in behaviour compatible with this goal. Changing perceptions and changing behaviour is the bread-and-butter work of personnel practitioners and is central to the achievement of environmental responsibility in work organisations.

■ Changing Perception through a Systems Approach

The benefits of a good systems model to those who are involved in it can be summarised as follows:

> They feel that it makes sense of their experience, of the situation and its context; they can commit themselves to it as a framework around which to co-ordinate their actions; when they do so they find it useful and realistic.[1]

Since the 1950s, when systems theory was imported from the natural and mechanical sciences to be used to develop ways of exploring social phenomena,[2] social scientists have been applying these theoretical concepts to help to explain organisational behaviour. The systems approach is familiar territory to personnel practitioners, and they are ideally placed to foster the adoption of a more complete systems approach to further environmental objectives.

Describing something as a system is partly a subjective process: it is a matter of how one perceives a particular set of circumstances. It can be a powerful way of changing people's perception of the world around them and specifically their relationship within the natural environment.

■ Developing a 'One-System' View

The most common everyday use of a systems approach by personnel practitioners, managers, consultants and academics alike manifests itself in the diagrammatic portrayal of a particular problem, or set of circumstances, through a number of discrete and in some cases overlapping circles. This particular mutation of the Venn diagram can be found scribbled on flipcharts and whiteboards throughout academic and corporate institutions. In its casual construction, it invariably fails to acknowledge the 'universal set' within which everything else operates: that is, the ecosystem. If portrayed at all, the ecosystem is represented as one of a number of systems.

This 'many-systems view' is part of the presentation of the world as discrete and isolated areas of knowledge where highly-specialised and uni-disciplinary approaches predominate. This disintegrated approach, while diminished somewhat in recent years, is still an important factor in shaping our perception. A simple adjustment in this common portrayal could acknowledge the ecosystem as the universal set within which all other constituents are subsystems. This could encourage a change in the prevailing perception which acts as a constraining influence on our ability to relate to the environment. Such an adjustment might help to mitigate the strong anthropocentric perspective which places our species at the centre of the 'universe'.

By viewing the environment as one system (where each subsystem is both connected within its own elements and interconnected with other sub-systems and, therefore, ultimately the whole system) could begin to encourage behaviour that implicitly and explicitly acknowledges these interdependencies instead of behaviour that seemingly ignores them.

■ Work Organisations as Natural Systems

We know that living organisms have a tendency to preserve and re-establish a steady state if allowed to do so: the condition of 'homeostasis'. By conceiving of work organisations in terms of homeostasis, and by encouraging a goal of the maintenance of a steady state, the function of the organisation would be to sustain equilibrium within its environment. This would encourage a perceptual framework very different to the one that prevails today. Such a goal would need to be underwritten by changes in economic objectives, which, at a macro level, would require the subordination of GNP and, at a micro level, the development of wider measures of success than simply profit.

Natural systems have decentralised 'control' mechanisms and are interrelated in complex networks of mutual support. Perceptions of work organisations in these terms would encourage decentralisation of power and replacement of hierarchical control with loosely-knit, flexible and temporary groups bound together in informal mutually-supporting networks: characteristics more suited to the dynamic conditions of today.

If such adjustments in systems thinking can be successfully promulgated, this could act as a catalyst for further developments. Systems thinking could be multi-dimensional: not just recognising the interconnectedness of different subsystems within a current time frame, but also encouraging a recognition of the interconnectedness of subsystems over time.

■ Facilitating Behaviour Change at Work

A systems approach that produces a change in perception provides no guarantee of changes in behaviour; nor is it a prerequisite. Perception may lead to behaviour change. Equally, a change in behaviour may cause, over time, a change in perception, attitude and, eventually, values, so as to reduce any cognitive dissonance caused by the contradictions between thought and action. It is a two-way street, and the sequence in which the ideas have been presented here should not be construed as suggesting any simple linear relationship.

If personnel practitioners are to begin to enable the behavioural adjustment of people within a complex of subsystems, they will need to further develop understanding of the inter-relationships between these different subsystems. They will need to seek out allies, nurture supporters and create networks of problem-solvers willing to act to change the status quo. If this sounds subversive, it is. There is a pressing need to usurp the prevailing hierarchical power structures that are stultifying our ability to adjust to a new set of conditions that would facilitate not the management of the environment, but our continued existence within it.

The kind of work organisation that emerges will be very different from the kind that has evolved from traditional bureaucracies. It will be one where power is diffused throughout and moves according to need and circumstance, but is certainly not centralised permanently at the top of the organisation or among élite groups of specialists. It will be one where traditional vertical and horizontal divisions give way to a looser, more ephemeral organisation structure. It will be an organisation where there are networks across disciplines and within different levels and departments, giving rise to temporary collaborations between groups of people. It will be one that is underpinned by holistic principles and propelled by lateral thinking—adaptable, responsive, flexible organisations, less concerned with status and control and more concerned with bringing the requisite competencies to bear on the complex problems that we face. It will encourage a more integrative, multi-disciplinary approach to problem-solving.

The many rallying cries for organisational change over recent years have met with limited success. One of the reasons for this is the centralisation of power in work organisations and the operation of power in our wider society. The personnel practitioner needs to be willing to seek creative processes that begin to diffuse this power.

■ Leading by Example

Oscar Wilde was attributed as saying: 'What you are screams so loudly in my ears I cannot hear what you are saying.' Personnel practitioners should avoid such recriminations by ensuring that their immediate domain is free of blatant abuses of the environment. There are many ways in which this can be achieved. An audit of the workplace could be undertaken to include all aspects of physical resource and working conditions. Actions such as re-use and recycling of materials, energy conservation, and review of supplier policy could be pursued. Staff travel could be reviewed to minimise car use and encourage the use of public and non-motorised transport. Environmental issues could be promoted through the staff magazine, by staff suggestion schemes, in briefing and brainstorming meetings; by encouraging staff to become involved in community environmental projects. There is a plethora of interventions at this local level. Importantly, such actions help to avoid accusations of double standards when advocating wider adoption of such behaviour. Probably one of the best publications containing a multitude of ideas in the form of easily-accessible checklists is the Winter model.[3]

Of course, any such possibilities need to be considered and assessed in terms of what is feasible at the time, and while such initiatives can be important, the main contribution for personnel practitioners is through their substantive functional role.

■ Setting the Corporate Framework

The mission statement has become a popular means of encapsulating the organisation's purpose and providing a flavour of its values. Many personnel practitioners have the opportunity to influence this document and could do so by the inclusion of an environmental statement. For example:

> We recognise that our activities consume limited natural resources and may harm the environment upon which we all rely for our existence. In all our operations we shall strive to minimise the damage to the environment. This objective is a central goal and one that involves all of us in a process of continuous learning and improvement. We shall seek to enact these intentions through our dealings with all stakeholders and particularly through our personnel policies and practices.

In isolation, such a statement is merely platitudinous but, combined with appropriate and consistent action, it can provide an important foundation from which environmental responsibility can be developed. Apart from its content, the process of constructing the statement is significant in determining its success. It is much better to have a participative process involving dialogue with representatives of all stakeholders than top-down imposition where the statement is presented as a *fait accompli*.

A policy could then be developed setting out in more detail how the general aim of environmental responsibility is to be followed. Such principles need to be translated into behaviour that, eventually, could lead to a culture change so that environmental responsibility permeates everything the organisation does. However, mission statements and policies can only be a small step in achieving the desired behaviour change.

■ Using Standard Performance Interventions

The existing personnel responsibility for health, safety and welfare can provide an ideal opening into environmental matters. Through legislative requirements and the organisation's health and safety policy, the personnel practitioner has many points of intervention. Employee assistance programmes have already seen a broadening of their remit. This could be further developed to include environmental health as a key factor. Counselling on personal health and welfare could extend to education and training in lifestyle to encourage environmentally-benign behaviour. Safety training could include prevention of damage to the environment as well as dealing with personal safety. In many ways, these kinds of changes would be a 'natural' extension of this traditional area and one that could be seen as legitimate for the personnel practitioner to pursue.

Most larger organisations have a sophisticated performance appraisal process in which the environment could feature throughout. Environmental objectives could be included in the performance targets. These can often be expressed quantifiably and could be directly linked to bottom-line performance. Opportunities could be taken to enhance awareness and engender motivation in respect of environmental issues; to identify environmental training needs; to provide information and feedback on the organisation's environmental achievements; and generally to reinforce a culture of environmental responsibility among the employees. (These ideas are explored in more detail in other chapters of this book.) A similar approach could be taken when dealing with peripheral workers such as agencies, contractors and consultants. Remuneration policy, if linked with performance appraisal, could underpin these environmental objectives.

Pay policy could, in addition, stand alone as an incentive for environmentally-responsible behaviour: either as an ongoing pay-performance link or through event-based reward—for example the use of bonuses for suggestions and innovations.

Resourcing policy could be adjusted to give priority to labour supply from the local catchment area and thereby minimise travel-to-work distances and engender a closer sense of community. This in turn could foster among the workforce more concern and involvement in local environmental issues. It would help to reduce the void between work and home, and so potentially soften the boundaries and lead to congruent behaviour in both areas. If people were encouraged to behave in an environmentally-responsible manner at work, then they might do so at home as well. Positive action programmes could be used in recruitment. We should see adverts stating that:

> applications are particularly welcome from environmentally-responsible individuals as this group is under-represented in our workforce.

Training policy can be infused with environmental issues at every level. There is, of course, a need to provide knowledge, awareness and an understanding of how to adhere to the policy together with practical skills to carry it out. In addition, the environment can be assimilated into most organisational training events, either by inclusion of explicit content or implicitly by the setting and manner in which the training is carried out. For example, The Body Shop reviewed its training policy and introduced environmental dimensions to projects such as its outward bound leadership programme by making the actual task one of conservation. It has also included environmental elements into its team-building.[4]

Apart from internal training policy, personnel practitioners have the opportunity to influence wider educational practices where their organisations are involved in sponsoring students at educational establishments. This is compatible with the proposals of the Toyne report, which assessed the strengths and weaknesses of current environmental provision in further and higher education. One of its key recommendations was that:

> all professional institutions should seriously assess...the place of environmental issues within those Higher Educational courses for which they control or influence the curricula, and take action to promote the appropriate changes...based on adequate consultation.[5]

As important clients of educational establishments, personnel practitioners can ensure that they are part of this consultation process.

Some organisations have created mechanisms through their grievance procedures that allow employees to report anonymously unethical practices to senior management. In the UK, there are only two companies known to operate internal 'whistle-blowing' telephone lines: the National Westminster Bank and Lucas Aerospace.[6] It is more commonplace in the USA, where 'whistle-blowing' involves employees reporting their organisations to the relevant authorities and where such action is often protected by law. This practice could become more widespread and incorporate environmental misdemeanours. Reciprocal arrangements through disciplinary procedures could be introduced to allow employers to take action against their employees.

In employee relations, it could be demonstrated that environmental issues are a legitimate part of the agenda in collective and individual bargaining. Employee communications could inform and involve employees in environmental issues: in job design, equal opportunities, contracts of employment, in fact in every area of activity in which personnel practitioners are involved, there is an opportunity to raise the environmental profile.

■ An Organisational Development Approach

While the functional interventions mentioned above potentially have a beneficial effect, and, collectively they may have a significant effect, they are unlikely to have a decisive or enduring impact upon the goal of environmental responsibility if left to stand alone. They are the classical instruments of organisational control. If applied prescriptively, they will tend to reinforce the prevailing centralised power hierarchy and its associated characteristics of role specialisation and operational segmentation that produces the kind of inflexibility that has been so damaging to the efforts to achieve organisational change. A less content-driven, less prescriptive approach is called for. While there are no easy answers, organisational development (OD) can help set the appropriate conditions. By focusing upon *processes*, it can help to develop within people the capacity to change—not only to accept change, but rather to initiate it in a continually-adaptive process to meet new circumstances as they arise.

OD has grown from the foundations of the human relations school in the 1920s. It has sought to encourage work to be viewed in a wider social context and to treat people as complete human beings, rather than just cogs in the machine.[7] It acknowledges that individuals themselves have open-system characteristics and relate to each other and to organisations in ways that are appropriate to such systems.

Many organisations have sought ways of changing to meet current circumstances. One kind of response has been to lumber from one change programme to another using traditional methods of structure and task redefinition, implemented through conventional command and control mechanisms. Invariably, when the organisation has reached its original goal, the goalposts have moved and another strategy has to be devised, followed by another and another. Not surprisingly, against this backcloth of strategic failure, organisations are seeking a different model within which to achieve change—a model that produces a continuing capability to adapt. OD is such a model.

OD requires a focus upon process and, in consequence, a reduction in the preoccupation with content. As Marshall McLuhan said, 'the medium is the message'.[8] Content-driven interventions perpetuate the outdated aspects of Kurt Lewin's conception of change: that of unfreezing and refreezing, with its implicit rigidity and assumptions of periods of stability.[9] Intervening at the level of task and structure—or engaging in authoritarian attempts to manipulate the soft subsystems such as culture—perpetuate the existence of a model that only partially and temporarily functions, whereas focusing upon process helps to set conditions in which suitable behaviour can emerge to fit the prevailing circumstances at the time—whatever these may be. Any resultant cultural shift can then be experienced as an emergent, rather than imposed, change.

The dominance of rationality to the exclusion of other dimensions of people's psychology, the preoccupation with task efficiency and the reductionist approach to human motivation, all contribute to work being an alienating experience for most people. This alienation denies free expression of feelings and emotions, and reduces work to an instrumental commitment and a calculative contribution. If OD could be successfully applied so that the experience of work was based on an holistic approach that liberated people to make a fuller and unconstrained contribution, then this would sanction behaviour that emanated from more than simply instrumental considerations. Behaviour that was more encompassing would involve expression of the latent concerns that most people have about the deteriorating condition of the natural environment. OD involves people in taking on new values and new behaviour more relevant to their own needs, to that of the workplace upon which they depend, and, in consequence, to the environment, upon which everything depends.

By failing to cater for the 'whole person', work organisations are becoming an anachronism. The trends in the broader society are gradually moving towards an holistic approach. Certainly, the environmental movement advocates this: some aspects of politics and economics foster holistic principles. Many of the professions are beginning to reduce the boundaries surrounding their particular disciplines. Yet work organisations still expect people to leave at the gate all the aspects of their humanity that are not seen as relevant to the productive process.

The promotion of an holistic approach in dealing with people at work requires the development of a different set of assumptions within a full systems model.

Figure 1 categorises management assumptions about employees according to whether these assumptions are 'regressive' or 'progressive'. While there have been encouraging signs of change in a number of organisations, the regressive assumptions are still dominant in most cases. Employees are treated as children, their actions are carefully monitored and controlled. They are fed edited and limited information and subjected to an increasingly sophisticated array of performance devices in an effort to engender desired behaviour. This enforced regime will always have a counter-productive effect upon the aim of environmental responsibility. It excludes essential aspects of people's humanity and thereby denies them the opportunity to relate to the environment in a caring and responsible way.

Those organisations that have tried to apply progressive assumptions have generally done so through task and structural changes. However, decentralisation of operations and functions is insufficient without the concomitant devolvement of power. Empowerment needs to include not just discretion over how the tasks are carried out to achieve particular goals, but also a say in what the goals are. Structures should be transitory to accommodate new problem-solving processes, involving temporary collaboration

Regressive Assumptions

- Employees are like children and need to be treated accordingly.
- Employees need to be carefully controlled to achieve desired outputs.
- Employees readily concede to subordinate relationships.
- Employee communications should be rational, expedient and mainly top-down.
- Employees need incentives to learn and develop.
- Employees require external stimuli to be motivated to apply their skills.
- Employees' commitment has to be managed through structure and performance techniques.
- Employees are unconcerned about how their work affects the environment.

Progressive Assumptions

- Employees prefer to be treated as adults.
- Employees want to control their own work and exercise personal discretion over what and how they contribute.
- Employees prefer to participate in decisions that affect them.
- Employees are entitled to know what is going on and should be permitted to communicate feelings and emotions as well as 'harder' cognitive aspects.
- Employees are intrinsically motivated towards growth and development.
- Employees naturally want to use their skills and abilities to solve problems.
- Employees will demonstrate commitment to what they believe is important and where they are given a choice.
- Employees' natural concern for the environment will emerge if permitted to do so.

Figure 1: *Environmental Responsiblity*

between individuals and groups. The core-periphery notion of labour supply—which seeks to protect the inner sanctum of employees from the ravages of the dynamics of the outside world and promotes the illusion of stability—would need to be set aside in favour of a more fluid and transient workforce. Contractual arrangements, remuneration policy and other personnel practices would have to be adjusted. Social policy would need to be devised to provide economic security under such new arrangements.

Progressive communications assume that people are entitled to know what is going on in the organisation. They should be allowed to communicate fully with each other and this communication should include 'soft conditions', such as emotions and feelings as well as 'harder' cognitive aspects of rationality. The more communication can become genuinely participative, the less susceptible members of the organisation are to manipulative techniques. This would create greater openness in general and promote notions of interdependency at the level of the work group and through all other levels—including interdependency within the ecosystem itself.

The progressive assumption that people want to learn is not just concerned with knowledge, but also learning new perceptions, attitudes and values. However, such things cannot be taught: they need to emerge through interaction to form new normative patterns of behaviour. Such learning requires openness: a willingness to exchange ideas and feelings and to deal with the conflict that may be generated. The learning process can become endemic in the organisation only if people feel safe to engage in the kind of interaction that facilitates learning.

The personnel practitioner would need to support a liberalisation of conditions and help to deal with the resultant implications. It would involve a substantially different kind of workplace. The mechanisms of intervention are those of the process consultant, and the original work of Edgar Schein and others elaborates on the skills involved in this role.[10] A powerful rationale for the central involvement of personnel practitioners is their existing expertise in the exercise of these process consultancy skills.

■ A Return to Professionalism

While the individual personnel practitioner can work as a process consultant, using such techniques as systems theory and organisational development, there are changes needed in the wider context of personnel management itself if such an environmental role is to be fully realised.

Through the influence of Human Resource Management (HRM), the personnel function has, in recent years, shifted direction from that of an emerging profession and instead has sought closer allegiance with management. It has done so in the quest for power and to enhance its effectiveness by reducing the traditional ambivalence of the function. It has used its expertise to pursue managerial goals of profitability and efficiency through maximising labour utility. As a result, it has become a natural ally to the economic system, which is a significant force in perpetuating our destruction of the environment. HRM, in unequivocally supporting managerial goals, places the personnel function in an amoral position—one unconcerned with either demonstrating or encouraging behaviour that emanates from a moral base. Without a value system there can be neither claims to professionalism nor the effective pursuit of OD principles in facilitating change towards environmental responsibility.

At the core of the notion of a profession is that the group should underpin its behaviour with a set of values: an ethical code of conduct that purports to serve the 'public good'. At times, this will involve actions that conflict with managerial interests. Traditional personnel management was prepared to wrestle with this dilemma. HRM has no such pretensions. Torrington and Hall sum up the position:

> ...we can suggest that personnel management potentially can have the independence and standing and authority of a profession, but human resources management cannot, as it is inevitably an integral part of general management and the job holder becomes a manager first and a personnel specialist second.[11]

This increasingly unprofessional approach to the personnel function and its consequential amoral stance makes it difficult to perform the kind of environmental role that has been argued here. The environmental position has to be underpinned by a set of values that is anathema to HRM.[12]

While the shift to HRM was understandable for a number of reasons, it must only be a temporary phenomenon. For personnel to fulfil a catalytic role in developing behaviour towards environmental responsibility, there will need to be a return to the tolerance of an ambivalent role and the development of a set of professional standards that emanate from a moral base. This will require an acceptance by personnel practitioners that their power will derive from a professional rather than a managerial source.

While a return to the pursuit of values and an ethical code of conduct under a professional guise would be a beneficial move, not all attributes of professionalism would have such a welcome effect. Overall, the way in which professional knowledge is compartmentalised works against the nurturing of any environmental responsibility. This disintegrating effect denies the essential interdependency of the ecosystem and the requirement of an integrated response in addressing our relationship within it. While there have been minor moves to break down some of the traditional barriers of specialisms to conceive a more eclectic approach to problem-solving, there are still very strong vested interests in preserving 'professional purity'. In advocating 'professional interventions' in pursuance of environmental goals, these strong partisan characteristics of professions need to be combated.

■ A Need for a New Paradigm

Of course, the workplace is just one of the major institutions that has to change if we are to develop a new way of relating to the environment.

Ultimately, there will need to be a change in the paradigm itself—a move away from the dominance of narrowly-conceived market economics and its promise of endless growth in consumerism. There will need to be an extinguishing of the myopia of the professions; a liberalisation of democracy towards more participation and away from over-reliance on representative mechanisms; a transformation in the judiciary, in education, in government, in the church—in fact in every major institution in society. There needs to be the development of a common perception of the problem and general agreement of the kind of behaviour needed to ameliorate it. This process of institutional change will be both driven by, and be an influence upon, the development of a new set of values based on sustainability. We need to move at a rate compatible with the urgency of the situation.

The *approach* to change itself needs to change. We cannot afford to be weighed down by the rigidity of compartmentalised thought, which produces fragmented action. We need to challenge the conventions that lead us to rely upon scientific and technological solutions to what are more complex issues involving social, spiritual and ecological dimensions. There is a need to move away from the stultifying effect of the dominance of individual professions; to break down the barriers between accounting and philosophy, between economics and sociology, and between politics and religion. By developing such interlocking relationships, we have the chance to produce a more eclectic approach—one that recognises that such complex problems are not solvable through conventional linear thinking.

What is essential is that we make a start on the transformation in the workplace now. In so doing, we may avoid the necessity for more coercive measures in the future. The longer we ignore the need to change this most vital institution, the more likely that society in general will fail to make the necessary transformation. The consequences of failure will probably be a fundamental loss of freedom and quality of life in the panic that ensues.

■ Notes

1. R. Carter, *et al.*, *Systems Management and Change* (London, UK: Harper & Row, 1984).

2. See, for example, J.T. Dunlop, *Industrial Relations Systems* (London, UK: Holt, Reinhart & Winston, 1958); H.A. Simon, *Models of Man* (London, UK: Wiley, 1957).

3. See G. Winter, *Blueprint for Green Management: Creating Your Company's Own Environmental Action Plan* (London, UK: McGraw-Hill, 1995).

4. Cited in S. Anthony, 'Environmental Training Needs Analysis', in *Training Officer*, Vol. 29 No. 9 (November 1993), pp. 272-73.

5. P. Toyne, 'Environmental Responsibility: An Agenda for Further and Higher Eduction' (Report of a Committee appointed by the Department of Education and the Welsh Office; London, UK: HMSO, 1993).

6. Cited in J. Pickard, 'Prepare to Make a Moral Judgement', in *People Management*, May 1995, p. 24.

7. See, for example, W.L. French and C.H. Bell, *Organisation Development* (London, UK: Prentice Hall International, 1990); J. Swieringa and A. Wierdsma, *Becoming a Learning Organisation* (Reading, MA: Addison-Wesley, 1992).

8. Marshall McLuhan's ideas are discussed in N. Postman and C. Weingartner, *Teaching as a Subversive Activity* (Harmondsworth, UK: Penguin, 1969), ch. 2.

9. Originally described in K. Lewin, 'Frontiers in Group Dynamics: Concept, Method and Reality in Social Science: Social Equilibria and Social Change', in *Human Relations*, Vol. 1 (1967), pp. 5-41.

10. See, for example, E. Schein, *Process Consultation. Volume 2: Lessons for Managers and Consultants* (Reading, MA: Addison-Wesley, 1988); *idem, Process Consultation. Volume 1: Its Role in Organisational Development* (2nd edn; Reading, MA: Addison-Wesley, 1988).

11. D. Torrington and L. Hall, *Personnel Management: A New Approach* (London, UK: Prentice-Hall, 1991).

12. For a more detailed account of the destructive influence of HRM, see T.J. Hart, 'Human Resource Management: Time to Exorcise the Militant Tendency', in *Employee Relations*, Vol. 15 No. 3 (1993), pp. 29-36; and for some counter-arguments, see D. Torrington, 'How Dangerous is Human Resource Management? A Reply to Tim Hart,' in *Employee Relations*, Vol. 15 No. 5 (1993), pp. 40-54.

⑨

Women, Environmental Management and Human Resources Management

Angela Mawle

WITHIN THE environmental NGO sector, an all-female working environment can pose challenges and complexities of human resource management, which range, daily, from the exciting to the destabilising. The uniqueness of this working environment is largely a result of a combination of factors, some of which are common to all voluntary-based organisations and others that arise from its focus upon women and the environment. These can be identified as:

- Volunteers forming the greater part of the everyday working group
- Scarce and diminishing financial resources, leading to inadequate infrastructural resources, materials, etc.
- Women as managers
- Feminist and ecofeminist principles and philosophy
- Project-oriented and ad-hoc work schedules

Because these factors play so significant a role in determining the success or failure of the human resource management within the organisation, they are examined in greater detail below and will be referred to as a background for the specific situation described in the later sections of this chapter

◼ Volunteers

Individuals decide to engage in voluntary work for widely differing reasons. Some are eager to fill a potential gap in their CV with a meaningful and structured work experience which will lead to the acquisition or improvement of skills. Others seek the opportunity to achieve a change in career direction by gaining experience in the chosen field and moving on to paid employment within that sector later. Recent graduates often welcome the chance to apply their academically-based knowledge within a practical setting, while women returners generally find the voluntary sector offers a comparatively non-threatening work environment in which they can build up both skills and confidence with which to enter the marketplace. Additionally, there are volunteers who prefer the lifestyle and ethos to that of a legally-enforceable, contractually-based relationship. Such individuals express the opinion that they enjoy the flexibility of volunteer hours and commitment and have little or no desire to work within a formalised and controlled framework.

■ Scarce and Diminishing Financial Resources

Ever-increasing numbers of voluntary organisations are in life-and-death pursuit of funds from contracting and closely-guarded revenue sources. The greatest destabilising effect that this has, in management terms, is the inability to core-fund such vital posts as administration and human resource management. Furthermore, the insecurity that inadequate funding promulgates throughout the organisation, in terms of ability to continue to fight the cause and finance the vision, can lead to tensions and failures of confidence which are the natural breeding grounds of distrust and intrigue. Add to this the day-to-day necessity of vying for the shared use of aged IT systems and other limited resources, and it becomes self-evident that huge strains can be placed upon staff relations. Financial constraints inevitably limit the physical resources available, including desks and floorspace.

An all-important sense of belonging is dependent on the feeling of value derived from access to essential resources and personal space. Meting out these scarce resources calls for tact, time and understanding, all of which may well be in short supply in the absence of infrastructure posts specifically focused on these management areas. The sense of value implicit in having rightful access to these essential resources is especially important to volunteers who may be suffering problems with confidence and self-esteem and who have no monetary value by which to define their worth. Erosion of self-esteem can be further exacerbated by ill-defined and under-resourced personnel management, which invariably leads to the stronger personalities within the group gaining unequal access to the limited facilities available.

■ Women Managers

Much has been written about the different personal qualities that male and female managers bring to their jobs. Such differences are usually attributed to dissimilarities in the early socialisation experiences of females and males that form the foundations of expectations for adult working life and relationships.[1] However, dispute exists as to whether these socialisation experiences necessarily lead to differences between male and female managers. It is argued that women who succeed in the management role reject their gender stereotype and identify with the masculine norm. Furthermore, a team of researchers at the US-based Center for Creative Leadership have concluded that 'The basis for claiming differences between executive women and executive men—whether used to exclude or encourage women into these ranks—is suspect at best'.[2]

Others claim that the early socialisation process results in male and female managers conforming to gender stereotypes and behaving accordingly in the management role. Margaret Hennig and Anne Jardin have concluded that men are advantaged managerially by the early socialisation experiences and 'bring to the management setting a clearer stronger and more definite understanding of where they see themselves going, what they will have to do, how they will have to act, and what they must take into account if they are to achieve the objectives they set for themselves'.[3] Carole Beale, Professor of Psychology at the University of Massachusetts, has undertaken extensive studies into the gender-based socialisation of young children, and concludes: 'Even if parents are very careful, the way girls and boys are brought up means that girls will suffer a disadvantage which stays with them throughout their life.'[4] On International Women's Day, March 1995, we learned that the total women on the boards of major British companies is 3.72%; that women make up just 2.8% of senior managers and 9.8% of managers. What is more, women managers earn 16% less than their male counterparts.[5]

Nevertheless, Rosener[6] has identified an 'interactive leadership' associated with women managers which has arisen specifically from women's shared experience as women. This interactive leadership draws upon qualities generally considered to be 'feminine' and is characterised by the demonstration of more positive interactions with subordinates, by the encouragement of participation, by sharing power and information and by stimulating excitement about work. This application of femininity is thought by some to be essential in fully developing the 'people potential' in today's workplace.[7]

Loden's work has identified a resentment of autocratic management practices among today's workers which, together with changes in the nature of the global economy could, if ignored, lead to a crisis within corporate America. She concludes that organisations must make greater use of the feminine leadership model, relying on team structures and collaborative decision-making rather than a masculine leadership model that relies on hierarchical structures and autocratic decision-making.

Of further interest, in the context of this chapter, are the findings of Dobbins,[8] who distinguishes different responses to poor performers by male and female leaders. In laboratory studies, male leaders' responses were based more on a norm of equity. They were inclined to punish subordinates who performed poorly because of lack of effort and to provide extra training to subordinates who performed poorly because of lack of ability. In contrast, female leaders responses were based more on a norm of equality. That is, they appeared not to discriminate between the two categories (lack of effort; inability), but were more likely to punish or train subordinates who performed poorly, regardless of whether the poor performance was attributable to lack of effort or lack of ability. No analysis appears to have been made of likely reasons for this lack of discrimination, although presumably it could be associated with a reluctance to acknowledge openly negative attributes within subordinates. However, the research did identify that female leaders tended to be less punitive and more supportive of *female* subordinates.

■ Project-Oriented and Ad-Hoc Work Schedules

The difficulties in obtaining core funding demand that every effort is put into seeking the sponsorship of project work that can support a percentage of administrative costs. Commonly, projects are based around the appointment of a key worker with specific and well-defined tasks relating to the achievement of measurable targets and an overall project aim. Thus opportunities arise for the advertising and recruitment of a paid worker who might or might not be drawn from the current stock of volunteers. What is more, because the project has attracted external funding and the organisation is accountable to the funders, there is a very real prospect that other work within the organisation will be subordinated to the demands of the project. Thus the creation of a paid post and the apparent priorities imposed by the project can lead to a serious imbalance within the organisation, largely resulting from a perceived de-valuing of unpaid members of staff and the funded work taking precedence over other campaign and research issues.

The need for constant exposure to the media (in order to maintain a high public profile and to exploit the consequent funding opportunities) can also result in sudden and dramatic changes of emphasis in the work undertaken by the organisation. This imposes severe pressure on the staff and again can result in the temporary abandonment of any current work that is not the subject of media interest. This of course can lead to resentment and loss of self-esteem in staff who are not directly associated with the high-profile activity.

■ Aspects of a Feminist Approach to Management

■ Feminism

Feminism has many definitions, but common to them all is that feminism must consistently try to change the sociopolitical, economic and cultural contexts that bring about systematic harm or disadvantage to women.[9] Feminism values mutuality and interdependence, inclusion and co-operation, nurturance and support, participation and self-determination, empowerment and personal and collective transformation.[10] Feminist *practice* emphasises connectiveness, co-operation and mutuality over separativeness, competition and individual success. It aims to produce conditions that benefit women and other out-group members.

A focus on co-operation cannot mean an absence of difference, conflict, competition or hierarchy. Rather it means a de-emphasis on winning and losing, status differences and invidious comparisons. Members of the team are encouraged to pursue excellence and personal fulfilment for the sake of their growth and development, rather than competitively seek to achieve the highest ranking among colleagues.

Co-operative management encourages competitiveness only through the growth and success of the whole organisation, not through the individuals working within it. Collaborative leadership focuses on achieving conflict resolution within organisations through strategies of collaborative negotiation.

Becoming fashionable is the notion of a 'web', or circle of relationships replacing the concept of the traditional hierarchy. A web of concentric circles around the director gives employees a sense of connectedness without the negative feelings associated with comparative hierarchical standing and worth. A change of job within the organisation means a change to a different locus on the circle—not a promotion or demotion in perceived hierarchical terms.[11] An extension of this principle is the active promotion of democracy and participation within the workplace. Self-governance and freedom of speech are basic tenets of democracy, as is the right to dissent without incurring the risk of retaliation or punishment. Feminist managers are under obligation to exercise authority carefully and to share information resources and opportunities.

Feminism encourages managers to have a 'hierarchical-up' focus, where 'superiors' are judged by how well they use authority to direct, support and facilitate the work of their 'subordinates'. Feminist managers should nurture and care for their staff, acknowledging them as men and women with spouses and dependent children, with obligations and lives that extend beyond their work.

Ecofeminism

The term 'ecofeminism', first coined in 1974 by Françoise d'Eaubonne, developed as a critical philosophical and social movement within North America and Australia and refers to a diverse range of women's environmental activities. It arose from what had hitherto been two different social movements—the environmental movement and the women's movement—and, within the latter, draws especially upon the women's peace and spirituality movements.[12] This movement straddles both mainstream religious traditions as well as new religions or faiths, such as neopaganism. Its aim is to develop a new and inclusive religious and spiritual practice.

Ecofeminists believe that the current state of the global environment is a direct result of belief systems and practices that are predicated upon the dominance and exploitation of each other and of the Earth. Patriarchy is seen to be the root of this destructive set of relationships, and ecofeminism seeks to expose and analyse this underlying philosophy. It aims to achieve a holistic harmony by creating or re-instating belief systems that will nurture and protect the planet. Ecofeminists wish to reconstruct a new understanding of the place of human beings within the natural world, and, in particular, to situate women, nature and men in a more balanced relationship with each other.

Eisler[13] has identified a 'partnership society' which is 'a way of organising human relations in which beginning with the most fundamental differences in our species—the difference between female and male—diversity is *not* equated with inferiority or superiority.' Diamond and Orenstein[14] state that ecofeminists 'consciously create new cultures that would embrace and honour the values of caretaking and nurturing—cultures that would not perpetuate the dichotomy by raising nature over culture or by raising women over men. Rather they affirmed and celebrated the embeddedness of all the Earth's people in the multiple webs and cycles of life.'

Another fundamental tenet of ecofeminist belief is the connectedness to the Goddess. Goddess cultures dominated pre-history where ancient traditions revered the natural cycles and where the Earth was held as sacred. Starhawk[15] suggests that 'The imagery of the Goddess...can become doorways leading out of the patriarchal cultures, channels for the powers we need to transform ourselves, our visions, our stories...'; and:

> Ecofeminism challenges all relations of domination. Its goal is not just to change who wields power, but to transform the structure of power itself. When the spirit is imminent, when each of us is the Goddess, is God, we have an inalienable right to be here and to be alive. We have a value that can't be taken

away from us that doesn't have to be earned, that doesn't have to be acquired. That kind of value is central to the change we want to create. That's the spell we want to cast.[16]

The acknowledgement of the Goddess and the connectedness of everything within and through Nature is the spiritual wellspring of ecofeminism, which sees environmental degradation as the direct consequence of the world's enslavement to science and technology. Humanity has become separated from Nature, with the Western religions identifying with a deity in whose image we are deemed to be uniquely made and which proclaims dominion over the natural world.

■ *Environmental Management?*

The heading of this chapter and the context in which it is read might lead the reader to construe that there is a practised form of management that conforms to 'environmental' principles. In terms of physical resource use and management, there is a definite trend within commerce and industry to devise corporate environmental policies and to implement environmental management systems. However, these are almost exclusively focused on the reduction of environmental impacts, the conservation of resources and the minimisation of waste within corporate activities. If employees are included in this strategy, it is usually only in terms of their participation in the operational process, e.g. 'Employees will be trained to enhance their understanding of environmental policies and to promote excellence in job performance and all environmental matters';[17] and 'Employees are generating innovative solutions which are creating competitive and economic advantage. To integrate green performance, environmental objectives are being set for employees against which they are being evaluated.'[18]

Organisations such as The Body Shop, however, have demonstrated that a serious commitment to the implementation of environmental management in the conventional sense can lead to the development of a human resource management philosophy that attempts to value and measure 'stakeholder' input. For this reason, the company is in the process of establishing social audit systems that more fully involve both employees and the community in influencing corporate operations.

Within the NGO sector, there are certainly examples where equity and egalitarianism is promoted as the underlying philosophy intended to frame and inform all organisational policies and practices, particularly those governing human resource management. However, many larger environmental NGOs generally operate according to the traditional management model.

■ Managing the Environmental NGO

Feminists and ecofeminists have a natural distrust of any terminology such as 'management' or 'control'—hence the substitution of 'co-ordination' for what must remain a function of taking responsibility for, and therefore to some extent, power over, issues of financial and human resource management. Co-ordination or management can be seen as representing a balancing informing function that facilitates and takes responsibility for the smooth running and operation of a project or venture and, as such, fits well with the concept of the web previously described. Leadership as such is not recognised as a necessary quality. Rather, the manager or co-ordinator is expected to empower such that the realisation of the potential of the self gives rise to the fulfilment of organisational needs and goals.

However, such skilled personnel and resource management requires levels of understanding and experience that are not readily available to underfunded and overstretched NGOs. Within a corporate situation, even to operate traditional hierarchical systems, high levels of resources are invested in creating teams of professionally-trained and regularly-updated human resource managers to ensure the smooth running of the organisation. Yet within the NGO, struggling to aspire to the ideal of consensual and interactive leadership that drives and sustains the web, it often falls to the Director and maybe one or two other members of staff to nourish and preserve the wellbeing of the group.

Inevitably, this same small core of people are charged with the financial management of the organisation as well as with maintaining the public image such that adequate funds are attracted and appropriately discharged to fuel and develop the vision. 'Vision' is an appropriate term, for most people are attracted to environmental NGOs for the opportunity they offer to work towards protecting the planet and ensuring a harmonious and holistic future. Women are attracted to working in an all-female environment in the belief that they can achieve a better way of working together and develop systems and relationships that can be an example to the world. If these women are feminists or ecofeminists, they will also be looking for a radicalising of the workplace and the world at large, and will consciously seek fulfilment of these ideals within the working environment.

So we have a potent and dynamic mix of motivated and often idealistic people who are joined together by a generalised common aim, but who often bring with them widely differing sets of expectations and ideologies which they anticipate will be satisfied through their connection with their chosen organisation.

Motivation, commitment and zeal within the working group are powerful combinations and require exceptionally skilled management to: (i) maximise fulfilment of the realisable; and (ii) minimise the disillusion that is the inevitable accompaniment of the pursuit of ideals. Furthermore, such motivated and inspired individuals can be very driven and determined, often overshadowing less forceful colleagues who can visibly diminish in such a presence. If these strong individuals gather together over a particular issue, and inadequate systems are in place to counter a domination of the overall group, then serious imbalances can occur.

Here we need to analyse the functioning of the web. Caring, nurturing and supportive human resource management can only operate within a web dynamic if there are no blockages or distortions around the circuit. The web must be predicated on a mutuality and trust between all of those involved. Essentially, the web represents a distribution or sharing of power, and its smooth and empowering operation is dependent upon the fair and honest use of such power. If abuses do occur, then they are not immediately apparent, as is the case within the hierarchical system, and can even masquerade as apparently genuine attempts to open up or question the validity or integrity of the system.

Furthermore, the commitment to democratic processes dictates that all dissent should be fully acknowledged and explored, which can lead to serious disruptions in the functioning of the web and therefore, by definition, the organisation. Add to this the presence of a woman manager, fully committed to participative and collaborative management, attempting to resolve the issues at the same time as handling overall administration and public relations, and it is obvious that chaos will soon ensue.

The web has to respond to yet further demands in an ecofeminist environment. Spirituality and the holistic development of the organisation is a sacred trust espoused by all, but specifically significant to the ardent ecofeminist. It finds particular expression in the incorporation of ritual within the operation of the web. Ritual is defined by Starhawk[19] as '...the way culture enacts and affirms its values'. She goes on to describe how ritual '...can become free space, a hole torn in the fabric of domination...we stand one step beyond the institution's control...And so the everyday changes, deepens, until the sacred, like an underground stream wears away control from below.' A similar approach is taken by Wehrmeyer and Parker in this book (chapter 7), who argue that corporate cultures have a powerful yet tacit influence on decision-making and environmental performance. Thus, if the perception of the sacred is shared by the whole and is common to each member of the web, then there can be a mutual challenge to external systems and power structures.

If however, the perception is shared by only a few within the web, then it can be argued that it is the web or organisation itself that is threatened. For those few can, if they feel the sacred to be under threat, challenge the control of the organisation itself.

The above features are obviously related to an all-female environmental NGO, but we have to add to these those specific circumstances encountered by all voluntary sector organisations.

In human resource management terms, problems usually occur around the ability to recruit volunteers with the skills mix and experience necessary to ensure a fair and equal distribution of the workload. Paid posts are normally project-related or of a very specific and tightly-defined administrative function, which dictates that all other positions are staffed by volunteers. Continuity of commitment in an economic climate in which the need for paid work is an immediate and undeniable imperative can entail the sudden and unpredicted loss of key workers and hence major holes in workplans.

Furthermore, the NGO cannot normally offer a career structure, and, once voluntary staff are trained and experienced, it is inevitable, and arguably desirable, that they seek paid employment elsewhere. Thus their skills and expertise are lost both to the organisation and to their work colleagues who would benefit from the 'in-service' training that could be developed around them. Some volunteers, with personal incomes or understanding partners, are able to offer a form of long-term commitment. However, this can mean that presence in a post can be a question of personal resourcing rather than suitability for the job.

Of course, personal development programmes for volunteers and other staff are of a first priority, ensuring as they do that opportunities exist for career progression and growth of the individual. However, the maintenance and development of such programmes is uniquely difficult to sustain where human and physical resources are under constant pressure.

A further consideration must be 'Who nurtures the nurturers?' Basically, whether one is at the centre of the web or the top of a hierarchy, it is essential that the systems of nurture and care should resource at every level. Energies of goodwill and consideration should flow between everyone involved in caring for and developing the organisation. However, NGOs are usually 'managed' by Boards of Trustees or Directors, and there is no guarantee that the individuals making up these boards see themselves as responsible for the active and responsible human resource management of those accountable to them.

■ Conclusion

Throughout this chapter we have looked at the some of the unique factors influencing women as human resource managers in the 'environmental' setting as well as attempting to assess 'environmental management' as it is currently practised.

A basic tenet underlying both feminist and ecofeminist philosophy is the emphasis on 'connectedness' and 'interdependence'. Furthermore, the science of ecology is described as 'the study of organisms and their environment—and the inter-relationship between them'.[20] Maurice Strong, Secretary General to the UN Conference on Environment and Development, exhorted the world's governments and citizens to acknowledge that '...A new world order, as we move into the 21st century, must unite us all in a global partnership—which always recognises and respects the transcending sovereignty of nature, of our only one Earth.'[21]

Thus recognising the critical importance of 'connectedness', 'interdependence', 'inter-relationship' and 'partnership' appears to be fundamental to any strategy aimed at achieving global health and harmony. Consequently, it could be argued that management systems that conform to these principles should be implemented *de facto* within the 'environmental' organisation. The concept of the 'web', as discussed earlier, is key to both ecofeminist and feminist philosophy and again is mirrored in ecological terms: 'the central significance of webs is derived from the fact that the links between species are often easily identified and the resultant trophic scaffolding provides a tempting descriptor of community structure.'[22]

The web, as described for organisational management purposes, does seem to offer a model for operating an open system that places equal value and recognition on each individual contribution, and where information and decision-making is shared throughout the system. However, any system such as this is dependent upon an ability to distribute power among the individuals making up the web. Such power is usually manifested in the form of greater access by one or more individuals making up the web to knowledge, resources, experience, etc., all of which have invariably been hard fought for in a harsh external and male-dominated world.

Moreover, because of its strong association with notions of patriarchy, feminists have great difficulty in acknowledging the concept of power— hence, nowhere is the true nature and just application of power fully addressed. Therefore, although in principle the feminist or ecofeminist management model offers a vision of true 'environmental' management, it is difficult to see how such an approach can function holistically, isolated as it will be, within a social and economic system that positively fosters competition and individuality and where success and power is measured in monetary terms.

Furthermore, a feminist management approach requires an in-depth understanding of the complex and subtle interplay between many psychological and sociological variables and demands a degree of sophistication in application that is very rarely available to the overstretched management of the small and under-resourced NGO. Nevertheless, it is just these small NGOs who, because of their freedom from hierarchy and tradition, together with an inbuilt vision of change, are in a position to explore and develop the concept. Conversely, the large corporation, replete with human resource managers, training budgets and staff development programmes, are bound by hierarchical systems and company procedures that preclude any real exploration of new philosophies of management. The old system thus replicates itself through time and perpetuates the very hierarchy that the feminist management approach seeks to change. Thus we have small organisations who can initiate new and vitally important ideas, such as those associated with feminist management, but who are doomed to fail in their application because of lack of competencies and resources; and the large well-resourced organisation, often seriously in need of new approaches to management, deliberately avoiding the resourcing of such ideas.

Clearly, to succeed in achieving a just and humane society that nurtures and protects our living environment, humankind must acquire a unity of purpose and effort which can develop only when we fully acknowledge the interdependence between both ourselves and the ecosystems of the Earth on which we depend. It seems of paramount importance, therefore, that environmentally-based organisations should seek to develop systems of management based on these same principles, leading by example as we move towards a 21st century marked by a society in harmony with itself and the natural environment.

■ *Notes*

1. See Gary N. Powell, 'Managing People', in *Women and Men in Management* (London, UK: Sage, 1993), p. 158.

2. A.M. Morrison, R.P. White, E. Van Elsor and the Center for Creative Leadership, *Breaking the Glass Ceiling: Can Women Reach the Top of America's Largest Corporations?* (rev. edn; Reading, MA: Addison-Wesley, 1992).

3. M. Hennig and A. Jardin, 'Patterns of Difference and their Implications', in *The Managerial Woman* (New York, NY: Anchor Press, 1977), p. 63 .

4. Reported in *The Observer*, 18 June 1995.

5. Reported in *The Guardian*, 8 March 1995.

6. J.B. Rosener, 'Ways Women Lead', in *Harvard Business Review*, Vol. 68 No. 6 (1990), pp. 119-20.

7. See M. Loden, 'The Case for Feminine Leadership', in *Feminine Leadership, or How to Succeed in Business without being One of the Boys* (New York, NY: Times Books, 1985).

8. G.H. Dobbins, 'Effects of Gender on Leaders' Response to Poor Performers: An Attributable Interpretation', in *Academy of Management Journal*, No. 28 (1985), pp. 587-98.

9. See K.T. Bartlett, 'Feminist Legal Methods', in *Harvard Law Review*, No. 103 (1990), pp. 829-88.

10. See P.Y. Martin, 'Feminist Practice in Organisations: Implications for Management', in E.A. Fagenson (ed.), *Women in Management* (Vol. 4; London, UK: Sage, 1993).

11. See Martin, *op. cit.*

12. See Susan Baker, *The Principles and Practice of Ecofeminism: A Review* (Rotterdam, The Netherlands: RISBO, 1993).

13. R. Eisler, 'The Gaia Tradition and the Partnership Future: An Ecofeminist Manifesto', in L. Diamond and G.F. Orenstein, *Reweaving the World: The Emergence of Ecofeminism* (San Francisco, CA: Sierra Club, 1990).

14. *Op. cit.*

15. Starhawk, *Dreaming the Dark: Magic, Sex and Politics* (2nd edn; Boston, MA: Beacon Press, 1988).

16. Starhawk, *Truth or Dare: Encounters with Power, Authority and Mystery* (San Francisco, CA: Harper & Row, 1990).

17. Simon Engineering plc, 'Simon Engineering Corporate Environmental Policy Statement, 1992', in Confederation of British Industry, *Corporate Environmental Policy Statements* (London, UK: CBI, June 1992).

18. Bill Birchard, 'Corporate Environmentalism and Du Pont: An Interview with Edgar Woolard, CEO', in *Greener Management International*, No. 2 (1993), pp. 64-69.

19. Starhawk, 'Power, Authority and Mystery: Ecofeminism and Earthbased Spirituality', in Diamond and Orenstein, *op. cit.*

20. R.J. Putman and S.D. Wratten, *Principles of Ecology* (London, UK: Croom Helm, 1985).

21. In an address to the Conference of Governmental Delegations, 1992.

22. R.T. Paine, 'Food Webs: Linkage, Interaction, Strength and Community Infrastructure', in *Journal of Animal Ecology*, No. 49 (1980), pp. 667-86.

10

Employees Give Business its Green Edge:
Employee Participation in
Corporate Environmental Care

Leon Klinkers and Nico Nelissen

*I*NTRODUCING a corporate environmental care programme does not
necessarily mean that it will be implemented. Implementing an environmental care programme in a top-down approach without employee
participation will probably have limited success. By involving employees in
the decision-making process, grass-roots support for environmental measures
can be found. Environmental policies must not be seen (and experienced) as
a top-down measure, but as a series of decisions that must rely on the
support of everyone within the company.

This chapter describes a research project in which different levels of
participation were established for four campaign types. By means of
questionnaires in both pre- and post-measurement, the influence of
environmental campaigns was assessed with regard to: employees' environmental awareness; employees' intended environmental behaviour; and
employees' actual environmental behaviour.

The main conclusion was that involving employees in decisions on
corporate environmental care proved to be most effective in improving
environmental awareness and intended corporate environmental behaviour.
Involvement increased their commitment to the issues, maximising the
success of environmental policies within the business. Based on these
conclusions, ten principles were generated for successful environmental
campaigning on the crucial basis of employee support.

■ Introduction

In the world of business, many changes are taking place that are influencing
organisations. Where once standard procedures and solutions sufficed, a
new set of answers to external changes needs to be found. These changes
require a re-evaluation of existing business strategies.[1]

Care for the natural environment is one of the external issues driving fundamental change within businesses. In this particular field, strategic opportunities as well as threats are on the increase. External pressures include increased government legislation; internally, businesses are discovering the financial benefits of environmental protection: that improving environmental performance can be cost-effective. Business management must include environmental considerations in its strategy, involve environmental care in all decision-making processes and make it an internalised business goal.[2] However, for implementation of environmental care within a business to succeed, employee support is of the utmost importance: environmental awareness and environmental behaviour of employees is essential.[3] But how can we improve employees' environmental awareness and behaviour? What corporate strategies do we need to develop? What role can environmental campaigns play? What role should employees play in these environmental campaigns?

In this chapter we will present research findings concerning the participation of employees in the implementation of environmental care within businesses. The central research questions will be formulated (1); the experiments with employee participation will be described (2); the results will be presented (3); and, finally, recommendations will be given to improve the role of employees in environmental strategies (4).

■ 1. Research Questions

Many businesses are in the process of introducing environmental care programmes. The introduction of these programmes, however, does not necessarily mean that they have reached the implementation stage. Participation of employees in the actual implementation processes of environmental care programmes is essential. Therefore, the central research question posed in our study is: what is the influence of the participation of employees during the implementation of environmental programmes within business *vis-à-vis* their environmental awareness and environmental behaviour?

Our findings are based on research carried out at eight companies in the metal industry in the Netherlands. All businesses included in the research programme produce different metal products, such as transformers, scaffolding, compressors and screws. They can be classified as small and medium-sized enterprises, with the number of employees ranging from 5 to 85. Some of them can be seen as 'family' businesses. Due to heavy competition, these businesses are struggling for survival. In these companies, different kinds of environmental campaigns were implemented, varying in the degree of employee participation. By means of pre- and post-measurement we have assessed the influence of environmental campaigns on employees' environmental awareness, employees' intended environmental behaviour and employees' actual environmental behaviour.

■ Data

The pre-measurement consisted of a survey among employees concerning environmental awareness, intended environmental behaviour and actual environmental behaviour and was taken in each of the eight companies. After this measurement, an environmental campaign was conducted at five of these businesses and a post-measurement was taken. The post-measurement consisted of the same survey used in the pre-measurement. In three out of the eight businesses, no environmental campaign was conducted and only pre- and post-measurement surveys were implemented. These businesses functioned as a control group.

In total, 194 out of 317 pre-measurement surveys were returned; a response of 61%. At the post-measurement stage, 139 out of 283 surveys were handed in; a response of 49%. The difference in the number of issued surveys in pre- and post-measurements is due to the fact that only the members of the workshop received a survey (see experiments with employee participation, below).

■ Environmental Awareness and Behaviour

What do we mean by environmental awareness and environmental behaviour, whether intended or actual? Environmental awareness in this study has been defined as an attitude towards the natural environment.[4] This attitude is a hypothetical construction based on employees' comments on how they relate to the natural environment. Intended environmental behaviour has been defined as the degree to which one is prepared to act in an environmentally-correct way, to what degree one is incited to act in an environmentally-correct way and to what degree one takes these incentives into consideration. Actual environmental behaviour has been defined as those individual actions that have a positive effect on the natural environment. Next to the employees' personal environmental awareness, intended environmental behaviour and actual environmental behaviour, we were interested in employees' views concerning corporate environmental awareness, intended corporate environmental behaviour and actual corporate environmental behaviour.

■ Measurement of the Central Concepts

The following central concepts were used and measured: Environmental Awareness (EA); Intended Environmental Behaviour (IEB); Environmental

Behaviour (EB); Corporate Environmental Awareness (CEA); Intended Corporate Environmental Behaviour (ICEB); and Corporate Environmental Behaviour (CEB).

■ 2. Experiments with Employee Participation in Environmental Programmes

The starting point of this study was to examine the four degrees of participation of employees (including non-participation) in environmental campaigns. Participation is defined as the influence employees have on decision-making concerning internal corporate environmental policy. This resulted in four kinds of campaigns with different focuses.

The campaign with an **awareness-raising** focus on environmental issues concerns the confrontation of the respondents with a questionnaire related to their (corporate) environmental consciousness, intended (corporate) environmental behaviour and actual (corporate) environmental behaviour. This action was based on the idea that filling out the questionnaire draws attention to environmental issues. The campaign with an **informative focus** concerns the degree of participation facilitated by management in which the employees become aware of internal corporate environmental policy by means of information and education. The third campaign, with a **consultative focus**, concerns the degree of participation in which management not only informs and educates its employees, but also consults them on how the environmental care programme can be formulated. Finally, the campaign with a **co-decision-making focus** concerns the degree of participation in which management not only gives employees the role of 'co-knowing' and 'co-thinking', but also gives them the opportunity to communicate, hold discussions and take actual decisions on intentions and plans concerning the elements of corporate environmental care that are to be introduced.

The degree of participation in the campaigns can be seen as a 'ladder' of participation, starting from **non-participation** (drawing attention to), through **information** and **consultation** to **co-decision**. Each step on the ladder means a higher level of employee participation in the decision-making process on environmental policy.

■ Environmental Campaigns as a Series of Steps

What kind of environmental campaigns were developed and what were the stages of implementation? The campaigns consisted of the following ten steps. Not every campaign, however, was designed to address all steps; the type of campaign dictated which steps were to be taken.

Step 1: Awareness-raising. A questionnaire was handed out to the employees; this was used as a pre-measurement.

The first step is the part of the campaign that focuses on raising awareness about the environment (**non-participation**). In three companies only Step 1 was taken.

Step 2: Announcement. A tripod was placed in the company displaying a large poster that read: 'Environmental Campaign' and the name of the company. On the poster a company logo was also placed. Together with the large poster, smaller posters with the company's logo were put up in different areas of the company, reading 'Take action in improving the environment!' All these actions focused attention on the environment and the role of the company in this area.

Step 3: Speech. At a carefully chosen time and place, the board of directors and the employees were assembled to listen to a speech from the manager concerning the implementation of an environmental campaign in their company, after which the manager detailed the strategy and content of the campaign.

Step 4: Showing a video. A videotape was shown, addressing the importance of environmental care in the industry sector, i.e. the metal industry.

Step 5: Planting a tree. After the speech and the video, a tree was planted outside the company as a symbol of the company's environmental action.

Step 6: Environment newsletter. In the course of the campaign, three newsletters were issued. The first one concerned control of energy use; the second corporate waste; and the third concerned 'good housekeeping'.

Step 7: Environment barometer. An 'Environment Barometer', monitoring the weekly consumption of water and energy within the company, was installed during the campaign. This performance indicator enabled employees to become more aware of how their behaviour within the company affected the consumption of resources.

The seventh step concludes the **informative** part of the campaign. Information and education of employees were the main goals of this stage of the campaign. In one company all seven steps were taken.

Step 8: Suggestion box. The first newsletter mentioned the installation of a suggestion box in those companies where a campaign with a consultative focus or a focus on co-decision making was introduced, giving employees the opportunity to communicate their own ideas about how to improve care for the environment within the company. Employees with creative ideas were rewarded with a t-shirt with a print that read: 'Take Action in Improving the Environment!' on the back and the logo on the front.

Step 9: Response. In an extra edition of the newsletter, a diagram was printed for employees to fill in, asking them to identify those production processes within the company with significant environmental effects. Employees could also point out which production processes needed improving.

The ninth step, with a focus on response, concluded the **consultative** stage of the campaign. Emphasis was not only put on information and education, but also on allowing employees the opportunity to offer advice and ideas on the implementation of environmental care within the company. In one company all nine steps were taken.

Step 10: Workshop. The workshop consisted of two sessions: a problem-diagnosis segment and a problem-solving segment. In the diagnostic segment, an inventory was made of the influence of production processes on different environmental aspects such as noise, energy, waste, soil pollution and water pollution. In the second problem-solving segment of the workshop, small groups addressed a range of environmental issues and discussed solutions. The suggested solutions were listed and presented as a package.

After concluding the workshops, a supplementary edition of the environment newsletter was issued in which the results of the workshops were reported to the employees.

In the companies where all ten steps were taken, employees were given the opportunity to hold discussions and to take decisions about the intentions and plans concerning corporate environmental policy. This particular campaign focused on **co-decision-making**. The full ten steps were taken in three companies.

In order to measure the impact of the different campaigns, a post-measurement was held, using a questionnaire with the same set of questions as in the pre-measurement.

■ 3. Results of the Experiments and Comments

What were the influences of the different degrees of employee participation on the environmental campaigns? How did the campaigns affect Environmental Awareness (EA), Intended Environmental Behaviour (IEB) and actual Environmental Behaviour (EB) of the individual employees and the company as a whole (CEA, ICEB and CEB)?

Figure 1 (overleaf) shows the differences in the key variables before and after the various degrees of employee participation in the different types of campaigns. The figures are based on a five-point scale, with 5.00 representing the highest point.

On the basis of this overall table the following conclusions can be made.

■ *a. Employees are concerned about the natural environment.*

It is often suggested that employees pay little attention to the ways in which their company deals with the natural environment, and only management is aware of the importance of this concern. In our study, we have found that this viewpoint needs to be adjusted. Employees do take the environment seriously, as indicated by Environmental Awareness, Intended Environmental Behaviour and Environmental Behaviour, especially the environment surrounding their own workplace, as indicated by Corporate Environmental Awareness, Intended Corporate Environmental Behaviour and Corporate Environmental Behaviour. This conclusion provides a solid basis for the introduction of an environmental care system in businesses that relies on employees' support.

■ *b. Employees have a more positive image of the way in which their company deals with the natural environment than of their own actions with regards to the environment.*

The scoring of the employees' image of the way their company deals with Corporate Environmental Awareness, Intended Corporate Environmental Behaviour and Corporate Environmental Behaviour is at a higher level than for their own Environmental Awareness, Intended Environmental Behaviour and Environmental Behaviour. Why employees feel this way is still not fully clear. We think the results could have been influenced by the characteristics of the research instrument. The statements that were put before the employees concerning Corporate Environmental Awareness, Intended Corporate Environmental Behaviour and Corporate Environmental Behaviour addressed quite concrete aspects of managerial issues. It could be possible (and our observations confirm this) that the businesses that have been the subjects of our research have already implemented the necessary environmental measures. Therefore, the employees experience the measures taken in their workplace on a daily basis and thus describe the company's way of dealing with the environment as a 'proper' one. One also needs to take into consideration the fact that the companies involved in the study represent the more environmentally-aware side of the metal industry. This factor can also explain the relatively high scores on Corporate Environmental Awareness, Intended Corporate Environmental Behaviour and Corporate Environmental Behaviour.

Campaign type	Mean pre-measurement EA	Mean post-measurement EA	Change	Mean pre-measurement IEB	Mean post-measurement IEB	Change	Mean pre-measurement EB	Mean post-measurement EB	Change
Non-participation	3.20	3.12	-0.08	2.71	2.99	0.28	2.73	2.80	0.07
Informing	3.19	3.11	-0.08	2.87	2.90	0.03	2.86	2.91	0.05
Consulting	3.21	3.18	-0.03	2.91	2.91	0.00	2.80	2.83	0.03
Co-decision-making	3.20	3.12	-0.08	2.93	3.13	0.20	2.97	2.96	-0.01

Campaign type	Mean pre-measurement CEA	Mean post-measurement CEA	Change	Mean pre-measurement ICEB	Mean post-measurement ICEB	Change	Mean pre-measurement CEB	Mean post-measurement CEB	Change
Non-participation	3.58	3.50	-0.08	2.79	3.10	0.31	3.56	3.78	0.22
Informing	3.42	3.53	0.11	2.75	3.06	0.31	3.48	3.84	0.36
Consulting	3.53	3.55	0.02	2.70	2.83	0.13	3.41	3.64	0.23
Co-decision-making	3.38	3.64	0.26	2.87	3.11	0.34	3.86	3.87	0.01

Figure 1

■ *c. The effects of the campaigns are limited, but worthwhile.*
If we observe the effects of the different types of environmental campaigns, some striking remarks can be made. First, the effects of the campaigns are surprisingly limited. No extreme changes took place, although every change in a positive direction is to be welcomed. Environmental Awareness was slightly influenced; Intended Environmental Behaviour improved through the 'awareness-raising' and the 'co-decison-making' parts of the campaign. Environmental Behaviour was slightly influenced by the campaigns.

The relatively small changes can be explained by several factors. The environmental campaigns are to some extent 'one-shot' approaches of communication, based on the assumption that a one-off incentive related to the environment will have some effect. The general experience in communication, however, shows that real changes in attitudes and behaviour only take place through intensive and long-term emphasis on values, and the breaking through of systematic barriers that frustrate environmental behaviour and the radical improvement of the conditions for environmental behaviour. It can be concluded that one should not have high expectations of short-term environmental campaigns.

The environmental campaigns were successful in relation to their impact on Corporate Environmental Awareness, Intended Corporate Environmental Behaviour and Corporate Environmental Behaviour. The campaigns with an informative focus had the biggest influence. An explanation could be found in the fact that the campaigns were directly related to activities in the business itself and not to home activity.

■ *d. Every type of environmental campaign has some effect.*
An important conclusion for corporate environmental policy is that almost every type of campaign has its positive effects. In nearly every environmental campaign we see a difference between pre- and post-measurement, indicating that most campaigns have a positive influence on the way employees deal with the environment.

■ *e. Co-decision-making campaigns have more effect.*
From our research data, we can draw the conclusion that environmental campaigns have more effect when employees are part of the decision-making process concerning the implementation of environmental policy. To stimulate Environmental Awareness and Environmental Behaviour, campaigns that are based on co-decision-making prove to be most successful in improving Corporate Environmental Awareness and Intended Corporate Environmental Behaviour. However, the impact of this campaign type on Corporate Environmental Behaviour was zero. One of the explanations

could be that the degree of Corporate Environmental Behaviour is already so high that it cannot be improved by campaigns. The involvement of employees in decision-making processes concerning environmental measures will increase their commitment. Involved and motivated employees will do their best to make environmental policies a success within the business.

■ 4. Recommendations
What recommendations can be made on the basis of our research results?

■ a. Environmental campaigns are of importance.
Even though employees' level of concern for the natural environment is already reasonably encouraging, actions and incentives are still necessary to keep people motivated. By organising campaigns and through other measures, awareness of environmental issues is maintained. This not only works to the advantage of the company (e.g. lower cost of waste processing), but also to the advantage of the employees (e.g. working environment and safety).

■ b. Environmental campaigns yield the best results if they are consistent with companies' everyday situations.
One has to make certain that the environmental campaigns are industry-specific and, if possible, company-specific. Experience teaches us that campaigns have the best results if they are consistent with the company's everyday situations. When attention is drawn to the possibilities of taking action to improve the environment of their own workplace, employees are likely to take the initiative. The opportunity to be proactive and improve matters will generate a positive response.

■ c. Environmental campaigning is a precise mechanism.
Companies differ. This is also the case in internal corporate environmental policy. Environmental care needs a tailor-made approach. In some cases, a model from one industry sector was copied without taking the specific situation of the company into consideration. Also, mention must be made of the different groups of employees within the company, which each have a different relation towards environmental issues. The way in which assembly-line employees are confronted with environmental issues differs from the way in which administrative personnel, transport personnel or sales people are confronted with these issues. Workshops in which employees of the same department or with the same kind of duties were gathered resulted in more specific and focused treatment and suggestions for actions toward environmental issues.

■ d. Environmental campaigns can be effective without consuming excessive time and money.

Companies that are thinking about instigating an environmental campaign in their organisation will probably ask themselves how much time and money is involved. Generally speaking, environmental campaigns do not have to be costly, nor do they have to be time-consuming. Of course, there are costs related to personnel, materials, etc. that are needed for the preparation and actual implementation of the campaign. Possibly, this task can be performed by an environmental co-ordinator, or a quality manager, but it is also possible (and even desirable) to hire an external advisor (or organisation) that is specialised in this field. The actual costs vary, depending on the nature of the campaign. With less intensive campaign types, one needs to think in terms of about US$5,000. In more intensive campaigns the cost will be higher. It is important to stress that this money will be more than cost-effective because of decreasing energy consumption, recycling, responsible processing of waste, etc.

■ e. Involve people in the decision-making process.

The introduction of an environmental care programme does not mean, as we have stated before, that it will actually be implemented. By involving employees in the decision-making process, the grass-roots support for environmental measures can be found. Environmental measures must not be seen (and experienced) as top-down measures, but as decisions that must rely on the support of everyone within the company.

All things considered, we can state that environmental campaigns do contribute, in a small way, to increasing the sensitivity of employees towards the environment. Given the small effort these campaigns require, it is reasonable to state that the cost–benefit comparison balances out positively for environmental campaigns. One must not expect miracles from these campaigns: they are a modest contribution to a more positive attitude and behaviour towards environmental issues within the company. More importantly, environmental campaigns lead to a number of environmental initiatives during the duration of the campaign that would not otherwise have happened.

■ Notes

1. See C.W.H. Hill and G.R. Jones, *Strategic Management: An Integrated Approach* (Boston, MA: Houghton Mifflin, 1989).

2. See J.T.A. Bressers *et al.* (eds.), *Millieuzorg van Directietafel naar Werkvloer* (Alphen aan de Rijn, Netherlands: Samson H.D. Tjeenk Willink, 1991).

3. See L. Klinkers and N. Nelissen, *Werken aan ons Milieu* (Nijmegen, Netherlands: Katholieke Universiteit Nijmegen, 1993).

4. See N. Nelissen, P. Scheepers *et al.*, 'The Need for Information about Environmental Consciousness and Behaviour', in *Business Strategy and the Environment*, Vol. 2 (1992), pp. 13-25.

Part 3

Training and Skills towards Environmental Improvement

11

Training for Environmental Improvement

Alison Bird

THE INSTITUTE of Environmental Management has organised and conducted a series of training workshops for environmental managers. This chapter identifies best practice from these workshops and the experiences managers brought to them.

When we began the series, our perceptions on the subject were somewhat rigid. The word 'training' had a formality about it which conjured up a classroom-type process—albeit a practical one—in which the teacher imparts knowledge and skills to the pupil. We found that our preconceptions were echoed by many workshop participants, but we also found that those who had taken the most flexible and imaginative approaches had achieved the best results. These individuals had begun by asking themselves the questions: What is training for? What is the primary training objective? The answers most had come up with may seem obvious—to provide individuals with the wherewithal to enable them to play an effective part in the achievement of the organisation's (and their own) environmental aspirations.

The participants had then asked themselves what was required to achieve this objective. In general, it was agreed that there are two principal elements involved. The first is to provide insights to individuals that will motivate them—this was generally termed 'awareness-raising'. The second was to equip the motivated individuals with the skills required to ensure that they are able to operate in a way that matches these aspirations.

Formal classroom approaches did not tend to work. Managers who had the greatest success were those who had gone further and asked how the two elements involved in achieving the overall training objective could best be delivered. Invariably, the key was to understand individual perceptions and motivators within the organisation and to focus the approach with these in mind; also to ensure that training was paralleled by visible environmental action and improvement within the organisation.

The approaches taken as a result of these types of analysis were extremely diverse, ranging from the use of computer-based packages to informal coffee-break discussions: participants considered that all of these approaches formed a part of the ongoing training process which had both formal and informal components. An outline of some of these approaches is contained later in this chapter.

■ Why is Eco-Literacy Important?

The environment has not generally been seen as a mainstream business issue, and, although this perception has shifted significantly over the last decade, there is still a long way to go before environmental considerations are fully integrated into business management and development. A real impediment to progress remains a low level of understanding about the inevitable, but often unpredictable, impact that physical environmental issues have on the way we run and develop our lives and our businesses. For example, environmental law and the way it evolves is generally underpinned by a real need to safeguard aspects of the physical resources on which we all depend. Pollution of water, air and land and uncontrolled use of water, energy and other resources will increasingly impact on the way business is carried out—these are the real issues. Customer pressure, laws, financial instruments—these are all reflections underlying the real tangible environmental issues, and yet it is the former that exert pressure on business and which are themselves all too often considered to be the drivers. To a degree, the real longer-term significance of, for example, environmental laws in a deregulatory climate, financial instruments in the context of fierce international competition, and customer pressures when the customer so often puts price above all else, can be played down if the true physical drivers are not understood. All too often this fundamental understanding is absent.

In other words, the eco-literacy of those in business, and, in particular, managers, needs to be improved. What is clear is the close correlation between success in environmental management and eco-literacy within the organisation—this was repeatedly made clear during the workshops. In the IEM's recent examination, there was also a definite relationship between candidates' understanding of the principles behind the current debate on sustainability and their grip on specifics in areas such as environmental law and management and the way in which these could best be tackled. All the evidence points to the fact that a competent environmental manager needs to be eco-literate.

■ What is Environmental Training for?

Environmental training enables individuals to carry out their work in a way which minimises significant impacts on the environment. This is likely to take the form of:

- Motivation built on the back of a sound awareness of the relevance and importance of environmental issues for the individual and organisation
- The building of skills and knowledge necessary to allow activities and decisions to be executed in a way that minimises environmental effects

■ How are Training Needs Identified?

Motivation and a sound awareness of the significance of key issues for the individual and organisation are relevant to everyone. However, different individuals have different priorities and awareness-training needs to relate environmental protection to these priorities. Necessary skills and knowledge will vary according to the individual's role, the type of activities they undertake and the decisions they make. A management system should have identified ways in which the organisation intends to control its environmental effects. It should be determined what skills and knowledge are required to implement the system.

Many of the most serious impacts are unplanned. Training individuals to carry out procedures alone is unlikely to be sufficient. Training should, where possible, help individuals understand the issues and potential ways of dealing with them. It is preferable that individuals have the skills to recognise an actual or potential affect and take appropriate action. All individuals make decisions. Where these have a significant potential to impact on the environment, the individual should have the necessary awareness to understand these potential impacts. For example, senior managers will need to understand the implications of decisions they make when establishing corporate direction and policy. However, it should be remembered that all individuals, not just managers, make decisions and these should be made in an environmentally-informed way. For example, a decision by a painter to dispose of a waste solvent down a surface water drain could have serious implications. It should be identified where decision-making is key to minimising effects and determined how best one can help the relevant individuals make informed decisions through training.

There will also be an environmental component to skills required by all individuals in the execution of their work. For example, environmental aspects of design should be an integral element of a designer's work. Equally, high standards of solvent handling should be part and parcel of the skills required by a competent spray painter. Effective environmental managers evaluate where environmental aspects to individual skills are important, and try to extend existing training to integrate environmental considerations into it.

In some cases, specific environmental training will be required. For example, it is likely that environmental managers will require specific training to help them understand the broad range of environmental issues that affect the organisation and how best to tackle to them. Similarly, those involved in waste management or the operation of pollution control and monitoring equipment will probably require specific environmental training to develop their skills. Indeed, where a waste management activity is involved, the law may actually require an operator to hold a WAMITAB (Waste Management Industry Training and Advisory Board) certificate, for example.

■ How is Training to be Undertaken?

There is no one fixed approach to training. Training needs to be geared to the circumstance to make it relevant to the individual and organisation and to persuade people to take it seriously. Figure 1 outlines some key considerations that practitioners have found useful in ensuring that training works and that it results in improved awareness and skills and a reduction in the organisation's environmental effects.

■ How are Environmental Managers Making Training Work?

Some of the main challenges faced by workshop participants involved overcoming the 'well, that's all very interesting but it's nothing to do with me' attitude, which may be held by both management and shopfloor levels. One manager said that, following a particular session of training, he felt that he had now experienced 'most aspects of indifference'. The following training ideas were some of the most successful in countering such indifference.

■ 1. Keep it Simple

The environment is a very complex topic. Key tips on helping the message to stick were:

- Keep the message simple—e.g. select four main areas and drum them home.
- Keep the focus relevant—e.g. select the four most relevant areas for the audience and reinforce these.
- Keep sessions short.

Do senior managers understand:

- The way in which environmental issues affect the business and its principal environmental effects?
- Key environmentally-driven trends?
- How to incorporate environmental considerations into business planning and decision-making?

Do middle managers understand:

- The way in which environmental issues affect the business, and in particular the area with which they are most involved?
- The significant environmental effects caused by the activities they manage, the reason they are significant and their means of control?
- The environmental significance of decisions they make?
- The role of individuals they manage in ensuring environmental protection and the skills they require to be effective in those roles?

Does the workforce understand:

- How environmental issues affect them and their jobs?
- Their actual and potential contribution to the organisation's environmental effects?
- Steps they might (or should) take to minimise these effects?

Do those who undertake specific environmentally-related tasks understand:

- What is required to be done in normal and abnormal operating conditions and why?
- The importance to the organisation and the environment of any failure to undertake their tasks properly?
- The legal implications of breaches—both for corporate and personal liability?
- How their task fits into the wider activities of the organisation, its policy and objectives?

Does the environmental manager understand:

- The organisation's significant environmental effects and why they are deemed significant?
- Techniques that might be applicable to control these effects?
- Trends in the development of significance and their relevance to business development?
- How to champion environmental issues within the organisation?
- How to keep informed?
- The principles and practices of environmental management, as defined by the Institute's Associate Membership criteria?

Figure 1: *Knowledge Requirements for Environmental Decision-Makers*

- Keep groups small.
- Keep the message consistent—do not change the message halfway through.
- Get the timing right—do not introduce a training programme when there are too many deep-rooted changes going on in the organisation.
- Keep the training going informally—through steady exposure to environmental information—do not let the environment stop being an issue once formal training has stopped.

Many people said that they felt they were teaching the wrong people the wrong things at the wrong time. Tony Jaggers of Rolls Royce said: 'If you are giving environmental training to a wide range of people, one of the problems to watch out for is that you are not simply teaching 5% of an audience while 95% nod off. You need to think very carefully about who you're talking to and make it relevant.' Many people at the workshops had learned the hard way that long sessions communicating complex ideas to large audiences is unlikely to be effective.

2. Get People to Do it Themselves

'Tell them and they'll forget; show them and they'll remember; involve them and they'll understand.' This sounds like straight 'management speak', but it was a maxim that came up repeatedly as a key motivator.

Train people in basic risk assessment. Ian Housley of National Power introduced his trainees to the ideas of basic risk assessment; this enabled them to come back to him with their assessments of key environmental effects and ideas for action. 'This seemed a good way to engage people's intelligence in the task of implementing good environmental management at all levels,' he said, 'and we got some very good ideas on reducing risk thrown in!'

Liberate people's intelligence. Keith Smith of Carson Office Furniture Systems said that liberating people's intelligence was crucial: 'People think very narrowly about task-related training—they seem to forget that for every pair of hands you employ, you get a brain for free—and people do have lots of ideas if you seek them. Get their suggestions and input—you can't do it all yourself!'

Engage the individual's own vision of success. Nicolette Lawson of Lucas Industries asked her trainees: 'What does the perfect environmentally-responsible company look like?' She then asked how far away they thought the company actually was from that, and how progress might be made towards it. This way she felt that she had engaged people in a vision of their own making of good environmental performance.

Get key individuals to deliver the training. Getting the sceptics involved in the actual training was one way a manager from a paper mill engaged people's interest. 'One of the key problems is getting people's—especially managers'—time. By involving them in the delivery of training at least you can ensure their commitment to the session.'

Get people thinking critically. Rather than simply imparting knowledge, some managers used the training sessions to instil a critical attitude in people, i.e. to make them always ask themselves questions about the way things should be, could be and are undertaken. Training managers to become their own 'critical customers' was the term used.

Pre-empt excuses. Anticipate scepticism, and even avoid it, by getting people to develop their own action plans. If people write their own procedures and plans, at least you will know that they have read them and that they think they'll work! Meeting and developing plans and programmes in this way was seen as a form of training in its own right.

▌ *3. Be Imaginative*

'People are getting bored with training,' said one environmental manager from a large manufacturing organisation. 'I feel there is a need to change people's perception of training—from both the trainers' and the trainees' point of view. We need to think laterally as well.' This view was reflected in the variety of different techniques that people were using—to great effect— to communicate the environmental message. It is the outcome of training that is important, and informal training can often yield the best results.

Use technology. National Power developed a programme that was very simple and fun to use, introducing key elements of the organisation's environmental policy and site operations. Initially they let staff know of its existence through their electronic mail system—it was then left up to people to motivate themselves to use it. 'We found that in less than a week of having the programme on the system, a staggering 75% of employees at a single plant had used it. We also had the added benefit of automatic documentation of who had used it when for our training records.'

Use competition. Dr George Howarth, of Smith & Nephew, used a video to inform different sites across Europe of four key areas of environmental management: environmental management systems; waste minimisation; energy saving; and pollution control. His four cornerstones of environmental improvement were used to inspire competition between the plants for environmental excellence, an environmental award going to the most outstanding achievement. 'The video had distinct advantages of easily communicating to vast numbers of staff across Europe simple cornerstones of environmental thinking; it has helped to instil a sense of the corporate environmental culture; and has inspired whole plants to become involved in the need for good environmental performance, and to learn new ideas from sister plants,' said Dr Howarth.

Use formal and informal meetings. What constitutes training anyway? One manager logged meetings with senior managers or the Board to talk about specific aspects of environmental management as *training* because he was helping keep the individuals informed. 'Having only ten minutes with key decision-makers is an ideal time to train—it helps you keep focused on what's important too.' Carson Office Furniture used coffee breaks to talk about particular issues: 'It breaks down the barriers: people are more comfortable and feel less conscious about asking questions. It also helps the environment become a more normal part of everyday conversation.'

Use normal mechanisms. Stan Battle in his work with Inveresk—which has won awards for its environmental training materials—actually logged his memos, keeping others up to date with new environmental legislation and trends, as 'training', because they were part of *keeping people informed*, which he saw as 'part of the drip drip drip' of environmental training. Other normal communication mechanisms, such as publications, newsletters, circulars, noticeboards, etc., were utilised by many as training materials.

Use free external expertise. 'There are all sorts of people that I bring in to tell others about the environment,' said a manager from a small label manufacturer. 'The regulators are a good source of information and they're experts on difficult legislation! Local environmental pressure groups and interest groups, such as the RSPB, have helped people become aware of the organisation's local impact on the community, both in terms of actual impact and perceived impact. Some very important lessons have been learned in such sessions—how could it be anything but training?'

Use photographs. Nicolette Lawson of Lucas Industries quoted instances where photographs were used over time to show how improvements had and had not been made since the last training session, and how such *incontrovertible evidence* could be used in refresher training.

Use the audit. Along similar lines, the 'close-out' meetings at audits had also been logged as training, while one organisation actually used the results of the annual audit to formulate the year's training programme. 'Following an audit, the identification of training needs on a yearly basis stares you in the face,' said the manager.

Use drama. 'Using drama and real-life examples makes the message stick,' said Kathy Rogerson of Bristol-Myers Squibb. 'Training needs to be remembered. It makes sense, therefore, to make messages memorable.'

Make training dynamic. 'No two of our training courses are the same. We continually evolve them and take account of employee input,' said Allan Brown of Jetstream BAe.

■ 4. Getting the Language and Focus Right

A key problem voiced by many workshop participants was how to get through to specialist staff, i.e. those who do not perceive themselves or their department to have any impact on the environment. Getting the language and focus right was considered key to the ability to persuade otherwise reluctant participants of the relevance of the environmental issues to the business.

Look for the main drivers. 'We look at what drives the department that we are trying to train,' said Nicolette Lawson of Lucas Industries, 'and then use those drivers to translate how the environment affects their department.' One such group of people might be the purchasing department: 'A key focus here is likely to be suppliers' costs, and particularly continuity of supply. The potential effect of business interruption is one that is taken very seriously by senior managers,' she said.

Customise the message. 'The challenge,' one manager said, 'is to make the hole in the ozone layer, for example, relevant to the individual. If people realise that they can make a difference it helps to create an active culture.' Liz Allen of Albion always includes as part of her training session on a particular topic—whether on energy, waste reduction or transport—what people can do at home about the issue: 'You've got to make it relevant to the individual or else you lose the real potential for people to understand and tackle the issue.'

Getting through to contractors. A particularly common problem area, voiced by many, was how to persuade contractors to be more environmentally responsible when they have no clear allegiance to the organisation. 'We always give our contractors our company policy video to watch as an induction to their work, but it doesn't really seem to make much impact,' said one manager in the healthcare sector. One organisation, however, was actively addressing what they saw as a key problem area in terms of training: 'We teamed up with others in the area who used the same contractors and then following the video let them know that any environmental slip-ups (collectively) would be seen as something of an endorsement on their "contractual licence": three endorsements and their contract wouldn't be renewed. The language of non-renewable contracts helped to focus their attention,' said the environmental manager.

■ *5. Find Champions*

Most environmental managers attending the workshops did not undertake all the training themselves, but brought others up to speed to enable them to train their own departments. Finding local champions—'the movers and shakers' in the organisation—is crucial. Candidates are not always obvious, however!

Use peer group trainers. 'We selected people throughout the organisation to lead training in different departments. We trained up "teams" of potential trainers so they could give each other support,' said one manager in an organisation too large to train all by himself. 'Most people would train up the head of the department: it's important to get them on your side, but don't just go for the obvious individual. Try to involve others in the department—the forklift truck driver and the office manager, for example— but do look for people with kudos and whom peers generally respect.'

'We get all kinds of staff to head up project teams,' said Keith Smith of Carson Office Furniture. 'Getting people involved in projects is an excellent way of training while actually moving things forward. Projects like reducing energy usage, water reduction, paper recycling show them they can make a difference.'

Use key influencers. A popular tactic was to convince key influencers in the organisation. 'We spend a lot of time focusing on the budget-holders and the purchasers,' said one quality, health and safety manager.

Find out who is motivated. One organisation had an environmental vacancy. After advertising internally, they found out pretty quickly who the key motivated players were in the organisation. The requirement for an essay on the environmental impact of the organisation confirmed the level of knowledge of the candidates and a key peer group training team was selected automatically. Even though only one person actually filled the post, the majority became involved in undertaking environmental training in the organisation while becoming more motivated in general. Another manager found that a suggestion box for environmental improvements quickly gave him an idea of the key people to train up to train others.

■ 6. Integrate the Environment into the Organisation's Culture
In practice, shifting the perception of the organisation as a whole towards positive environmental management is difficult and will take time. It will certainly not be the result of a single training programme, but over time is likely to emerge if one is persistent, consistent and focused in one's efforts.

Avoid making the environment an extra burden. 'People need to see good environmental performance as part and parcel of doing their job well,' said Ingrid Osterburg of Seton Healthcare, 'not simply as an add-on that's an extra burden to an already heavy workload.'

Be resourceful. For any training that is already undertaken, whether induction or on-the-job, ask: Is the environment included? Can it be included adequately? How should it be included? Try to integrate the training as much as possible. If the environment is seen as *extra* to the type of training that is already being undertaken, then it will not be seen as an essential part of the organisation's overall performance, but simply something new that needs to be complied with. 'Very few people have a huge budget to train everybody. You have to be resourceful and use the means to hand,' said a manager in a small-to-medium-sized operation.

Use the dominant ethos. 'We try to work within the current culture, which is one of Quality, and to ensure that the environment goes hand in hand with that. Otherwise we are inventing a whole new way of thinking that is external to the way the organisation already operates,' said Tony Jaggers of Rolls Royce.

Promote common ownership of the environment. If the organisation has a culture where common ownership of the environment is accepted, then environmental training will yield results as a matter of course. However, it is a difficult culture to create, as one manager discovered. 'I work in a small manufacturing organisation where the MD is very environmentally conscious, so I could not understand why the potential for environmental improvement hadn't been realised. After some investigation, we realised that everybody thought that the company was already in good hands—they knew that the MD was keen and that there was a very able and competent environmental manager. Basically, they saw responsibility for the environment as being dealt with. A change in emphasis at the next Board Meeting, when the other members of the Board—e.g. finance, purchasing and production directors—were all given environmental responsibility for their function, resulted—almost overnight—in a change in attitude.'

Focus on what can be delivered. One word of caution emerging from the workshops, however, was to focus now on what it is possible to deliver. Try not to be over-ambitious—it may only be a culture of compliance that can be fostered for the moment!

■ 7. Back it with Action and Audit Success

No training will be worthwhile unless it is backed by action. Most managers at the workshops felt that they were very unsure about the effectiveness of the training they had implemented and were keen to measure success so that they did not feel that they were 'training for training's sake'.

Do not make it fit then forget. As Tony Jaggers of Rolls Royce said: 'Make it relevant and then support and enable initiatives.'

Do not lose the initiative. 'Once you've raised the awareness, it is important not to lose the initiative. Keeping the process going is so important: even though it takes up a lot of time, it will pay off in the long run,' said Tim Pinder of Ready-Mixed Concrete.

Know the final results. According to Allan Brown of Jetstream BAe: 'The theory of setting up a training programme is easy. Step 1: Why do we want to implement training? Step 2: Where are we now? Step 3: Where do we want to be? Step 4: How are we going to get there? Step 5: Once things are under way, how are we doing? But the classic mistake people make is that they tend to leap to Step 4 without having thoroughly considered earlier steps. The usual scenario is to launch awareness sessions, set up a few teams and wonder why it fizzles out in twelve months!'

One needs to be clear about the training objectives so that the training results are easy to monitor and therefore support. There needs to be ongoing results from the training, not a simple spurt for action towards a single goal.

Look for tangible outcomes. Following the training, what improvements have been made? 'I like to audit the outcomes of my training a month afterwards. If there is no demonstrable change, then something has gone wrong and training has been unsuccessful. If people see me walking round asking questions regarding progress, they'll take it more seriously,' said an environmental manager in the metal coatings sector.

Look for successes, but also look for failures. 'Follow up any non-conformances found in the audit or any complaints from the public and find the cause. That'll be a fair measure of success, or rather lack of it—and you'll end up with key areas for targeted training!' said Russell Foster of Searle.

Get senior management commitment. Training has to be seen to be backed by demonstrable company commitment. Give rewards and recognition for successes backed by senior management—some managers were particularly keen on environmental performance appraisal. 'Praise goes a long way,' said one senior manager, 'but so does a financial incentive: we reduce bonuses following training if environmental performance is poor.'

Use the previous year's training. 'I always go back to the previous training as a starting point for refresher training,' said one manager. 'It's an excellent gauge for how far have people progressed since, and I test them on what they learned then and what they have actively done since.' This also helps focus the need for specific training on a rolling programme.

Use end-of-training testing. 'Testing at the end of a training session is unpopular but it helps focus attention,' said Ian Russon of British Steel. 'We always test engineers after induction training.'

Link training targets and objectives to successful outcomes. 'Our targets were initially linked to the delivery of training, i.e. when, where and to whom, and not to the outcome,' said one manager. 'It satisfied the documented records and therefore, to a certain extent, the certifier, but I wasn't sure of its effectiveness. Next time round I'll build in key learning outcomes and I'll test them periodically.'

■ Case Study: Training and Procedures for Training at Carson Office Furniture Systems

Carson Office Furniture Systems is a manufacturer of wood-based office furniture, employing 200 people and is part of the Acco-Rexel group. Carson was one of the first companies to be registered to BS 7750 in March 1995. Their environmental manager, Keith Smith, presented his approach to environmental training at the Institute workshop at the Engineering

Employer's Federation in London. Carson Office Furniture has placed great emphasis on training within the environmental management process, and many of Keith Smith's approaches have been outlined above. Training coverage has been extremely broad-reaching throughout the organisation, both in terms of awareness-training and specific job training. The emphasis has been on *in-house* training, and responsibility for this has been jointly assumed by the environmental and personnel managers—between them they organised a training programme which is reviewed annually. One of the first steps was to develop an objective and target for the training process. The objective for the training programme was 'Environmental Awareness' and the target was 'All Employees'. The target date was 31st July 1994 (the starting date was 30th March 1994).

Awareness-training needs were identified during the preparatory environmental review. The content of this part of the training programme was set and tried out on the environmental site team (which was already established) using VCR and OHP equipment supported by a presentation from Keith Smith. From this trial, a training session was devised that lasted for twenty minutes. Ten minutes were added for questions, making a session that would last for half an hour—time enough to get the message across, but not too long to be tiresome. The whole organisation was then divided into groups of no more than twenty people, including directors and managers. Twenty is an ideal number, because with a group that size one has a more personal approach and production can be geared accordingly. Training was held in the canteen and was spread over a four-month period. Now that the initial awareness-training has been completed, it is included in their new employee induction programme, along with quality and health and safety.

Specific job training needs were also identified and a training programme organised in conjunction with the heads of the departments concerned. This process is ongoing. Job training included design engineers, maintenance managers and contractors. According to Keith Smith:

> However well prepared we thought we were, we still received a non-conformance during our assessment to BS 7750 that read: 'Training needs are not defined for personnel developing and implementing projects.' Our project leaders were highly-skilled people so what more could we do? We asked the assessors. 'They may be highly skilled academically, but what do they really know about the projects they are leading? Have you defined the specific training required to handle the waste paper project, for example?' We had to go back to each of our objectives and targets on which the projects were based and define specific training needs. They included quite simple activities at the end of the day, but we needed to address them.

Details of the training process, its goals, how it is documented, carried out and audited and reviewed are contained in Carson's detailed Training Procedure below.

1. Purpose

1.1. To increase all employees' awareness of environmental impacts of their work and the legal and financial liabilities of Carson Office Furniture Systems.

1.2. To ensure all employees are aware of the Company's environmental policy and their respective roles and responsibilities in contributing to its development and implementation.

1.3. To secure commitment to the implementation of the environmental policy.

1.4. To ensure that only competent personnel should work in activities which have (or may have) a significant impact on the environment.

2. Responsibility

These procedures apply to all employees, at all levels within the organisation.

3. Documentation

3.1. A register of formal training is kept in the Personnel Department, and copies of training certificates.

3.2. An informal single-sided chart to record training is kept in the offices of heads of departments in the factory.

3.3. An informal single-sided chart to record training is kept by the Works Engineer.

3.4. An informal single-sided chart to record training is kept by the Design and Development department.

3.5. A Course Appraisal Sheet is issued to candidates attending courses to report their comments on the quality and effectiveness of the course.

4. Procedure

4.1. Components of the training strategy are shown in an Appendix.

4.2. The Personnel Manager and the Environmental Manager shall be responsible for identifying and organising environmental awareness-training.

4.3. Heads of departments shall be responsible for all *on the job* training.

4.4. The Personnel Manager shall formally notify all heads of departments, at least annually, that all employee training needs must be reviewed.

4.5. The Departmental Managers shall consider each subordinate's training needs and return to the Personnel Manager a list of employees who would benefit from formal training and the weakness to be addressed.

4.6. The Personnel Manager shall keep Departmental Managers informed of available external courses which might be appropriate to the department's needs.

4.7. The employee shall be advised of the identified weakness by the Departmental Manager, and notified of the external course which would benefit them. The employee shall be advised of the course content, location and duration.

4.8. If the employee is agreeable to receive training, the Personnel Manager shall be informed. The Personnel Manager shall book the employee on to the next available course and co-ordinate the training arrangements with the Departmental Manager and employee.

4.9. The Departmental Manager, having established that an individual within the department requires informal *on the job* training, shall be responsible for organising the necessary training.

4.10. Informal training shall normally be conducted by a competent person, having the necessary expertise and training ability to carry out the task.

4.11. Suppliers may be invited to conduct internal training within their sphere of activity, e.g. furnace maintenance.

4.12. The Departmental Manager shall inform the Personnel Manager of all informal training given to employees, which is then recorded on the employees' personal file.

4.13. The Personnel Manager shall review the effectiveness of external courses by requesting those attending to complete a Course Appraisal sheet at the end of the course. The appraisal shall require comment upon the course duration, assessment of venue and facilities provided, relevance of the instruction given, and overall assessment of the course. They shall also be asked to comment upon other subject matter which might have been included.

5. Appendix: *Components of Training Strategy*

5.1. General awareness of global and local environmental issues and of the environmental management system and responsibilities at all levels.

5.2. Awareness of environmental impacts and issues arising from operational activities of the business, including the environmental policy which must be understood at all levels within the organisation.

5.3. Individual environmental responsibilities relevant to each employee within their daily work and routine tasks.

5.4. Emergency procedures: what to do when there are abnormal operating conditions, emergencies, incidents or when accidents occur.

5.5. Building in appropriate understanding for specialist and strategic managers.

5.6. The environmental manager will also require training and regular updating on legislative, scientific and market developments.

5.7. Particular emphasis needs to be placed on the training needs, and the training of design engineers to be able to consider such activities as: alternative materials; product lifecycle; sources of raw materials; sustainability of raw materials; minimum use of energy; etc.

■ Trainer Train Thyself

Training, raising awareness, identifying training needs and keeping people informed are all commonly assumed to be part and parcel of the environmental manager's job. However, what about training for the environmental manager? What sort of knowledge does this person need, and how can it be developed?

■ What Does the Environmental Manager Need to Know?

Many queries to the Institute from new environmental managers open with variations on: 'I have just been given the remit for the environment in my organisation: what do I need to know, and how can I develop that knowledge?' Until the establishment of the Institute's knowledge and competence standards, there have been no clear goals to which the environmental manager could aspire, or against which to measure his/her own portfolio of skills. One of the initial tasks that the Institute undertook, therefore, was to determine, through wide consultation, the scope of knowledge required by an environmental manager.

The Institute's consultation exercise with over 300 individuals, trade associations and professional bodies covering industry, commerce and local government, resulted in the criteria for Associate Membership. The criteria, now familiar to members, cover three main knowledge areas:

- Environmental management.
- Environmental legislation and policy.
- Facilities and operations.

The criteria are now acknowledged as the professional *scope of knowledge* representing the principles and practices of environmental management.

Gaining Associate Membership status aims both to satisfy employers that their environmental staff have reached a recognisable standard of competence, and to give practitioners a recognisable status and transferable qualification. In June 1995, the Institute ran its first open book assessment for Associate Membership and had over 100 applicants. The Associate Membership criteria satisfies the first of such members' queries, i.e. 'What do I need to know?' However, until now, the Institute did not have a satisfactory answer to the second question, i.e. 'How can I develop that knowledge?'

■ How can the Knowledge be Developed?

The Institute has just launched a scheme called the Signature of Commitment, which encourages trainers to deliver courses compatible with the Institute's Associate Membership criteria. The Institute of Environmental Management will be regularly publishing the list of the courses that sign up to the scheme and will be testing their effectiveness in delivering to the criteria by their independent assessment, via open-book examination, twice a year.

Until the foundation of the Institute, there has been a woeful lack of clarity in the UK as to the standard of knowledge for successful environmental management, which has resulted in a plethora of environmental courses offering often wide-of-the-mark syllabuses. The Institute's scheme aims to help raise the standard of courses to a level that people can recognise and trust in, and to help provide guidance to members who are understandably confused about which ones to choose. There are already a number of courses delivering pertinent environmental training, and the Institute wants to ensure that members know which ones these are.

Many members will already be skilled and knowledgeable in certain areas and may simply require focused training in other areas. Some will want the whole course, while others may simply require a short refresher course to top up their existing knowledge ready to take the exam. For this reason we have tried to be as flexible as possible regarding the types of delivery and course content to try to suit all needs. As an environmental manager, it is not imperative that one knows everything, but it is important that one knows where to find relevant information and, more importantly still, that one knows how to interpret and apply it.

■ *Appendix*

■ *Environmental Training at Bristol-Myers Squibb*

Induction training for new employees (policy); talk by co-ordinator and NRA's 'Pollution Pays' video

Awareness training for experienced employees (four times a year for all staff given by each department on four different topics (one-two hours' duration per topic, 10–15 individuals per session)

Specific environmental topics in addition to the above for individuals involved in environmental operations (10–20 training hours per year on topics ranging from operating the effluent treatment plant to specific waste disposal)

The Environmental Co-ordinator is herself required by the company to undergo forty hours of continuing professional development training annually.

Trainer: Kathy Rogerson, QA and Environmental Manager, Bristol-Myers Squibb

■ *Environmental Training at Ready-Mixed Concrete*

Environmental Policy and Management System: top-level course for fifty (one day)

Environmental auditing for staff with responsibility reaching 100 (one and a half days)

Environmental awareness for supervisory and other staff reaching around 2,000 people (half a day); limited to 10–15 individuals per session—training takes 10% of environmental manager's time

Trainer: Tim Pinder, Environmental Manager, Ready-Mixed Concrete

■ *Environmental Training at Rolls Royce*

Senior management: **awareness training** for commitment and responsibilities (1 hour; 8–9 individuals per session)

Site plant and process managers: **specific training** for legal obligations and good practice (long half-day duration; 12–15 individuals per session)

Other specialist managers: **specific training** for good practice and company future (half day; 10–15 individuals per session)

Other general managers: **general education** (good practice; one-hour duration; 24 individuals per session). Similarly, workforce in general for good practice, as above.

Trainer: Tony Jaggers, Company Environmental Manager, Rolls Royce

■ Environmental Training at Albion Group

Over a six-month period, six different topic workshops are held, looking at different areas of policy and environmental improvement for, e.g., waste reduction, energy, packaging, transport, and emissions to air and water.

Four workshops are held per topic, 1–2 hours each. They involve a mixed group of twelve people from the Chairman and Managing Director to the shopfloor in a single group.

Each session covers one issue: what is meant by it, what it means to the organisation, how it is being tackled, what roles are in tackling it, the targets and solutions, and, particularly important, why it is relevant to you as an individual and what you should be doing at home about it.

Trainer: Liz Allen, Environmental Co-ordinator, Albion Group

12

Environmental Training in UK and German Companies

Klaus North and Sabine Daig

*I*N RECENT YEARS, environmental training has become an increasingly important topic for companies in the UK and Germany as environmental issues now feature prominently on their strategic agendas. This change has been brought about by a multiplicity of driving forces that make companies care about their environmental performance, and, as a consequence, about the environmental capabilities of their workforce.

Environmental education and training is increasingly seen as a key tool to improved environmental performance by committing the entire workforce and providing the necessary information and skills.

Recent developments towards certification according to standards and procedures—such as the European Management and Audit Scheme, ISO 9000 Quality Standards or BS 7750—further enhance environmental training, both in the UK and Germany. In particular, BS 7750 asks for the following:

> The organisation shall establish and maintain procedures to ensure that its employees or members, at all levels, are aware of:
>
> a) the importance of compliance with the environmental policy and objectives and with the requirements of this standard
>
> b) the significant environmental effects, actual or potential, of their work activities and the environmental benefits of improved performance
>
> c) their roles and responsibilities in achieving compliance with the environmental policy and objectives, and with the requirements of this standard

d) the potential consequences of departure from specific operating procedures.

The organisation shall establish and maintain procedures for identifying training needs, and for providing appropriate training for all personnel whose work may have a significant effect upon the environmental performance. [...] Personnel performing specific assigned tasks shall be competent on the basis of appropriate education, training and/or experience, as required by legislation or regulation, if such exists, and by the organisation.[1]

■ Development and Design of Environmental Training

Effective and targeted environmental training and communication must lead to culture change within the organisation regarding the perception of environmental issues. It has to raise general awareness and it has to transfer skills and enable the participants to cope with the environmental challenges within their jobs. As one employee is able to undermine all of the good environmental work of the company as a whole, by causing, for example, a spillage resulting in an unconsented discharge, it is important that environmental training is provided to everyone directly and indirectly involved with the company's environmental performance.

The workforce has to understand and support the protection of the environment. People have to know about the driving forces that make the company care about this subject and they have to understand the link between the protection of the environment and their own job and their own life. This awareness is a cornerstone for the success of the environmental skills training programme.

The skills and knowledge required will vary from job function to job function and there will be some that need less knowledge than others. The environmental skills training has to be tailored to the needs of every company and has to be designed according to the company's target groups. It will be necessary to design various activities to enhance environmental skills according to the job functions of the participants. Key functions have to be identified and all individuals with a direct or indirect influence on environmental performance will have to be trained.

In order to develop meaningful environmental education and training, the following steps should be undertaken (compare also Fig. 1):

1. Set environmental targets.

2. Carry out an environmental training needs analysis.

3. Identify target groups.

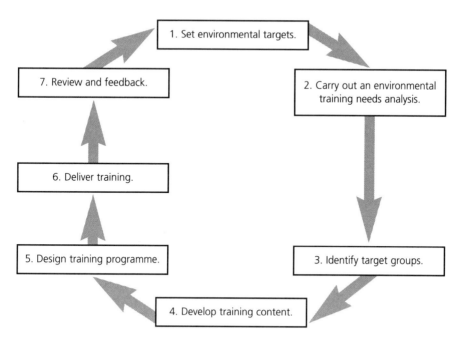

Figure 1: *Design and Implementation of Environmental Training*

4. Develop the training content.

5. Design the training programme.

6. Deliver training.

7. Review results.

(See also Chapter 17 Wehrmeyer and Vickerstaff 'Analysis for Environmental Training Needs'.)

The first step is to set **environmental targets**. Each company will have different targets depending on the business they are in or the stage of environmental action the company has reached. The company's driving forces will also play a role in setting environmental targets. The second step follows the identification of the company's **training needs**. The training needs vary from one company to another depending on such things as the environmental targets and business activities. It also depends heavily on the level of awareness, knowledge and skills regarding the environment that exists within the company.

The next step is the identification of the **target groups.** According to the company's internal structure, there will be various target groups with different training needs and levels depending on their job function. As soon as the target groups are identified, the **training content** will have to be developed. With the target groups known, it will be easy to estimate the rough content of the training programme and it will also be obvious that there should be several types of training activities according to the different target groups. The exact training content will then be developed as the process goes on.

A particular issue within this process is whether the company takes advantage of the expertise of consultants or not. The answer will depend heavily on the in-house expertise that is available and, again, on the environmental targets that are set. If, for example, the company aims to achieve an accreditation to BS 7750 or the European Management and Audit Scheme (EMAS), the advice of consultants will be needed. If the company's targets concern waste minimisation, it may be that consultancy is not necessary. This decision also affects the **design of the training programme** regarding trainers that are going to carry out the training sessions. If the company has human resources and expertise to do this, consultancy might not be necessary. On the other hand, one has to keep in mind that environmental training requires a broad skills base and sometimes an impartial viewpoint that could be provided most efficiently by external specialists.

Tools and methods to be used depend on the type of training that will be chosen. Presentations, discussions and case studies are the most usual ones. In a **review,** results of the environmental training are evaluated and fed back to programme development.[2]

■ In-House Training Programmes of UK and German Companies

In the following we will provide eight examples of how companies in the UK and Germany organise their in-house environmental training. Four companies located in Britain and four companies located in Germany have been paired, as they are subsidiaries of one multinational group, such as Vauxhall and Opel, competitors, or work in similar businesses. The comparison is guided by the seven steps, explained above, for developing environmental training. As none of the companies had developed a specific review system, this point is not dealt with separately. Information on the companies was gained from company reports, information leaflets and interviews with environmental and training officers at the various companies. Similarities and divergencies will be discussed under 'Conclusions'.

■ *Vauxhall Motors*

Since 1925, Vauxhall Motors has been part of the world's largest vehicle manufacturing company, General Motors (GM). In 1993, Vauxhall Motors occupied a 17.09% share of the UK car market. The company employs over 4,250 people at its Ellesmere Port plant and the plant produces a total of around 130,000 cars and vans per year.

Driving Forces. To counter pressures from European legislators and consumers, GM Europe decided that every plant in Europe will achieve either a BS 7750 or an EMAS accreditation within the next few years. The plant in Ellesmere Port was chosen to be the first of the GM plants in Europe to do so and aimed for a BS 7750 certificate. It has four main business activities, namely the vehicle assembly, sub-assemblies, pressings and the V6 engine plant. Due to its outstanding position among the European plants, Ellesmere Port became the pilot project for Europe. The next plant expected to achieve an accreditation is Opel Bochum in Germany, which is aiming for EMAS.

Environmental Targets. The main target was to achieve accreditation under BS 7750. The company began with the implementation of BS 7750 in March 1994 and in 1995 Vauxhall Motors at Ellesmere Port became the first automotive company in the world to receive an accreditation by the British Standards Institute for its Environmental Management System. To achieve the certification, Vauxhall Motors used an external consultancy— Arthur D. Little—but created internal ownership at the same time.

Training Needs Analysis. In order to identify the environmental responsibilities within Vauxhall Motors and to find out about the training needs, a consultant carried out interviews with the plant managers, the health and safety managers, workers from the shopfloor and maintenance. The knowledge acquired helped design future training for the workforce.

Target Groups. In order to communicate the BS 7750 objectives and procedures to the entire workforce, managers, environmental specialists and individuals in key functions, such as employees in contact with hazardous substances, were informed and provided with specific training.

The first group to be addressed was senior management. This was done within various meetings and discussions and with the help of a thirty-minute environmental awareness presentation. Once the support from the managers was gained, other groups were addressed.

Training Content. The training content depended on the target group. Senior management, who were trained first, were given information on BS 7750, the background and driving forces. The auditors who had the in-house responsibility for the project were trained about the environmental audit process, environmental legislation, waste and water management and management of hazardous materials.

The training content for the rest of the workforce was designed according to their work. Everybody was informed about BS 7750 and its implementation. In addition, an environmental awareness presentation included information on legal requirements, the environmental effects of the plant, the emission control programme, and what the company wanted the participants to do.

Mechanisms of Delivery. When the structure of environmental responsibilities was clear, one planning engineer became the first internal auditor and was made responsible for the process. He gathered people from every key area in Vauxhall Motors so that a group of ten environmental auditors was formed. This group held weekly meetings where environmental issues within Vauxhall Motors, such as returnable packaging or waste segregation, were discussed. With this group, and the influence of every member in it, environmental issues became an internal matter of concern from the outset. These auditors were sent on a two-day training course, provided by the consultants.

Besides the ten auditors, seven environmental programme co-ordinators were selected. They were chosen on the basis of their specialist knowledge of environmental issues and were made responsible for implementing action plans covering the main environmental issues at the plant.

The next step was the development of an environmental manual, as required in BS 7750, and this was delivered by Arthur D. Little. Copies were issued to every one of the 245 supervisors, and it was revised and improved as the process went on—an easily-accessible computer-based version was installed, along with an environmental legislation database. To ensure the best use of this system and to encourage people to use it, computer training is offered, either for individuals or for small groups in twenty-minute sessions.

Methods and Tools. As it would have been too time-consuming to train the remaining part of the 4,250-strong workforce in small groups, it was agreed to give presentations to large groups—600 to 800 at a time—in the company's presentation facility. The auditors themselves gave these presentations using the thirty-minute environmental awareness package, also used to train the managers earlier in the process.

To support this information, environmental responsibility sheets were created. These sheets give a brief summary of what should be understood to meet the requirements linked to a particular job or what the employee needs to know in general. There are environmental responsibility sheets for Unit/Department Managers, Supervisors, Maintenance Managers, Shift Managers and all employees. Another instrument is an environmental incident report form.

As Vauxhall Motors sees staff motivation and active awareness as a key part of any successful environmental management system, communication of the environmental initiatives and progress was taken very seriously. Apart from leaflets and newspapers, posters were produced on issues such as how to save energy or water and how to segregate waste. Material usage and cost charts are displayed in each unit of the plant and employees are further encouraged to participate through the company's environmental suggestion scheme. Every new employee within Vauxhall Motors receives an environmental introduction pack that details Vauxhall Motors' environmental policy and activities.

■ *Adam Opel AG*

Adam Opel AG has been part of the world's largest vehicle manufacturing company, General Motors (GM), since 1929. The company produced 830,829 automobiles in 1994, of which 215,050 were produced in Rüsselsheim. 47,335 people were employed in 1994, including 26,449 in Opel Rüsselsheim, and the turnover of Adam Opel AG in 1994 was DM25.6 billion.

Driving Forces. One of the main driving forces for Adam Opel to protect the environment is the pressure coming from competitors in the automotive industry. Besides the fact that Adam Opel is committed to the environment to ensure the least possible impact, the market pressures regarding the environment are now considerable in Germany. However, the public image of the company with regard to the environment is positive and the company aims to maintain this.

Environmental Targets. The environmental targets of the company are to ensure the best environmental practice possible, to produce as little waste as possible and to use the best technology available. This helps to lower the risk of environmental accidents and also provides cost-saving potential in day-to-day business. More environmental targets will be set within the framework of the EMAS, for which accreditation is planned for 1996/97.

Training Needs Analysis. A training needs analysis as such was not carried out in Opel Rüsselsheim. The environmental training courses or modules were developed as an integrated part of other training courses that aimed to inform about, for example, a new process being installed.

Target Groups. The target groups for environmental training are mainly the operators in charge of environmentally-hazardous substances. They will receive environmental training as a part of their training for new processes and projects. The foremen attend refresher courses regarding environment and health and safety on a regular basis. Employees who aim for a master craftsman's diploma get a one-day environmental training course about the protection of land, water and air, which includes field trips and presentations. Apart from this, every apprentice is educated in environmental protection.

Training Content. The training content covers the protection of land, water and air as well as legislation relevant for day-to-day business. Environmental awareness training as such is not carried out. Environmental issues are integrated within the training given with all new processes and projects. This training aims to use examples from within the factory, visiting different plants where specific problems can be seen and explained. The training content will be more specified as the environmental audit process is carried out in the year 1996/97.

Mechanisms of Delivery. The training courses are conducted by the environmental specialist or people in charge of the implementation of special processes. They communicate with the supervisors in charge of this process and they explain to them how the new process will affect the current business. This is done by presentations for groups of 20–25 participants. If the training course covers a special subject, such as the protection of water according to VAWS,[3] it will be conducted by external trainers, e.g. from the Chamber of Commerce.

The environmental manager at Rüsselsheim has written an environmental manual containing essential information on environmental protection. The manual covers legislation, environmental responsibilities, internal organisation and regulations for day-to-day business, and is available to plant managers for reference purposes. Apart from this, environmental issues are communicated in the internal house magazine to all employees.

Methods and Tools. To impart the training content, the company mainly uses workshops, in which the number of participants never exceeds 25. During these work-shops, presentations and discussions are used to get the message across to the participants. If convenient, trips to other plants are undertaken.

■ General Electric Company (GEC)

The General Electric Company (GEC plc) has worldwide interests in power generation, telecommunications, avionics, defence systems, shipbuilding, electronics and household appliances. The company employs 95,000 in the UK and, in 1994, had a turnover of £10 billion, with pre-tax profits in excess of £900 million.

The GEC Management College is a training institution that provides training and consultancy to a wide range of clients from all business sectors, mainly for its largest client, the subsidiary and joint venture companies of GEC plc, but also for local government and public sector organisations. GEC plc has 140 companies and the GEC Management College provides consultancy support in environmental matters as well as in other subjects.

Driving Forces. There are various driving forces affecting GEC, but the main ones are:

- Legislation in the United Kingdom and the European Community
- Customer pressure, as the Ministry of Defence or NATO require environmental issues on the company's agenda
- Shareholder pressure

The environmental initiative within GEC companies was started top-down: the GEC management decided that action had to be taken regarding the environmental issues within GEC.

Environmental Targets. The environmental targets have to be worked out by each GEC company individually. However, GEC plans to carry out an audit of every site within the next year to gather information about the actual situation and the main environmental issues. Apart from that, as an overall target GEC wants to lower the risk of environmental accidents and to raise environmental awareness within the 140 companies in the group.

Training Needs Analysis. The training needs analysis has to be carried out by each GEC company individually. However, the need for environmental awareness training was quite obvious. Therefore the GEC Management College designed an environmental training pack for GEC companies.

Target Groups. The managing directors chose within their companies an environmental director who became responsible for environmental issues.

These environmental directors are from various departments: personnel, manufacturing or quality, depending on personnel skills and internal structure of the company. From these departments an environmental manager was also selected, and these managers attended three full-day training courses carried out by the GEC Management College. The first training session took place in 1993 when 120 training courses were carried out, followed by 22 training courses in 1994 and 80 in 1995 up to the time of writing. More target groups were identified according to the internal structure of the various GEC companies.

Training Content. The Environmental Managers Training Programme includes various subjects. At the first session, the subject was environmental legislation, BS 7750 and the Environmental Management System. Following this initial session, the managers went back to their companies and conducted a review. Armed with this information, they joined the second training session, dealing with issues such as waste management and transport as well as air emissions. These topics were explained in terms of best practice and how to monitor them. The third and last section was spent in discussion of treatment of waste water, ground water, communications, awareness-raising and risk management.

Mechanisms of Delivery. The first step was to bring the 140 managing directors together in two meetings of 70 individuals to inform them about environmental driving forces and environmental legislation. When they returned to their companies, the MDs had to organise their own method of responding to the environmental challenge. As well as the training course attended by every environmental manager from all GEC companies, each company carries out its own internal training programme, depending on specific needs.

However, other initiatives are undertaken under the auspices of the GEC Management College in order to make environmental improvements: for example, workshops for designers on environmentally-friendly design. In these workshops, designers from two different companies examine each other's product with regard to their environmental friendliness. The exchange of opinions and knowledge generates new ideas for both teams.

As another initiative, the GEC Management College invites specialists from different departments, e.g. research and development, design, manufacturing, purchasing and others to meet in a special interest group. The meeting lasts one day and is attended by 30 to 50 people.

Methods and Tools. The environmental training course attended by all the environmental managers was presented in three parts over four weeks so that the participants had the chance to go back to their companies after each training session and integrate the new information into their work, and also to collect information to bring to the next training course. GEC Management College also provides an environmental training pack for the GEC companies, which comprises:

- A three-part VHS video entitled *Why Should I Care?*
- Participative tasks
- Facilitation notes
- A glossary of environmental terms

The materials in the pack have been prepared in such a way that every employee will gain a better appreciation of global and local environmental issues and their crucial role in making improvements, both at work and at home. The pack is delivered to all GEC companies and will be presented to every employee in 1995/96.

■ *Siemens*

Based on sales and the number of employees, Siemens is one of the world's largest companies in the field of electrical engineering and electronics. Almost 60% of the company's business is with international customers, and Siemens has manufacturing and sales organisations in more than 190 countries. Electronic products and systems now account for well over half of total sales. Sales in Germany in 1994 were DM35.8 billion and the number of employees stood at 222,000

Environmental Targets. The environmental targets within Siemens are set according to the company's environmental protection guidelines. According to Siemens' *Initiatives for the Environment*, 'We are committed to conserving the environment and treating natural resources with care and respect. This applies as much to our production processes as to our products. The assessment of the environmental effects of our products begins as early as the development stage. It is our aim to go beyond legal requirements to prevent environmental pollution or to reduce it to an absolute minimum.'[4]

Training Needs Analysis. The department for in-house training and the committee for environmental protection assess the needs of the workforce and develop environmental training courses accordingly.

Target Groups. Every employee within Siemens receives some environmental training. However, the main target groups are: employees in charge of the correct treatment of hazardous waste and dangerous substances, and specialists who want to broaden their knowledge. An introductory course is designed for employees who have no knowledge on environmental issues, but are going to need it for future tasks. For the sales staff, Siemens developed a training course on environmental protection in the context of product and sales management.

Training Content. The training courses offered cover a whole range of environmental topics:

- Introduction to environmental protection
- Soil protection and water management
- Waste management
- Treatment of water-polluting substances
- Emissions
- Environmental protection in the context of product and sales management
- Environmental auditing

The training content varies from training course to training course, but one important topic in all of these training courses is environmental legislation and regulations. Another important topic is the internal organisation of environmental responsibilities advising participants as to who is able to provide further information when necessary. Further topics include possible waste-avoidance measures, environmental aspects in case of a fire, and the EMAS.

The 'Introduction to Environmental Protection' course covers the following topics: organisation of environmental responsibilities within Siemens; legislation; management of chemicals and hazardous substances; water, waste and air management; and costs

Mechanisms of Delivery. Environmental protection at Siemens is organised on three levels, with responsibility lying, respectively, with a member of the Corporate Executive Committee, the Group Presidents, and plant managers. They receive technical support from the Corporate Office for Environmental Protection, the environmental protection officers at group level, and environmental specialists at each location.[5]

Environmental training is part of the in-house education and training programme within Siemens. Training courses last at least one day and take place during the working hours. The one-day training sessions are conducted by in-house trainers, whereas specialist training courses on, for example, fire prevention,[6] are carried out by external trainers, e.g. from the Chamber of Commerce.

Every year around 5,000 suggestions on how to further optimise work processes are made by plant employees. This indicates that environmental protection is 'not a matter for a few selected individuals, but a concerted action promoted wholeheartedly throughout the company, at all levels from board members to our newest trainees.'[7]

Methods and Tools. In the training sessions, presentations are given and discussions initiated. Blackboard and video support the trainers' presentation.

■ European Gas Turbines (EGT)

EGT designs and manufactures industrial gas turbines for power generation and mechanical drives for the on-shore and off-shore industry. EGT has five sites in Lincoln, three of which are manufacturing sites. The company employs approximately 2,400 people in Lincoln, and also has manufacturing sites in France and Germany. EGT is a GEC company.

Driving Forces. Driven by BS 7750 and the Environmental Protection Act 1990, the management decided to deal more thoroughly with environmental issues within EGT, and in 1992 an audit of the three manufacturing sites was made by a GEC consultant. The audit investigated legal compliance and record-keeping, and made suggestions for improvements to production. At the same time, the issue of employee environmental awareness was addressed.

Environmental Targets. As environmental protection is a progressive process, the company believes that targets should be constantly reviewed. Environmental training of the entire Lincoln workforce is planned for completion by April 1996. Another target is to set up a waste minimisation programme. Whether EGT will try to achieve BS 7750 or EMAS accreditation will be decided in the near future.

Training Needs Analysis. EGT plans to carry out environmental training using the Environmental Training Pack from GEC Management College. The environmental manager from EGT Lincoln is anticipating valuable information on further training needs through feedback from participants of these training courses, which will be used to design in-depth training courses.

Target Groups. Training started with 120 senior managers attending four half-day workshops in groups of thirty. They then relayed the information to their departments and cascaded the training down. At the same time, employees were free to seek further information from the environmental manager of EGT. The entire workforce will receive basic training from the Environmental Training Pack provided by GEC Management College.

Training Content. For senior managers, the training content was: environmental driving forces and legal background; the company's environmental impact regarding emissions into air, soil and water; the company's environmental commitment; and the required support from all employees. The GEC Management College Environmental Training Pack is as described above.

Delivery, Methods and Tools. These are as described in the section on GEC.

■ ABB (German Branch)

ABB is one of the world's leading companies in the field of electrical and power engineering and environmental control technology. The company's turnover in 1994 was DM10 billion and at that time the company employed 34,000 people. Important power generation activities are located in Germany. ABB currently has no EMS and does not carry out regular environmental training. The company is actually in the process of developing an environmental training programme for the whole company, which will start in January 1996.

Driving Forces. Driving forces for ABB are market pressures and competitor pressure. The company policy guidelines emphasise the best possible protection of natural resources.

Environmental Targets. The main environmental target of ABB is to ensure the best possible protection of the environment, on the basis that prevention is better than cure. In addition, the company is convinced that a full environmental review will also lead to improved business practice. Environmental protection within ABB begins with the product design and is continued through the whole process.

Training Needs Analysis. A training needs analysis as such was not carried out in ABB. However, every location has a local environmental controller ('leco') who is in charge of the site's environmental performance. The leco also has to develop the training content and to consider the best way to deliver the information to the workforce.

Target Groups. The target groups are all employees and, in particular, supervisors, plant managers and managers. Everyone has to integrate environmental protection into their day-to-day business to ensure the best possible practice with regard to the environment. As well as environmental skills training, environmental awareness training is planned.

Training Content. Managers will have to understand the long-term environmental targets of ABB and will have to integrate them into their work. Managers need to ensure that their departments do everything necessary to protect the environment. Staff working with hazardous materials will receive training about how to handle them, as well as environmental awareness training. This awareness training will include the company's environmental policy, company targets, and waste and water management. The emphasis will be on the question 'What can I do?'

Delivery: Methods and Tools. Environmental training will be combined, where convenient, with health and safety training. The leco at each site will propose mechanisms of delivery as well as methods and tools appropriate for the target groups.

■ *ICI*

ICI is a world leader in chemicals, producing paints, industrial chemicals, materials and explosives. ICI employs over 65,000 people, has manufacturing facilities around the world and has a turnover of over £8 billion.

Driving Forces.[8] The main driving force for ICI C&P to improve the environmental performance is pressure from competitors and customers. Apart from that, the ICI management believes that environmental protection makes good business sense and offers opportunities to improve the business as a whole. Compliance with environmental legislation is another driving force.

Environmental Targets. ICI is committed to the environment and has issued annual environmental reports since 1991. To focus their efforts on environmental improvement, they set themselves four main objectives in 1990:

1. ICI requires all its new plants to be built to standards that will meet the regulations it can reasonably anticipate in the most environmentally-demanding country in which it operates that process. This will normally require the use of the best environmental practice within the industry.

2. ICI will reduce waste by 50% by 1995, using 1990 as the baseline year. The company will pay special attention to wastes that are hazardous. In addition, ICI will try to eliminate all off-site disposal of environmentally-harmful wastes.

3. ICI will establish a revitalised and more ambitious energy and resource conservation programme, with special emphasis on reducing environmental effects so that they can make further substantial progress by 1995.

4. ICI will encourage recycling within its businesses and with the customers.[9]

The second target especially attracted public attention and this is also the area on which ICI particularly focuses.

Training Needs Analysis. A training needs analysis as such was not carried out within ICI C&P. It was generally understood that the first training should raise awareness, followed by more specific programmes.

Target Groups. Information on ICI's environmental activities and necessary action was cascaded down to the entire workforce layer by layer. The first target group addressed was senior management.

Following this, environmental specialists were sent on an intensive environmental training course to acquire the necessary knowledge for their new job.

A selection of managers and supervisors on site attended a one-day introductory training course, which was designed to raise environmental awareness of those who were not experts on environmental issues. Plant managers formed another target group receiving special environmental information.

Every operator attended a training session on Integrated Pollution Control (IPC). IPC seeks to ensure that the Best Practicable Environmental Option (BPEO) is chosen in situations where there are emissions into more than one environmental medium.[10]

Training Content. Training for senior management included background and driving forces behind ICI's commitment to the environment. Environmental targets were explained along with plans of how to achieve them. Senior management was asked to support the environmental initiative and to inform their managers about it.

The five-day training course attended by environmental specialists contained information on ICI policy and legislation, the impact of manufacturing on the environment, technical aspects and current environmental practice, management techniques for environmental improvement and an outlook to future development.

The one-day introductory training course for managers and supervisors covered issues such as legislation, environmental site policy, environmental contacts, lifecycle analysis, IPC, waste minimisation and risk assessment. Plant managers were supplied with information on IPC and the environmental impact of their plant, and operators received a training session on IPC conducted by plant managers during which they set targets according to the process they were working on.

Methods and Tools. The five-day training course for environmental specialists was followed up with various types of feedback. Members were contacted at intervals of three weeks, three months and one year to ensure that the course content was kept fully relevant to their needs. During the course itself, a variety of methods and tools was used: presentations, discussions, case studies, exercises, field trips, and a plenary session. The training sessions for the operators were carried out as presentations with a discussion about targets that were to be set afterwards.

In 1992 ICI began its training activities with a distance-learning programme which included three booklets on water pollution control, air pollution control, and disposal of waste. These booklets were designed by environmental specialists from ICI and distributed to the plant managers.

■ BASF

The BASF Group is one of the world's largest multinational chemical companies. Its operations extend from oil and gas to high-tech chemical products and consumer goods.[11] The company employed 65,549 people in Germany in 1994 and had an annual sales turnover of DM11.98 billion.

Driving Forces. BASF is committed to the environment and wants to reduce its environmental impact. Environmental initiatives are seen as an investment in the future with the aim of saving resources for the next generation.

BASF has moved from end-of-pipe technology towards process improvement, where the entire lifecycle of a product is taken into consideration. This means that design and production already aim to lower the impact on the environment, e.g. with regard to recycling. This will result in lower energy usage and therefore cost savings for the company as well. BASF believes that the best practice approach cuts both ways: it will deliver the best protection for the environment and realise the best business practice possible.

Environmental Targets. BASF views environmental protection and industrial safety as an ongoing challenge basic to its work.[12] The company adheres to the following guidelines:

- It does not give economic considerations precedence over environmental protection and safety.
- It minimises any adverse environmental impact of production, warehousing, transportation, distribution and product use.
- It promotes environmental and safety awareness among all employees.
- It promulgates knowledge on environmental protection and product safety through open dialogue with the public; exchanges knowledge and experience with authorities, trade and governmental associations, policy-makers and the scientific community.

BASF has various environmental targets, namely: to economise on energy use; to make the workplace a safer place; to reduce waste and emissions; and to promote technological innovation.

Training Needs Analysis. The training needs within BASF are investigated with the aid of the internal suggestions scheme: every employee has the opportunity to make suggestions regarding environmental improvement. As an incentive, the best suggestions receive prizes. Apart from the general suggestion scheme, plant managers are asked to identify their personal training needs or the training needs they perceive necessary for their staff.

Target Groups. The target groups for environmental training are managers, supervisors and plant managers. According to BASF's 1994 Environmental Report, 'BASF's works managers will be attending a new regular briefing on the latest status of environmental protection and safety. The new advanced training programme will provide extra know-how in this field for all BASF employees who need to have a detailed picture.'[13] Plant managers attend various training courses in context with environmental protection and health and safety.

Training Content. The new training course for work managers will be based on the updated Environmental Protection and Safety Guidelines, adopted by the company in 1993. They lay down that employees must be provided— through practical and theoretical training and briefings—with all the facts on environmental protection and safety they need for their jobs. The heart of the new BASF advanced training plan is a quarterly briefing for works managers in research, production and engineering. At the meetings, the latest trends in the industrial safety and environmental protection fields—in environmental legislation, for example, or the law concerning wastes or hazardous substances—are presented and discussed.[14]

Methods and Tools. The methods used in the environmental training courses are mainly interactive. The trainers require the participants to be active, e.g. to carry out a case study rather then just listen in a formal situation. The case study is a popular tool for illustrating the process of licensing a new plant and is used in instructing plant managers. To raise environmental awareness, trainees are given the opportunity to simulate accidents with so-called 'mini-plants'.

■ *Conclusions*

The eight British and German based firms described above have each developed their own environmental training system. In Figures 2 and 3 we have summarised important features of the relevant training approaches in order to facilitate a comparison. While all companies are committed to environmental protection, the way this is translated into management and

	Vauxhall	Opel	GEC	Siemens
Environmental targets	Decision by GM Europe		Individual targets of 140 GEC companies within overall company policy	Detailed company-wide targets
	BS 7750 accreditation	EMAS accreditation		
Training needs analysis (TNA)	Interview by external consultants	No specific TNA	a) individually b) by GEC Management College	No specific TNA
Target groups and training approach	■ Awareness training for senior management ■ Training for auditors ■ Specific skills and awareness training for staff	Skills-oriented training for specialists and operators	■ Top-down approach ■ GEC Management College: Training Pack as awareness training ■ Specific programmes in each company	■ Bottom-up approach ■ Wide-ranging course programme (awareness-, legally-, skills- and process-oriented) ■ Integral part of in-house education and training programme
Delivery	Short awareness training and longer skills training	One-to-several-days training course	By GEC Management College and/or 'cascading down'	By training department and/or consultants

Figure 2: *Comparison of Training Provisions in UK and German Companies*

	ICI	BASF	EGT	ABB-Germany
Environmental targets	Company-wide targets; going beyond legislation	Detailed company-wide targets	Company-wide policy and specific targets for sites	Overall policy and specific targets of subsidiaries
Training needs analysis (TNA)	No specific TNA	Review with plant managers	Initial courses used to define training needs	TNA by local environmental co-ordinators ('Iecos')
Target groups and training approach	Combination of top-down and bottom-up approach Programmes for management, specialists and operators	Combination of bottom-up and top-down Wide-ranging training	■ Top-down ■ Awareness training of senior management and cascading information to lower level ■ Skills training to be developed	Awareness and skills training in a combined bottom-up, top-down approach
Delivery	Phased training with feedback, action learning	Courses, simulation of accidents in mini-plants	GEC Package: 'cascading down'	Decentralised training on all levels

Figure 3: *Comparison of Training Provisions in UK and German Companies*

staff training differs widely. The paired firms are not necessarily any closer to each other regarding environmental targets and training than firms belonging to another pair. Also, there is no clear Anglo–German divide. Below we will first discuss environmental systems of company pairs, followed by an evaluation of Anglo–German differences.

Although Vauxhall's and Opel's overall environmental targets are similar, namely to attain either BS 7750 or EMAS, approaches to environmental training differ. At Vauxhall, training is a tool to prepare for BS 7750 in a top-down process. Opel has a longer history of environmental involvement in a bottom-up manner. Preparation for EMAS is seen as guidance to fill up training gaps and to systematise what has been achieved up to now.

While GEC represents a decentralised approach to environmental management, Siemens opts for detailed company-wide targets which are put into practice by a bottom-up and all-embracing training approach. Even though environmental targets are set by GEC subsidiaries, awareness training is provided in a top-down approach, based on the training pack from GEC Management College.

Both ICI and BASF give top priority to improving environmental performance of their human resources. It seems that, due to the characteristics of chemical industry, these two companies coincide more than other pairs in their environmental training. Their training is geared towards integrated pollution control in a combined top-down and bottom-up approach. Given their responsibilities, plant managers play a key role in defining training needs, selecting target groups and initiating programmes. Operators of key processes, along with those in charge of material handling, form target groups for a permanent training where action learning features prominently.

In our company pair, EGT and ABB (Germany), in the first instance environmental training is driven by the desire to attain either BS 7750 or EMAS, while at ABB environmental performance is linked to business performance. The group is even lobbying for tighter environmental legislation to promote sales of their equipment. To be consistent, therefore, environmental awareness and skills of human resources are considered an important asset. Environmental training at EGT is standard-driven using a top-down approach. ABB pursues very much a decentralised and bottom-up approach which is consistent with its overall organisation.

The differences in environmental training systems of the paired companies may lead to the conclusion that adherence to a specific business does not induce similar approaches, particularly if environmental concerns are of importance but not a top priority. On the contrary, the two examples of the chemical industry demonstrate that in a sector where environmental protection is vital for survival, and where processes widely determine company organisation, in these cases training systems seem to converge.

We might argue that perhaps Anglo–German differences are more pronounced than sectoral ones. What, then, are these Anglo–German differences?

The idea of in-house training in regard to environmental protection is newer to British than to German companies. The German companies analysed, in general, offer wide-ranging environmental training as an integral part of their in-house training programme. Training sessions there usually take not less than one day. The British companies tend to use modules of environmental training that take less time. All British companies agreed that environmental awareness training is necessary as well as environmental skills training. Apart from ABB-Germany, no German company plans to carry out separate awareness training or is currently doing so. In the UK, top-down approaches are more common, while

German companies rely more on a bottom-up training approach. UK companies tend to perceive training as a tool for attaining BS 7750, while German companies seem to develop their own specific agendas, less driven by attaining a standard procedure, even though EMAS is becoming more influential.

Companies in the UK and Germany mentioned similar driving forces, such as legislation, competitor and customer pressures and the wish to lower the risk of environmental accidents. However, legislation was mentioned as the major driving force for British companies, whereas German companies take a more proactive view, indicating that they want to go behind legislative requirements (also mentioned by ICI in the UK sample) and that their aim is to cause the lowest impact possible for the environment. This statement is interesting, insofar as environmental legislation is stricter in Germany than in the UK.

The training content comprises a whole range of subjects, depending on the target group. One big issue for British and German companies was waste and water management. As the target groups are slightly different, the training content also varies. British companies include general driving forces into the training as they believe that it is necessary to raise awareness among the workforce. BS 7750 is another topic that does not play a role in German training. The company's environmental policy or the corporate guidelines are part of training in both countries.

Concerning the mechanisms of delivery, we find in general a different approach. German companies have well-structured training activities. Environmental training is part of the internal training programme as other training topics are. In Germany, companies are used to offering environmental training of longer duration than in the UK, and they offer a wider range of environmental training. This is partly due to the fact that German legislation demands environmental specialists where a company has more than a specific amount of employees. The companies in the UK, on the other hand, show more enthusiasm in regard to environmental training and they find more and unusual ways to put the message across.

German companies seem to believe that skills training that is relevant to an individual's work will simultaneously raise awareness and change behaviour. On the other hand, UK companies tend to believe that, first, a more general state of awareness should be reached before skills training is started. Consequently, UK companies try to create a top-down movement where BS 7750 is often used as guide book. German companies approach the subject more in the manner of 'learning by doing'.

We suggest that the differing approaches to environmental training can be explained by three factors: the state of environmentalism; management and corporate culture; and adherence to a specific business sector. The type of business and the state of environmentalism in a country determine to what extent a company is concerned and, consequently, how important environmental awareness and skills are for the success of a firm. Management and corporate culture shape the approach to HRM in general and environmental training in particular.

Effectiveness of environmental training, therefore, depends on whether companies are able to link all three factors in building an environmental training system. With mounting pressure to attain EMAS, training approaches may converge in both countries in the future. According to Peattie and Ringler,[15] there is, however, a danger that, with the desire to attain BS 7750, UK companies are focusing their attention too strongly on issues of systems, procedures, audits and manuals. The same could also happen for German companies regarding EMAS.

◼ Notes

1. British Standards Institute, *Environmental Management Systems: BS 7750* (London, UK: BSI, 1994).

2. Compare also Alison Bird in chapter 11—'Training for Environmental Improvement' pp. 238-39.

3. Verordnung über Anlagen zum Lagern, Abfüllen und Umschlagen wassergefährdender Stoffe.

4. Siemens, *Initiatives for the Environment* (Munich, Germany: Siemens, 1995), p. 15.

5. Siemens, *op. cit.*, p. 15.

6. 'Brandschutzbeauftragte'.

7. Siemens, *op. cit.*, p. 15.

8. The following information refers to ICI coat and paintings (C&P), Runcorn.

9. ICI, *ICI Environmental Performance 1994* (London, UK: ICI, 1994), pp. 4 and 5.

10. GEC Management College, *Environmental Training Pack* (London, UK: GEC, 1994), p. 24.

11. BASF, *Annual Report 1994* (Ludwigshafen, Germany: BASF, 1994).

12. BASF, *BASF Group Corporate Guidelines* (Ludwigshafen, Germany: BASF, 1994), pp. 14 and 15.

13. BASF, *Environment Report 1994* (Ludwigshafen, Germany: BASF, 1994), p. 32.

14. *Ibid.*, p. 32.

15. K. Peattie and A. Ringler, 'Management and the Environment in the UK and Germany: A Comparison', in *European Management Journal*, Vol. 12 No. 2 (1994), pp. 216-25.

13

Managing the Learning of Ecological Competence

Peter Dobers and Rolf Wolff

*T*HIS CHAPTER elaborates on the problem of managing the ecological challenge from a competence point of view. The aim of this chapter is to discuss a set of competence areas from a management perspective, which together form the concept of 'ecological competence'. Conceptual reflections about ecological competences establish a first step in specifying descriptions of an ecological learning process and may serve as an analytical tool for researchers interested in exploring this subject more deeply. Empirical data from Sweden demonstrates learning elements of emerging 'ecological spaces'.

■ Introduction

Ecological issues have traditionally been viewed as problems mainly caused by industry. The last decade's compliance with legislation has been the major driving force for investment in ecologically-sound technology.[1] The business community now faces new driving forces to take ecological issues seriously and not only accepts, but increasingly seeks, the challenges of ecological business opportunities. Empirical studies demonstrate that business leaders conceive individuals' demands for ecologically-sound strategies and products in general and employees' demands in particular as crucial.[2] However, the execution of this challenge is difficult and must be analysed thoroughly.

The challenge for human resource management is to create conditions for the necessary competence to be created and maintained. The aim of this chapter is to develop a set of competence types, which together form the concept of ecological competence. We argue that the key to successful establishment of ecological competence lies in the ability to organise for and to modify competence, that is to create and maintain conditions for organisational learning.

The chapter starts out with a discussion of the relationship between competence and strategic decision-making. The empirical case study of a government-initiated ecological reform demonstrates the need for an organisational learning framework. The case study is based on interviews of participants and extensive examination and analysis of reports and documents. The chapter then further examines the organisational learning framework. Organisational learning theories explore the transformation mechanism that contribute to meaning and learning. Finally, the concept of ecological competence establishes a first step in specifying useful descriptions of an ecological learning process and may serve as an analytical tool for researchers interested in exploring this subject further. A process view, based on empirical data and case studies in Sweden, will demonstrate the learning elements and steps of how organisations can handle and integrate the problem of ecological competence into their day-to-day business.

■ Competence and Strategic Decision-Making

The Oxford Dictionary defines competence as 'being competent', which in turn is to have the 'ability, power, authority, skill, knowledge, etc. to do what is needed'. Put simply, competence is the ability to handle a situation satisfactorily and to act accordingly.[3] Conceptual frameworks of competence relate to elements such as ability, knowledge, culture, framework, and mentality.[4]

The term 'competence' also relates to the word 'compete'. If a person is perceived as competent, it must be a subjective viewpoint in relation to others. In organisational literature, the concept of 'competence' first appeared at the end of the 1950s. Selznick[5] discusses how companies develop a 'distinctive competence' to compete with other companies. Argyris[6] and White[7] assume learning to take place on the individual level, whereas Hall[8] develops a concept combining the organisational and the individual level. Competence is also one of the newer aspects of business strategy research.[9] According to this approach, 'a core competence is...a source of competitive advantage, in that it is competitively unique and makes a contribution to value and or cost', and '...is just what the name implies, an aptitude, a capability, a skill'.[10]

There are still many questions related to the issue of whether corporate ecological strategies really do contribute to competitive advantages. There are few empirical studies available, but these tend to be contradictory.[11] 'The business of business is business.' This could imply that ecological knowledge will only play a part of organisational life if and when it is perceived as being directly relevant to its business. Obviously, ecological considerations will influence organisational decision-making if they present business opportunities. But, as Walley and Whitehead argue,[12] at present ecological compliance is mainly induced through the legislator and leads to costs rather then benefits.

Evidently, the ecological challenge, seen as one problem or challenge among many, has to compete with other problems for the attention of the manager. Once they receive this attention, ecological problems gain potential relevance in a decision-making context. Acknowledgement is a prerequisite for organisational learning. Top management attention is the bottleneck in organisations. If top management devotes attention to a strategic uncertainty (for example, ecological issues) and engages the organisation in learning about this uncertainty, a basis is created for the embodiment of new competences in the organisational mind. Once the learning of new procedures has successfully been implemented, routines are established and maintained as programmed control. Programmed control can be delegated to staff and translated into manuals and programmes. Organisational learning thus opens the door for new strategic responses (see Fig. 1).

The concept of 'interactive control systems' has been developed by Simons[13] and contrasts strategy formulation as a process of learning with the technology of strategic planning.[14] Strategy in a company emerges as a response to continuous uncertainty. Interactive control is top management's response to the constant flow of new strategic issues that are genuinely uncertain. Single issues are addressed, dealt with and incorporated into the organisation's body of knowledge.

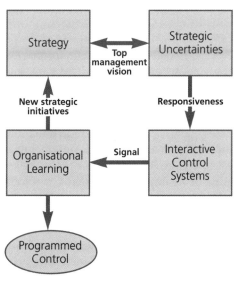

Figure 1: The Environmental Challenge

Source: R. Simons, 'The Role of Management Control Systems in Creating Competitive Advantage: New Perspectives', in *Accounting, Organization, and Society*, 1990, pp. 127-43.

■ A Shift in the Problem-Solving Paradigm: The Environmental Project at Gothenburg

Following a proposal by the Minister of Environmental Affairs, the Swedish parliament decided in 1987 to appoint a delegation to 'initiate and co-ordinate actions to make the Gothenburg region essentially cleaner over a ten-year period'.[15] The delegation named itself the Environmental Project Gothenburg (EPG) and the work proceeded between 1st January 1988 and 1st June 1989, when they also published a Swedish Government official enquiry report.[16] The EPG created a learning arena, in which it was possible to establish new competence types necessary to combat newly-defined ecological problems.

The EPG was initiated in a period in which the Swedish environmental policy was being challenged. During the 1980s, ecological issues entered the agendas of the Swedish political parties.[17] The existing administrative perspective of ecological control reached its limits. According to the Undersecretary of the Minister of Environmental Affairs at that time:

> The environmental projects were initiated at a time when we could look back on the results of the preceding environmental policy. One problem, however, was that there was no documenta-tion of the results. We had an inherent feeling that we had reached some kind of plateau with our actions. The admini-strative control apparatus that existed could not come to grips with the new problems it was facing.

Thus, it became clear that conditions were indicated in which a search for new solutions could take place. Three basic ideas guided the work of the delegation: (1) to formulate actions and to suggest innovative approaches that would lead to a significant decline in emissions in the Gothenburg area; (2) to ensure legitimacy for these projects in order to achieve a quick start; and (3) to implement essential projects, and to present the results of the work of the delegation over one and a half years in such a way that it could function as a model in Sweden.

A new facet of the EPG was an increasing awareness that administrative and legislative environmental regulations had limits. At the same time, the business community was increasingly accepting an active role regarding the search for and implementation of ecological solutions. Consumers started to put pressure on the retailing industry regarding the supply of ecologically-sound products. Enshrined in the directives was the concept of learning. End-of-pipe solutions had shown a growing effectiveness, but these measures did not cover non-point source emission. A complementary battery of solutions was therefore sought. The EPG was not the only regional experiment carried out, and was accompanied by three other similar projects: for the Dalälven River, for Western Skåne, and for the region of Sundsvall/Timrå.[18]

One feature in common is that all four directives were formulated openly, and that each delegation had far-reaching freedom to shape actions for ecological improvements. This shows an attempt to create new ways of how to manage ecological competence in a region that includes business organisations and the public sector. The project's launch was accompanied by a 'threatening image' of the ecological problems. Take, for instance, the Gothenburg region as pictured by the Minister of Environmental Affairs:

> Hisingen [an industry area] in Gothenburg is one of the nation's most exposed areas regarding ecological pollution to the air.[19]

Or:

> The Sundsvall region [...] is one of the oldest and most exploited industrial areas in our country. The activities at large process industries have, since the breakthrough of industrialism, led to considerable emission accumulating in soil and water.[20]

While over-accentuating the problem in such a way, the minister achieved various effects. First, attention was drawn to the diffused regional ecological problems. An intensive debate within the local political system began on whether this picture really was justified. Secondly, by defining the problem as the minister did, she also indirectly criticised what the preceding environmental policy had accomplished. Whether or not this was due to existing regulations and not to efficiency of the local agencies, it was still perceived as criticism. Several actors, such as the Swedish Environmental Protection Agency (EPA) and the local social democratic party were surprised by the minister's initiative. While the party actively supported the process, the EPA maintained a critical attitude throughout the project.

Legitimacy on a local level was achieved primarily through the work of the delegation. The project secretary of the EPG delegation had an extensive personal and professional network within the ecological profession in western Sweden. He had a background in Greenpeace Sweden, in the county administrative board, and was known in the industry as an expert on pollution issues. The chairwoman of the delegation (a social democrat) worked intensively to meet agencies, industry and others concerned and to play a part in the social network of the project secretary. In sum, credibility for the work of the delegation was accomplished not so much politically, but because of perceived staff competence and professional project management in the implementation phase. This led to a general acceptance of their work in the Gothenburg region.

Concerning contact with, and credibility with, industry, the delegation chose to work with those consultants upon which industry already relied. This was done in order to benefit from the perceived competence of professionals who had established a reputation in non-environmental subject areas. Thus, credibility among industry was secured, and the traditional conflict between a state-initiated delegation and the commercial sector could be avoided.

■ Towards Ecological Competence in Business: An Organisational Learning Perspective

Organisations are becoming increasingly competence-intensive,[21] but most organisations lack ecological competence, since it is a new field of knowledge and action. Organisations can be treated as knowledge systems,[22] and the specific knowledge base of an organisation can be characterised as the 'organisational mind'.[23]

Ecology is primarily a subsidiary of biology and explores the inter-relation between life and nature.[24] As a science, ecology is directly connected with other disciplines such as medicine, engineering, social sciences and business administration. All disciplines are embedded in an ecosystem, and ecology is the body of knowledge concerning the functioning of our ecosystem.[25] Here, we use the term 'ecological', since it narrows down the meaning of the general environment to the natural environment.

There are many different positions and theoretical developments explaining the learning process and adaptation of organisations. Some approaches describe learning in terms of adaptation, information processing, development of theories-in-use, and the institutionalisation of experience in the organisational context.[26]

In a recent book,[27] Mintzberg builds a bridge between organisational learning perspectives and the development of organisational strategies. Organisational learning (OL) is critical for the formulation and evaluation of organisational strategies. For our purposes we have to ask whether specific OL perspectives are able to enhance our understanding of the empirical phenomena in which we are interested; the adaptation of ecological norms into the organisational decision-process and strategy, and hence the evolution of ecological competence.

Cyert and March[28] label adaptation as 'organisational learning' and describe three different phases of the decision-making process: adaptation of goals; adaptation in attention rules; and adaptation in search rules. With regard to ecological adaptation, the goal adaptation will inevitably be problematic from a definitional point of view. 'Ecological adaptation' is *per se* an ambiguous, complex and vague concept. It focuses on a problem and not on a goal. Adaptation in attention refers to the selective attention that an organisation bestows on different parts of the environment. When studying 'ecological demands', we have shown[29] that organisations are controlled by external demands, and develop processes and institutions by which they are able to handle conflicting demands. In the case of Volvo, Schwartz[30] describes how the company de-couples[31] the production system from these demands, by creating a legitimating function, i.e. public affairs. The public affairs function deals with the ecological demands from the outside, and by doing that enables the production system to create new modes and solutions of production. De-coupling enables selective attention and the development of new solutions.

The basic structure of the Cyert and March[32] perspective is external. Other theorists focus on organisations in which members have the capacity to learn to predict changes in their environments, identify the influences of these changes, search for relevant strategies, and develop appropriate structures for implementation.[33] With regard to ecological learning, organisations have to question their assumptions of what they do. They have to unlearn and develop new views and solutions. An internal learning theory is needed to explain what is going on within the organisation, when its dominating theories-in-use are in question, and how and when old knowledge is replaced through processes of unlearning.

Usually an organisation responds to external signals by successively correcting its core theories-in-use. The basic assumptions of these theories are rarely questioned. The continual and concerted sharing and meshing of individual assumptions, of individual images of self and others, of one's activities in the context of collective interaction, maintains the organisation's theories-in-use.[34] The construction and modification of these theories through individual and collective inquiry is what can be labelled 'organisational learning'.[35] The point here is that individuals are agents of organisational actions and learning. It is when a mismatch is detected in the organisation, between predictions of outcomes of action theories and actual results, that a search process emerges and basic assumptions are questioned. At best, new assumptions are developed and new theories-in-use emerge.

With regard to ecological learning, the question is whether there are any mismatches between predicted results and actual outcomes of organisational actions. Some preliminary research findings from the oil industry indicate that, at least in investment decision-making, assumptions are not fundamentally questioned when ecological demands enter the decision arena. Rather, these demands are incorporated into a loosely-organised decision-making process.[36]

The effectiveness of organisations is a function of their long-term strategic choices, choices of transformation processes, and the administrative structure that support these processes.[37] Organisational choices are based on the knowledge-base incorporated in the organisational mind. The organisational mind is the accumulation of the experiences and the knowledge of its individual members. However, the organisational mind is more than the sum of its individual minds, as knowledge is perpetuated despite the fact that individuals enter and leave the organisation.

Duncan and Weiss define organisational learning as the process within the organisation by which knowledge about action–outcome relationships and the effects of the environment on these relationships is developed.[38] This knowledge is distributed across the organisation, is communicable to its members, has consensus validity, and is integrated into the working procedures and administrative structures of the organisation. With regard to ecological learning, the threats to learning occur as a consequence of organisational ideologies, rigid structures, historical performance standards and established legitimating standards.

When confronted with ecological demands, a company has to judge whether this demand is a threat to the elements of the knowledge-base, or whether the threat can be met by its established routines. The first type of threat would require what Argyris and Schön would label 'double-loop learning'; the other would require learning that can be classified as 'single-loop learning'.[39]

The strategic decision model presented in the previous section illustrates the awareness of company leaders with respect to ecological issues and their strategic dignity. We now have to take a look at the mechanisms that make companies adapt ecological knowledge into their knowledge system.

A merging of learning situations[40] in combination with Mintzberg's concept of 'emerging strategies'[41] enables us to structure the history and present status of ecological learning in Swedish business. Following Weick,[42] a simple stimulus-response structure for learning situations can be distinguished (see Fig. 2).

The 'S' represents the organisation's mechanism for 'seeing'. Perception and filters are based on what we could call 'the theory of business'. Responses ('R') are the organisation's instrumental answers to the theory of business and represent the 'action portfolio' that a company possesses. The simple structure enables us to distinctly differentiate four learning situations.

Learning situations	Stimulus (S)	Response (R)
I.	Same	Same
II.	Same	Different
III.	Different	Same
IV.	Different	Different

Figure 2: Stimulus-Response Structures for Different Learning Situations

Source: K.E. Weick, *The Social Psychology of Organizing* (Reading, MA: Addison-Wesley, 1979).

Type I learning: Same S Same R

If the theory of business remains the same, our responses do so as well. The organisation focuses on the continuous improvement of standard operating procedures (SOPs).

Type II learning: Same S Different R

The theory of business remains the same, but new responses are needed. For example, new market segments are exploited with old products and services. However, the changes needed are implemented within the previous frame of reference. Therefore, this situation may be characterised as 'single-loop learning'.

Type III learning: Different S Same R

This learning type occurs when companies' action do not match the actual business situation. Companies often continue to apply old measures and strategies, although over time the basis for business has changed. A deadlock occurs and, at best, a new theory can be developed to define new strategies. At worst, the company disappears from the market.

Type IV learning: Different S Different R

A genuine 'double-loop learning' situation arises when both the theory of business and the measures taken are not stable. In a situation like this, a company has to start a radical process of discovering its future basis for survival. It has to search for a new theory of business and related strategies are needed.

If we use this structure to develop a frame of reference for 'ecological learning in business', both the time dimension and the various technologies for planning can be added. Figure 3 gives an overview.

The 1960s mainly focused on regulatory measures by which companies were forced to improve their processes (standard operating procedures). Learning equalled improvement of existing processes.

The 1970s forced companies to re-define their processes due to changing cost structures as a consequence of taxation. Re-defining processes created single-loop learning, questioning actions and technologies, but not the basic assumptions of the business theory in operation.

The mid and late 1980s can be characterised by 'learning by failure'. Swedish companies often acted with a marketing orientation, communicating 'ecological' images, rather then really re-evaluating processes and products. These initiatives very often backfired and forced companies into serious reflection about their ecological strategies. Strategies were re-evaluated, environmental policies defined, ecological managers employed and thus the process of learning about the ecological environment started.

In the 1990s top managers have changed their attitudes. Now, ecological issues are really treated strategically. However, uncertainties are overwhelming. There are few reliable decision models at hand; and ecological problems are complex, so the tools employed have to reflect this complexity.

Transformation	Theory of business	Triggers of change	Defining strategic responses	Organisational learning	Environmental strategy formulation
1960s	Same	Regulation	Same	Refinement	Improvements in Standard Operation Procedures
1970s	Same	Taxation	Different	Single-loop learning	Adaptation of processes and technologies
1980s	Different	Management's attitudes, image, competition	Same failure	Learning by	Re-evaluation of strategies
1990s	Different	Strategic re-orientation	Different	Double-loop learning	Planning as discovery

Figure 3: Ecological Learning in Business

Source: R. Wolff and O. Zaring, *Organisational Learning. The Creation of Ecological Minds in Organisations* (Paper presented at 'The 1994 International System Dynamics Conference'; Stirling, UK: University of Stirling, 1994).

The 'theory-of-business' is questioned, re-evaluated, changed, and planning procedures are adapted that help discover new possibilities and restrictions. Of course, the above analysis is a simplification. The phases reflect the Swedish experience. It can be expected that time differences exist between countries or between specific industries, although the contents of various phases seem to be similar in the broader European context.[43]

■ Four Elements of Ecological Competence
The necessity to develop an ecological competence confronts companies and public organisations with new management challenges:

1. Making use of an inter-disciplinary scientific knowledge-base.
2. Managing inter-organisational relationships.
3. Integrating ecological technology into multi-technology operations.
4. Creating and maintaining a value-driven discourse.

■ Making Use of an Inter-Disciplinary Scientific Knowledge-Base
To control ecological pollution, politicians and agencies need reliable knowledge about the problem. Detailed legislation often prevents both the controlling agency as well as the controlled business company from learning. In this type of system, companies stick to compulsory learning of the latest emission norms[44] and agencies control their compliance. Experimentation is not given space, the political system does not learn and no new ecological solutions are developed. Knowledge of past control results allows agencies to formulate present and future means of control,[45] which tend to induce traditional, already-tested, controlling behaviour. This also prevents an adversary position between industry and environmental groups.

The environment—as with many other complex problem areas—suffers not from a lack of solutions, but rather from the fragmentation of knowledge. The organisation of research and development on the one side, and the separation from basic and applied research on the other, contributes to the disintegration of a body of knowledge that could constitute the 'ecological theory'. The expert society needs a management function that integrates knowledge about the ecological system.

Non-point source and invisible pollution need innovative solutions. Instead of closing learning processes through simple control philosophies, the process of developing complex ecological solutions must utilise as much existing knowledge as possible. The concept of 'ecological space' refers to the fact that ecological problems are 'regional': regions can be cities, counties or countries. In order to manage these ecologies, the whole body of existing knowledge has to be accessible.

To make sense of ecological knowledge within a given ecological space is therefore a management task. It involves many different actors, with different roles, interests and knowledge-bases.

■ *Managing Inter-Organisational Relationships*

The concept of 'ecological space' implies that there are many actors involved in the solution of ecological problems. Different actors define the problem differently, and also which solutions are necessary, as they represent different spheres of interest.[46] As a growing number of actors interact in an ecological arena such as in the EPG, the organisational quality of ecological problems rises to the surface. A social competence is needed in every actor system.

In the EPG, the secretary of the delegation possessed a number of competences, which were essential for the work of the delegation: the ability to manage such a project; the scientific knowledge-base to formulate and evaluate ecological problems; and the capacity to make priorities. His foremost skill, though, was to bring the various actors together and enable them—at least to some extent—to conclude that they all owned the problem.

Instead of control, communication between different actors is a prerequisite for the development of ecological solutions. In the case of the EPG, social networking by a dedicated person was appropriate to facilitate improvements. As demonstrated in other cases, mass communication via unconventional means such as art, music and poetry can be utilised to start a process of inter-organisational communication and problem-solving.[47]

Municipalities, for instance, represent one actor among many in an interdependent system with individual companies, different agencies with ecological responsibility, researchers with different backgrounds and orientations, and citizens lobbying against pollution.[48] In accordance with industry, municipalities need to acknowledge the strategic quality of ecological issues. In the future, the importance of local agencies in ecological policy will increase, according to the directive on the future role of the Swedish EPA.[49]

> [...] the central role of the Swedish EPA in the total ecological reform work will be strengthened and its organisation must be adjusted to a goal- and result-oriented control, as well as a conscious decentralisation and integration of the ecological reform work in different societal sectors.[50]

'Joint vision' is perhaps a concept that better grasps the change in the conditions of managing and controlling inter-organisational relationships.[51]

The 'joint vision' will contribute to:

> [...] joint competence development of actors that are not fully
> informed and that partially have competitive roles. Joint vision
> demands a leadership that encourages open undertakings and
> self responsibility, not order and control of others.[52]

Education towards an adaptation of more ecologically-sound operations is currently taking place in all parts of the society. Business companies realise that the 'business of business is not only business', but involves also the ecological conditions under which the business process is taking place. Local agencies realise that their role contains both control aspects and co-operative measurements. Politicians are becoming aware of the diffused character of their role: they have to control; they should push technology development; and they should co-operate with different actors. All these changes in responsibility and roles are due to a shift in implementation structure:

> Only local representatives, in 'horizontal co-operation' with
> other competence areas, can systematically create local presence
> which is a necessary (but not a sufficient) prerequisite to define
> and attack costly ecological challenges.[53]

■ *Integrating Ecological Technology into Multi-Technology Operations*

Legislation against pollutants has become stricter in two respects. First, permanently-decreasing emission limits are implemented. Secondly, regulations cover an increasing number of pollutants. Thus, the performance of existing cleaning technology reached a certain point where new technological solutions had to be developed.[54] In a field study of ABB Fläkt, up to ten different cleaning technologies were installed in their most sophisticated integrated cleaning systems. ABB Fläkt could guarantee an availability of 95% for each subsystem.[55] However, to guarantee a 95% availability of an integrated cleaning system with ten interdependent cleaning technologies, each of these must show a 99.5% availability ($0.995^{10} = 0.95$). The complexity of handling technological developments increases drastically and the management of multi-technology companies face new problems.[56] When rejecting a well-tested and safe technology in favour of a new, untested, technology, managers are confronted with two types of risks. One risk concerns the technological uncertainty in itself; the other is related to the envisaged emission levels—whether or not the new technology is able to deliver the promised results—as well as the uncertainty of interaction of the new technology with existing older technology.

The problem is reinforced by the fact that modern products require the management of many different technological competence areas simultaneously. It is said that mobile telephones contain fourteen different technological knowledge areas. Thus, to produce these telephones, fourteen different production areas have to be managed. On top of that, ecological technologies have to be developed that both take care of pollution during the production as well as the use and waste process.

■ Creating and Maintaining a Value-Driven Discourse

We are thus in the beginning of an area of total re-engineering of our industrial life. We have to re-invent our modes of production and consumption.

Many of the changes to come will not be initiated on the basis of simple cost–benefit analyses. There are still very few reliable decision-supporting models at hand that could deliver the arguments managers need in order to convince their boards that ecological investment is, or could be, profitable for the company, both in the short and long term. The uncertainty is still excessive with regards to what competitors are really up to. Finally, we know little about the triggering mechanism that motivates consumers to purchase ecologically-sound products and services.

What we *do* know is that business leaders in Scandinavia consider the environment to be a strategic challenge that will persist.[57] The initiative to develop positive ecological solutions has thus been taken over by the business community. This change is value-driven and will subsequently be awarded by the incidence of business opportunities. The growing importance of 'green private labels' in the Swedish retail industry is a good example of the growing market potential.

It is important that this process is kept alive. We should encourage and support business leaders to search for ecological solutions. As employees and consumers, we have considerable influence on businesses' ideologies and decisions. As researchers, we have an obligation to support the management of ecological spaces with decision-making tools, case studies and thus engage in the continuous creation of relevant knowledge.

■ Conclusions

Our own research clearly indicates that the Swedish business community has not yet fully incorporated ecological considerations into their strategic decision bodies. So far, there is a dominance of ecological managers in charge of companies' compliance to ecological demands and legislation. In order to organise for ecological competence, ecological management has to be incorporated into daily operations and strategies. This will lead to scientifically-driven decisions, to the management of relevant inter-organisational relationships, and to the use of new integrative ecological technologies. However, the most important transformation mechanism will be the gradual change towards ecological values in management.

What this contribution wants to highlight is the need of management research to engage in ecological issues. Organisation and management theory are important complements to other sciences, which have so far dominated the field. However, there are a lot of myths circulating regarding the environment. Contradictory scientific results contribute to managers' continuing uncertainty. Management research and collaboration with both public and private sector actors will improve our capacity to develop complex solutions for the fast-growing complex problems in our respective ecological spaces.

Proponents of an 'ecological' re-orientation of business have to consider the transformation mechanism involved by which a re-orientation of business is triggered. An organisational learning perspective contributes to the understanding of the knowledge creation processes (and unlearning processes) that are needed to adapt 'ecological' knowledge into the present industrial competence system. The research task is to shed light on the specific challenges that companies face, depending on their contingencies. The discussion of ecological adaptation of business thus has to go beyond simplifications and generalisations.

The strategic decision aspects presented argue for a combination of strategic decisions, tools and implementation, taking into account the constraints companies face. Here a collaborative approach between the regulator and business will be appropriate considering the complex problems we face during the next decades.

Finally, the organisational learning perspective advocates industry research collaboration and is a vote in favour of looking at what is possible to accomplish on the actual base of knowledge in a given situation and at a given time.

■ Notes

1. See, for instance, P. Dobers, 'Legislation-Induced Bubble Markets: Driving Forces of Air Pollution Control Technology in the Area of Waste Incineration', in *Scandinavian Journal of Management* (forthcoming 1996; Special Issue on Business and the Environment).

2. See E. Terrvik and R. Wolff, *Svenska Miljöbarometern Företag 1993 (The Swedish Environmental Business Barometer [EBB])* (GRI Report 1994:4; Gothenburg, Sweden: Gothenburg Research Institute [GRI]/Stockholm, Sweden: WWF, 1993).

3. See K. Keen, 'Att rekrytera och utveckla kompetens' ('To Recruit and Develop Competence'), in *Personal*, Vol. 5 (1987).

4. See S. Ohlsson and A. Targama, *Offensiv PA för affärsmässig förnyelse (Active Human Resource Management for Business Renewal)* (Lund, Sweden: Studentlitteratur, 1986); J. Sandberg, *Att utveckla och bevara kompetens. Organisationsuteckling sett ur ett kompetensperspektiv (To Develop and Maintain Competence: Organisational Development from a Competence Perspective)* (FE-Report 274; Gothenburg, Sweden: Gothenburg University, 1987).

5. P. Selznick, *Leadership in Administration: A Sociological Interpretation* (New York, NY: Harper & Row, 1957).

6. C. Argyris, *Personality and Organization* (New York, NY: Harper & Row, 1957).

7. R.W. White, 'Motivation Reconsidered: The Concept of Competence', in *Psychological Review*, Vol. 66 (1959).

8. J. Hall, *The Competence Process: Managing for Commitment* (Bromley, UK: Chartwell-Bratt, 1980).

9. See P. Hamel and G. Heene, *Competence-Based Competition* (Chichester, UK: Wiley, 1994).

10. *Ibid.*, pp. 18-19.

11. See R. Wolff and O. Zaring, *Business Strategy and Ecological Adaptation: A Research and Learning Challenge* (GRI Working Paper; Gothenburg, Sweden: Gothenburg Research Institute [GRI], 1994).

12. N. Walley and B. Whitehead, 'It's Not Easy Being Green', in *Harvard Business Review*, May/June 1994, pp. 46-52.

13. R. Simons, 'The Role of Management Control Systems in Creating Competitive Advantage: New Perspectives', in *Accounting, Organization, and Society*, Vol. 15 No. 2 (1990), pp. 127-43.

14. See H. Mintzberg, *The Structuring of Organizations* (Englewood Cliffs, NJ: Prentice Hall, 1974).

15. Miljö- och energidepartementet (Swedish Ministry of Environment and Energy), Dir 1987:57, *Kommittédirektiv, Åtgärdsprogram för Dalälven (Activity Plan for the Dalälven River)* (1987).

16. Miljö- och energidepartementet (Swedish Ministry of Environment and Energy), SOU 1989:32, *Miljöprojekt Göteborg: För ett renare Hisingen (Environmental Project Gothenburg: For a Cleaner Hisingen)* (Statens offentliga utredningar [Public Enquiries], 1989).

17. See M. Bennulf, *Miljöopinionen i Sverige (Environmental Opinions in Sweden)* (Göteborg Studies in Politics nr. 30; Lund, Sweden: Dialogos, 1994).

18. See Miljö- och energidepartementet (Swedish Ministry of Environment and Energy), Dir 1987:57, *Kommittédirektiv, Åtgärdsprogram för Dalälven (Activity Plan for the Dalälven River)* (1987); Miljö- och energidepartementet (Swedish Ministry of Environment and Energy), Dir 1989:5, *Kommittédirektiv, Åtgärdsprogram för Västra Skåne (Activity Plan for Western Scania)* (1989); and Miljö- och energidepartementet (Swedish Ministry of Environment and Energy), Dir 1989:9, *Kommittédirektiv, Åtgärdsprogram för Sundsvall-Timråregionen (Activity Plan for the Sundsvall-Timrå Region)* (1989).

19. Miljö- och energidepartementet (Swedish Ministry of Environment and Energy), Dir 1987:59, *Kommittédirektiv, Miljöprojekt Göteborg, (Environmental Project Gothenburg)* (1987).

20. Miljö- och energidepartementet (Swedish Ministry of Environment and Energy), Dir 1989:9, *Kommittédirektiv, Åtgärdsprogram för Sundsvall-Timråregionen (Activity Plan for the Sundsvall-Timrå Region)* (1989).

21. See K.-E. Sveijby and A. Risling, *Kunskapsföretaget (The Knowledge Company)* (Malmö, Sweden: Liber, 1986); M. Alvesson, *Ledning av kunskapsföretag. Exemplet ENATOR (The Leadership of Knowledge-Intensive Firms. ENATOR)* (Stockholm, Sweden: Norstedts Förlag AB, 1989); E. Gummesson, *Yuppiesnusk eller Ledarskapets Förnyelse? (Yuppie Mess or the Renewal of Leadership?)* (Stockholm, Sweden: SNS, 1990).

22. See R. Wolff, *Der Prozess des Organisierens: zu einer Theorie des organisationalens Lernens (The Process to Organise: A Theory of Organisational Learning)* (Spardorf, Germany: Wilfer, 1982).

23. See Wolff and Zaring, *op. cit.*; B. Hedberg and R. Wolff, *Strategy as Learning, Learning as Strategy* (unpublished working paper; Gothenburg/Stockholm, Sweden, 1995).

24. See M. Kirchgeorg, *Ökologieorientiertes Unternehmensverhalten: Typologien und Erklärungsansätze auf empirischer Grundlage (Ecology-Oriented Company Behaviour: Typologies and Explanations on an Empirical Basis)* (Wiesbaden, Germany: Gabler, 1990).

25. See H. Strebel, *Umwelt und Betriebswirtschaft: Die natürliche Umwelt als Gegenstand der Unternehmenspolitik (The Environment and Business Administration: The Natural Environment in the Corporate Policy)* (Berlin, Germany: E. Schmidt, 1980).

26. See R.M. Cyert and J.G. March, *A Behavioral Theory of the Firm* (Englewood Cliffs, NJ: Prentice Hall, 1963); C. Argyris and D.A. Schön, *Organizational Learning: A Theory of Action Perspective* (Reading, MA: Addison-Wesley, 1978); J.G. March and J.P. Olsen, *Ambiguity and Choice in Organisations* (Bergen, Norway: Universitetsforlaget, 1979); B. Hedberg, 'How Organisations Learn and Unlearn', in P. Nystrom and W.H. Starbuck (eds.), *Handbook of Organizational Design* (Oxford, UK: Oxford University Press, 1981); P. Shrivastava, 'A Typology of Organizational Learning Sytems', in *Journal of Management*, Vol. 20 No. 1 (1983), pp. 7-28.

27. H. Mintzberg, *op. cit.*

28. *Op. cit.*

29. B. Schwartz and R. Wolff, *Environmental Affairs: A Case Study* (GRI Report, 1991:1; Gothenburg, Sweden: Gothenburg Research Institute [GRI], 1991).

30. B. Schwartz, *The Public Affairs Function and the Environment* (Unpublished manuscript; Gothenburg, Sweden: Gothenburg Research Institute [GRI], 1994).

31. See K.E. Weick, *The Social Psychology of Organizing* (Reading, MA: Addison-Wesley, 1979).

32. *Op. cit.*

33. See March and Olsen, *op. cit.*; Hedberg, 'How Organisations Learn and Unlearn'; Wolff, *Der Prozess des Organisierens*.

34. See Shrivastava, *op. cit.*, p. 12.

35. See Argyris and Schön, *op. cit.*

36. See O. Zaring, *The Greening of Capital Investment Decisions: An Oil Industry Case Study* (GRI Working Paper 1993:2; Gothenburg, Sweden: Gothenburg Research Institute [GRI], 1993).

37. See R. Duncan and A. Weiss, 'Organizational Learning: Implications for Organizational Design', in *Research in Organizational Behavior*, Vol. 1 (1979), pp. 75-123.

38. *Ibid.*, p. 84.

39. Argyris and Schön, *op. cit.*

40. See Hedberg and Wolff, *op. cit.*

41. Mintzberg, *op. cit.*

42. *Op. cit.*

43. See Dobers' analysis of 'bubble markets' (Dobers, *op. cit.*).

44. See O.P. Olson, 'Reform as a Learning Process', in: N. Brunsson and J.P. Olsen (eds.), *The Reforming Organization* (London, UK/New York, NY: Routledge, 1993), pp. 176-90.

45. See J.L.R. Proops, 'Ecological Economics. Rationale and Problem Areas', in *Ecological Economics*, No. 1 (1989), pp. 59-76.

46. See B. Flyvberg, *Rationalitet og magt. Bind I: Det konkretes videnskab (Rationality and Power. Part I: The Science of Concreteness)* (Odense, Denmark: Akademisk Forlag, 1992); *idem, Rationalitet og magt. Bind II: Et case-baseret studie af planlægning, politik og modernitet (Rationality and Power. Part II: A Case Study of Planning, Politics and Modernity)* (Odense, Denmark: Akademisk Forlag, 1993).

47. See Miljö- och energidepartementet (Swedish Ministry of Environment and Energy), Dir 1989:5, *Kommittédirektiv, Åtgärdsprogram för Västra Skåne (Activity Plan for Western Scania)* (1989); Miljö- och energidepartementet (Swedish Ministry of Environment and Energy), SOU 1990:93, *Miljön i Västra Skåne. År 2000 i våra händer (The Environment in Western Scania: Year 2000 in our Hands)* (Statens offentliga utredningar [Public Enquiries], 1990).

48. See P. Dobers and R. Wolff, *Political Control Technologies and Environmental Spheres: Towards a New Paradigm of Environmental Control in Sweden* (Gothenburg Research Institute [GRI]; Paper accepted for publication in *Technology Studies* [forthcoming]; Special Issue on Technology and the Natural Environment).

49. Miljö- och energidepartementet (Swedish Ministry of Environment and Energy), SOU 1991:32, *Naturvårdsverkets uppgifter och organisation (The Tasks and Organisation of the Swedish Environmental Protection Agency)* (Statens offentliga utredningar [Public Enquiries], 1991).

50. Miljö- och energidepartementet (Swedish Ministry of Environment and Energy), Dir 1990:67, *Kommittédirektiv, Naturvårdsverkets uppgifter och organisation (The Tasks and Organisation of the Swedish Environmental Protection Agency)* (1990).

51. See B. Hjern, 'Är lokal demokratisk miljöpolitik egentligen demokratisk?' ('Is Local Democratic Environmental Policy Really Democratic?'), in: B. Kullinger and U.-B. Strömberg (eds.), *Planera för en bärkraftig utveckling (Plan for a Sustainable Development)* (Stockholm, Sweden: Statens råd för Byggnadsforskning, 1993), pp. 177-86.

52. *Ibid.*, p. 183.

53. *Ibid.*, p. 183.

54. See Dobers, *op. cit.*

55. See P. Dobers, *Driving Forces of Environmental Technology. The Development of Waste Incineration Air Pollution Control Technology* (GRI Working Paper 1993:1; Gothenburg, Sweden: Gothenburg Research Institute [GRI], 1993).

56. See O. Granstrand and S. Sjölander, 'Managing Innovation in Multi-Technology Corporations', in *Research Policy* (1990), pp. 35-60.

57. See E. Terrvik, R. Wolff, J. Ulhøi, H. Madsen and B. Ytterhus, *The Nordic Business Environmental Barometer (N.B.E.B)* (Oslo, Norway: Bedriftsøkonomens Forlag, 1995).

14

The Greening of European Management Education

John P. Ulhøi and Henning Madsen

*T*HIS CHAPTER addresses the extent to which the increasing demand for corporate environmentalism has penetrated institutions of higher business and management education. The study presents the results of an empirical study in four EU member states, based on an analysis of several thousand pages of material collected from forty business schools and universities, twenty of which were visited and interviewed. The sample of business schools was selected with the assistance of 78 leading European experts in the field of environmental management, thereby ensuring that cases were chosen from the leading edge of curricula greening. It is concluded that management education has some difficulty in living up to its primary responsibility of 'showing the way', and in providing contemporary and adequate management models and tools.

■ *Introduction*

During the past couple of years, there has been an increasing tendency to talk about the greening of industrial processes, products, etc., in Western economies—most notably in the US and northern Europe—in a way that may delude the rest of the world into believing that this is a well-established and widespread trend in these parts of the world. However, as argued by Pedersen,[1] this is still largely wishful thinking: the reality is that the greening of industry, which is a very complicated and continuous process, actually only started less than a decade ago in a minority of large enterprises (LEs).

Two reasons in particular may account for this. Firstly, there is a lack of knowledge about the precise limits of nature's carrying capacity. Secondly, managers and educators know little about the responsibilities, roles and opportunities created by growing environmental concern in society at large.

With an expected doubling of the world population and a four- to five-fold increase in economic output projected for the coming decades, meeting social needs without transgressing biophysical limits will require no less than a paradigm shift in the way people interact with and exploit the natural environment. Such a radical process of change will involve, and need, the active participation of all social partners, and, in particular, the provision of appropriate higher education and training. This puts decision-makers of tomorrow (both in government, public administration and industry) in a strong position. Due to their potential influence on future business leaders and policy-makers, such institutions are in a unique position to help society in general, and industry in particular, adopt environmentally more sustainable paths of development. Put differently, it might also be argued that, if business schools and universities want to maintain their leadership in preparing future managers for corporate employment, they must respond swiftly and adequately to the markets they serve. At a recent INSEAD conference on 'Educating Business Leaders of Tomorrow', involving representatives from European business schools, some of the consensus was aptly summed up by the following statement:

> ...environmental issues are not currently considered an essential component of a business education. Although there are isolated instances of institutional commitment to environmental management education, in European schools especially, there is a clear gap between corporate and academic priorities.

Similar conclusions were reached at EU Round Table meetings in Rome in 1992 and Dublin in 1994.

■ Methodology

The main elements of the overall approach include:

- An extensive literature review; interviews with key representatives of both national and international organisations with a long history of involvement in the topic

- A postal survey of existing researchers and other resource persons in the field

- An analysis of several hundred pages of course material from forty higher managerial education and research institutions—of which approximately half were visited and interviewed

The interviews, which were based on a semi-structured approach, were carried out with professors responsible for environmental programmes and/or courses.

To assist the research team in choosing the most progressive examples in the four countries concerned, a list of leading international researchers was compiled in collaboration with both national and international colleagues. These resource persons were then contacted and asked to give examples of the leading, most innovative, and environmentally-oriented business schools both inside and outside the four Member States (3–4 examples from industry, 2–3 examples from higher education, and 1–2 examples from other full-time educational courses). This resulted in a list of 40 institutions of higher education, selected on the basis of their environmental initiatives, which strongly supports the belief that the four selected countries (France, UK, Germany and Denmark) are among the most progressive in the Community in this area. All available material from these institutions, which also includes some examples from outside the four selected EU countries, has been submitted to extensive analysis.

■ Results
In the majority of institutions visited and/or analysed, graduate courses in environmental management-related issues are typically disciplinary and specialised in nature. None of the 'normal' institutions offering an MSc degree have fully integrated the environment into existing curricula. In a few cases, however, a more interdisciplinary strategy has been implemented.

For all forty institutions, the key characteristics of existing management education were analysed with respect to:

i General information

ii Current environmental courses

iii Teaching approaches and existing teaching materials

iv Existing research activities (topics, aims, people involved, publications, etc.)

For the seventeen management education and research institutions visited, the following were also included:

i General information

ii The role of management education institutions

iii What should educators prepare students to do

iv What should be taught

v What deserves special attention

vi The 'ideal' curriculum

vii Barriers to the further greening of curricula

vii Expectations for the future

More specifically, the study found that:

- There are some positive signs of change and a growing emphasis on environmental education in business schools and other institutions of higher education, though still in a minority.

- The majority of institutions visited and/or analysed offer graduate courses in environmental management-related issues, typically disciplinary and specialised courses.

- Environmental courses typically have a limited number of participants partly due to a lack of interest among students (in a few cases) and due to pedagogical considerations.

- None of the 'normal' institutions offering a Master's degree have integrated the environment into existing curricula.

- The key educators in environmental management in the selected sample come from a variety of professional backgrounds, none of which can exactly be said to be 'tailor-made' for the job.

- Social sciences, technical sciences and natural sciences are represented, with a predominance in the former.

- The most frequently-mentioned driver was that of one or two internal professors who were dedicated to the environment.

- Environmental courses are relatively new due to a rather late recognition of the importance of the environment at the included institutions of higher education.

- Environmental concern is typically incorporated into existing programmes in an unstructured, non-integrated way.

- The institutions included in this study offer environmental courses both at undergraduate, graduate, and postgraduate level, typically as electives among other (degree-relevant) courses.

- Environmental courses are often based on the interactive participation of the individual participant.

- Environmental courses have close ties with local industry (students are often required to do their assignments in collaboration with local firms).

- Environmental courses are characterised by a multitude of teaching methods, only using the 'traditional' one-way-communication approach to a limited extent.

- Institutions were generally mentioned to have a very important role as opinion-makers and in having political influence.

- The greening process has been delayed by various kinds of barriers, ranging from external barriers, such as scientific communities and providers of research funds, to internal barriers, such as colleagues and (particularly in the older and larger institutions) institutional inertia.

■ Current research activities at these institutions are characterised by being specialised and by being carried out in isolated research environments (no, or very few international collaborators).

■ Current research activities tend to be both carried out and described in an ad hoc manner, presumably unconnected with local major research plans and/or programmes.

■ Only in one of the surveyed countries were any major planned and interdisciplinary programmes with researchers from other countries noted.

■ With regard to the future, there was general optimism among the respondents that the greening process will continue.

■ Discussion

A study of a selected sample of 210 environmental managers[2] found that all but 5% had been educated to degree level or above, typically from the 'established sciences'. The study concluded that no more than a handful of these environmental managers had undergone any kind of rigorous training to prepare them for the job. It was also found that desirable educational characteristics included:

i An understanding of the [environmental] issues.

ii The ability to motivate fellow employees.

iii A good understanding of the business.

With regard to age and sex, the majority of E-managers were young males (only 8% female). An ILO study[3] also stressed the need for interdisciplinarity in environmental training, thereby enabling the student to understand complex systems and their elements, the causes and effects of environmental phenomena and their interaction with human activities, and the need for environmental ethics. In this study, educational and training programmes were seen to relate to different levels, each fulfilling a specific need. Training institutions, it is argued, are best equipped to offer occupation-specific environmental knowledge and skills, whereas individual enterprises are best equipped to provide environmental training tailored to the job.

At a recent workshop in Dresden[4] it was found that, as regards teaching practices and curricula, the teaching methods included the interactive involvement of the students, case studies, and various audio-visual facilities. Concerning curriculum development, several participants reported that modification of individual course units presented few problems, whereas institutional approval was normally required for major new courses.

According to Moser and Arnold,[5] business schools and universities have four levels of commitment to curriculum greening. The first level consists of a non-systematic grass-roots integration of environmental issues into existing courses in management, accounting, production, finance, etc. This level has been found in several of the institutions surveyed in the present study. The drawback of this approach, however, is that it does not give the student a broad introduction to environmental issues.

At the next level, a single elective course is devoted to environmental management. Although this approach ensures a much broader coverage of the issues (one of the senior members of this research team has been running such a graduate course for years), it invariably only appeals to the 'converted', i.e. students who are already interested in environmental issues. This is the dominant approach among the surveyed institutions.

At the third level, the degree programme allows the student to take several courses in the environment and still graduate within a traditional discipline (e.g. business administration). This approach has also been found at a couple of the surveyed institutions.

Finally, some institutions have both faculties of business administration and technical and/or natural sciences, which offer a joint programme. This was found in only one case in this study (a joint PhD programme in Denmark).

This study supports the assertion that we are far from achieving the full integration of environmental concern into higher education curricula. As already indicated, there may be several reasons for this:

- An insufficient understanding of the interactions between population growth, human activities, and the environment
- An insufficient understanding of the practical, economic, and social limitations
- The organisation into areas of specialised knowledge, and established disciplines fighting to keep and/or increase their 'share of the cake'
- The hegemony of the positivistic model of science (PMS) in contemporary natural and social science, which, among other things, allows mainstream economics to view the economic system totally separated from the biophysical system

■ (As a result of the above) the imminent PMS-led career structure within the academic world, which, among other things, makes it hard to 'swim against the tide'. As one interviewee, an internationally-recognised university academic, stated: 'You need to have a couple of well-recognised publications in your belly before you dare (and succeed) to publish a non-mainstream article'.

For these reasons, academic institutions are predisposed to turning out traditionally specialised graduates, and, at best in most cases, only offer environmental courses as a voluntary add-on to existing programmes. The 1990 INSEAD conference report on Environmental Resource Management concluded that there is a need for champions, success models, funding, and curricula materials if change is ever to take place in institutions of higher education.[6] This study has shown that, if not for individual champions, the environmental greening process would never have got started in educational institutions. As for funding, interviewees have pointed to an alarming lack of funding of sufficiently educated colleagues and educational materials. With regard to the latter, the authors of this report are, almost on a daily basis, reminded of this through the various international electronic networks to which they are connected. The first two requirements of the INSEAD report are thus no longer the most critical aims, while the others, e.g. lack of funding and resistance from the scientific (economic) community, have assumed much more importance.

As pointed out by Cortese,[7] there is still a need for a variety of highly-educated and trained professionals. Demographers are needed to understand the trends in population growth and to develop strategies to stabilise population levels; scientists are needed to understand the natural world and the efficacy of environmental improvement strategies; health specialists are needed to understand and document the toxic effects of pollution; engineers are needed to develop cleaner technologies; lawyers and policy-makers are needed to develop appropriate environmental regulations; economists and management specialists are needed to evaluate the costs of pollution and to develop preventative managerial strategies; geographers, planners and sociologists are needed to develop solutions to environmental problems that are both socio-economically, sociopolitically and socioculturally feasible; and, finally, humanists and philosophers are needed to evaluate the values and motivations (inhibiting as well as catalysing) involved in the implementation of environmentally-sustainable developments.

According to UNEP,[8] industry has five major environmental education needs:

i Greater all-round environmental awareness

ii Environmental education for present and future managers

iii Training programmes for environmental specialists

iv Environmental education for engineers and other professionals

v Worker education and training

> International co-operation can greatly enhance the reach and effectiveness of environmental education and training for industry, for example through the sharing of experience between countries. [...] Industry's environmental education and training needs are immense.[9]

This study reflects the state of the art of contemporary environmental and resource management education in Europe. It is based on empirical findings from a selected sample of institutions of higher education and other institutions providing environmental management courses of longer duration, and thus has no explanatory or generalising power for other managerial educators in the countries concerned, only for those at the 'cutting edge' in the Community. Unfortunately, these are still a very small minority.

The inclusion of environmental concern into management curricula can be described as a multi-stage process. The various educational implications of this process are illustrated in Figure 1.

According to the definitions in Figure 1, the majority of managerial educators are close to Stage 3. This is surprising, since, after all, they are expected to be ahead of developments in trade and industry, and should thus have been clustered around Stages 4 and 5.

The main findings of this study lead, among other things, to a central question: is the development of a harmonised and joint approach to environmental management education and training in the EU feasible, and can financial incentive schemes to encourage this be recommended? With regard to paradigmatic resistance within the scientific community, it is assumed that this can best be changed by the researchers themselves.

Arguments in favour of such a joint strategy include:

- It has cost-effective potential.

- It has potential synergetic effects.

- It will lead to faster development and dissemination of the greening process within the educational system.

- Individual institutions will not have to 're-invent the wheel', but can concentrate on adaptation and refinement.

Criteria	Stage 1	Stage 2	Stage 3	Stage 4	Stage 5	Stage 6
Contribution of the educational institution to sustainable development	None	None	Minimum/ moderate	Moderate	Active	Maximum
Institutional commitment:						
General mindset of educators	Environmental management is ignored.	Environmental management is viewed as an add-on.	Environmental management is a worth-while, albeit subordinate discipline.	Environmental management is an important teaching discipline.	Environmental management is the most important discipline.	Environmental management is integrated into all teaching activities.
Resource commitment	No resource commitment	Minimal resource commitment	Consistent yet minimal	Moderate funding	Generally sufficient funding	Open-ended funding
Administrative and/or college support	No support	Piecemeal involvement	Piecemeal involvement	General commitment	General commitment and active involvement	Full commitment and active involvement
Environmental curricula or courses	None	Few ad hoc	Few ad hoc	Few, but ongoing	Several ongoing	Included in all disciplines

Figure 1: *Evolutionary Stages of Higher Environmental Management Education*

■ Giving students an 'EU' education will ease the mobility of human capital.

Arguments against a joint approach include:

■ It will have to cope with significant cultural and qualitative differences.

■ It may put a brake on innovative new approaches.

■ It will put considerable strain on a few key educators for a period of time, which might force them to neglect their home institution.

Alternative options are:

■ New funding (programmes) for new and innovative environmental education approaches

■ Follow-up research to evaluate and assess the growing number of unconnected experiences among managerial educators

■ The establishment of an EU database, containing environmental management services, for the quick distribution of new teaching materials, curricula, experiences, etc.

The results of the study clearly show that, as regards incorporating environmental issues into existing managerial disciplines and functions, the leading 'green' institutions responsible for educating corporate managers lag far behind leading 'green' companies. The question is: what can be done to bridge the gap?

This is a very important question, since it bears directly on the *raison d'être* of management education institutions, which are expected to provide state-of-the-art knowledge and tools to the business community. As such, it is only fair to expect them to be at least a little ahead of the 'customers' who are supposed to 'buy' their products.

There is no single satisfactory explanation for the state of affairs described in this study. Rather, as the study has amply documented, there are several important factors, which have different weights from one institution to another. Apart from the factors already discussed in this report, it is important to consider how the dialogue between educators and managers can be improved. Several options are frequently suggested: commissioned and sponsored research projects; sponsored chairs and/or departments/ centres; corporate representatives in publicly owned educational institutions; mutual exchange of professors and managers; compulsory trainee periods for students in real-life companies during their education. As long as the money and influence of the business community is not directly involved, then most educators will probably have no objections. Opinion is divided on the money issue.

Arguments in favour of a strong corporate relationship to business educators include:

- A higher degree of correspondence between expectations and results
- Better funding potentials
- Shared responsibility for the direction of management education.

Arguments against involvement include:

- A weakening of the scientific autonomy of educational institutions
- It will be harder to develop new ideas that deviate radically from present knowledge and experience.
- It will be more difficult to criticise company practice.

■ Conclusion

...educational institutions should integrate environmental and developmental issues into existing training curricula...[10]

With respect to the individual company, Agenda 21 urges industry to '...include an environmental management component in all relevant training activities',[11] and '...to promote an understanding of the interrelationship between good environment and good business practices'.[12]

Environmental training relates to a variety of jobs and occupations. By its very nature, i.e. complexity, training has to be interdisciplinary. Environmental issues and human activities are intimately interwoven, and often lead to potential conflicting interests. Continuous education and training are crucial for instilling the knowledge and skills necessary for putting into effect measures that are compatible with sustainable development.[13]

The radical process of change required over the next fifty years, that was suggested in the introduction to this chapter, will put institutions of higher education, which produce the key decision-makers of tomorrow (both in government, public administration and industry), in a strong position. They have—and will continue to have in the future, along with the increasing demand for life-long training and education—an important role to play in the educational, research, and policy developments of society. This gives the various social partners a profound responsibility to increase the awareness, knowledge and skills needed to realise an environmentally more sustainable future. Institutions of higher education have long been able to provide highly-competent and well-tested frameworks and approaches for handling such complex tasks.

Due to their influence on future business leaders and policy-makers (through their present students) and existing leaders (through their alumni), institutions of higher education are in a unique position to help society in general, and industry in particular, adopt environmentally more sustainable paths of development. Before this can happen, however, they need to undergo a period of self-examination in which they make some important changes in both the process (e.g. the existing organisation and career structure, and teaching approaches) and content (i.e. the specialised content) of the courses they offer.

This is also supported by the study, which has found that, while industry's environmental responsibilities and involvement have increased rapidly, the management education system has generally lagged behind. As a result, managers who are today responsible for incorporating environmental concern into business operations and planning are 'self-made' and environmentally highly-committed individuals, who experience daily conflicts with colleagues who lack any kind of environmental concept in their professional vocabulary.

Institutions of higher education have a responsibility, also emphasised during the interviews, to stay ahead of developments in order to provide the business community with the necessary means to cope with problems both before and after they occur. This implies that it is not sufficient just to teach what is practised. On the other hand, it should also be clear that, in order to disseminate the concept of environmental management to as many companies as possible, post-graduate training courses based on existing practices will be required for years to come. Due to national differences in management style and practice,[14] training activities will almost certainly have different contexts and scope. However, in order to avoid tedious discussions on the outcome of environmental management, it is important that a harmonised approach be adopted as quickly as possible.

Put another way, this study has provided evidence that seriously questions whether the management education system lives up to this important role. The sooner this documented mismatch in the present educational system is corrected, the sooner it will be able to produce graduates better equipped to handle reality as it is and not as it is supposed to be.

■ Notes

1. J. Pedersen, 'Towards the Greening of European Business' (Paper prepared for The European Summer School for Advanced Management, Århus, Denmark, 29 June–9 July 1994).

2. Environmental Data Services Ltd, *Environmental Managers in Business* (London, UK: ENDS, 1993).

3. R. Gagliardi and T. Alfthan, *Environmental Training: Policy and Practice for Sustainable Development* (Geneva, Switzerland: ILO, 1994).

4. See United Nations Environment Programme, *Training Approaches for Environmental Management in Industry: An Interagency Workshop for European Training Institutes* (Dresden, Germany, 18–21 September 1994).

5. M. Moser and H. Arnold, 'The Greening of Business Schools', in *Industry and Environment*, Vol. 16 No. 4 (1993), pp. 17-21.

6. See Moser and Arnold, *op. cit.*

7. A.D. Cortese, 'Building the Intellectual Capacity for a Sustainable Future', in *Industry and Environment*, Vol. 16 No. 4 (1993), pp. 6-10.

8. UNEP, *op. cit.*

9. *Ibid.*

10. United Nations Conference on Environment and Development, *Agenda 21* (Rio de Janeiro, Brazil: UNCED, 1992), ch. 36.16.

11. *Ibid.*, ch. 36.17.

12. *Ibid.*, ch. 36.20.

13. See Gagliardi and Alfthan, *op. cit.*

14. See, for example, K. Peattie and A. Ringler, 'Management and the Environment in the UK and Germany: A Comparison', in *European Management Journal*, Vol. 12 (1994), pp. 216-25.

This project was was funded by an EU grant (0130/93-3030-74).

15

Working in Environment:
Skills, Expertise and New Opportunities

Joyce Miller

THIS CHAPTER is based on the discussions and proceedings of a one-day conference on 'The Evolution of the Environmental Profession in Europe: Needs, Competences and Future Trends', convened on 30th June 1995 in Geneva, Switzerland, under the leadership of the European Environmental Management Association (EEMA) and the European Association for Environmental Management Education (EAEME). This conference brought together experts working in the environmental field at the cutting edge of new concepts with the potential to revolutionise employment in this area. All quotations not otherwise referenced are taken from the Conference's Executive Report.[1]

Career opportunities have expanded as a result of the increasing importance and relevance of the environment for all sectors of economic activity. Analysts estimate that more than two million people will be employed in the environment industry within the European Union by 2000 as the result of new policy initiatives and continuing public pressure to clean up the environment. While interest in working in the environmental field is at an all-time high, it is important to recognise that:

■ Expectations regarding future career opportunities in environment need to be grounded in the reality of how companies are actually utilising environmental expertise.

■ Demand is growing mostly for those who can play integrative roles within organisations with respect to environmental aspects.

■ As environment becomes more integrated into traditional business activities, working in this area can become a route to general business management.

- Within a context of 'eco-efficiency', which aims to operationalise the concept of sustainable development on the part of companies, environmental employment, as such, may ultimately disappear.
- Training is emerging as one of the largest needs and is a tremendous area of opportunity for the future.

What, then, are the specific skills and competences required by individuals working in a world where environment is equated with competitive advantage in order to remain at the leading edge? Where exactly are the growing career opportunities related to environment located, and what trends are now emerging that will affect future job opportunities in this area?

> I am wildly optimistic. The future still needs to be invented, and there are therefore enormous opportunities for those working in the environmental field.
> *Dr Juan Rada, Managing Director, The Environmental Partnership*

■ We are being told that career opportunities related to environment are expanding.

ECOTEC, a UK-based research and consulting firm, estimates that more than two million people will be employed in the environment industry within the European Union by 2000 as the result of new policy initiatives and continuing public pressure to clean up the environment (see Fig. 1).

Professor Philippe Bourdeau is former Director of Environmental Research in the European Commission, and now Chairman of EAEME, an association of fifteen European universities which has been operating since 1991 with the support of the European Union to offer a new European master degree in environmental management to address the emerging need for training in this area. He indicates that

> both EU and national legislations have become increasingly concerned with environmental issues, with major implications for all aspects of the economy. This trend will only accelerate as environmental considerations become integrated into all policy areas. In this process of change, there are still many tools that need to be developed to translate these concepts into daily practice.

Career opportunities seem to be expanding as a result of the increasing importance and relevance of environmental issues for all sectors of economic activity, and interest in working in the environmental field is at an

Environmental Sector	Expenditure within EC[1]	Numbers employed (thousands)				% EC jobs[4]
	1992 prices (billion Ecu)	1992	2000	Increase	Increase %	
Environmental Protection	48[2]	370	636	266	72	34
+ Exports[3]		92	192	100	50	
Industry Environmental Management[5]		168	288	120	72	15
Public Authority Environmental Management	15	333	573	240	72	30
Water Supply		226	389	163	72	21
Total Environmental Industry Employment		1189	2078	889	72	100

1. Environmental Protection and Environmental Management are taken as being 75% and 25% respectively, of 'Total Environmental Expenditure'.

2. Adjusting for imports of 9% (OECD estimate [OECD, 1992]) the estimate for EC *production* for the environmental protection industry is reduced to 43 billion Ecu.

3. Employment associated with exports to non-EC countries is estimated at 92,000 in 1992 and 192,000 in 2000 (calculated using an OECD estimate of a 20% additional output for non-EC markets and an ECOTEC estimate of a 'doubling' of jobs by 2000 due to export potential). While employment associated with exports may not be as directly influenced by EC policy as production for the internal market, it is impacted by the range of EC environmental, industrial and employment policies, and is therefore considered appropriate for inclusion in the overall employment figures in this table.

4. Refers to relative employment numbers when exports are excluded from the Environmental Protection figures. The inclusion of exports would increase the relative importance of the Environmental Protection market to 39% of total employment in the environment industry.

5. Refers to *internal* management activities; for example, in 'sensitive industries'.

Figure 1: *EC Environmental Expenditure and Direct Employment 1992–2000*
Source: Monica Hale, *Sustainable Growth and Environmental Employment in Europe: The London Guildhall University 'Careers in Environmental Initiative'* (London, UK: London Environmental Centre, 1995); adapted from estimates by ECOTEC, *Sustainability, Employment and Growth* (Birmingham, UK: ECOTEC, 1993)

all-time high. In France alone, 850 'masters' or university training courses in the field of environment, are putting 20,000 graduates into the labour market each year.

■ What is environmental employment, and are there environmental professionals?

While it is clear that environmental legislation is growing, and increasing numbers of new graduates are being trained in environmental management, it is perhaps important to identify precisely where all these new job opportunities related to the emerging environmental pressures are located.

Actually determining what constitutes an 'environmental job' and an environmental professional is, in fact, quite a difficult task. Currently, a range of varying definitions exist for environmental employment. James Medhurst of ECOTEC[2] has defined environmental employment as: jobs in environmental protection, water supply, the environmental management activity in industry and public authorities; and 'soft' activities, which include conservation and the provision of environmental services. Alternatively, the OECD has identified three types of 'environmental service' jobs, falling broadly into: technical engineering, environmental consulting, and management services. More recently, in an attempt to define more precisely what environmental managers actually do, the UK Institute of Ecology and Environmental Management (IEEM) suggests these individuals are:

> Professionals who have a sound knowledge of ecology and environmental management through academic studies or professional training, and who have a minimum of three years' experience. In particular, professional ecologists and ecological managers should be competent to apply their ecological knowledge (in a direct or advisory capacity) to study, classify, protect and manage ecosystems, their constituent species, and to processes which affect ecosystems.
>
> This must be understood as applying ecological principles to strategic considerations as well as those relating to the implementation of policies and projects. The practice of ecology and ecological management is not solely a scientific and technical one. At senior level in particular, it involves competence in management and mediation among many interests. It draws on innovative and creative capabilities in developing and managing solutions to problems as well as evaluating them. It requires a sensitive awareness of political and ethical issues as the profession is typically practised in complex institutional contexts.

Monica Hale, Director of the London Environment Centre at London Guildhall University, observes that

> the past decade has witnessed a startling change in the perception of environmental careers and the nature and status of such work. The environmental careers market has been transformed from what was often regarded as an amateur, predominantly voluntary employment sector, to a highly professionalised area of specialist expertise.

Hale asserts that trying to determine how many available environmental jobs exist is a matter of guesswork and prediction. One of the difficulties is that environment has not been established as a separate profession in its own right. Also, there is now a perceptible move both by employers and in higher education to integrate environmental considerations into a range of economic and managerial activities.[3]

■ How are companies currently utilising environmental expertise?

Definitions of environmental employment are unhelpful in determining whether this field is simply the newest fashion or whether it is, indeed, a sustainable professional future. To gain more insight, it is useful to look at how companies are actually using environmental knowledge and skills in their operations.

Based on recent empirical research, Peter James, Head of the Environmental Leadership Research Programme for the Ashridge Management Research Group, reports that there are three categories for environmental staff in industry:[4]

- **Pure environmental specialists**: staff who undertake specialised environmental activities, such as auditing or emission monitoring

- **'Environment and...' specialists**: staff who have environmental competence but work in functions such as research or marketing with a mandate to increase environmental awareness

- **Environmental integrators**: executives with some business experience and/or well-developed business awareness and considerable environmental competence who work to integrate environmental aspects across the entire business

James notes that, in the Anglo-Saxon world especially, the balance within companies is tilting away from specialists and towards generalists, and that most senior environmental managers see the secret of success more within their general management abilities, company and industry understanding (which is often related to scientific and technical background) and top-level support, than in environmental knowledge *per se*. This is because improved environmental performance depends upon the actions of line managers and non-environmental staff, who usually cannot be ordered to take action but must be persuaded. With twenty years of experience in environmental management, Ronald McLean, Director of Arthur D. Little's Environmental Management Section in Europe, additionally observes that as environmental management becomes more integrated with other business activities, it could, in fact, become a route to general business management for environmental professionals.

■ Demand is growing for those who can play more integrative roles within organisations.

Increasingly, companies seem to be hiring in pure environmental specialists' expertise on a contract basis, and the demand for those who can play more integrative roles is growing considerably. James[5] remarks:

> there have been few attempts by governments and other bodies to balance supply and demand. Some professional initiatives are now beginning. Too many environmental courses are just turning out narrow specialists who believe they will find jobs in companies but who lack the business skills which they are also looking for.

There is evidence of a trend away from specialist expertise, with companies looking for those with more generalist background and increasing emphasis on interpersonal rather than purely technical skills. Of course, one of the challenges in moving towards this is ensuring a certain level of quality within a generalist field. Existing professional bodies, whether in the field of law, accountancy, or personnel, have all experienced difficulties in performing quality control among their members, in defining required interpersonal skills, and in providing continuous professional training and development.

Moreover, the way in which universities and training institutes are currently operating seems to result in a supply of inappropriately skilled future employees. Joyce Tait of Scottish Natural Heritage observes that

> interdisciplinary studies are under threat in the [British] University system because of funding constraints and yet, in practice, there is a trend towards more integrated approaches to decision-making. There is a serious need to teach people how to carry out this integration rather than assuming, as is currently the case, that they will pick it up as they go along.

Currently, many of the environmental positions available in companies are being taken on by engineers, as companies feel that they best fit into the mainstream of business. Christoph Nitschke, Director of the Institut für Umweltbildung im Beruf in Berlin, reports that

> the majority of environmental job vacancies in Germany are addressed to engineers, and they are increasingly being called on to have a wider understanding of their tasks or even to perform new complex tasks combining elements of research, planning, policy-shaping, administrative pollution control, and consulting.[6]

This trend is even more prevalent in the German public sector as well as the private service sector (environmental consulting). Furthermore, Nitschke has gathered empirical evidence that environmental demands are increasingly becoming a component of existing positions, and that new qualifications such as flexibility, communication and organisational abilities, 'mediation competence', and 'integrated thinking' will be *the* critical skills for environmental professionals. The ability to think about a range of causes and effects, different disciplines and different interests at the same time, and to reconcile these to different contexts within which the choice of an optimal solution may vary, will be key competences for the future. Nitschke has identified a range of factors that seem to contribute to the evolution of integrated tasks:[7]

- The existence or creation of small working units, e.g. small business, profit centres, project teams
- Taking on leadership tasks
- Removal of 'intersection lines' between different responsibilities
- Conversion from end-of-pipe to preventative approaches
- Introduction of 'institutional self-reflection' by which organisations question their decisions more deeply
- Following new paradigms or ideals such as 'open planning'
- Single-case orientation
- Customer orientation

Nitschke concludes that 'the environment requires a new approach to learning, a new approach in methods, organisation, action, and infrastructure.'

■ New opportunities to improve environmental performance can be found through the integration of complex systems and applying the principles of industrial ecology.

Juan Rada, Managing Director of The Environmental Partnership, also advocates adopting a different approach to dealing with environmental issues. Rada believes that the solutions to many environmental issues—and thus many of the future opportunities for environmental professionals—can be found through integrating diverse activities, technologies, and disciplines. He contends that

> the field of opportunities is constantly increasing, with some very interesting new requirements for people, particularly in relation to the integration of complex systems. One of the

major constraints we confront is the classical inertia of the system. Numerous measurements and systems have been developed over the decades that are actually contrary to the environment. For example, a water company is rewarded for selling water, not conserving it!

Rada also points to the development of standards as a barrier to innovation. He explains:

> this provides a monopoly to certain technologies. For instance, the catalytic converter is an example of legislating emission control for an internal combustion engine rather than setting an emission level, and this effectively destroyed any further innovation in this respect. The way that project management is currently conceived is also a barrier. It is not creative and synergistic. It has simply been developed as a tool to ensure that things get done on time and on budget.

Rada advises those individuals working in the environmental field not to think about their careers, but rather to address the problems that need to be solved.

The concept of industrial ecology also represents new potential for employment and achieving a better environment. Over a period of 25 years, four large Danish companies in Kalundborg began systematically to exchange their waste in such a way that the by-products of the 'metabolism' of one company were being used as material or energy resources in the other companies. Kalundborg thus became one of the world's first functioning industrial ecosystems and a model for many of the eco-industrial park projects that have subsequently been developed. This concept is also a model for companies thinking about how to operationalise the idea of sustainability.

According to the industrial ecology analogy, the present industrial system looks like an unsustainable juvenile ecosystem, in which matter passes through rapidly. There is a high consumption of energy and raw materials, and large quantities of *unused waste* are generated. Suren Erkman, a Geneva-based science journalist, states that 'the objective of industrial ecology is to make the industrial system resemble a mature ecosystem, with a very efficient use of materials and energy.' Moreover, Erkman contends:

> industrial ecology is a proactive, private-sector-driven approach that will create new career opportunities, particularly for experts in industrial metabolism and symbiosis and designers

of new industrial processes that can utilise secondary raw materials of variable quality. This concept represents a fundamentally new approach for companies where managers try to optimise and valorise the total flows of energy within a company and throughout the entire lifecycle, and not focus only on developing environmentally-friendly products, reducing pollution, and minimising waste.[8]

■ Environmental pressure groups are focusing on collaboration and developing solutions, which also calls for new skills on the part of business.

Historically perceived as being at crossed purposes with industry, environmental pressure groups are increasingly interested in engaging in positive dialogue and are looking for industry partners in sustainability—which carries some interesting implications for those people working in the area of corporate environmental management. With 4.5 million members, offices in more than thirty countries, and an operating budget of $US150 million, Greenpeace represents a powerful force for environmental protection. Colin Hines, Economics Unit Co-ordinator for Greenpeace International, acknowledges that

> many people want us to do the 'stick' work, which focuses public attention on problems, but we also have a 'carrot' side, and this is growing. We've won the battle persuading the public, business, and governments that there are environmental problems. The key battle area now is: what are the solutions?

One solution—and one victory—for Greenpeace was the development of 'Greenfreeze', a CFC-free refrigerator.[9] After identifying 16,000 people in Germany who said they would buy such an appliance, Greenpeace commissioned the development of a prototype that uses hydrocarbon gases. Now, most of the German refrigerator manufacturers are producing CFC-free models, and they are taking this new technology to developing countries, such as China, with the support of the World Bank. Hines observes: 'otherwise, the developing world would have been sold the wrong technology!' Greenpeace is now talking openly with the financial community about specific industry sectors and specific companies. For instance, on the climate change issue, Greenpeace is holding joint meetings with the insurance and re-insurance industries.

■ *Industry says it needs technical expertise, but environmental sensitivity and management skills will also be increasingly called upon, and expected!*

At the forefront of environmental performance improvement, the chemical industry has pioneered the implementation of comprehensive environmental management systems. Vivian Sheridan, Public Affairs Manager in DuPont Europe, notes that while this drive is profound and revolutionary, it does not call for the wholesale recruitment of environmental specialists, or even consultants. He explains:

> On the contrary, it relies almost exclusively on sensitisation and training that builds on the skills of industry specialists drawn from virtually every role and function. In the past, we hired top-class engineers for their technical skills. We will still need these people, but we will also be looking for individuals with the same or better levels of expertise—plus a specialised environmental formation—not the other way around. These people are needed in research and development, plant engineering and management, product and process development, raw materials procurement, and in the whole area of logistics and transport. As well, we need talented chemists and scientists who create products that not only enhance the quality of life, but which can also be made, used, and disposed of in a way that is fully in line with our goals of sustainability.

Sheridan indicates that communication skills will also be highly valued in the coming years, and adds that

> DuPont's emphasis has been on sensitising employees at every level to what environmental performance means for the industry, its customers, and for society. In this, the role of the communicator is critical. It calls for commitment, idealism, creativity, as well as a broad awareness of national and international environmental developments, and a working knowledge of products and processes which, in the chemical industry, can only be learned on the job.

Primary industry is witnessing a similar phenomenon in terms of increasing demand for environmental sensitivity and management skills, in addition to technical expertise. René-François Bizec, Environment Director for Usinor Sacilor, Europe's largest steel producer, observes that:

people in charge of environmental matters are expected to be co-ordinators rather than operators and to take environmental protection into account by working as part of a cross-disciplinary team. To carry on producing in the future, enterprises must produce 'cleanly' and develop lines of environmentally-sound products, which are non-aggressive towards health, nature and, above all, the urban and social surrounding. Developing these products requires researchers and engineers who have *continuous* training in environment.

■ 'Eco-efficiency' calls for a new kind of environmentally-literate professional

Initially coined by the Business Council for Sustainable Development (BCSD) in *Changing Course*, its report for the 1992 Earth Summit,[10] the 'eco-efficiency' concept has been adopted by a number of leading companies. Manfred Wirth, Director of Environmental Programmes for Dow Europe, explains:

> while there are many ethical definitions for sustainable development, it's important for companies to look for a useful and actionable definition of the concept. Rather than just continue talking about it, Dow has tried to develop a model for action.

This model involves a 'triple balance of securities': ecological security, which is necessary to maintain the Earth's capacity to support healthy life systems; socio-economic security, which is related to adequate education, sanitation and technology; and resource security, which is being squandered by 'living off the planet's capital instead of its dividends', affecting environmental quality and the quality of life.

Wirth explains:

> this triple balance of securities translates into business language. The sustainable corporation must transform materials and provide competitively-priced goods and services that people value for their contribution to the quality of life and the protection of the environment, while progressively reducing their environmental impacts and resource intensity throughout the entire lifecycle to a level at least in line with the Earth's estimated carrying capacity.

Eco-efficiency requires a break with traditional thinking and different skills, especially on the part of those involved in product development.

Wirth remarks:

> in Dow, we're looking for network thinkers: people who can
> operate across different organisations and cultures, who
> understand business alignment and value creation and who
> know lifecycle analysis, environmental impact assessment, and
> how to account for externalities.

Jan-Olaf Willums, Executive Director of the WBCSD, believes that eco-efficiency calls for a new type of environmentally-literate professional. He explains:

> business expects certain key skills and expertise from these
> professionals. Companies are looking for people who have the
> skills to work in multi-functional teams and communicate
> across disciplines; the ability to visualise long-term impacts of
> current activities; the capacity to be an agent for change within
> an organisation and industry sector; a willingness to form
> creative partnerships to achieve shared environmental objectives
> with very different organisations; the creativity to develop and
> implement new decision-making tools in co-operation with
> regulatory agencies; and the ability to communicate these ideas
> across institutional and cultural boundaries!

Larry Kohler, Focal Point for Environment and Sustainable Development in the International Labour Office (ILO), also believes that specialists in environment will be on the decrease. He indicates, moreover, that

> there are no clear definitions about what are environmental
> jobs and professions. Environmental jobs do not equal environ-
> mental professionals, and all jobs will not be 'green' jobs. The
> focus now is on traditional professions—welders, labourers,
> truck drivers, economists and so on—who are all gaining a
> new component to their jobs. These are the people who are
> integrating environment into their daily work activities. They
> will need to be aware and competent to deal with the
> environmental aspects of their roles in purchasing, finance,
> distribution, public relations, communications, engineering,
> etc. This will require not only that managers be better trained,
> but that *all workers* are better trained to protect the environ-
> mental reputation, credibility, and competitiveness of enterprises.

■ *What can be learned from this range of experience and perspectives?*

While interest in working in the environmental field is growing, with an abundance of specialised graduates being turned out each year across Europe, the nature of work in this area is evolving rapidly, based on the experience and insights of a number of experts working in this field. It no longer seems to be the domain of pure specialists. At present, the largest demand in the marketplace—and some of the most challenging new career opportunities—are for those individuals who have demonstrated management skills and environmental sensitivity, in addition to technical expertise. Environmental professionals are being asked to improve a company's business and environmental performance, shape its future strategic direction, even drive a step-wise change in corporate culture.

Working in the area of environment is, in fact, increasingly becoming a strong training ground for general business management, given the everyday practice in: handling ambiguity; managing complex stakeholder relationships; motivating others to act without wielding formal authority over them; forming non-traditional partnerships to achieve shared objectives; and being able to visualise the future impact of current activities, and develop creative and strategic responses—often within a transnational context.

■ *Those wanting to identify new career opportunities need to look at how companies are actually using environmental expertise.*

Clearly, expectations regarding future career opportunities in this field need to be grounded in the reality of how companies are actually responding to environmental issues and using environmental expertise. More and more individuals are, in fact, simply gaining a new 'environmental' component to their jobs or they are being asked to integrate environment into their daily roles and functions. They are being asked to interact with environmental pressure groups, financial agents, governments, the media, local communities, and others in their own industries in developing more sustainable solutions and approaches.

■ *The concept of environmental employment is fast eroding.*

Responsibilities that were previously carried out by environmental specialists and consultants are increasingly becoming the tasks of teams of individuals charged with operationalising a company's environmental policy and achieving measurable environmental performance improvement. Within a context of 'eco-efficiency', which aims to operationalise the idea of sustainable development on the part of companies, environmental employment, as such, may ultimately disappear. The drive is for all employees to become environmentally-literate professionals.

■ Training is one of the largest needs and an enormous area of opportunity for the future.

As environmental responsibilities are integrated into existing roles, functions, profiles and tasks, significant new requirements for continuous training are emerging. Ongoing programmes of sensitisation and training will be required to equip these individuals with the competences and skills to deal with the environmental aspects of their roles in engineering, designing, purchasing, manufacturing, distribution, marketing, negotiation, communications, and so on. The practical problem for educators, then, is how to equip environmental professionals with both environmental and business skills, which are much broader than those provided by traditional training programmes.

Continuous environmental performance improvement relies heavily on harnassing the efforts of line managers, non-environmental staff, and individuals across all levels of organisations. Building the capacity of individuals and organisations to protect the environmental reputation, credibility, and competitiveness of enterprises is one of the most significant challenges we face today, particularly given the inadequacy of existing training programmes, institutions, and approaches.

■ Notes

1. *The Evolution of the Environmental Management Profession in Europe: Needs, Competences and Future Trends* (Conference proceedings; Lausanne, Switzerland: EEMA, 30 June 1995).

2. ECOTEC Research and Consultancy Ltd, *Sustainability, Employment and Growth* (Birmingham, UK: ECOTEC, 1993).

3. See Monica Hale, *Sustainable Growth and Environmental Employment in Europe: The London Guildhall University 'Careers in Environmental Initiative'* (London, UK: London Environmental Centre, 1995).

4. Peter James and Stephanie Stewart, *The European Executive: From Technical Specialist to Change Agent and Strategic Co-ordinator?* (Berkhamsted, UK: Ashridge Management Research Group, 1995).

5. *Op. cit.*

6. Christopher Nitschke, *Environmental Professional Profiles: Public Sector Needs and Competences* (Berlin, Germany: Institut für Umweltbildung im Beruf, 1995).

7. *Op. cit.*

8. For more information on industrial ecology, see Suren Erkman's forthcoming book, *Industrial Ecology, Industrial Metabolism and the Service Economy.*

9. See Joyce Miller and Francisco Szekely, 'Tradeoffs Not Always Necessary to Protect the Environment: The CFC-Free Fridge Example', in *MIBE Newsletter*, Vol. 2 No. 4 (May 1994).

10. Stephan Schmidheiny and the Business Council for Sustainable Development, *Changing Course: A Global Business Perspective on Development and the Environment* (Cambridge, MA: MIT Press, 1992).

Part 4

Case Studies

16

Learning to Change:
Implementing Corporate
Environmental Policy in the Rover Group

Suzanne Pollack

*T*RANSPORT is in transition as we approach the 21st century. As our roads become increasingly congested, governments, businesses and individuals are wrestling with how to deal with road congestion and other vehicle-related impacts, such as emissions, noise pollution and disposal. Globally, some 50,000 vehicles are disposed of every day.

This chapter looks at how one vehicle manufacturer—Rover Group—is making environmental issues a key component of its business strategy. In striving to make its manufacturing processes and its product more environmentally responsible, the Rover Group has launched a company-wide training and awareness programme. The programme seeks to raise environmental awareness from the CEO to shopfloor, so that all Rover Group associates are engaged in the organisation's drive to improve its environmental performance. The overall aim of this chapter is to draw out the learning points from the Rover Group experience for other businesses wishing to improve their environmental performance.

In order to understand the rationale behind the Rover Group environmental policy, an overview will be given of the environmental issues they perceive to be relevant in their operating environment (primarily Europe). This overview will be followed by a description of the Rover Group environmental policy; how it fits with their other business systems; and the learning points that have emerged to date. At present, the Rover Group is involved in a 'learning about the environment' cascade. A 'cascade' is a process by which one group of associates delivers training to another, having tailored the original training to meet the needs of their audience more closely. In other words, the training is cascaded through the organisation, as trainee becomes trainer.

The learning points considered here relate to:

■ The commitment and awareness of senior management

■ Strategic Human Resource Management (SHRM)

■ Tensions in implementing environment policy

■ Cascade programmes

■ Building Cars towards the Millennium

As 2000 approaches, the automotive industry is subject to increasing turbulence, caused by increasing competition, oversupply in the marketplace, changing technology, increasing fuel prices, concern for the environment, legislation and more demanding and discerning customers. All of these factors are significant in that they demand change within the industry. So, for example, we have recently witnessed Ford restructure its business on a global basis. We have also seen significant investment into alternative fuels for vehicles, such as gas, electric and solar, and car plants have become highly-automated, sometimes robotically-controlled, manufacturing plants. Underlying this turbulence is a groundswell of opinion that questions the principal legitimacy of the car industry.

The Rover Group perceives environmental improvement as important on ethical grounds and a source of competitive advantage in a turbulent marketplace. Competitive advantage is seen to come from:

■ Reductions in waste

■ More efficient use of raw materials

■ More efficient use of energy

■ More employee (associate) commitment

■ Staying ahead of environmental legislation

■ Producing cars that are more desirable to customers (e.g. more fuel-efficient, more environmentally responsible in manufacture, lower emissions, more competitively priced)

■ Being able to respond to the requirements of corporate purchasers of cars (i.e. fleet buyers)

If we examine the context in which the Rover Group operates, we can see that competitive advantage is not the only driver for improved environmental performance (see Fig. 1). Looking at each category, we see the following:

■ Legislation and Government

European car manufacturers have to comply with an increasingly stringent and comprehensive range of environmental legislation. This legislation relates both to the manufacturing process and to the product itself. Over 250 directives have been passed by the European Union (EU). These directives relate to water quality, waste disposal and industrial air pollution. The EU directives demand cleaner and more efficient standards of manufacturing, together with an increasing demand for companies to make public the impacts that they have on the environment. European organisations are additionally having to invest more time in complying with legislation due to the deregulation of enforcement agencies and the subsequent creation of new enforcement agencies in the Member State.[1]

In terms of their products, car manufacturers are also subject to more and more stringent legislation. For example, in California a series of laws has been passed with respect to vehicle exhaust emissions, ultimately aiming for 99% 'clean' exhaust emissions by 1998.[2] As it becomes increasingly clear what this means, pressure against this law rises and it is now quite unlikely that the target will be met. This may, of course, simply become a niche market.

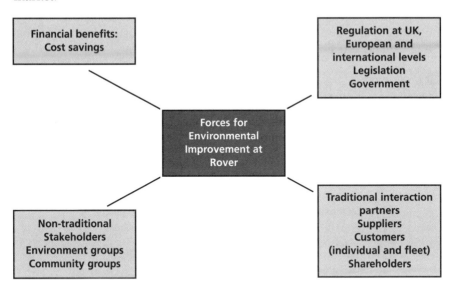

Figure 1: *Forces for Environmental Improvement for Rover*

Source: *Rover Group Core Package* (Cowley, UK: Rover Group, 1994)

Indications of further legislation are contained in the 1994 UK Royal Commission Report on Environmental Pollution.[3] In order to cope with a forecast doubling of cars on the UK's roads between now and 2025 (from 20 million to 40 million), the report recommendations include the introduction of:

- Urban and motorway tolls
- Higher fuel taxes
- Controls to reduce carbon dioxide emissions from vehicle exhausts by 2020 to no more than 80% of the 1990 level
- Lower speed limits for improved fuel efficiency and lower emissions of nitrogen oxides
- Switching a third of people who currently use private vehicles to public transport by 2020, i.e. 12% more than in 1994
- Tightening EU emission limits for all new vehicles
- Increasing vehicle excise duty for less efficient cars

European car manufacturers also export to the US where vehicle emissions standards are even higher. In the US, for example, a vehicle has to pass the emissions limits both when brand new and after 50,000 and 100,000 miles.[4] Germany and the UK also include emissions testing in their annual MOT vehicle tests for vehicles over three years old.

■ Customers

The phenomenon of the 'green' consumer is filtering into the purchasing decisions of private car owners. Research conducted by Rover Group[5] indicates that UK car purchases are:

Confused
about environmental issues

Cynical
because of some of the 'hype' surrounding 'green' products

but also

Willing
to make 'green' purchases if they can be 'proved' to be 'green'

The confusion customers exhibited was related to their understanding of environmental problems. They did not have a clear picture of what all of the problems are and how they relate to each other. This, of course, is hardly surprising because a complete understanding still eludes experts. The point is: if you are not sure what the problem is, you will probably not feel confident about the action you should take to solve it.

The cynicism exhibited was related to the feeling that consumers can be misled by business. In other words, products are endowed with 'green' attributes that are merely marketing 'hype'—for example, selling washing powders on the basis that they are 'phosphate-free', when they have always been phosphate-free, or promoting the recycled paper aspect of toilet tissue, when it has always contained a significant proportion of recycled paper.

The third category—the 'willing' aspect of customer behaviour—was indicated by the fact that only 5% of those questioned would *never pay* extra for environmental performance, while 12% said they were obliged to spend the extra, and the rest of the sample either wished they could spend the extra, said that they ought to, or that they 'could' spend a little extra—i.e. 95% showed some tendency towards paying extra for a 'green' car.

In terms of fleet purchasers (still a significant market in the UK), fleet managers have become much more concerned with fuel efficiency, emissions levels and the safety of the vehicles they purchase. For example, The Body Shop's fleet criteria can only be satisfied currently by the VW Golf Umwelt Diesel.

■ Pressure Groups

Frances Cairncross, Environment Editor of *The Economist*, writes in her book *Costing the Earth*: 'The groups most courted and feared by managers are the green lobbying organisations like Greenpeace and Friends of the Earth, which can, with a single press release, condemn a product or a company.'[6]

In the 1990s, some pressure groups have worked more closely with business to try to help them improve their environmental performance. However, the issue of transport into the next century is such a contentious one that car manufacturers need to be mindful of the results of pressure group action both at the local and the global level. For example, Greenpeace has actively brought instances of business polluting UK rivers to the public's attention by filming their scientists taking water samples at manufacturing outlets discharging into UK waterways. Both the water test results and the pollution as it occurred were plain for all to see on national television. One manager at a UK car manufacturing plant told the author: 'Greenpeace haven't appeared at our factory gates yet and we want to keep it that way.' In Germany, BMW is actively involved with environmental groups to ensure that it is clear that they are taking environmental problems seriously.

Another example of a pressure group in action is the Twyford Down Pressure Group. The Twyford Down group successfully held up the completion of the London–Dover motorway link by some ten years and at a cost of several million pounds. The motorway link was originally to have been completed in time for the launch of the Channel Tunnel in 1994. As hostility to the building of new roads continues, car manufacturers need to be seen to be contributing positively to the transport debate.

One way in which the industry is demonstrating its commitment to reducing its environmental impact (and hence promoting a positive public image) is through 'recovery programmes'. Recovery programmes involve collaboration between different car manufacturers to recover as much of used vehicles as possible, so that they can be re-used, recycled or remanufactured. Recovery programmes in Europe and the US are listed in Figure 2.

Recovery programme	Companies involved
Pravada 2	German and other manufacturers
Partnership	Renault, Fiat, BMW, Rover
Fare	Fiat
French industry	Renault, PSA, Citroën
Recycling BV	Netherlands
CARE*	UK manufacturers
US	Ford, GM, Chrysler

* CARE is about to be expanded across Europe and it will involve Rover, BMW, Peugeot, Ford and Fiat.

Figure 2: *European and US Recovery Programmes*

At the local level, this also means reducing the negative environmental impacts of manufacturing operations. The influence of some local community groups on local government is now quite substantial, and it can be extremely time-consuming to resolve local difficulties. Businesses are recognising this, however, and some are taking positive initiatives to improve the environment in which they operate. For example, the Rover Group planted 200 deciduous trees at its Graydon site to commemorate its partnership with BMW. One can argue this was just another PR exercise—perhaps it was—but it can also be argued that, if the preferred method of generating favourable publicity is through positive environmental action, then this is an encouraging sign. At its Longbridge plant, Rover Group rescheduled its rail deliveries during the night to reduce the noise pollution experienced by local residents.

■ Shareholders and Financial Benefits

Financial benefits can accrue from improved environmental performance through:

- Reduced costs of handling and disposing of waste
- Reduced requirements for raw materials
- Reduced stock control
- Increased energy efficiency
- Increased sales
- Reduced insurance premiums

In addition, shareholders can be more confident that their investment is more secure. Environmental liabilities can be extremely damaging to the prosperity of a business. Moreover, as Frances Cairncross points out, 'wise companies' recognise that 'to wait for the regulations and then try to act may be more expensive than to try to anticipate them and build them into new investments'.[7] The idea that 'pollution prevention pays' was first conceived by the chemical giant 3M. It is, however, fair to say that this is not always the case in strictly financial terms. Not all environmental protection 'adds value' in the consumers' eyes or saves cost to producers. For example, to eliminate the harmful emissions from painting cars with solvent-based paint, car manufacturers need to introduce paint shops that spray water-borne paint, rather than solvent-based paint. In the UK, the cost per new paint shop is a minimum of £10 million. Legislation controlling air and water emissions, however, requires that such a change is made. This instance highlights the role of legislation very clearly. It can be argued that shareholders' primary interest is usually to maximise their investment by satisfying customers' needs. However, if purchasers are not going to *demand* water-borne paint (because the issue is too obscure, too complex or too poorly communicated to rouse public opinion), then it must become governments' responsibility to *legislate* against solvent-based paint.

■ Conclusion

Thinking more broadly, one can see that similar operating contexts apply to many industry sectors today. It is therefore surprising that environmental improvement appears to be happening somewhat slowly and haphazardly. However, once one realises that continuous environmental improvement in organisations needs to happen in a fundamental and all-embracing way, it is perhaps not so surprising. Implementing environmental policy requires the ability and will to learn to change throughout the whole organisation.

■ *Implementing Corporate Environmental Policy in the Rover Group*

Year in, year out, environmental damage causes financial losses on a stupendous scale in Europe, along with the destruction of irreplaceable resources whose value cannot be expressed in money terms. This is the challenge which industry is facing: to restore the environment with the same panache with which the European Community was rebuilt after the Second World War. This challenge can only be met on the basis of an environmentalist approach to business management, which for a variety of reasons is also in the firms' own immediate interest.[8]

The Rover Group employs 35,000 people, at seven locations in the UK and has a turnover of £4.3 Billion. In 1994, it held approximately 12% of the UK car market and just over 3% of the European market. In addition, the Rover Group sold 12,000 4×4 vehicles in the US. Until recently, the Rover Group was owned by British Aerospace. It is now part of BMW, the German car manufacturer. Over the past 5–10 years, the Rover Group has turned itself round from a loss-making concern into a high-quality marque, prestigious and profitable enough for BMW to wish to acquire.

Quality is the 'engine' that drives the company. It does not have a Board, as is more usual in Europe; instead it has a Quality Council, which directs the overall operation and strategy for the Group. In other words, the shared values, style, systems and strategy of the Rover Group are similar to those to be found in Japanese manufacturing companies. Indeed, until 1994, the Rover Group was closely linked with the Japanese car manufacturer, Honda. It still has some joint projects, which are continuing despite the Rover Group's change of ownership from British Aerospace to BMW.

The Quality Council acts in a similar manner to a Board of Directors, although there is more emphasis on all associates having responsibility for the Rover Group's success. It may also be that the Quality Council takes a longer-term view of the direction in which it believes the Rover Group should go. This would certainly be supported by the proactive stance being taken on improving Rover's environmental performance. There is no doubt that this is a significant undertaking that requires commitment in the short, medium and long term.

The company describes its mission as to:

> Produce and sell distinctive and desirable products, known for their robustness and driver appeal. Our aim is improve continually our products and services, to satisfy our customers and make a profit. This will allow us to prosper as a business to the benefit of our customers, dealers, suppliers, shareholders and employees alike![9]

The Rover Group adopts a Quality approach across all its business functions and operating units. Thus marketing, finance, purchasing, research and development, personnel, and so on, all have specific responsibilities as well as a general responsibility for implementing the Quality Policy. The Quality Policy is broken down as follows:

- System
- Organisation
- People
- Product and programme planning
- Product specification
- Purchasing
- Product manufacture
- Customer satisfaction

The Quality Policy is summarised on a poster that is displayed throughout the organisation and it is an integral part of the way Rover Group conducts its business.

As well as highlighting the Quality responsibilities in the organisation, the Quality Policy also details the ten environmental values of the Rover Group. Figure 3 is an extract from the Quality Policy Document, and contains these environmental values.

Figure 4 is interesting because it shows how the Quality approach, as displayed on the Quality Policy Document, is applied to the Environmental Policy. Just as the environmental values appear on the Quality Policy poster, so the Quality Policy Statement appears on the Environmental Policy Document. Of course, showing on a policy document how the environmental values can be brought to life is not the same as convincing all 35,000 associates that the Rover Group is as serious about its Environmental Policy as it is about its Quality Policy. The argument put forward for Quality is often extremely powerful—if the organisation does not change then it will go bust.[10] In the context of environmental improvement within the Rover Group, two aspects of Quality are fundamental. First, that each and every individual is able and willing to assume responsibility for his/her actions. Secondly, that they strive for continuous improvement (or 'Kaizen', as it is referred to in Japan).

Quality was launched within Rover as a turnround strategy: i.e., change or go bust. There is no doubt that Rover has changed and that it is now a valuable marque (valuable enough for BMW to pay £800 million for the Rover Group in 1994). However, the Environmental Policy has not been

1. **'Whole-life' strategy**
   The company's environmental strategy covers all aspects of the company's business, from developing and manufacturing vehicles through to distribution, servicing, repair and performance throughout their lives and eventual disposal. It is a 'cradle-to-grave' approach.

2. **Legislation is the minimum**
   Legislation and conditions stipulated by the authorities must be considered as minimum requirements. By making use of any scope that may exist between demands made by law and what is financially reasonable, the highest standards must be sought.

3. **Best practice**
   The environmental consequences of any action must be considered, even when no legal requirements are involved.

4. **Decision factor**
   Environmental aspects must be considered in the selection of any strategy. When investment and purchasing decisions are made, both the environmental impact and any associated risks should be clearly highlighted. The route with the smaller environmental impact must be given priority over alternative proposals which are in other aspects equal.

5. **Everyone's responsibility**
   Responsibility for environmental protection lies with all members of the company. The management of each area should clearly establish, define and communicate these responsibilities.

6. **Expertise**
   Well-founded expertise must be developed on the extent and risks of the environmental impact resulting from company operations and its products.

7. **Shared experience**
   The cross-company exchange of experience and learning between areas with similar or complementary tasks is of great value to both the individuals involved and the company, and must be encouraged.

8. **Public face**
   Where feasible, both the authorities and the local community must be informed of the company's operations, its planned improvements and actions in the event of an emergency.

9. **Priority at a breakdown**
   When the normal process is interrupted by a breakdown, the highest priority must be given to the protection of health and the environment ahead of restarting the process.

10. **Regular monitoring**
    The impact of all processes must be evaluated and performance regularly checked.

Figure 3: *Ten Environmental Values*

Source: Extract from the *Rover Group Quality Policy Document* (Cowley, UK: Rover Group, 1994)

Relationship to the Quality Policy
This policy document details and specifies the environmental protection procedures required by the Rover Group Quality Policy and specifically identified in directives A14 and G08.

Statement of Policy
It is the policy of the Rover Group to conduct its operations in a manner that reflects a commitment towards the protection of the environment and compliance with all applicable environmental laws and regulations

Scope and Key Implications

- The implementation of this policy must recognise the environmental impact of both products and processes in use and disposal as well as manufacture
- Inherent environmental rights as well as those given by law should be protected
- It is intended to make consistent, measurable improvements in the environmental performance of company operations and its products

This should be achieved through:

- improvements in energy efficiency
- reduction in pollution (including waste, air and water as well as noise)
- increasing the recyclability and/or biodegradeability of all materials

This policy recognises a long term commitment to update company practices in the light of advances in technology and new understandings in health and environmental science.

Figure 4: *Extract from the Rover Group Environmental Policy Document*

launched with the same fanfare nor the same resources. Although the Rover Group's Quality Council believe that it must address environmental issues and that this is in the company's best interests, if asked to prioritise the key business challenges they face, one wonders if the environment would come before or after changes required in technology, working practices, increased efficiency, cost reduction, and so on. This is not to say that environmental improvement is not part of these changes. The issue is more: do individuals really understand and believe that it is? Moreover, are they encouraged to seek environmental improvements? For example, do associates share in the benefits of their suggestions for environmental improvement? Is environmental improvement part of the appraisal scheme? There is evidence that this is beginning to happen, but not yet on anything like the scale that it does for the Quality Policy.

One example of an incentive scheme for environmental improvements exists at the Cowley manufacturing site. It is a suggestion scheme whereby savings gained from ideas that are implemented are shared with the person who put forward the original idea. If the savings are over a certain sum, the individual is presented with a new Rover car.

Understanding of environmental issues does vary enormously within the Rover Group, as it does in most organisations. There are considerable misunderstandings about the impacts business has on the environment and lack of awareness that these impacts *can* and *must* be reduced. If the Rover Group's potential car buyers are 'confused', 'cynical' but 'willing',[11] the same can certainly be said of the Group's associates. Some are extremely knowledgeable and committed to the organisation's environmental values, while others remain to be convinced of the need for environmental improvement and their senior management's commitment to it. This spectrum of views was displayed by the individuals consulted by the author in preparing the first stage of the cascade and by the participants in the first stage of the cascade.

These are two vital hurdles to overcome if the Rover Group is going to be able both to improve environmentally and to create competitive advantage for itself from this process.

■ Achieving Organisational Commitment

Rover Learning Business, the people and organisation development unit in the Rover Group, together with senior management (particularly those on the Environmental Strategy Committee) recognised the need for a process to galvanise associates into action. Thus, a Strategic Human Resources initiative was set in motion, whereby external providers were sought who could help to set up a learning cascade through the business. Rover Learning Business, the training and development function of the Group, took responsibility for the setting up of the cascade programme, together with the environmental committee. The learning cascade is called 'Learning about the Environment' and the first phase has been completed. The first phase involved the development of learning modules related to five key topics linked to Rover's business:

1. The natural environment
2. The pressures for change
3. Management systems
4. Technical systems
5. Future trends

Each module was supported by one or two learning events involving delivery from Brunel University (the lead external provider), associates of the Brunel Environment Programme and Rover Group personnel.

The participants in Phase 1 of the cascade helped both in the design and the delivery of the modules. The Phase 1 participants were deliberately selected across all functions and business units, with variable levels of knowledge about the environment. The intention was to give ownership of the initiative to as wide a spectrum of associates as possible. At the same time, it was recognised that this first group could not be too large because it was important to ensure that they received an in-depth understanding of the environmental forces for change. Thus, the participants in Phase 1 numbered fifty associates, eleven of whom are part of the environmental committee.

Having completed Phase 1, Phase 2 involved the original participants (the core group) in the development of a core package which they could then tailor to meet their individual function/business units' needs. Phase 3 is just beginning and involves the original group in the delivery of their tailored core packages to their function/business unit. The process is designed to be iterative, so that each tier in the cascade can deliver to the next tier the essence of the core package, together with the messages that are particularly relevant to each audience.

■ The Learning Points

> I have never seen a stronger force for coalescing the organisation about a common purpose than the environment.[12]

The theory may sound simple, but the cascade programme is taking longer than anticipated to move through the organisation. This is partly due to the fact that many of the associates delivering the second stage of the programme have not been involved in training before. Therefore, tailoring the core package has taken them longer than anticipated, as has their personal preparation for running their part of the cascade.

As the programme is not progressing as quickly as anticipated, it is somewhat difficult to give too many examples of its results. Some of the early indications of progress are:

■ Clearer targets for environmental improvements. For example, the Cowley manufacturing site now knows that it uses 3,500,000 gallons of water per week at a cost of £7,000 per week. This figure is being disseminated throughout the site, to see if the Longbridge manufacturing site reduction in water usage of 30% in a two-year period can be achieved at Cowley.

■ Rover will be joining the European CARE initiative concerned with recovering parts and materials from used vehicles.

- Rover associates involved in the first tier of the cascade are being asked to contribute to public training programmes concerned with environment improvement. They are also being contacted by other business people who are setting up environmental improvement initiatives in their organisations.
- There is already a greater awareness in the Rover Group of the environmental policy than there was eighteen months ago. For example, including the participants in the first stage of the cascade programme, some 500 associates have now been involved in environmental training.
- 'Spin-off' training activities have been initiated: for example, at the Longbridge manufacturing site Environmental Impact Assessment workshops have been developed and run, including auditing on part of the Longbridge site.

These are small indications that the environmental cascade programme is having an effect. Whether this effect, at this stage, is more or less significant than other factors (such as legislation) it is difficult to say. It is always possible that some things may have happened without the development initiative. Equally, it is difficult to argue that informing individuals and giving them space to review Rover's environmental impacts will never lead to environmental improvements.

In any event, the purpose of this chapter is to document some of the lessons learned thus far. The learning points fall broadly into four categories: the commitment and awareness of senior management; strategic human resource management; tensions in implementing an environmental policy; and cascade programmes. These learning points are now discussed.

The Commitment and Awareness of Senior Management

Senior managers need to: recognise the need for change; be able to articulate why change needs to happen; point to processes to enable change; insist on integration to proven existing systems and procedures (as mentioned, in Rover's case, their Quality systems and procedures); commit resources to developing commitment; and to adopt a long-term perspective. It is important for senior managers to recognise the need for change—in this case, environmental improvement. If they do not recognise this as an issue relevant to their business, then they will not attach importance to achieving environmental improvement. This, of course, then has a number of knock-on effects. The issue is given low priority, few resources and low prestige. Therefore, incentives for other, less senior personnel, to put significant effort into the issue are lacking.

Figure 5 shows the strategic position the Quality Council (Rover's senior management team) has adopted which creates the impetus for environmental improvement. In other words, the Quality Council believes that Rover should be developing strategies to move them significantly towards being a sustainable business. The Environmental Policy indicates how change should occur. The 'Learning about the Environment' cascade is a significant undertaking both financially and in man-hours. For example, in the first tier of the programme, fifty associates spent seven days being trained—i.e. 350 working days were 'lost' to training. However, Rover believed that a thorough understanding of environmental issues and their relevance to Rover was vital if the Tier 1 participants were really going to engage with the subject and be motivated and confident enough to pass their knowledge and commitment onto other Rover associates, some of whom would be their superiors.

Having progressed this far, a significant challenge to the Quality Council is to ensure that they keep a long-term perspective. Short-term financial pressures are potentially seductive in diverting senior management's attention from the benefits of long-term change programmes, such as the implementation of the Environmental Policy. This, of course, is one of the classic problems in organisational learning, although more so of Western-style businesses than Eastern-style businesses. It, perhaps, highlights the limitations of transferring an operating ethos (Quality) from one culture to another. The Rover Group may have a Quality Council, but in the final analysis it still has to perform well in the short term, otherwise its value on the London Stock Exchange will fall. This in turn will create pressure on the organisation to focus on short-term measures to improve performance, such as, cutting costs. Cost-cutting measures invariably affect longer-term projects whose benefits will probably not be achieved in the immediate future. It has also led to 'downsizing' (losing payroll headcount) on an extraordinary scale. One can, of course, argue that this is necessary for the long-term survival of businesses such as IBM, Rank Xerox and British Telecom, to name but a few. Equally, one can argue that downsizing can be taken too far, with too little regard for its impact on a business's ability to innovate and grow.

■ Strategic Human Resource Management

Strategic Human Resource Management (SHRM) is central to Rover's approach to establishing improved environmental performance as a critical business success factor. The reader can be forgiven for experiencing 'jargon fatigue', but, on examination, it can be seen that SHRM is a valuable concept for enabling senior management to effect organisational change.

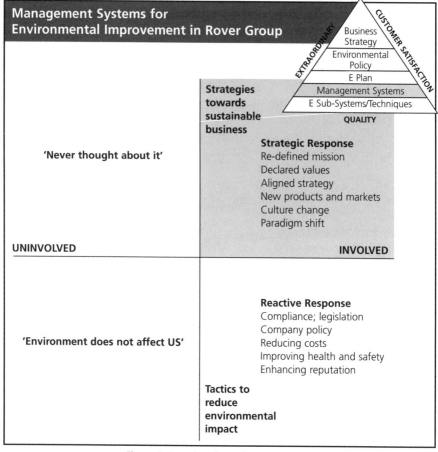

Figure 5: *Learning about the Environment*

© C. Hutchinson, 1994

The extent to which an organisation is engaged in SHRM rather than personnel management can be measured using John Storey's SHRM proforma.[13] The proforma measures the extent to which:

- There are underlying beliefs and assumptions channelling behaviour in an organisation

- Human Resources (HR) issues are core, rather than peripheral, to strategic decision-making

- Line managers are involved in the development and delivery of HR practices

■ Key levers are identified and harnessed to deliver business strategies

In the case of Rover, it can be seen that both their Quality Policy and their Environment Policy are designed to provide beliefs and assumptions that channel behaviour. Also, it has been recognised that the strategic decision to compete on the basis of environmental performance and to improve environmental performance cannot be achieved without reference to the HR issues this raises. For example: how are people to be rewarded for the environmental improvements they initiate? How are they to be made aware of the issues and encouraged to act in a positive manner. These two issues are not fully addressed yet within Rover, but initiatives are being taken—for example, the Longbridge incentive scheme mentioned above. The cascade programme is, of course, itself an example of raising awareness and encouraging change.

In terms of key levers, it can be seen that the cascade is in itself a lever and that, additionally, it is a lever operating through, and being directed by, associates in line management positions. The shift from personnel management to SHRM is significant. Moreover, given that this shift needs to be ongoing, one can argue that it exemplifies the shift that organisations need to make if they are going to move from 'end-of-pipe' solutions towards sustainability. John Storey in his 1992 research project[14] found that Rover seemed to be one of the organisations that had more fully adopted SHRM. Perhaps this is why they have been so proactive in their implementation of their environment policy.

A key feature of SHRM in Rover is 'Rover Learning Business' which provides development facilities and solutions to the core Rover businesses. 'Rover Learning Business' was able to facilitate the cascade in many ways.

■ It assisted with the selection of a training and development provider with relevant knowledge of the environment and business (Brunel: The University of West London). The methodology adopted was to draw up a shortlist of organisations that could deliver the training to the Tier 1 participants. These organisations were then asked to design a programme related to a written brief developed by Rover Learning Business in consultation with the environmental committee. Each organisation presented their proposals, after which Brunel University was awarded the contract to run the training for the Tier 1 participants.

■ It advised that the first tier of participants in the environment cascade should, as far as possible, cover all functions and business units— deliberately steering the organisation away from over-reliance on associates with existing environmental responsibility. Environmental co-ordinators have a vital role to play, but this is perhaps best seen as an advisory/change agent role if long-term organisation-wide environmental improvement is going to happen. This is because change needs to happen at a fundamental level. All associates do need to be involved and committed to change.

■ It ensured that senior management was involved in some of the delivery of the cascade and that they will receive cascade training too. Senior management are participants in the second tier of the cascade.

■ It provided development for associates involved in running workshops for the second tier of the cascade, many of whom did not have previous training experience.

■ It acted as the interface with Brunel University, ensuring that all the Tier 1 participants (the core group) were able to input into the design and delivery of the first tier of the cascade (i.e. the five learning modules).

■ It helped find solutions to unexpected difficulties. For example, having taken part in the first tier of the 'Learning about the Environment' cascade, the core group experienced some difficulty in developing the core package they wished to deliver to Tier 2. Thus, one of the Brunel University Associate Faculty involved in Tier 1 was engaged by Rover Learning Business to help with this process.

▮ Tensions in Implementing an Environmental Policy

Individuals involved in the implementation of an environmental policy can usefully employ a force field analysis[15] to improve understanding of the tensions within which they are trying to work in order to improve the organisation's environmental performance. Figure 6 shows the view of the author of some of the tensions in the Rover Group.

Drawing up a force field analysis enables individuals to think about the things that they can use to help move their initiative forward and the things they need to overcome. For example, identifying the Rover Group Quality Policy as a force pushing for environmental improvement is important. This means that, wherever possible, connections are actively sought to the existing Quality systems and procedures. Thus, the intention is to raise awareness that the environmental improvement is in fact already the responsibility of all associates and that, in many instances, existing systems and procedures can be used to achieve environmental improvements. At the same time, it is useful to be aware that the Quality Policy may not be perceived as including environmental performance and it was launched with a much higher profile than the Environmental Policy. This could lead to the Environmental Policy being perceived as the 'poor relation' to the Quality Policy.

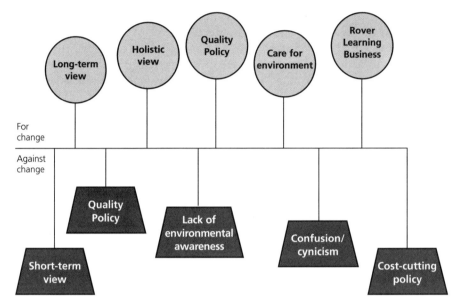

Figure 6: *A Force Field Analysis of Implementing the Rover Group Environmental Policy*

▰ Cascade Programmes

In embarking upon a cascade programme, it should be noted that it is a time-consuming process. Since it is about gaining commitment, individuals need to be given time to become familiar with the aims and objectives of the cascade, to feel that they have contributed to the process and, therefore, to feel that they 'own' the process and the resulting behaviour and actions that the cascade aims to produce.

For the Rover cascade, a '7C' audit was done. The seven Cs are:

- ▪ Commitment
- ▪ Clarity
- ▪ Consistency
- ▪ Communications
- ▪ Continuous
- ▪ Cross-fertilisation/Cross-functions
- ▪ Courage

The '7C' audit picks up on the values that the organisation believes are important for the cascade to succeed. In this case, it was about Rover having the courage to get ahead of its competitors and do something radical with respect to its products and processes; about Rover recognising the need for a clear, consistent message to be communicated and embedding the values in the organisation's existing systems and procedures, so that it will continue after the first flush of enthusiasm. The seven Cs assume that the organisation is prepared to make the necessary financial commitment to the cascade programme. This may be a dangerous assumption—it may be better to talk of the eight Cs and include cash as the eighth factor!

■ Conclusion

> An image as an environmentally responsible company is becoming an essential part of a Competitive Strategy.[16]

This chapter has described one organisation's progress in implementing its environmental policy. Although the project discussed—an environmental cascade programme—is still in its early stages, it is nevertheless valuable to share the methodology used and the learning points gained to date with a wider audience. It can be seen that once again the importance of senior management understanding of the changes they desire, and the commitment to see it through, are vital. It also shows how developing commitment through to organisation is resource-intensive, but invaluable if real progress is to be made.

Further tracking of the initiative needs to be done, as does further research into how organisations can engage fully with environmental issues.

■ Notes

1. See Environmental Law Department, *Overview of Environmental Law* (London, UK: Simmons & Simmons, 1994).
2. See Rover Group, *Environmental Brief* (Cowley, UK: Rover Group, 1992).
3. *Transport and the Environment* (Document 0101267428; London, UK: HMSO, 1994).
4. See Rover Group, *op. cit.*
5. Rover Group, *The Role of Environmental Issues in Relation to the Automotive Industry* (Cowley, UK: Rover Group, 1994).
6. Frances Cairncross, *Costing the Earth* (London, UK: Economist Books, 1991).
7. Cairncross, *op. cit.*
8. Georg Winter, *Business and the Environment: A Handbook of Industrial Ecology with 22 Checklists for Practical Use* (New York, NY: McGraw-Hill, 1987), p. 17.
9. Rover Group, *Quality Policy* (Cowley, UK: Rover Group, 1994).

10. See Tom Peters, *Thriving on Chaos* (London, UK; Pan, 1987); J.M. Juran, *Juran on Planning for Quality* (London, UK: Collier MacMillan, 1988); W.E. Deming, *Quality, Productivity and Competitive Position* (Cambridge, MA: MIT Press, 1982).

11. Rover Group, *The Role of Environmental Issues...*

12. Edgar Wooland, CEO of Du Pont, quoted in S. Schmidheiny and the Business Council for Sustainable Development, *Changing Course: A Global Business Perspective on Development and the Environment* (London, UK: MIT Press, 1992).

13. John Storey, *Human Resource Management* (London, UK: Routledge, 1995).

14. *Ibid.*

15. See C. Carnall, *Managing Change in Organisations* (London, UK: Prentice Hall, 1990).

16. *Business Week*, 18 June 1990.

This chapter © 1996 Suzanne Pollack

17

Analysis for Environmental Training Needs

Walter Wehrmeyer and Sarah Vickerstaff

*I*T IS widely recognised that the training and development of staff has a vital role to play in any organisation's attempt to improve its environmental management. The need for employee training *per se* will typically be expressed in corporate environmental statements or in textbook principles of good environmental management.[1] However, detailed discussions of how an organisation might assess its training and development needs in this area are much thinner on the ground. This chapter attempts to set out a number of different ways in which an organisation could conduct an analysis of environmental training needs and improve its delivery of training in this area. Throughout the discussion, due consideration is given to the likely constraints that organisations might experience in implementing such approaches. To further ground the discussion in a practical context, we provide a case study of an organisation that has undertaken such an analysis. We will begin by reviewing some of the general requirements for a systematic approach to the management of training and the identification of training needs.

■ What Needs to be Learned, by Whom and When?

Any organisation aiming to improve its environmental management must first recognise the importance that staff training has, in both raising employee awareness of environmental issues and in equipping them with the appropriate attitudes, knowledge and skills to function effectively, efficiently and safely in terms of the firm's environmental requirements. Marshall and Mayer see the need for such environmental training primarily in the costs of not training, expressed in the higher likelihood of environmental prosecution, greater environmental control costs and, generally that 'properly trained, environmentally aware employees are the key to making correct day-to-day decisions...environmental training can reduce the possibility that an employee will make a costly decision because of an incomplete understanding of environmental regulations.'[2]

The resulting training needs of staff will obviously vary widely from industry to industry and from one level in the organisation to another. A training needs analysis's primary aim is to provide the organisation with answers to the questions: what needs to be learned, by whom and how quickly? The ease with which any organisation can answer these questions will in part derive from the strength of their existing training systems. Training needs in the environmental area are in principle no different from other areas that may require a training response such as equal opportunities, moves to improve quality, introduction of new technology or systems for example. Therefore the first question to pose is how does the organisation manage its training effort and how does it determine its training needs in other areas?

A systematic approach to the management of training and development in any organisation requires the cycle of activities seen in Figure 1. This

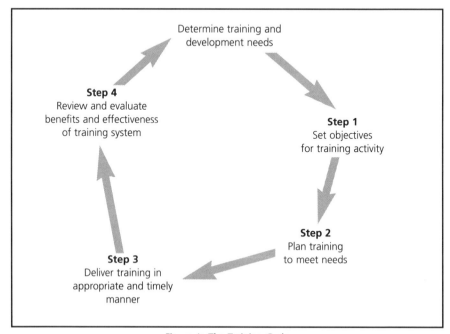

Determine training and
development needs

Step 4
Review and evaluate
benefits and effectiveness
of training system

Step 1
Set objectives
for training activity

Step 2
Plan training
to meet needs

Step 3
Deliver training in
appropriate and timely
manner

Figure 1: *The Training Cycle*

clearly sets the training activity in a continuous process of planning and review and reinforces the point that the successful management of training and development requires a proactive approach.[3] We will consider each part of the process in turn.

■ Training Needs Analysis

The classical approach to a Training Needs Analysis (TNA) suggests that an organisation needs to develop systematic methods for monitoring and reviewing training and development needs at three levels.[4] In practice, many organisations' training function will be much more reactive than this, responding to training needs at the job and individual levels as and when they become obvious.

For many organisations, the issue of training staff for environmental considerations may first emerge as part of a wider green audit or environmental baseline review of existing operations and procedures. Such a process will typically involve a root and branch evaluation of the organisation's activities and a consideration of the environmental risks and hazards associated with each area or section of work. This review would provide an opportunity to assess the current level and adequacy of training as in the case study that follows.

At the organisational level, corporate planning activities may provide the focus for proactive consideration of environmental threats and opportunities. In theory, this should also permit the consideration of the staffing and training implications of medium-to-long-term developments. A change in the organisation's activities in the medium term, or the expectation of changes in legal or regulatory frameworks, as examples, may signal the need for changes in staff attitudes, knowledge or skills. The lead time on major training activities—for example, reskilling the workforce to operate new machines, or operate within new safety standards—may be considerable; a sound training system would identify these needs well in advance of the actual change. Also, at the corporate or organisation-wide level, training may figure as part of broader cultural or awareness policies. The introduction of new environmental programmes and their dissemination is likely to require both general awareness-raising as well as specific skills development. The former might typically be undertaken for the organisation as a whole.

There may also be other existing initiatives that provide a ready forum for environmental issues: for example, communication programmes, continuous improvement schemes, TQM or other quality initiatives. British Telecom, for example, see environmental performance as a quality issue.[5] Health and safety arrangements may be the main existing focus for environmental issues and can provide a basis for reviewing and updating training requirements. Milliman and Clair (Chapter 2) quote the example of Duke Power which has a corporate environmental training committee overseeing and investigating environmental training needs.[6] The advantages of such a structure within a large company are the opportunity to think strategically about longer-term training needs as well as immediate concerns and to co-ordinate efforts across the organisation. It also signals to the organisation, and especially other managers, that environmental training is important and has significant resources devoted to it.

Thus, for any organisation seeking to introduce or improve its effort, an audit of existing training systems, activities and resources—corporate-wide— is the starting point for any analysis of environmental training needs. A corporate environmental committee, if one does not already exist, should be established as a suitable body to steer the environmental training system. It is vital that such a committee has representatives from human resource and/or training specialists, as well as environmental professionals and other executives or senior managers.

Following the review of training needs at a corporate or strategic level, the next stage to be considered is the job level. Identification of training needs for each occupation requires a job analysis. Put simply, such an analysis requires 'the process of examining a job in detail in order to identify its component tasks'.[7] A typical outcome of a job analysis would be some form of job description which is a 'broad statement of the purpose, scope, responsibilities and tasks which constitute a particular job'.[8] If job descriptions already exist, then they could be reviewed to see if they adequately define the environmental issues that impact upon the job. There may be a need to work with line managers to review and amend job descriptions. The significance of the job review is to define the factual job activities providing the basis for assessing whether particular job incumbents have the skills, attitudes and knowledge necessary to perform the job effectively. Some organisations will also produce personnel specifications that define the skills and experience requirements of the job holder. Thus, these activities provide the basis for defining human resource needs in the recruitment and selection process. They also fulfil a diagnostic role in keeping under review how jobs are designed and how duties, responsibilities and relationships between jobs are defined.

Another way of approaching job training needs is via performance management systems. How does the organisation monitor and review performance: does it measure productivity, quality, wastage, accidents, etc., and how is this information used to inform human resource management activities? In addition, this can involve asking employees, supervisors and managers about the job, what it entails, how it is performed and difficulties that are encountered. Focusing on the job should allow an analysis of the needs for general awareness of company policy and the approach to environmental issues; any specific health and safety requirements; specific materials handling and environmental protection concerns.

A typical method for assessing and reviewing training needs at job level is to undertake a training audit which involves interviewing staff about the training they have received, its perceived adequacy and further training they would like or feel they need. As in the case study reported below, this may be done as part of a wider environmental audit that has identified the areas of work activity of actual or potential environmental concern. This provides a means for determining how recent and appropriate existing training is, the training gaps and the impact of other systems such as health and safety or TQM on environmental training needs. If existing policies are used to define performance requirements and training needs in regard to other aspects of work, the organisation does not want to duplicate these with another set of procedures for environmental training needs analysis. As Anthony indicates reviewing the case of The Body Shop, the aim was to match the environmental performance process with the training process so that 'environmental policy and training policy can be interrelated to obtain a more co-ordinated approach'.[9]

The feasibility of skills audits will depend upon the size of organisation and/or the resources available to conduct it. In a small firm, numbers may permit this, but pressure of work can make it difficult to take people away, even briefly, from the operational activity. In a larger organisation, resources may permit, but it may be unrealistic to attempt to audit everyone, in which case a sampling method is required in order to cover a representative cross-section of the workforce. Audits and reviews of this sort may be treated with some apprehension or even hostility by staff, especially if they are unaccustomed to being asked what they think.[10] Some companies use staff attitude surveys as a regular method of tapping into employee awareness and feelings about work-related issues. This could provide another means for an initial assessment of environmental training needs.

As in the case study reported here, it is not untypical for an organisation to employ an external consultant to undertake such audits and surveys. The main advantages of outsourcing the process are the possibility of buying in specific expertise that the organisation does not have, and providing a legitimacy and objectivity for the process, as it is seen to be conducted by someone without a vested interest and with a fresh eye to review and assess existing activities. The downside of using an external consultant for many smaller organisations may simply be the cost.

However it may be conducted, by review of job descriptions, by survey or audit, it is necessary for the organisation to assess the environmental training needs at job level. It may be possible to do this in a phased way, starting with those work areas of most obvious environmental impact and working back over time to jobs of less environmental sensitivity. Alternatively, job descriptions could be systematically reviewed as jobs become vacant through turnover or promotion.

At the individual level, a TNA focuses upon the attitudes, skills and knowledge of the individual employee, whether by defining competencies or framing a personnel specification linked to a job description. This asks the questions: What does the employee need to know, and be able to do, to work efficiently, effectively and safely, and is there a gap between this and what the employee already can do? Training audits, appraisal systems, performance management and monitoring systems, mentoring, management development and career planning activities are all ways in which the organisation may already keep individual training needs under review. In short, they are ways of trying to match the individual's abilities to the requirements of the job and to respond to skills gaps by providing appropriate training and development. They also provide a means for evaluating past and existing training. After training, the individual's performance can be assessed by supervisors, in the context of an appraisal or through whichever performance management systems exist.

We can summarise this three-level approach to a Training Needs Analysis in Figure 2.

Level of analysis	Policy level	Focus	Main methods
Organisation	Strategic	Corporate-wide	Strategic planning Organisation review Audit of existing training system
Job	Tactical	Effective job performance	Job analysis Job descriptions Competence framework Skills audits
Individual	Operational	Personal capabilities/ potential	Appraisal Performance management Mentoring Career development

Figure 2: *The Three Levels of a Training Needs Analysis*

From this discussion of different approaches to conducting a TNA, we can identify key points in the human resource management cycle when environmental training may figure; these are shown in Figure 3.

At the recruitment and selection stage, the organisation has the opportunity to highlight environmental awareness and consideration as part of its corporate identity and to begin to structure expectations in potential recruits. It may be that an organisation wants to include sensitivity to environmental concerns as part of its selection criteria. Having selected new staff, the induction phase represents the first concrete training opportunity. A number of companies, such as The Body Shop, include environmental awareness in their induction programme. The next stage, namely training to do the job, should be based upon the job-level review and the attitudes, skills and knowledge identified as necessary in the job description.

Monitoring continuing performance of the job holder, however done, may periodically suggest the need for retraining or updating as the job, process or materials change. Development of staff for future roles also provides the opportunity to consider and assess the appropriateness of existing attitudes, knowledge and skills. Thus, throughout the human resource management cycle, it is possible to review, identify and assess the current adequacy of training in environmental issues and any gaps in provision that exist.

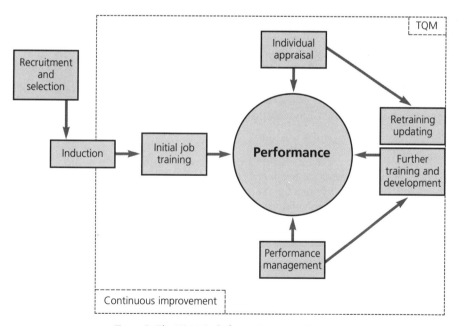

Figure 3: *The HRM Cycle for Environmental Training and Development*

■ Setting Targets for the Training Activity

The next phase of a systematic approach to training requires that the organisation set objectives for the training activity. Without such targets it is very difficult to evaluate the success of any training offered and whether the training should be repeated in the future and, if so, whether it should be modified in any way. How clearly targets can be set for training will depend inevitably upon the kinds of knowledge, skills and attitudes that the training is designed to develop. In the areas of materials handling, safety or quality, it may be possible to set a clear quantifiable target improvement following on from the training input. In the case of increasing general awareness about environmental issues, it may be impossible to define measurable objectives. Nevertheless, in the latter case, it is still important to specify what the intended outcome of the training is, even if it is only possible in qualitative or 'soft' terms. As Buckley and Caple comment, the setting of clear objectives for training activities helps the trainers choose appropriate methods of training and can give employees a sense of what they are aiming for.[11]

■ Plan the Training Response

Having identified training needs and set targets for the training activity, the organisation needs to plan its response. First, it is necessary to consider what resources are available and the timing of the training. Many organisations do not have a dedicated budget for training activities and therefore expenditure has to be agreed on an 'each-case' basis. Where a budget is allocated, its use may be in the hands of managers in different sections or divisions of the organisation. In the latter case, it is very important that managers at all levels understand and appreciate the need for environmental training if they have responsibility for implementing it. As Linnanen has noted:

> in many cases increasing the environmental orientation of the firm is easier for top management than for middle managers. While environmental policy for top managers means vision and careful calculation, for operational-level managers and workers it often means new restrictions, rules and things to take care of; in other words simply more work.[12]

Thus, adequate resourcing of the training effort is not just a financial issue, but also one of making sure that managers will pursue the training strategy effectively, release people for training and integrate the training effort into other human resource management processes, such as appraisal and performance management.

The next issue is the timing or sequencing of the required training. This requires consideration of the lead time necessary both to develop the needed awareness and skills and to cover the intended work group. As in the case study discussed below, this is likely to require some prioritisation of the skills needed and a rolling programme of training and development activities.

■ Choosing the Methods and Provision of Training

The organisation needs to consider how best to provide the required training. This includes the costs and benefits of providing in-house training activities as opposed to using existing courses provided by colleges or consultant trainers. Critical considerations here are how best the target group of staff are likely to learn the required skills, and what style and methods of training will be the most appropriate. It may be the case that the organisation can build environmental issues into its existing training provision. For example, health and safety training could be reviewed to include a specific environmental element; management development programmes could be redesigned to include environmental exercises. A considerable amount of environmental training may be accomplished by incorporating it into existing training and development activities. Alternatively or additionally, as we seen in the case study below, a mixture of external specialists may be brought in to provide tailored and relevant expertise.

■ Review and Evaluation

The final stage of a systematic approach to training requires the organisation to review and evaluate the success of the training and development it has provided. This process not merely justifies the resources that have been devoted to the training activity, but also feeds into the continuing process of defining training needs in the future. Research suggests that very few companies evaluate the contribution of training activities in strict quantitative terms. This is partly because of the difficulties in isolating the impact of training from other factors that affect performance. However, if objectives were set for the environmental training activity, then it is possible to assess the training given in the light of these. It is also desirable to get feedback from participants in the training as to how useful they thought it was and to review individuals' performance in the medium term to see whether skills and knowledge gained are being actively used in the job context. Management of the review process may be in the hands of a corporate environmental committee where such exists.

In the following case study we see a practical example of how a particular organisation came to review its environmental training needs and set about meeting them.

■ The Case

The organisation concerned is a department of an Australian Utility, then called the Engineering Services Branch (ESB).[13] The department provides repair, maintenance and construction services for auxiliary power plant machinery, maintenance of electricity sub-stations up to 330,000 volts and the construction of small power stations. Its corporate mission is, according to its Strategic Plan, 'To be the best at satisfying the needs and wants of our customers through our employees', which is achieved by focusing on these areas:

- ■ Customer satisfaction
- ■ Employee morale
- ■ Marketing culture
- ■ Continuous improvement culture
- ■ Financial management
- ■ Communication
- ■ Competitive and effective services

In 1994, it employed 344 full-time staff on site, representing about 8% of the State Energy Commission of Western Australia (SECWA) staff with an estimated $AUS40 million of expenditure and assets. In 1991, ESB undertook a review of its business to improve organisational capabilities before privatisation. As part of this, Continuous Improvement and Total Quality Management were selected as the key pillars of organisational and operational management. Since then, ESB has gained a reputation for providing high-quality services to its customers at apparently highly-competitive prices.

This emphasis on continuous improvement was also shown externally, as ESB is the first public sector department in Western Australia to be certified under the Quality Management Standard ISO 9000 (BS 5750), which was not only hailed as a significant success, but also laid down the path for more environment- and quality-related awards and accreditation in the future.

In 1993, during the annual strategic planning retreat of the management team, it was decided that environmental protection would be a Key Performance Area (KPA) for the next two years. Other KPAs were to gain the Annual Australian Quality Award and to be fully prepared for privatisation. Success in environmental management was to be measured as gaining BS 7750, the British environmental management standard which was offered through Standards Australia. Until then, environmental protection was not considered essential and was thought of as being dealt with under the health and safety procedures. This low profile was despite the fact that a number of work processes involved handling of asbestos; that the transformer stations held, until recently, PCB-contaminated[14] transformer oil; and that some work practices released substantial amounts of CFCs.[15]

The main motivation to adopt Environmental Management as a strategic KPA was that: 'we really should do it'; 'it improves staff morale'; and 'we can't have full Quality if the Environment suffers'. These are unexpected internal and environment-based pressures that were the prime motives in this case, rather than the more traditional pressures, such as market opportunities, a past accident or pending legislation. This was because such a market did not exist at that time, there had been no significant environmental accident and the TQM approach meant that they had been ahead of legislation anyway.

The recognition of the need for an improved environmental strategy was therefore proactive. This is a critical aspect of the rapid success of ESB in implementing BS 7750 and Environmental Management into the organisation, because: (a) the impetus for change came from staff themselves and not from legislative or regulatory threats, allowing a self-determined approach that was more easily accepted by staff and had less penalties attached; and (b) the existing TQM systems greatly helped the introduction of Environmental Management and specifically, as will be shown below, the development of a training programme. It was found subsequently that ESB would be in a key position to add environmental control technologies to its service portfolio, but this was not seen at the time.

The approach to BS 7750 is an unusual one: here, accreditation was used to learn about proper environmental management largely *before* environmental management had been introduced. Contrary to this, many BS 7750 firms already have an Environmental Management System in operation, which then is commonly improved to suit BS 7750. For ESB, BS 7750 is an internal performance target rather than an award of past system performance. The Quality Manager illustrated the difference:

> For us, BS 7750 is like a driving license. It doesn't show that you can drive, but it allows you to learn 'on the road' what driving is all about—and it at least shows that you know most of the theory of how to do it.

This is largely in line with BS 7750 which does not verify performance outcomes but is a management system toward continuous environmental improvement.

To gauge staff morale and motivation towards environmental management, to assess environmental management expertise, and to establish a baseline of environmental attitudes, the management team decided as the first step in 'greening the branch' to undertake a questionnaire survey of all staff, which was carried out by one of the authors. The survey showed strong but largely dormant support for environmental protection at work, in that the overwhelming majority would approve of it and perceived the need for it, but significantly fewer staff had expected such programmes to be initiated.

The second step was to undertake an initial environmental review, using an outside consultant familiar with the environmental management standard BS 7750. This review was required by the standard as a baseline for future environmental performance improvements, but it served the additional function of providing data for the environmental training needs analysis, and both aimed at establishing a baseline. Possible training needs were assessed using structured and semi-structured interviews with shopfloor staff and supervisors, assessing the accuracy, relevance and timeliness of knowledge mainly related to COSHH,[16] handling procedures and Health and Safety regulation. These could then be cross-referenced with some of the data from the attitude survey where it was shown that staff who had a high level of environmental awareness were in most cases also those who knew most about the Health and Safety procedures. Apparently, attitudes and knowledge were positively correlated.

After this decision, this Environmental Policy was decided:

> It is the Policy of Engineering Services Branch (ESB) to manufacture and deliver products and services in a manner that is not detrimental to the environment or to the health and safety of our people and to the community at large. It is our intention to implement an Environmental Management System, which sets out environmental targets for all our relevant activities. These targets and the results of our Environmental Management System will be made available to interested parties upon request...ESB's ongoing commitment to minimising the impact of its operations on the environment will be by means of a programme of Continuous Improvement.

This is followed by a number of specific environmental pledges most of which contain no quantitative targets.

After these initial steps, the involvement of ESB in other Key Performance Areas, such as seeking continued recognition in its TQM efforts in the Australian Quality Award, meant that the department could devote less time and resources to environmental management. Hence, a gap appeared between the management decisions and its eventual impact on the environmental performance of the branch. However, there were additional reasons for the discrepancy which could be attributed to environmental management itself:

- **Technical inadequacy.** In many cases, environmental effects could not be properly monitored. For instance, all electricity was measured on one meter—jointly with another branch. There were no possibilities to identify high and low water consumers across the site.

- **Managerial ignorance.** Little existing environmental data was collected and information was not brought to the attention of either the management team or the responsible decision-maker.

- **Environmental innocence.** In a number of cases, the environmental effects of work practices were not known by employees. The process identified training needs for Environmental Awareness and for Safe Work Practices.

- **Management time.** Immediately after the BS 7750 accreditation, attention temporarily focused on the application of ESB to the Australian Quality Award (AQA). Together with rising pressures towards privatisation, environmental management received less attention during that period, but after being commended by AQA, environmental protection has regained its priority level.

After the initial decisions on environmental management—namely the staff attitude survey, the initial environmental baseline audit and the Environmental Policy—the management team approached staffing of environmental management. Overall responsibility was given to the Quality Systems Manager and an Environmental Improvement Team was initiated. It consisted of representatives from most workshops, the Quality Systems Manager and the Health and Safety representative. The workshop representatives were volunteers who were selected from twice as many applications: some would call these staff environmental champions. The team of eight had the brief of continuously improving and facilitating environmental protection throughout the branch. In sessions with the external consultant who commissioned the survey, the team developed its own mission, Key Performance Areas, Key Performance Indicators for each area and an Action Plan. The Quality Systems Manager reported to the team as well as being accountable to the management team; all team members communicated environmental issues to and from their workshops.

To address training needs, the Environmental Improvement Team, which had a limited budget for environmental training, reviewed existing training provision and formulated new areas of training. To do this, team members 'went walkabout' on the shopfloor, asking questions about how materials were handled, what workshop staff saw as the relevant environmental effects, which safety precautions were known (and used) and which emergency procedures were applicable. These questions frequently evolved into informal discussions that furthered the profile of environmental management in ESB.

The information from these questions was used in two ways. First, the areas of environmental management were categorised according to existing environmental procedures, which originated from the COSHH and the Quality Manual instrumental and required by BS 5750. A similar approach is put forward by Marshall and Mayer[17] who reviewed Environmental Protection Agency (EPA) and Toxic Release Inventory (TRI) legislation and its training requirements. Not surprisingly, the training areas concentrated around the handling and operative procedures and environmental management generally:

> A: Emergency Response Procedure
> B: Chemical Handling Procedure
> C: Fire Response Procedure
> D: Explosion Response Procedure
> E: Chemical Spill or Leakage Procedure
> F: Wastewater Disposal Procedure
> G: Asbestos Handling Procedure
> H: First Aid Procedure
> I: Environment-Related Accident Procedure
> J: PCB Handling Procedure
> K: Environmental Education Procedure

As can be seen, the majority of these training areas relate to tactical and operational policy levels, as they are aimed at the job or the individual. The second use of this information was an assessment of the existing training needs (see Step 1 of Fig. 1). The training needs were categorised into:

✓ Training is perceived to be sufficient, with no training refreshment required. Staff not needing training refreshments were sufficiently aware of current procedures, implemented these, had a positive attitude towards environmental protection and thought of themselves as not needing further training as they felt confident in their environmental management skills and operative practices.

☐ Training is needed in this area. This category was assigned when new materials or processes had recently been introduced that were covered under a specific Quality Manual procedure requiring training, or when new procedures—such as the Environment-Related Accident Procedure—were introduced, but no training was yet provided.

○ Training has not been received, but is seen by employees as not necessary. This and the previous category were open, at times, to considerable discussion, where staff in this section felt that their on-the-job training was already of sufficient standard, or current work practices eliminated the need for such training anyway. A case in point is the PCB-handling procedure, where all PCB-contaminated materials are sent off for handling and disposal and a separate workshop took all compulsory transformer oil samples to be sent off for chemical analysis. In either result of this analysis, most staff did not come into contact with PCB.

✕ Not applicable. This conclusion was drawn when procedures did not apply to them (e.g. workshops who did not handle asbestos needed no training in handling it).

For the various workshops of the organisation, Figure 4 could be established, which is a table outlining the training and incorporates the categories described above. Please note that the classifications are for each workshop rather than for individuals. The roles of supervisors or other specific staff were then taken into account in the individual training needs analysis. The objectives for the training provision (Step 2 of Fig. 1) were to deliver the required training to all staff concerned in a cost-effective and practical manner. To this end, workshop-by-workshop sessions were

Name of Section	A	B	D	E	F	G	H	I	J	K	L
Workshop 1	☐	☐	☐	☐	○	✕	✕	✓	☐	✓	☐
Workshop 2	✓	✓	☐	☐	✓	○	✓	✓	☐	✓	☐
Workshop 3	☐	☐	✓	○	☐	☐	☐	☐	☐	✓	☐
Workshop 4	✓	○	☐	○	✕	☐	✓	✓	☐	○	☐
Workshop 5	✓	☐	☐	☐	☐	☐	○	✓	☐	○	☐
Workshop 6	✓	☐	✓	✓	☐	☐	✕	✓	☐	✕	☐
Workshop 7	☐	✓	☐	☐	☐	○	○	✓	☐	○	☐

Figure 4

prepared for those areas deemed suitable, whereas most training sessions were conducted across workshops. Identification of individuals for training was made by the respective representatives of the Environmental Improvement Team or else the individuals themselves volunteered. Decisions as to who should receive training were effectively made in discussions within the Environmental Improvement Team and between the team and the workshops.

The training sessions all took place in the company's own training centre using outside specialists who could provide relevant expertise in the field. For instance, the emergency, fire and explosion response procedure training was delivered with the help of the local fire brigade, the PCB and asbestos handling training was delivered with the help of the local Health and Safety office, and environmental education and awareness training took place using an outside consultant and a local university.

The training sessions were followed up (Step 4 of Fig. 1) a couple of months later using a follow-up survey of staff, where again all staff were surveyed using the same questionnaire as before. This allowed testing of the environmental attitudes, knowledge and awareness levels of staff.

■ Conclusions

As it can be seen from the above discussion, training needs analyses have a critical role in the establishment and promotion of environmental management. The main advantage of using a systematic approach towards training, of which training needs analysis is but one part, lies in the deliberate development of skills and knowledge throughout an organisation, in the avoidance of the costs of not training (which can be substantial in environmental management), and in the effects on motivation, quality of output and service delivery generally. The case showed one organisation that utilised training needs analysis as part of its TQM-dominated approach towards improving environmental performance and achieving the environmental management standard BS 7750.

Even though the case showed the benefits of a simple and clear approach particularly suited to small- and medium-sized enterprises, the background of ESB has probably influenced the shape and outcome of environmental management more than has been credited so far. That the department had no immediate environmental penalties to fear and that the environmental management adoption was entirely voluntary has certainly helped its implementation. Equally, the emphasis on getting staff involved and keeping processes simple has also assisted in the now broad acceptance of environmental management in the company. Also, the existing management style shaped by TQM is a significant contributor to ESB gaining BS 7750 within seven months of making the initial decisions towards accreditation.

The usefulness of training needs analyses quite often is a function of three distinct elements, one of which is the extent to which it is connected and related to other, already-existing management systems. The second element is the extent to which even complex issues are dealt with in an uncomplicated manner. The assessment by colleagues of staffs' knowledge and understanding of procedures through simple questions such as 'Where is the fire extinguisher?' and 'Show me how it works' may serve as an example. The third element indicated the extent to which processes and standards are not seen as final results but as stages in a developmental process of continuous improvement.

■ *Notes*

1. See, for example, British Airways, *1993 Annual Environmental Report* (London, UK: British Airways, 1993), p. 49; The Body Shop, *The Green Book and The Body Shop 1992/3 Environmental Statement* (Littlehampton, UK: The Body Shop, 1993), p. 14; R. Welford and A. Gouldson, *Environmental Management and Business Strategy* (London, UK: Pitman, 1993), p. 12; K. North, *Environmental Business Management* (Management Development Series, Vol. 30; Geneva, Switzerland: ILO, 1993), p. 82; J. Milliman and J. Clair, 'Environmental HRM Best Practices in the USA: A Review of the Literature', in *Greener Management International*, No. 10 (April 1995).

2. M.E. Marshall and D.W. Mayer, 'Environmental Training: It's Good Business', in *Business Horizons*, March/April 1992, p. 54.

3. For similar models, see R. Buckley and J. Caple, *The Theory and Practice of Training* (London, UK: Kogan Page, 1990), p. 26; and M. Armstrong, *Personnel Management Practice* (5th edn; London, UK: Kogan Page, 1995), p. 514.

4. See, for example, J. Kenney and M. Reid, *Training Interventions* (London, UK: Institute of Personnel Management, 1986), p. 26; and Armstrong, *op. cit.*, p. 514.

5. See R. Welford, *Cases in Environmental Management and Business Strategy* (London, UK: Pitman, 1994), p. 67.

6. Milliman and Clair, *op. cit.*, p. 38.

7. Buckley and Caple, *op. cit.*, p. 70.

8. Kenney and Reid, *op. cit.*, p. 157.

9. S. Anthony, 'Environmental Training Needs Analysis', in *Training Officer*, Vol. 29 No. 9 (1993), p. 273.

10. See J. Barnett and L. Graham, *Training for the Small Business* (London, UK: Kogan Page, 1995), p. 63.

11. Buckley and Caple, *op. cit.*, p. 103.

12. L. Linnanen, 'Market Dynamics and Sustainable Organisations: HRM Implications in the Pulp and Paper Industry's Management of Environmental Issues', in *Greener Management International*, No. 10 (April 1995), p. 119.

13. After the events described here, the State Energy Commission of Western Australia (SECWA) was privatised with one part becoming Western Power and the department described her becoming its Power Services Branch. As the case relates to the earlier events, its older name has been maintained.

14. PCBs are polychlorinated biphenyls, used in the past as pesticides and in transformer cooling oils to prevent flames and sparks. Their use was banned in 1979 by law. They are highly-persistent toxins and can cause damage in very low concentrations. Currently, they accumulate in the foodchain of many marine and land-based species such as seals, dolphins, otters and birds. Porteus calls it 'a classic example of a man-made compound being introduced without assessment of its environmental impact', A. Porteus, *Dictionary of Environmental Science and Technology* (Milton Keynes, UK: Open University Press, 1991), p. 261.

15. CFCs are chlorofluorocarbons, a class of chemical compounds commonly used as solvents, aerosol propellants, refrigerants and in foam productions. The gases are chemically inert, but short-wave radiation in the stratosphere breaks some of these chemicals up, which in turn break up ozone. The 1987 Montreal Protocol decided to phase out completely the use and production by 2000.

16. COSHH are the regulations for the Control of Substances Hazardous to Health.

17. *Op. cit.*

18

Action through Ownership:
Learning the Way at Kent County Council[1]

Stephen Rees

Thought creates a problem and then tries to do something about it while continuing to make the problem, because it does not know what it is doing.[2]

RECENTLY, local authorities in the United Kingdom have been undergoing a transformation in the way they operate. A plethora of new legislation, along with organisational change factors such as boundary changes, Local Government Reviews, Compulsory Competitive Tendering and public expenditure constraints have all served to alter and, arguably, undermine the nature and potential of local democracy. For better or worse, the public sector has also become influenced by private-sector ethics, which have not only led to a culture change but also to an identity crisis.[3] The following case study is based on the experience of a 'cutting-edge' local authority—Kent County Council. Kent County Council (KCC) is the largest business in the County of Kent, serving a population of 1.5 million people. This chapter will explore what changes KCC has experienced in human resource management and associated structures over the ten-year period of 1985–1995; the barriers these changes have created to integrating environmental management into the weft and warp of the local authority; and what lessons can be learned about creating a more sensitive learning culture willing and able to deliver sustainable solutions.

■ Evolution and Devolution: The KCC Agenda for Change
Back in the late 1980s, Kent County Council was, like many other local authorities, a very centralised organisation with power vested with chief officer barons and senior political magnates. Over previous years of relative

stagnation, KCC had remained inflexible, non-adaptable, and a large cumbersome organism of then nearly 45,000 employees, and seventeen departments with a £1.5 billion turnover. Many service and support functions such as finance and information systems were situated at the centre. Only the personnel function operated in a more devolved manner.

Then, with the appointment of a new Chief Executive, a culture change was initiated. The aim of the Chief Executive was to create a more proactive organisation to replace the reactive bureaucracy that had gone before. New chief officers took over, followed by a much more devolved approach to management. 'Risk taking' and 'flatter management structures' became the buzzwords for the evolution of a new multi-faceted organism where budget-holders took on greater responsibility and employees in KCC were no longer considered 'public servants' but now termed as 'service providers'.

'Devolution', 'total quality', 'getting closer to the customer', and 'management not administration' became the bywords of the new business ethos. With the onset of devolution, the main functions of finance, information systems, and other central support services devolved out into the departments, getting closer to customers by directly supporting service providers. Encouraged by the economic boom, KCC began to be more expansive, developing a EuroRegion link with Nord Pas de Calais, Wallonia, Flanders and Brussels City, while developing and supporting strategic projects and action programmes in partnership with a whole host of organisations. Stimulated by 'Pay Plus', a new performance-related pay scheme, the morale within the organisation appeared upwardly and outwardly mobile and dynamic. Through devolution, KCC seemed to be better placed to meet the challenges ahead.

■ The Central Government Agenda for Change

By the early 1990s, the proactive and independent ethos soon became problematic. Central government had its own agenda of new legislation, including proposals for Compulsory Competitive Tendering (CCT) and fundamental changes to service provision such as 'Care in the Community'. The central government agenda of deregulation and 'less government' soon began to take hold and challenge the nature and optimism of local government. At the time, although some of the initiatives, such as CCT, seemed to fit in well to the new KCC culture, the organisational changes generated a wide range of fears and insecurities, which were further heightened by the Local Government Review (LGR) of Kent[4] and public expenditure squeezes by central government.

By 1995, KCC had rationalised itself to thirteen autonomous departments, a system of purchasers and providers (the latter being in-house contractors and business units), employing 35,000 full-time employees, with a budget cut to £1.25 billion, and further dramatic cuts in the offing. The confident new culture of the organisation had been shaken to the core and swept away to reveal a divided, fragmented and very hesitant organisation hoping to gain credibility through providing quality services and action through partnership, rather than by direct leadership. Like most local authorities, KCC seemed to be taking on more and more work with less and less resources available and increasingly vague ideas about their role and purpose in the local regions. Maintaining the status quo became, at times, an ambitious target.

■ *Managing Change: Resource and Process Management Functions*

At the onset of devolution, all management systems in KCC were bound up in a Medium Term Plan (MTP),[5] whereby three-year plans were placed under an annual review cycle, shaping departmental and functional development. This longer-term approach to managing change not only enabled functions to adapt and co-ordinate better, but also allowed staff and business units to gear up to new risks, requirements and priorities. The MTP also recognised that core functions needed to work more closely together, especially in designing and delivering systems to support service and functional development within departments in a much more integrated and cohesive fashion (e.g. training, guides to best practice, tailored audit manuals and network development).

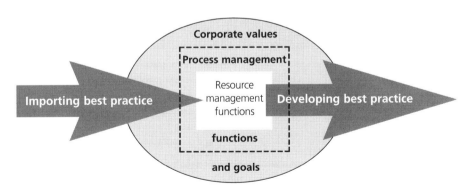

Figure 1: *Corporate Monitoring Framework: Meeting Corporate Standards and Improving towards Corporate Goals*

After devolution, KCC had a new, streamlined and much smaller organisational nerve centre (see Fig. 1). The Corporate Resource Department, aligned to the Chief Executive Department, was designed as the powerhouse for organisational management, dealing with the key resource management functions of property, personnel, information systems, finance and also the broader process functions of business planning, corporate review, democratic process, communication and purchasing. However, in reality, these central 'purchasing' functions were weak, with limited powers or resources to influence the now much stronger and more independent service 'provider' departments who had recruited many of the key personnel.

The personnel function, which had traditionally been devolved prior to devolution in KCC, assumed new powers within departments. For example, 95% of the corporate training budget was removed from the centre and devolved to departments to service their own training needs. The personnel function had conventionally dealt with people, pay and performance. However, in KCC there continued to be an emphasis on the management of people to deliver services in a reaction to short-term changes such as CCT and LGR, rather than the management of people in the sense of training and developing them to 'learn' in order to control change and lead through adopting best practice. For many devolved strategic functions (see Fig. 2) with limited powers (such as the new environment function), this has arguably prevented the local authority organisation from 'learning' effectively, limiting KCC's ability to realise its full potential and role.

Resource management ('must dos')	Process management (continuous improvements towards goals/values)
■ Finance ■ Personnel ■ Property ■ Information systems	■ Service delivery by departments ■ Business planning ■ Purchasing ■ Democratic process ■ Corporate review ■ Communication ■ Environmental Management (EMAS/BS 7750) ■ Total Quality (BS 5750)

Figure 2: *Strategic Functions*

Devolution continues to pose some practical difficulties for both the strategic functions still left at the centre and those devolved to or evolved from within departments. Devolution has lessened their ability to work together and to set and monitor performance and standards across the whole of KCC. As individual service departments have grown with devolution and become more autonomous, so other problems have arisen in relation to information systems, purchasing and strategic co-operation. Devolution has led to real barriers to communication,[6] loss of economies of scale and consumer power[7] and duplication of effort.[8] Core values, management systems and departmental service priorities have tended to conflict with each other, making the promotion of a new approach (such as environmental management) very difficult to organise or encourage. Managers and staff appear to have a range of individuals to respond to, ranging from line managers, corporate function monitors, internal auditors and core value practitioners, which arguably leads to confusion and the duplication of effort with a general lack of coherent approach. This has probably undermined the corporate ability of the organisation to deal with strategic issues such as sustainable development in an integrated and well-ordered fashion.

■ Management Feedback Mechanisms

Prior to the onset of the Local Government Review, the strategic corporate resource functions started to reassert themselves through a series of personnel initiatives called 'Making Connections' aimed at bringing together managers from all parts of the organisation, to understand better the process and direction of organisational change and its key elements. To overcome duplication and raise standards, other mechanisms were introduced, including a new corporate framework and more corporate fora on key issues such as training, income generation, public relations and medium-term planning. Corporate literature was also employed to help to inform managers and staff of what KCC was doing and where it was going. As the threat of the Local Government Review in Kent took hold, many of the new corporate management mechanisms took on greater importance. Feedback through personnel and corporate structures still remains dominated by the short-term agenda of central government with limited action to embrace new ideas and new ways of doing business. In essence, where 'change' should be a byproduct of 'learning', KCC managed to create an approach where 'learning' is the byproduct of 'change'—highlighting the lack of control a local authority has over its own destiny when trying to meet a central government agenda.

■ *The Environment Programme: Origins of Strategy*

From the late 1980s, KCC, through an inter-departmental review group, set up an environment programme of new action and obtained a corporate budget of £300,000 to pump prime new initiatives.[9] Given the culture of the organisation and the threat of the Local Government Review, propaganda by example was and remains very much the theme—making the environment pay and proving that action could be undertaken at low cost, no cost or even to generate savings. As public expenditure squeezes began to bite, so resource efficiency and competitive benefits became practical areas to progress.

In 1990 a small enabling and support function, the Environment Unit, was set up within the Planning Department. The Environment Unit's evolution from planning seemed a natural step, reflecting the expertise within the Planning Department and the close links with traditional issues such as heritage and countryside management. The Environment Unit (now grown from two to five people) was set up to manage the new budget and drive forward on propaganda by example—leading the way by promoting real and tangible action while providing support to departments and business units. Figure 3 outlines the spheres of influence of the Environment Unit in trying to integrate environmental management into the key roles and statutory responsibilities of the County Council. The Environment Unit was and is a devolved corporate entity, based within the Planning Department, subject to the Chief Planning Officer's control, and, as the environment function, attempting to develop strategic programmes of action, training and development in partnership with other departments through persuasion and practical support.

■ *Training Strategy*

In recognition of the changes that had affected KCC, the Environment Unit had to devise and develop its own strategy for human resource management. The corporate centre, although committed in principle to environmental issues, was not committed to environmental management, and had too many other priorities to address. Thus, the Environment Unit, a function with limited and relatively weak power, had at a time of great organisational change, to try to build up its role, identity and support services by careful tactics, while relying on the goodwill and commitment of key members and officers within the County Council. Without the central or departmental support from personnel functions to introduce environmental training to all staff in a structured manner, the Environment Unit attempted to develop its own strategy for training and development, using the Environment

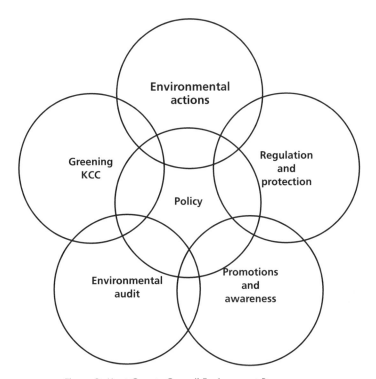

Figure 3: *Kent County Council Environment Programme*

Programme budget sparingly (£20,000 per annum) as a means to target key sections or individual. This includes activity on:

■ General awareness training undertaken by Environment Unit at low cost

■ Specific training for green teams, key officers or members often undertaken by specialist consultants and related to key issues

■ Green surgeries or issue-based training to help overcome barriers and blockages to developing best environmental practice: for example, the implementation of corporate environmental action targets

The emphasis of human resource management right at the start was to use training as a means to identify and implement action.

■ *Measuring the Corporate Pulse as the First Step to Ownership*

The first stage for the Environment Unit was to visit departmental management teams and try to set up a suitable network and structure upon which to progress environmental issues. Each management team was introduced to the overall strategy and benefits of introducing environmental management into the organisation. These are illustrated in Figures 4 and 5, outlining the overall strategy of translating state-of-the-environment auditing into a better understanding of how KCC can green and improve its own business activities. This auditing established a baseline for disseminating vital information on local environmental quality as the first step to empowering the decision-making process. Much of this information has been used subsequently to inform internal decision-makers such as politicians, planners, contract managers and service providers.

The first step of the environmental training strategy was to take a snapshot of the state of Kent County Council. Measuring the state of the environment is one aspect, but how often have the staff of an organisation been considered in the same way? Staff awareness, attitudes, behaviour and

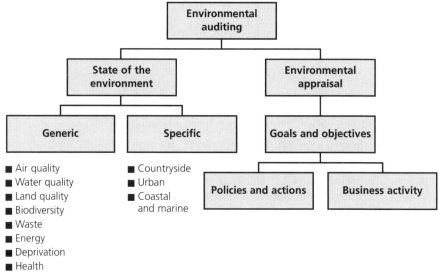

Figure 4: *Environmental Auditing*

values are rarely appraised or their concerns addressed. Yet, the *state of the organisation* will very much determine the success of environmental initiatives.

Following up the meetings with departmental management teams, green teams were set up in each department in 1992 and required, through a corporate target, to undertake an environmental review of the County Council's activities. This basic review identified environmental impacts arising both within departments and corporately and allowed a rolling programme of action to be implemented across the organisation. The environmental training of green teams proved to be the first step towards greening the organisation and changing its business culture.

> ■ Local stewardship—for its own sake
> ■ Public expectation
> ■ Good practice begins at home
> ■ Resource efficiency
> ■ Compulsory Competitive Tendering
> ■ Regulation and guidance
> ■ Highlights risks and liabilities
> ■ Prioritise action
> ■ Commitment of staff

Figure 5: *Why Audit?*

Each department responded in its own way to the request for a green team. Some asked for volunteers and obtained enthusiasts without necessarily the tools or access to senior management to make things happen. Others chose existing groups of senior managers to progress the issues, while other green teams were a mixture of both enthusiasts and key personnel. Which approach was, in environmental terms, more successful depended largely on the way in which each team used their personal and organisational influences. Nevertheless, a start was made, which would help shape the integration of environment into existing human resource management structures.

■ Training Programme: Targeting Movers and Shakers

The main focus of environmental training in KCC is to try to deal with organisational change and pressures by:

- ■ Making environmental issues relevant
- ■ Focusing on the needs of individuals
- ■ Developing ownership in the roles and responsibilities of those individuals
- ■ Developing skills and experience through learning through action

Each training session for green teams and key individuals (usually of half- or one-day duration) continues to be designed to progress environmental appraisal and environmental management through personal ownership. The first element of training explores the hopes, fears and misconceptions of County Council staff, provoking a wide-ranging debate, helping individuals to explode myths and avoid technical detail of little significance, while moving towards personal action that makes a cumulative difference. The introductory training also continually reinforces the environmental management loop now commonly recognised within the EC's Eco-Management and Audit Scheme proposals and BS 7750 (See Fig. 6). Questionnaires and green rating games have often been used as tools to help individuals to explore the issues and their personal relationship linked to their own roles and responsibilities.

The second element of training is designed to help staff appraise their own policies, practices, procedures and projects within their own departmental business plan, and identify short- and medium-term actions. The training ensures that any recommendations arising are specific, measurable, achievable, realistic and time-bound (giving rise to the acronym 'SMART'). The recommendations of green team members have been used to:

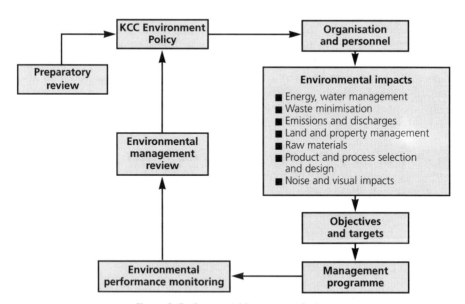

Figure 6: *Environment Management System*

- Identify targets in departmental business plans
- Alter departmental management systems to better reflect environmental impacts
- Integrate environmental standards and targets into functional monitoring and audits
- Develop generic corporate environmental action targets that help to promote best practice throughout the organisation

This has all helped to reinforce ownership while allowing green teams a sense that their recommendations and ideas are being acted upon. The training continues to be limited to the targeting of key staff and the transformation of their roles and responsibilities. This might include business managers, contract managers, school and property caretakers, and technical staff, where appropriate.

The Barriers to Environmental Change

The hopes and fears expressed through training sessions help to highlight the state and morale of an organisation. In KCC, organisational change and pressure posed a number of barriers to the ownership and development of environmental management. Members of staff readily exposed problems relating to:

- A lack of will and commitment by senior officers and politicians
- Entrenched cynicism about the relevance or importance of the issues
- A lack of time and resources
- Green fascism and green policing
- The development of a new bureaucracy
- Cost constraints
- Problems of communication and monitoring in a large devolved organisation
- Knowledge gaps

The Environment Unit had to devise and develop suitable support structures and services to overcome these problems.

The Outputs of Training: Propaganda by Example

By using training as a baseline from which to encourage action, various initiatives have developed to sustain the momentum of culture change in the face of huge organisational pressures. CCT, LGR, along with financial and statutory constraints, have all limited the receptiveness of individuals and business units alike in taking on environmental action. Seven years on, still only 1 in 500 staff have been effectively trained in a way that means that their role and responsibilities better reflect environmental issues. Thus, even in 1995, a typical survey of staff or a training session will still often reflect the need to develop a clear commitment, a sense of direction backed up by good support and networking structures and a well-defined management system.

Experience has shown that, in KCC, there are in effect four behavioural types: pragmatists, cynics, idealists and externally-motivated types, each requiring a tailored approach. The pragmatists want action rather than talk, better working practices and the opportunity for creative ways of problem-solving. The entrenched cynics need to be confronted and nurtured with issues of real importance to their own situation, while the idealists often need careful management so that they do not upset the pragmatists or cynics. The externally-motivated types are usually not bothered by anything and thus require special attention, sometimes even merely to persuade them to attend a training session. Thus the Environment Unit has to continually tailor its approach to influence key individuals and to work within existing management interfaces.

To better integrate environmental management into the human resource management of the organisation, many tools and levers have been used. They include:

■ The introductory training of all officers (public servants) in the core corporate resource department dealing with functions, standards and specifications on finance, purchasing, personnel, property and informa-tion systems—supported by five environmental action work groups, including issues such as energy efficiency and transport and the integration of environment into central monitoring functions

■ The training of elected members (politicians) in sustainable development

■ The targeted training of key decision-makers (e.g. £10,000 of training of school and social service homes caretakers in energy and water management securing estimated savings of £110,000)

■ Corporate environmental action targets on energy, purchasing, paper and management, helping staff in making personal contributions

■ The promotion of the environmental benefits of resource savings towards developing and maintaining a competitive edge

■ The environmental appraisal of policies such as the Structure Plan, Waste Local Plan and Transport Plan—with others to follow

■ The greening of contracts with better specification on supplies and on service delivery

- The inducement of action through using pump-priming budgets (Environment Programme Fund and Energy Loan Fund)—rewarding and supporting managers willing to take action

- The promotion of good action through reports, an environmental newspaper and other publications

- The constant provision of practical advice through green surgeries for staff, more training and through literature such as an environmental newspaper, *How Green is Your Office?* guide and the *Little Green Catalogue,* promoting environmentally-sensitive office supplies

- A wide range of support for departmental action covering green schools and environmental education, landscape and countryside projects, heritage projects, town centre management, urban regeneration, transport projects, recycling and waste minimisation initiatives, environmental monitoring, energy management and information delivery

The Future

As yet there remain many environmental areas that have not been addressed, though it appears that the easiest and least sensitive issues have been covered. The Environment Unit, in its devolved and weak position, has achieved much with limited resources. All in all, a comprehensive programme has been built up on environmental action. This has taken place, ironically, without sustainable development being the top priority and at a time of great transition where environmental issues have had to compete with a whole range of 'change' factors and competing management initiatives. Arguably, the full potential for investing in people to maximise social and environmental benefits has yet to be realised in KCC.

The Environment Unit is now moving from an 'Ownership Inducement Phase' to a 'Conflict Resolution Phase'. Kent County Council is yet to address properly its major environmental impacts, namely:

- The personal impact of officers and political members, i.e. the more thorough integration of environmental responsibility into people, pay and performance criteria

- The purchasing impact of KCC with its huge consumer power, limited by CCT in its ability to employ through contract caring, ethical and local companies

- The transport impact of staff, both commuting and during work, and the comparative impact of private and lease cars

- The strategic role of KCC in mobilising planning, economic development, social services, education, trading standards, transportation, waste disposal, libraries and information, and other services into embracing the sustainable development agenda whereby environmental and social costs and benefits are considered at the heart of decision-making

■ Lessons Learned from KCC's Experience

The Environment Unit continues to bind the fragmented functions and values of the organisation into one cohesive sustainability framework. This is no easy task, given the pressures that exist. A number of lessons have been learned over the last five years about harnessing the organisational changes in a local authority and in developing best practice for human resource management. The following factors are lessons for any organisation trying to introduce a new management approach and philosophy within a highly-devolved infrastructure with a weak, or arguably nonexistent, corporate centre.

■ Active Commitment

Top-down commitment, adequate resourcing and clear goal-setting are essential to help everyone know exactly where they stand, ensuring that communication, networking and opportunities for action are optimised. In a devolved organisation, this active and up-front commitment becomes even more vital. The way this commitment is communicated is critical. How personnel functions translate commitment into people, pay and performance criteria will be crucial to the success of management change. This active context includes the need for adequate resourcing where top management set an example and are seen to be putting money and support where their mouth is.

■ Overcoming Fragmentation and Competition

In a devolved organisation, lacking a strategic centre, competition and conflict may arise in the development of strategies and policy objectives. Conflict resolution mechanisms (fora, work groups and partnerships) need to be set up to address areas of duplication and/or competition, helping to provide cohesion and coherence, while allocating resources effectively. Human resource management here can develop integrated standards and best practice, and can help to address:

■ Conflict between core values and functional priorities

■ Conflict between core values and departmental priorities

■ Conflict between functional and departmental priorities

In each case, the organisation begins to confront the contradictions into its own management structures and move towards a more robust and integrated strategy for managing both material and human resources.

■ Democracy in Action

Selective fora can be used within the organisation to set policy, ratify commitment, agree on targets and objectives, improve education and networking, develop creative problem-solving, enact powers of embarrassment, monitor performance and encourage partnership projects. In KCC there has traditionally been a split between personnel and strategic functions. Personnel functions need to align their approach to people, pay and performance closely to the strategic and business management objectives, ensuring that staff training and development (learning through ownership) leads to appropriate organisational change and achievable action.

■ Agents of Change

Choose your (green) evangelists and teachers wisely. If the person trying to communicate is perceived by others as either naïve, idealistic or an (eco-)fascist, issues can readily become a threat rather than a positive challenge; the action required can be perceived as hassle instead of a worthwhile opportunity, and, sadly, staff may simply switch off instead of being turned on. Human resource management implications here would benefit from the effective training of trainers and motivators, helping to frame language, action and opportunities in both a non-threatening, positive, practical and user-friendly framework.

■ Target the Communication Interfaces

Once you have your agents of change they must target practical information and support to personnel at key communication interfaces where decision-making takes place and action results. In KCC this includes political, administrative, contractual, purchasing and training interfaces. By far the best way to encourage a learning culture is to ensure that (environmental) criteria are built into staff performance appraisal processes, stimulating manager and managed to justify what they have achieved in support of core concerns. For example, in terms of environmental management, writing environmental responsibility into everyone's action plan can make a dramatic difference—from the typist who saves paper and designs documents to the wordsmith who drafts policies or contracts. KCC is only just beginning to address this fundamental issue.

■ Management by Process

Do not re-invent the wheel—adapt existing management structures to embrace new goals. Strive for zero defects and quality, develop reward systems for desirable behaviour, and ensure that environmental reporting is built into all decision-making, monitoring and review processes. In human resource management terms, this will require the effective employment of incentives and disincentives to move people towards continuous improvements in performance—both personal and organisational.

■ Supporting Action

Consider a **partnership fund** to pump prime new initiatives with other organisations, generating income and action which otherwise might not have happened. Develop 'save to spend' incentive mechanisms so that budget-holders who make savings or create income from action can re-invest to optimise the success of their work. Develop 'spend to save' mechanisms to encourage devolved budget-holders to invest in reducing consumption and improving resource efficiency (e.g. energy loan and waste minimisation funds that pump prime action over manageable payback periods). Develop the skills of financial staff and managers encouraging long-term 'value for money' through recognising environmental costs, benefits, impacts, risks, fitness for purpose and durability. Use environmental and organisational review data to reallocate and reprioritise resources to areas of greatest need.

■ Staff Ownership and Networking

Use training as a direct tool to encourage action. Develop generic corporate action targets so that everyone can contribute (energy saving, waste minimisation, purchasing, etc.). Develop feedback mechanisms (e.g. newsletters, green surgeries, issue-driven promotions, task teams and attitude and awareness surveys) to encourage issue ownership. Encourage staff and contractors to develop enquiry-driven action (e.g. pilot projects) and develop centres of excellence on key issues and champions on key functions in support of staff in their everyday work. Make it easy for staff to act—provide practical information on solutions and facilitate good practice.

■ Monitoring Change

Where practical, it is vital to monitor performance. The information collected on performance monitoring can be used wisely to help improve performance, educate staff and raise awareness. Comparisons—i.e. benchmarking—can also be made with other personnel or organisations to verify performance. Performance monitoring between groups or departments can be used to encourage friendly competition helping to spread good practice or embarrass people into action. Outside the organisation, performance monitoring can be a sobering affair, highlighting where the organisation stands in relation to major competitors. In KCC, CCT now means that local authority staff compete with the private sector.

■ Customer Power to Drive Management Systems

Environmental management as a total quality management system is customer-driven. However, the customer is rarely empowered with enough knowledge and information to provide the vital feedback to ensure that products, services and performance are all improved. Staff thus have a vital role to play in raising the sensitivity of the corporate organism. With staff better able to communicate with the customer, so the customer will be able to have a greater influence on their own lifestyle and quality of life. Human resource management must try and allow staff to become closer to the customer while at the same time recognising corporate standards and limits to resources. There is also a minor point that consumer power relies on people being able to choose—which has not been traditionally the case in most local authorities.

■ Conclusion: 'Born-Again' Local Authorities

Kent County Council's experience with environmental training highlights that management, education and development of a large local authority business is no easy task. Competing management frameworks, competing priorities and problems in communication can weaken and even prevent the culture change necessary to deliver sustainable solutions. The KCC Environment Unit has had to create a number of tools to overcome such problems, targeting its own resources at people and management interfaces to exert the greatest effect.

In the old breed of local authorities, a new pseudo-podium—a strategic arm—is just emerging from the corporate body to embrace the development of Local Agenda 21 (see Fig. 7). This new projection into the unknown area of community participation in decision-making is shaped by a new language called 'eco-babble', driven by the Eco-Management and

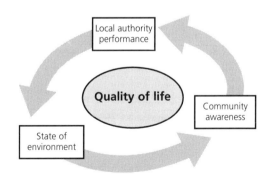

Figure 7: *Environmental Quality Management*

Audit Scheme and guided by new goals, targets and 'sustainability indicators'. This remains a tentative attempt to move employees and customers towards a state of perfection—sustainable development, 'where quality of life and the interests of future generations are valued above immediate material considerations and economic growth'.[10]

The new breed of local authorities can be seen as multi-celled organisms, each nucleus a devolved budget centre, each cell a corporate identity struggling to justify its existence, each membrane a barrier to change. In human resource management terms, the resource circulation and communication system that flows around to nourish these human cells is vital if the whole corporate body is to function properly. The modern-day human species, divided and conquered by cultural and organisational divisions, caught up in a stranglehold of individual wealth creation and locked into employment security, is often insensitive to the life-threatening changes that are occurring. Before we can take on the radical changes necessary to deliver sustainability, there is a need to invest time, energy and resources to make sure that the isolated cells within the body of humanity reach a critical mass and momentum whereby all people are empowered to act together. If we believe in the 'precautionary principle', setting up systems and structures that allow staff both time and opportunities to 'learn the way' is paramount. This learning should help people understand where they are and what they are doing wrong before moving towards constructive change. Current trends in local government suggest that such a learning approach, in the form of environmental management and community development (EMAS and Local Agenda 21 processes), are already being strangled at birth by individual, political, financial and organisational constraints. For local authorities like KCC, there is a question as to whether the organisation has the long-term security and management systems to deliver sustainable development—or will organisation and personnel alike be martyrs to short-term economics? The recent publication of KCC's core values (see Fig. 8) would suggest that KCC is moving to meet this challenge.

- ■ **Targeting those in need**
- ■ **'Care in the Community'**
- ■ **Caring for the environment**
- ■ **Strengthening Kent's economy**
- ■ **Improving quality of life**
- ■ **Improving local democracy**
- ■ **Quality and improving public services**
- ■ **Partnership: working together**
- ■ **Equal opportunities**
- ■ **Listening to and valuing staff**

Figure 8: *Core Values of KCC: Delivering Sustainable Development*

■ Notes

1. The views expressed in this chapter are those of the author and not those of Kent County Council.

2. David Bohm, *Thought as a System* (London, UK: Routledge, 1994).

3. See S. Rees and W. Wehrmeyer, *Sustaining the Unsustainable? Implementation of Sustainable Development within the UK Local Government* (Research report; Durrell Institute of Conservation and Ecology, University of Kent, UK, 1995).

4. The Local Government Review in Kent involved the county and fourteen district councils, with a Royal Commission questioning the validity of the existing two-tier structure to local government. Many districts want 'unitary' status and more powers, placing county and districts in direct conflict, while at the same time limiting partnerships and co-operation.

5. The Local Government Review had one profound impact: that of the Medium Term Plan, which bound together departments and functions in a loose but cohesive structure of business planning and resource allocation. The MTP became irrelevant as the county fought for its own survival, to sustain the status quo and promote its strategic role. The Local Government Review made KCC extremely insecure and short term, leading to an organisational emphasis on service delivery and promotional identity. Departmental service visibility became paramount.

6. For instance, departments purchasing information systems equipment that cannot communicate with each other; difficulties in monitoring performance across numerous devolved budget cost centres.

7. Centralised purchasing has been undermined and with it the ability to maximise consumer power.

8. The functional heads for health and safety, quality and environment all lie in different departments, all compete for resources separately and all have action programmes that are separate rather than integrated.

9. This fund did rise to a peak of £500,000 but has since fallen back to £300,000 with extra resources for projects being attracted through sponsorship or European funding. The bulk of these resources have been used to support action and partnerships on countryside heritage, recycling and environmental education initiatives. Very little has been employed in developing environmental management systems.

10. Local Government Management Board, *Sustainability Indicators Research Project* (London, UK: LGMB, June 1994).

19

A Global Challenge:
Environment Management in Cable & Wireless

John Beatson and Stephen Macklin

ABLE & WIRELESS is one of the world's leading international tele-communications groups, with operations in over fifty countries on five continents. The operations are centred around three regional hubs, namely Asia, the Caribbean and North America, and Europe. Group turnover for 1994/95 was £5.1 billion, and operating profit £1.1 billion. Worldwide the group employs approximately 40,000 people.

Cable & Wireless provides more than 120 different services in all of the telecommunications sectors, from basic voice to mobile communications, and advanced value-added services through a number of telecommunications networks. Part of the network consists of cables that are above the ground, below the ground or under the sea. Modern cables are fibre-optic, although co-axial and copper cables are also maintained. Other parts of the network are provided by means of wireless technology: for example, mobile phones, satellite, earth stations and microwave links. In order to support the provision of the telecommunications network and services to customers, Cable & Wireless undertakes a number of activities that are common to many other businesses, such as running offices and shops, operating and maintaining mechanical and electrical equipment, constructing access roads, running vehicle fleets and backup electricity generators, and storing fuels. Cable & Wireless Marine operates and maintains a fleet of cable-laying and repairing ships.

Because of the unusually dispersed geographical nature of its operations —literally all over the world—Cable & Wireless has faced a challenging task in developing both an environment policy and a coherent environmental management system for the group as a whole. The job is even more complicated by the diverse cultural backgrounds and different levels of economic development in the countries in which Cable & Wireless operates. These are the sorts of factors that have already been taken into account in employment policies, and this was one of the reasons why the group's human resources department was eventually chosen as the vehicle to implement the environment programme. In coming to this decision, it was recognised that in a service sector company such as Cable & Wireless, the environment function could well be placed in a finance department, in parallel with the risk and the audit function, or alternatively in a corporate affairs department reflecting the impact of environment on customer and stakeholder concerns. Probably the correct place is in the middle of all three, but human resources has the important advantage, at least in Cable & Wireless, that it also looks after the group safety function.

While the job is by no means complete, the basic policies, plans and processes are now in place to enable Cable & Wireless's constituent businesses to start to tackle what is for some a new and increasingly important part of their management task.

■ History

As with many large organisations, environmental improvement actions on the part of individual businesses preceded a group-wide policy. They were inspired by resource-saving programmes, community programmes, and, in many cases, a desire on the part of employees to improve their local environment. Examples include changes to the siting of dish antennae in Hong Kong to avoid areas containing endangered plant species, and a number of paper and other material recycling schemes often inspired by enthusiastic individuals and springing up in places as far afield as Australia, Hong Kong, Bermuda and the UK. In other businesses, local requirements, such as the need to conserve water supplies on a small island, have inspired actions that today might be part of the most forward-looking environmental programme. As will be seen below, the communication of best practice is recognised as an essential part of the environment programme and one of the spin-off benefits of a wide international operation.

While these localised initiatives were flourishing in the late 1980s, questions about various aspects of the group's environment policy were starting to be raised by individual shareholders, a number of investment funds, particularly those with green funds, and by environmental pressure groups. These enquiries were procedurally handled in the company secretary's department, and some limited investigation of the matters raised was undertaken as a direct consequence.

In 1990 a review was undertaken of the impact of the group's activities on the environment in the UK and in Hong Kong and, as part of that work, a survey was undertaken by interview of company staff attitudes to environmental matters. This marked the first time that environment was seen in the company as a matter centred on people rather than on physical or engineering actions or consequences. In 1994 the group's first published environment policy was made publicly available. Later that year a worldwide environment forum was set up, bringing together simultaneously by video conference staff from many parts of the world to share experience and expertise. Guided by working groups of that forum, a worldwide review of the effects on the environment of the Cable & Wireless group's activities was undertaken at the end of 1994 and the beginning of 1995. The new policy (see Fig. 1) and plan arising from that survey was published in 1996 and a work programme agreed. It will be implemented by an environment team reporting to the Group Director of Human Resources.

■ Cable & Wireless Environment Policy and Values

Like all commercial companies, the operations of Cable & Wireless give rise to environmental effects, although telecommunications operations inherently cause relatively few. Cable & Wireless believes that the telecommunications industry has just as much responsibility for promoting the long-term care of the environment as those industries in which pollution is a high risk. Indeed, in providing services that reduce the need for travel and the use of paper, the industry is well placed to provide positive environmental benefits. The new technologies of teleworking and video conferencing are particularly important in this area, making remote working a real option.

The Cable & Wireless environment policy includes a vision statement, eight objectives, and sections on policy application and implementation. The two central themes of the revised policy are the integration of environmental management into the business process and continual improvement of environmental performance. Also, the eight objectives allow for common standards of environmental performance to emerge on a global scale.

Within this global context, Cable & Wireless's businesses will adopt their own environmental plans as local companies, meeting domestic legal requirements with due regard to the demands of local customers, stakeholders and employees. Businesses will include in their plans a number of environmental standards (the same standards as referred to in the previous paragraph) that are agreed to be of global importance to the Cable & Wireless group as a whole. The implementation of such standards over specified timescales will be agreed by the businesses of the group. Thereafter they will be made mandatory across Cable & Wireless with regular monitoring and review. The businesses will promote the exchange of information around Cable & Wireless so that best practice can be universally

The Cable & Wireless environment policy:

■ Forms a basis on which businesses will continue to build their particular environment policies

■ Provides objectives against which businesses can measure their environmental performance with due regard to the local context

Aims
It is a fundamental aim of Cable & Wireless that its activities are undertaken with due regard to their effect on the environment. The company will integrate environmental management into its business processes, continually improve its environmental performance and, as a minimum, keep within regulatory control constraints.

Objectives
Cable & Wireless is committed to the following policy objectives that will promote the long-term protection of the world's environment:

■ Ensure that resources are not wasted and that, where practicable, materials and goods are re-used or recycled

■ Reduce the generation of wastes as far as is reasonably practicable and dispose of all remaining waste in a responsible manner

■ Identify and evaluate business environmental effects and control and manage those effects that have been identified as significant

■ Encourage suppliers of goods and services to operate in an environmentally-responsible manner

■ Communicate best practice

■ Encourage employees to take part in appropriate environment initiatives

■ Foster open communication with neighbours who live and work in areas local to Cable & Wireless facilities

■ Support international, national and community initiatives designed to protect and enhance the environment

Policy Implementation
Implementation of the policy will be supported by specific policies, standards, codes of practice and practical guidance, which will form part of the global environmental management system. The system also creates a network to support businesses worldwide and provides a channel of communication of best environmental practices.

Figure 1: *The Cable & Wireless Environment Policy*
Source: © 1996 Cable & Wireless plc

understood and implemented. Each business will therefore manage its own environmental affairs on a day-to-day basis, while Group Human Resources will maintain an overview of the local business's approach and environmental issues in order that:

- There is a point of co-ordination providing both a helpline and a conduit for information exchange as well as representation of the group as a whole when so required.
- Any policy contributions that might affect neighbouring businesses or the group as a whole are met with an appropriate central response.
- Future areas of environmental concern affecting the group or significant parts of it are anticipated and businesses informed.

■ The Environment Forum
In the developmental phase, the Cable & Wireless environment forum met quarterly, using video conferencing and voice to link members from a dozen businesses representing the main areas of operation of the group. The key purpose was to exchange information, share best practice, access the opinions of others and to set up task groups to develop common policies and standards and best practice guidance documents. The value of the forum was that it allowed geographically-scattered businesses to participate in development work and policy-setting in a way that is often not possible, and promoted a high level of 'buy-in', one of the prerequisites of successful policy implementation.

■ Managing Change
The different levels of cultural, developmental, regulatory and technical conditions present across the group create a challenge, but also an opportunity for rapid advance in the direction of effective sharing of information and expertise. Significant progress has already been made, and there is a growing realisation among employees that environment is an integrated part of the group's business management responsibilities. The approach to improving environmental performance is based on nurturing both businesses' and employees' environmental aspirations, and providing them with the knowhow to achieve these aims. This covers effective communication, sharing of best practice, organising for action, and catalysing business action.

■ Effective Communication
The environment policy objectives provide a clear direction and view of what the group wishes to achieve. This can only be achieved with the

commitment and support of all employees. To gain this support, the environment team has recently initiated an environmental awareness and training programme. This addresses both knowledge, skills and motivation, and will help guide future action. It is a particularly exciting challenge, in that the environment team must communicate effectively on a global scale, taking account of both language and developmental differences, including the way environment is culturally perceived.

■ Sharing of Best Practice

Growing competition and the need to respond rapidly to the ever-changing business environment means that group businesses cannot operate in isolation. To meet business needs effectively, all must have access to the full range of skills, knowledge and experience within the Cable & Wireless group. An important finding of the global environmental review was an increasing need voiced by employees for further practical guidance covering key improvement areas, and particularly for better information-sharing processes.

■ Future Plans

Future plans include the development and dissemination of practical guidelines, policies, standards, and codes of practice as well as an audit system. Experts and interested parties within Cable & Wireless have recently been invited to take part in task teams, which will address common issues, developing appropriate policies, standards and guidelines and, where appropriate, business support. Plans also include a network to support businesses worldwide, and a helpline service that will direct questions and requests for support to those with relevant expertise in the group. Cable & Wireless intends to adopt broadly the International Chamber of Commerce's approach to environmental auditing.

It is recognised that effective implementation is only possible in the longer term by integrating environmental management into the overall business process. This will involve businesses developing and implementing their own policies and plans within their existing business processes, and the present phase of initiating many environmental projects from the centre will change into one of providing expert help for limited parts of an ongoing process.

This chapter © 1996 John Beatson and Stephen Macklin

Author Biographies

Susan Barrett is Reader in Policy and Organisational Studies at the School for Policy Studies. Ms Barrett's work at Bristol focuses on processes of policy development and implementation and the management of change. Her work has included research, consultancy and teaching in the fields of land policy; changing professional roles in acute health care; managing the introduction of new information technologies (including consultancies for the UK Department of the Environment, Victoria State Government of Australia and the Organisation for Economic Co-operation and Development); and the development of social responsibility in public service organisations. She is currently directing a joint School for Policy Studies/*New Consumer* research project funded by ESRC on the implementation of corporate social responsibility policies in a sample of UK companies.

Alison Bird, MPhil, is one of the founding directors of the Institute of Environmental Management (IEM). She has been involved in environmental issues since the late 1980s. After regularly covering environmental liability issues for a London-based financial publisher, she launched and edited *EnviroRisk*, a monthly publication dedicated to risk management, liability and insurance issues. After moving to Scotland, she was brought into the successful 'Centre for Environment and Business in Scotland' team to address the growing demand for professional support for the individual environmental manager. This in turn culminated in the formation of the IEM.

Dr Judith Clair joined the Department of Organization Studies at Boston College as an Assistant Professor in 1993. She has consulted for organisations in the area of crisis management, natural environmental management, fraud detection and performance enhancement.

Sabine Daig holds a diploma in International Business Administration from Wiesbaden Business School. She has carried out environmental training needs analyses and designed environmental training programmes for several companies.

Peter Dobers is a research assistant at the Gothenburg Research Institute, Sweden. He is part of the research programme on ecological business and is writing a doctoral thesis on strategies for environmental reforms.

Tim Hart retrained as a personnel specialist following an early career in banking, and held personnel manager postions in local government. He spent ten years as a full-time academic, teaching accountancy and personnel management at professional and postgraduate levels. He now teaches part-time while engaging in writing, research and consultancy in managerial and environmental issues.

Peter James directs the Environmental Leadership research and teaching programme at Ashridge Management College, one of Europe's largest business schools. He has written extensively on environmental performance measurement, implementation of environmental policy and environmental benchmarking.

Leon Klinkers is academic tutor of the European Association of Environmental Management Education at Tilburg University, The Netherlands, and works as Management Consultant for Det Norske Veritas Industry.

Henning Madsen is Associate Professor in Statistics at the Aarhus School of Business, Denmark, and has a PhD in Business Economics. His specialist interest is in the application of quantitative methods at the strategic level.

Angela Mawle has a BSc in Environmental Sciences and an MSc in Environmental Technology from Imperial College, London. After a period as an environmental consultant, Angela returned to Imperial College as the Academic Administrator for the Centre for Environmental Technology (ICCET). In 1994 she became Executive Director of the Women's Environmental Network, a women-centred environmental NGO.

Joyce Miller has worked since 1992 as a Research Associate at the International Institute for Management Development (IMD) in Lausanne, Switzerland. She was involved in launching IMD's project on Managing the Industrial and Business Environment (MIBE), a joint venture with ten leading European companies to research and develop tools to integrate environment into daily business practice. She has spearheaded research to define what is 'green' by identifying the criteria, metrics, and systems that a range of stakeholders use to assess excellent corporate environmental performance. She has developed numerous case studies focusing on environmental management, business strategy, and alliances. She is an active member of the European Environmental Management Association (EEMA). Formerly, she worked with IBM in Canada, Sweden, and Germany.

Dr John Milliman is an Assistant Professor of Business at the University of Colorado at Colorado Springs. His reseach and consulting interests are in international human resource management and environmental management.

David Murphy is a PhD student in International Policy at the School for Policy Studies. He is researching business–NGO environmental partnerships as policy responses to sustainable development, with funding from the University of Bristol and the Social Science and Humanities Research Council of Canada. He is also working as a researcher on the SPS/*New Consumer* corporate social responsibility research project, and on course development for the New Academy of Business. Prior to his arrival at Bristol in 1993, Mr Murphy worked for many years with CUSO, Canada's largest international development organisation, including various assignments in West Africa and Canada.

Nico Nelissen is Professor in Public Administration at the Catholic University of Nijmegen and Professor in Environmental Issues at Tilburg University, The Netherlands.

Dr Klaus North is Professor of International Management at Wiesbaden Business School, Germany. His research covers international manufacturing management and environmental business management. He frequently consults with major firms and international organisations and teaches regularly in business programmes abroad. He has published widely on productivity, quality and environmental management topics, including the book *Environmental Business Management*, published by the International Labour Office in 1992.

Andrea Oates is a researcher in health, safety and environmental issues at the Labour Research Department, an independent trade union research organisation in London. She has also carried out research on work and environmental issues as a member of the Industrial Relations and Environmental Network Europe (IRENE), co-ordinated by the Wissenschaftszentrum Berlin (SZB).

Kim Parker MA, MSc, PhD, has a first degree in engineering and a masters and doctorate in control engineering. He worked for the Department of the Environment for eight years, developing a simulation model of world economic development, international trade and natural resource use. After working at the Technical Change Centre for three years, he moved to the University of Kent, UK, in 1984 as a Lecturer in Operational Research.

With a PhD from Henley Management College, **Suzanne Pollack** is co-editor of *The Environmental Management Handbook* (Pitman) and author of *Improving Environmental Performance* (Routledge). Based at Henley, she has produced two distance-learning courses and continues to write papers on business and environment issues, focusing on, and working closely with, major corporations. Her most extensive work so far has been the six-month modular environmental development programme at Rover Car Group.

Stephen Rees is a graduate in Environmental Science and has fourteen years' experience in developing environmental issues, specifically: land and estate management, community project co-ordination, waste minimisation, environmental education, training and promotions. Latterly he has been developing environmental appraisal and management with a large UK local authority at Kent County Council Environment Unit.

Stephanie Stewart is currently an environmental consultant with Price Waterhouse L.L.P. in New York. She has previously worked as an accountant, environmental auditor and environmental researcher in Europe and the USA.

Dr John P. Ulhøi is Associate Research Professor in Management at the Aarhus School of Business, Denmark, and holds a PhD in Business Administration. He is Editor-in-Chief of a Danish environmental management journal and editorial board member of a number of international journals and scientific associations. He has developed courses in the field of corporate environmental management at graduate, executive and doctoral level.

Dr Sarah A. Vickerstaff is Senior lecturer in Social and Public Policy at the University of Kent at Canterbury, UK. Her main areas of research interest and teaching are the labour market and the management of work and training. She has published widely on human resource management and training issues.

Walter Wehrmeyer is Lecturer in Ecological Management at the Durrell Institute of Conservation and Ecology, University of Kent, UK. He is editor and author of *Environmental References in Business* and *Measuring Environmental Business Performance*. He is Director of Graduate Studies at the *Business in the Environment* Research Degree Programme at the University of Kent.

Rolf Wolff is Professor in Business Administration, head of the Gothenburg Research Institute and is responsible for the ecological business research programme.

List of Acronyms

AQA	Australian Quality Award
BCSD	Business Council for Sustainable Development
BPEO	Best Practicable Environmental Option
BSI	British Standards Institute
CBI	Confederation of British Industry
CFCs	Chlorofluorocarbons
COSHH	Control of Substances Hazardous to Health
CPRE	Council for the Preservation of Rural England
CPSA	Civil and Public Services Association (UK)
CWU	Communications Workers Union (UK)
DOT	Department of Transportation (US)
DPG	German Communications Union
EAEME	European Association for Environmental Management
EAG	Environmental Action Group (of TUC)
EEF	Engineering Employers Federation (UK)
EEMA	European Environmental Management Association
EFQM	European Foundation for Quality Management
EHS	Environmental Health and Safety
EM	Environmental Management
EMAS	Eco-Management and Audit Scheme
EMIS	Environmental Management Information Systems
ENACTS	Environmental Policy Group of TGWU
ENDS	Environmental Data Services Ltd
EPA	Environmental Protection Act (UK)
EPA	Environmental Protection Agency (US)
EQA	European Quality Award
ESB	Engineering Services Branch (Australia)
ESRC	Economic and Social Research Council (UK)
EU	European Union

GEMI	Global Environmental Management Initiative
GMB	General, Municipal and Boilermakers Union (UK)
HMIP	Her Majesty's Inspectorate of Pollution
HRM	Human Resource Management
HSE	Health and Safety Executive (UK)
HSW	Health and Safety at Work Act (UK)
ICC	International Chamber of Commerce
IEEM	Institute of Ecology and Environmental Management
IEM	Institute of Environmental Management (UK)
ILO	International Labour Office
IMD	International Institute for Management Development
INEM	International Network for Environmental Management
IPC	Integrated Pollution Control
IPMS	Institute of Professionals, Managers and Specialists (UK)
IRSF	Inland Revenue Staff Federation (UK)
KPA	Key performance area
LA21	Local Agenda 21
LEC	London Environment Centre
LGEC	Local Government Environmental Co-ordinator
LGMB	Local Government Management Board
LGR	Local Government Review
LRD	Labour Research Department (UK)
MIBE	Managing the Industrial and Business Environment
MSF	Manufacturing, Science and Finance Union (UK)
NGOs	Non-Governmental Organisations
NUM	National Union of Mineworkers (UK)
OSHA	Occupational Safety and Health Administration (US)
PCBs	Polychlorinated biphenyls
PMS	Positivistic Model of Science
PTC	Public Services, Tax and Commerce Union (UK)
RCRA	Resource Conservation and Recovery Act (US)
RSPB	Royal Society for the Protection of Birds (UK)
SECWA	State Energy Commission of Western Australia
SMEs	Small to medium-sized enterprises
SOPs	Standard operating procedures
TGWU	Transport and General Workers Union (UK)
TQEM	Total Quality Environmental Management
TQM	Total Quality Management
TRI	Toxic Release Inventory (US)
TSCA	Toxic Substances Control Act (US)
TUC	Trade Union Congress
UNCED	United Nations Conference on Environment and Development
UNECE	United Nations Economic Commission for Europe
UNEP	United Nations Environment Programme
WAMITAB	Waste Management Industry Training and Advisory Board
WBCSD	World Business Council for Sustainable Development
WWF	World-Wide Fund for Nature

Index